ALSO AVAILABLE FROM 🌀 TOKYOPOP®

TOKYO MEW MEW

MIA IKUMI & REIKO YOSHIDA

VOLUME TWO

TOKYOPOP
LOS ANGELES • TOKYO • LONDON

Translator - Ikoe Hiroe
English Adaptation - Stuart Hazelton
Contributing Editor - Jodi Bryson
Retouch and Lettering - Tina Fulkerson
Cover Layout - Patrick Hook

Editor -Julie Taylor
Digital Imaging Manager - Chris Buford
Pre-Press Manager - Antonio DePietro
Production Managers - Jennifer Miller, Mutsumi Miyazaki
Art Director - Matt Alford
Managing Editor - Jill Freshney
VP of Production - Ron Klamert
President & C.O.O. - John Parker
Publisher & C.E.O. - Stuart Levy

E-mail: info@TOKYOPOP.com
Come visit us online at www.TOKYOPOP.com

A  Manga

TOKYOPOP Inc.
5900 Wilshire Blvd. Suite 2000
Los Angeles, CA 90036

Tokyo Mew Mew Vol. 2

ISBN: 1-59182-237-8

First TOKYOPOP® printing: June 2003

20 19 18 17 16 15 14
Printed in the USA

TOKYO MEW MEW

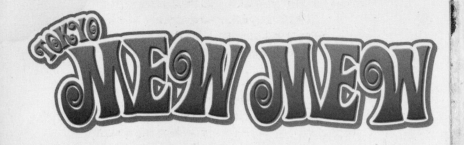

TABLE OF CONTENTS

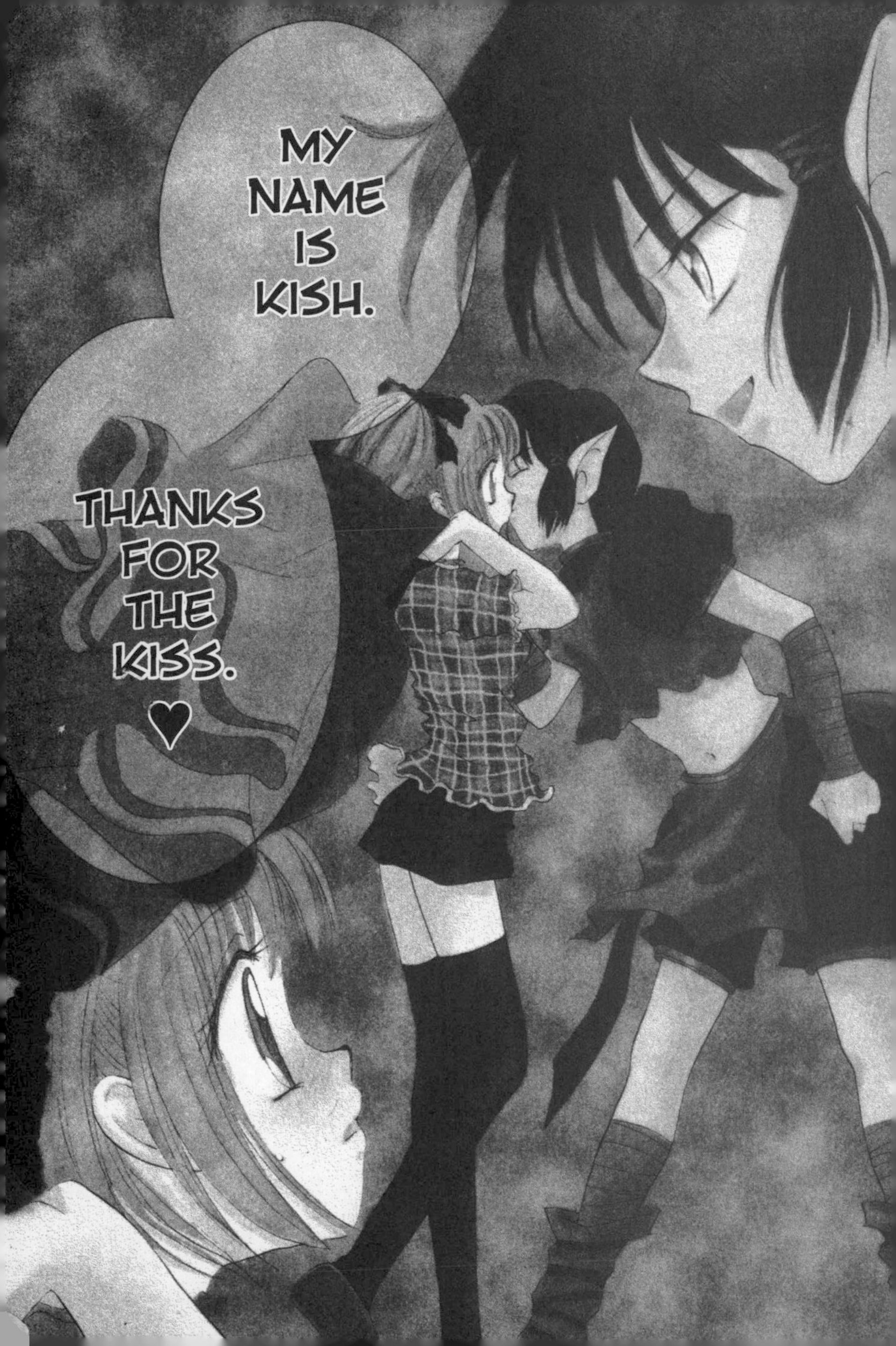
MY NAME IS KISH.
THANKS FOR THE KISS. ♥

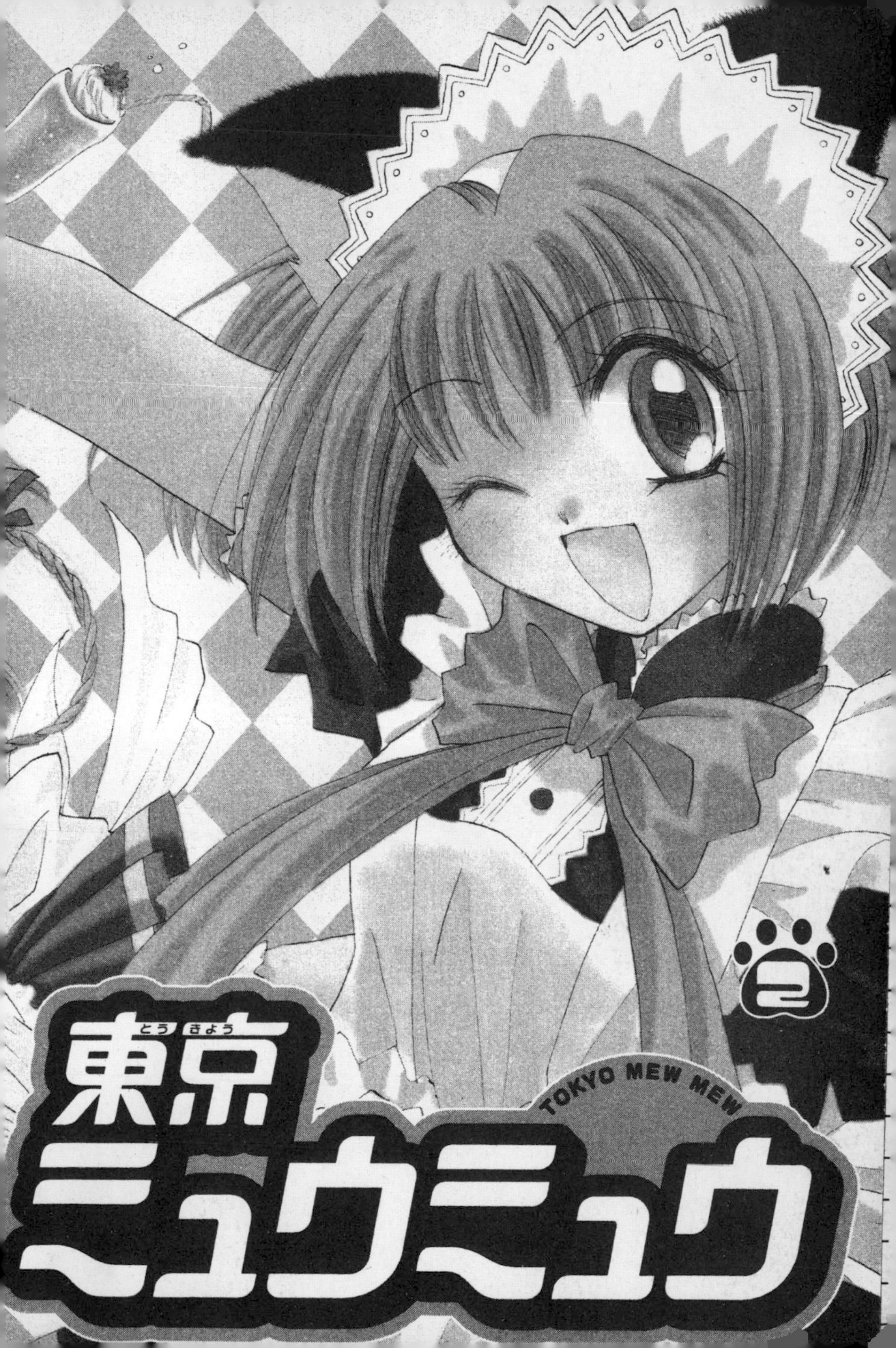
2
とうきょう
東京
TOKYO MEW MEW
ミュウミュウ

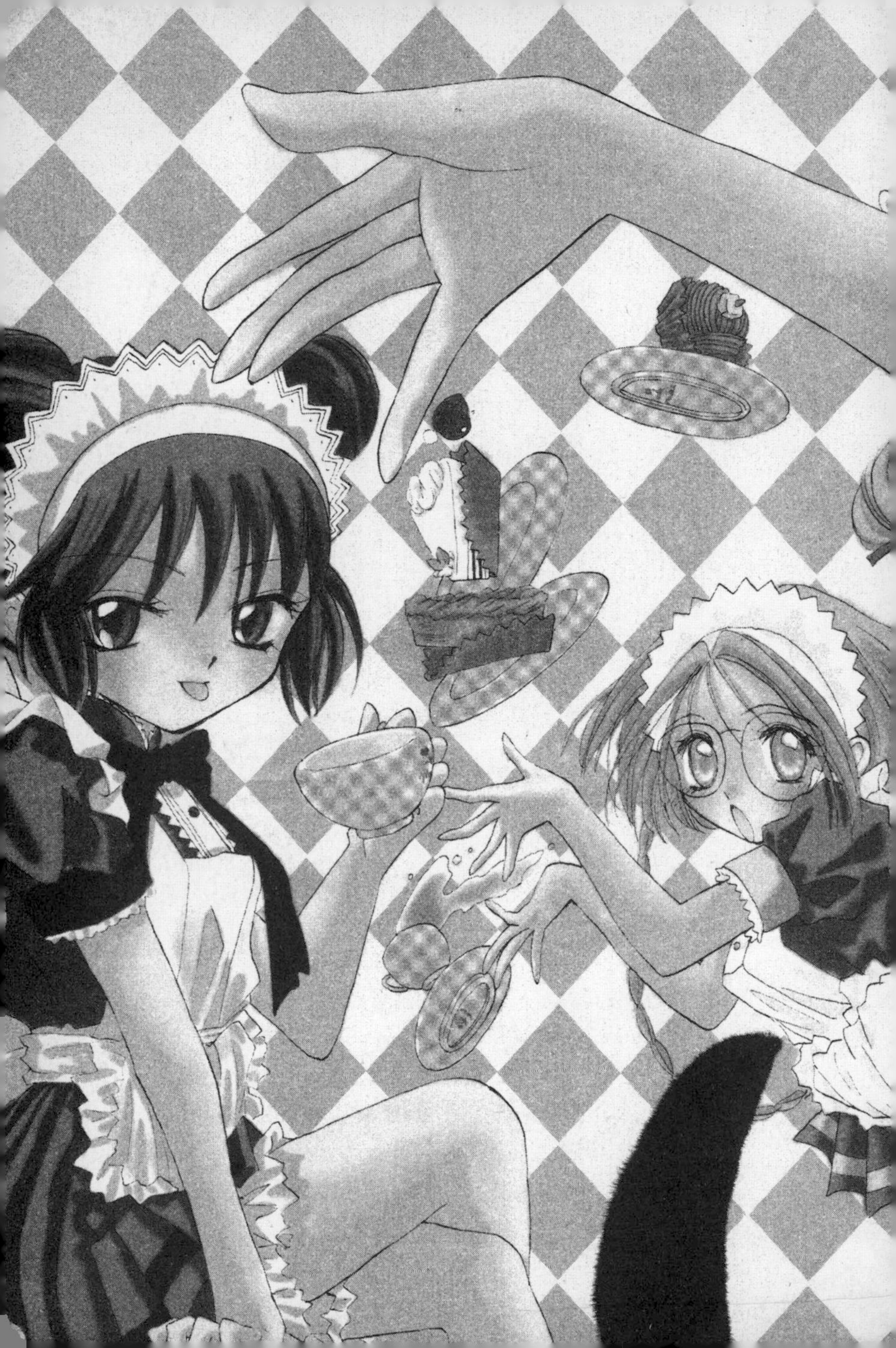

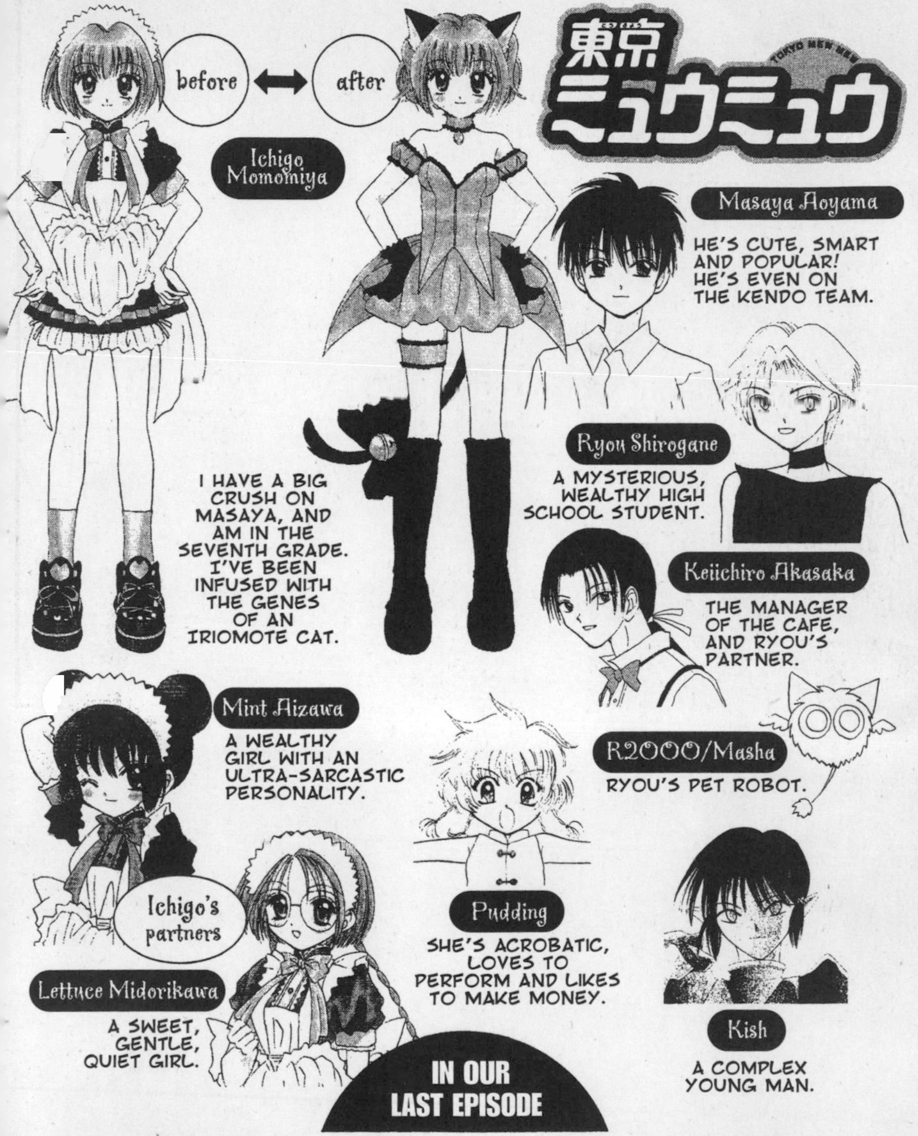

東京ミュウミュウ
TOKYO MEW MEW
before
after
Ichigo Momomiya
I HAVE A BIG CRUSH ON MASAYA, AND AM IN THE SEVENTH GRADE. I'VE BEEN INFUSED WITH THE GENES OF AN IRIOMOTE CAT.
Masaya Aoyama
HE'S CUTE, SMART AND POPULAR! HE'S EVEN ON THE KENDO TEAM.
Ryou Shirogane
A MYSTERIOUS, WEALTHY HIGH SCHOOL STUDENT.
Keiichiro Akasaka
THE MANAGER OF THE CAFE, AND RYOU'S PARTNER.
R2000/Masha
RYOU'S PET ROBOT.
Mint Aizawa
A WEALTHY GIRL WITH AN ULTRA-SARCASTIC PERSONALITY.
Ichigo's partners
Lettuce Midorikawa
A SWEET, GENTLE, QUIET GIRL.
Pudding
SHE'S ACROBATIC, LOVES TO PERFORM AND LIKES TO MAKE MONEY.
Kish
A COMPLEX YOUNG MAN.

IN OUR LAST EPISODE

Ichigo Momomiya is 11 years old. During a date with Masaya, a freak accident turned her into Superhero Mew Mew. Infused with the genes of an Iriomote cat, Ichigo must find her partners and save the planet from invading aliens!!

One day, on a date with Masaya, Ichigo's identity is revealed to a friendly, acrobatic girl. A mysterious young man called Kish surprisingly and boldly kisses Ichigo…!

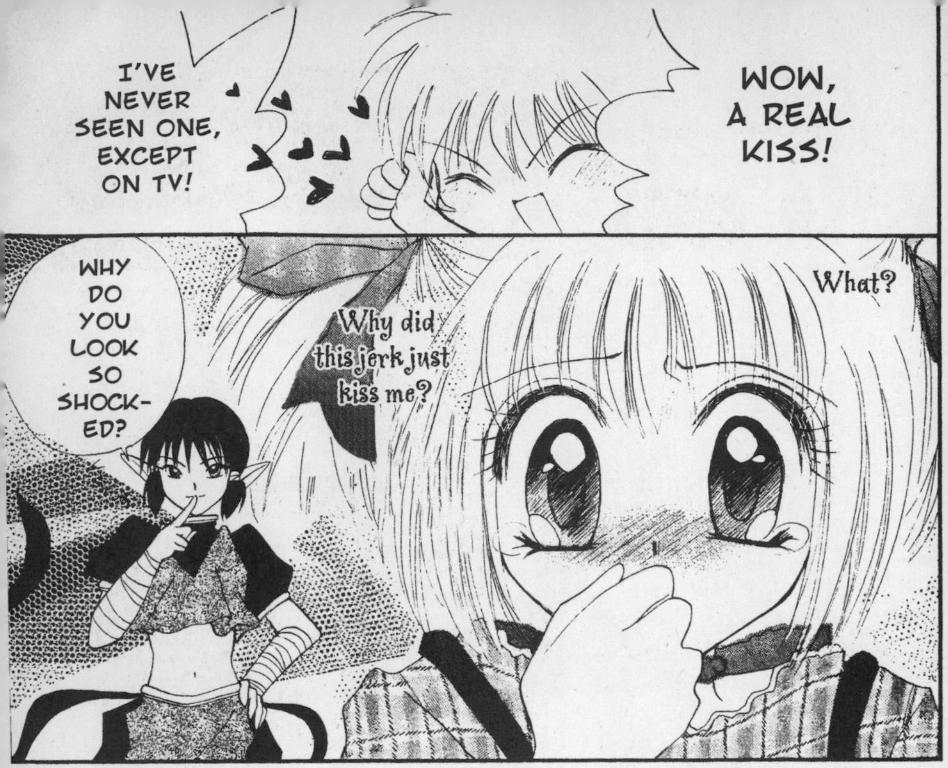
WOW, A REAL KISS!
I'VE NEVER SEEN ONE, EXCEPT ON TV!
What?
Why did this jerk just kiss me?
WHY DO YOU LOOK SO SHOCK-ED?

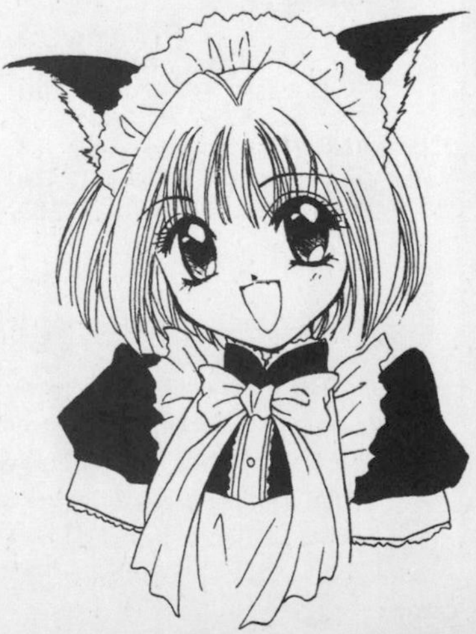

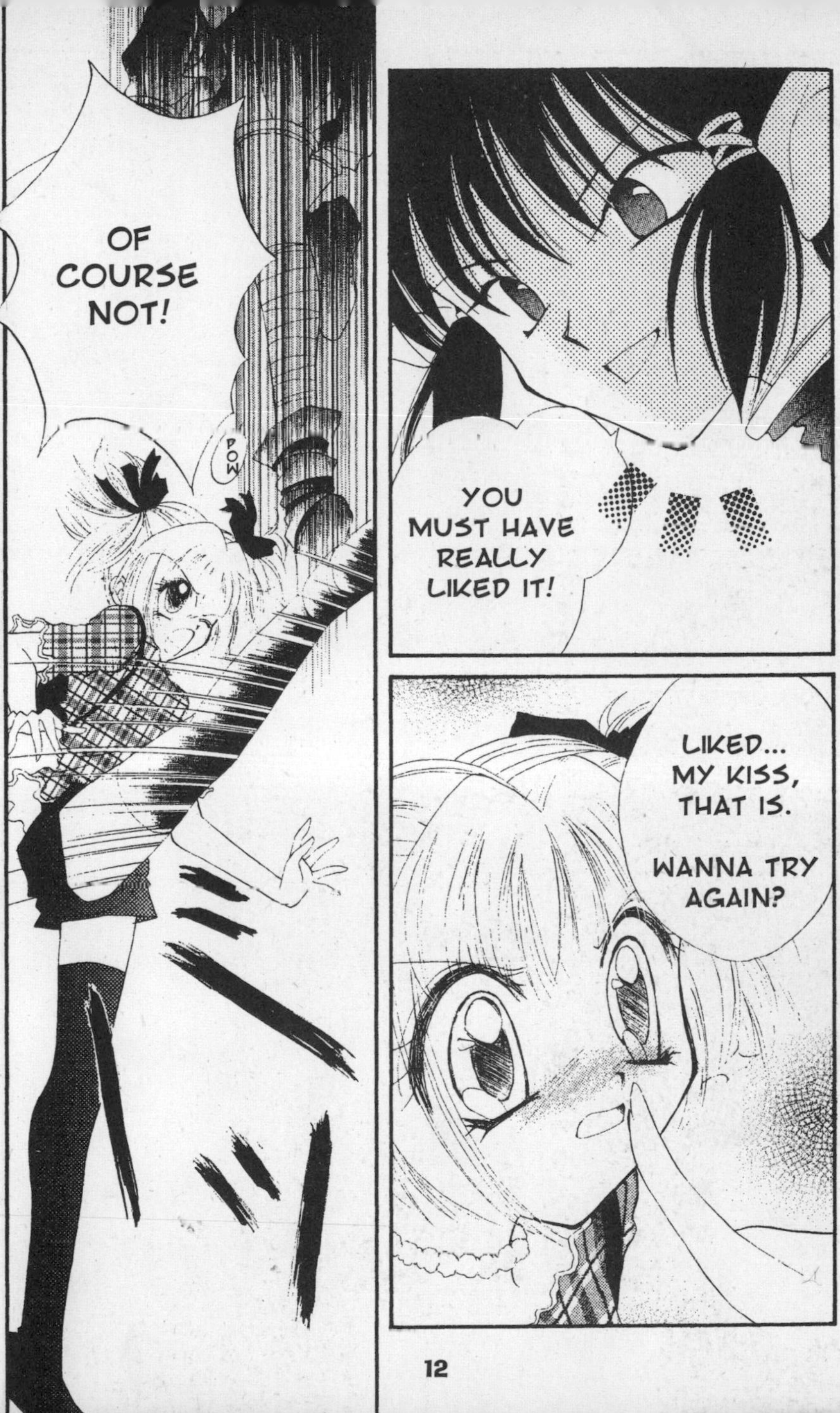
YOU MUST HAVE REALLY LIKED IT!
LIKED... MY KISS, THAT IS.
WANNA TRY AGAIN?
OF COURSE NOT!
POW

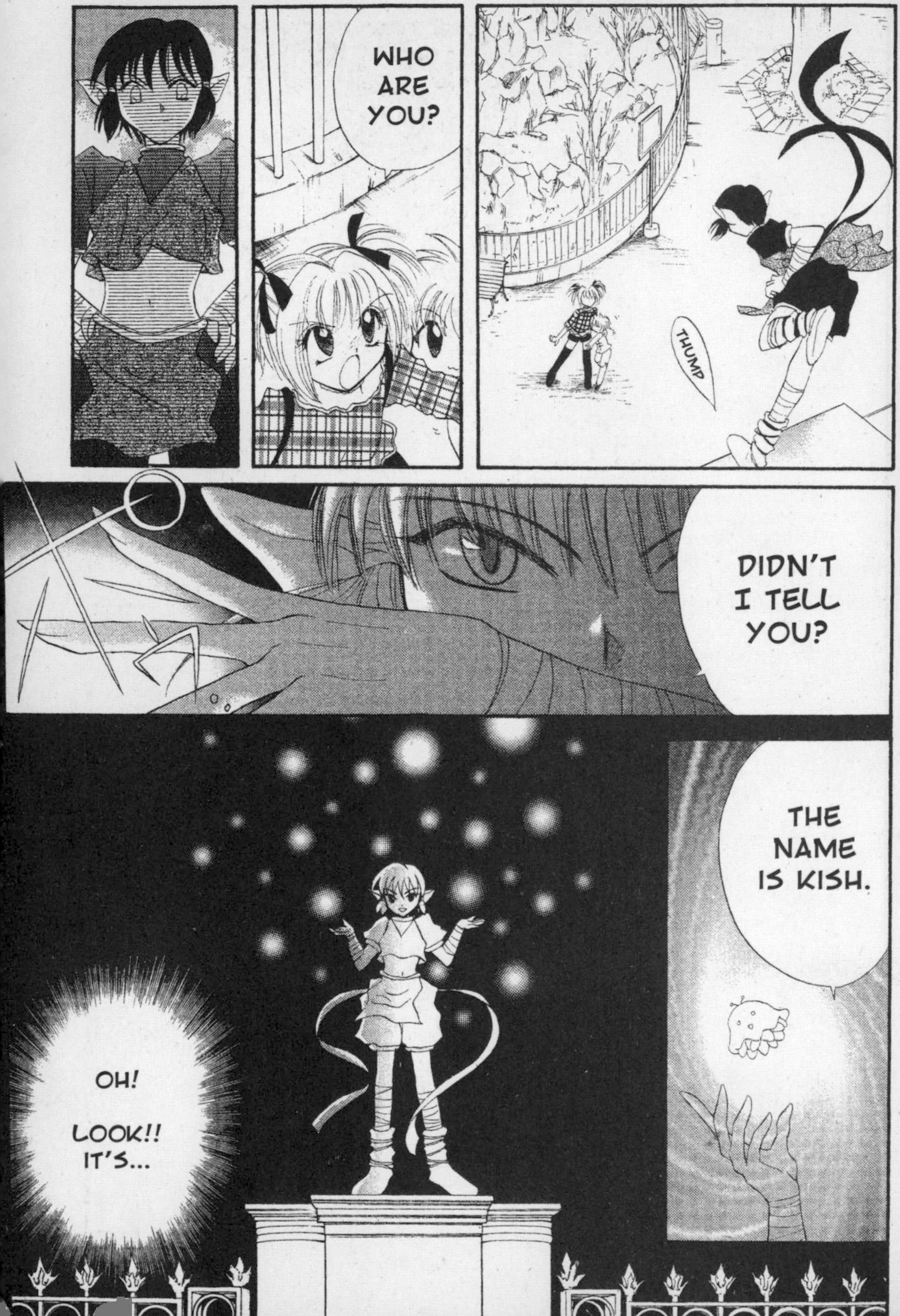
THUMP
WHO ARE YOU?
DIDN'T I TELL YOU?
THE NAME IS KISH.
OH!
LOOK!! IT'S...

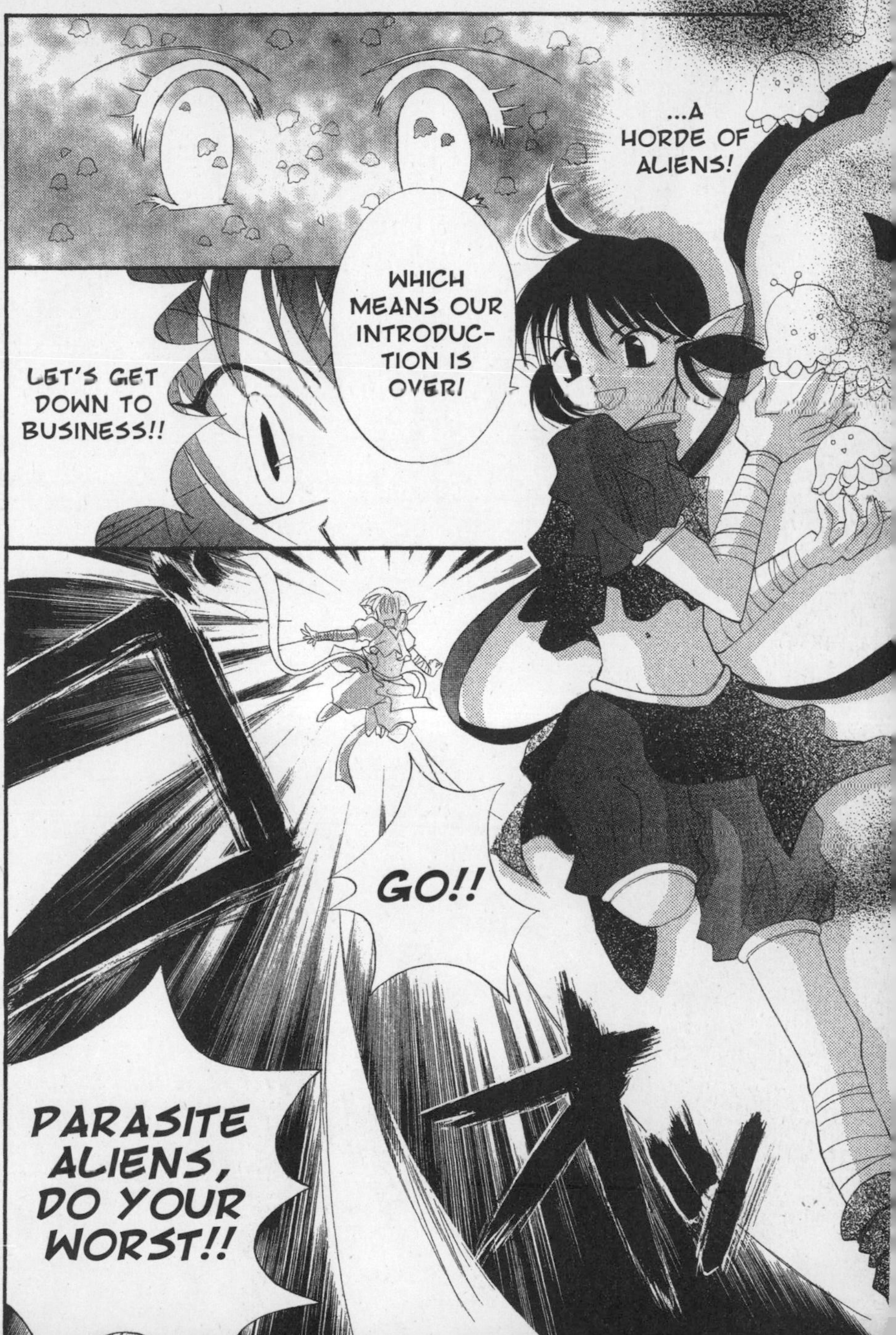
...A HORDE OF ALIENS!
WHICH MEANS OUR INTRODUCTION IS OVER!
LET'S GET DOWN TO BUSINESS!!
GO!!
PARASITE ALIENS, DO YOUR WORST!!

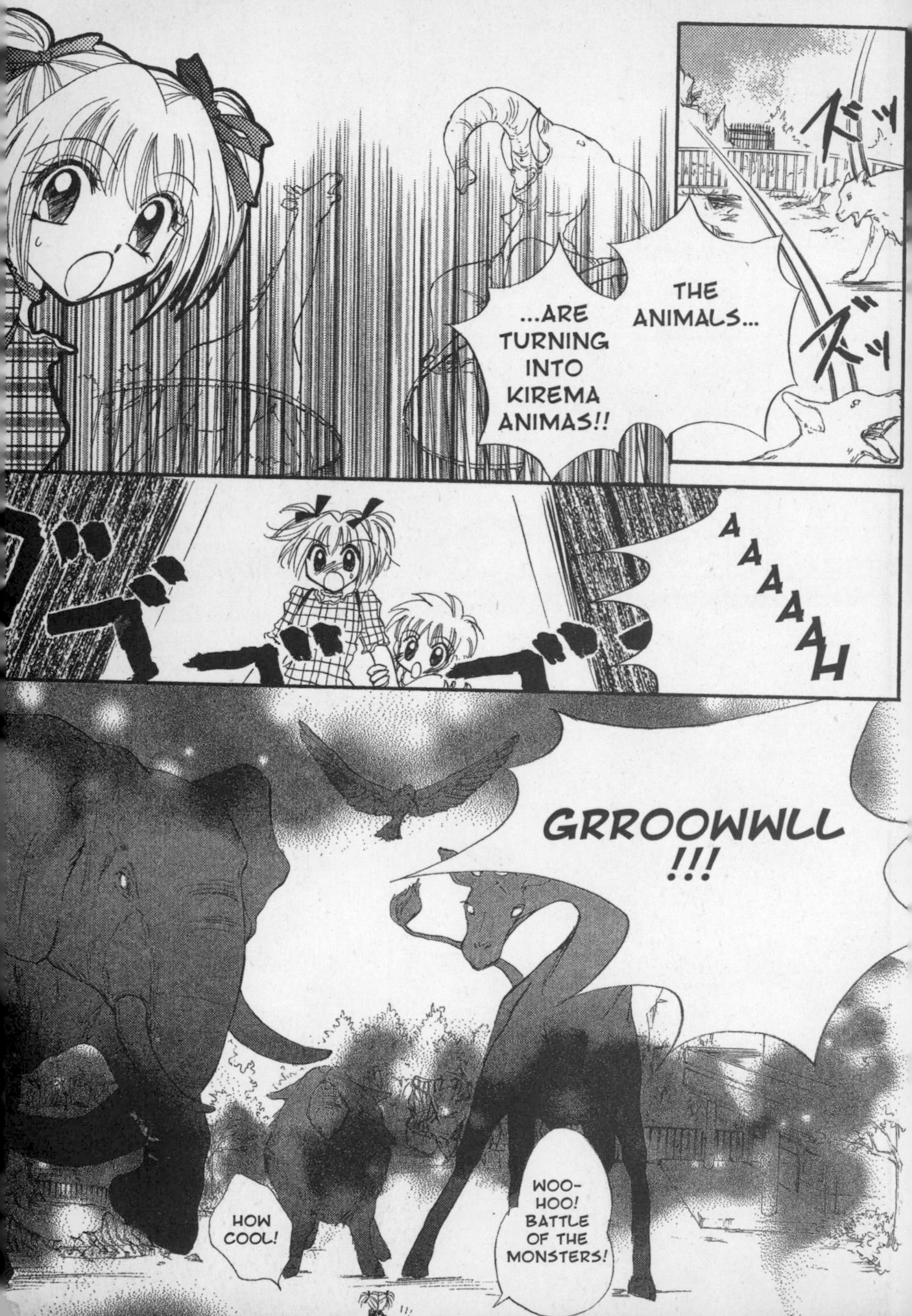
ズッ
ズッ
THE ANIMALS...
...ARE TURNING INTO KIREMA ANIMAS!!
AAAAAH
GRROOWWLL !!!
WOO-HOO! BATTLE OF THE MONSTERS!
HOW COOL!

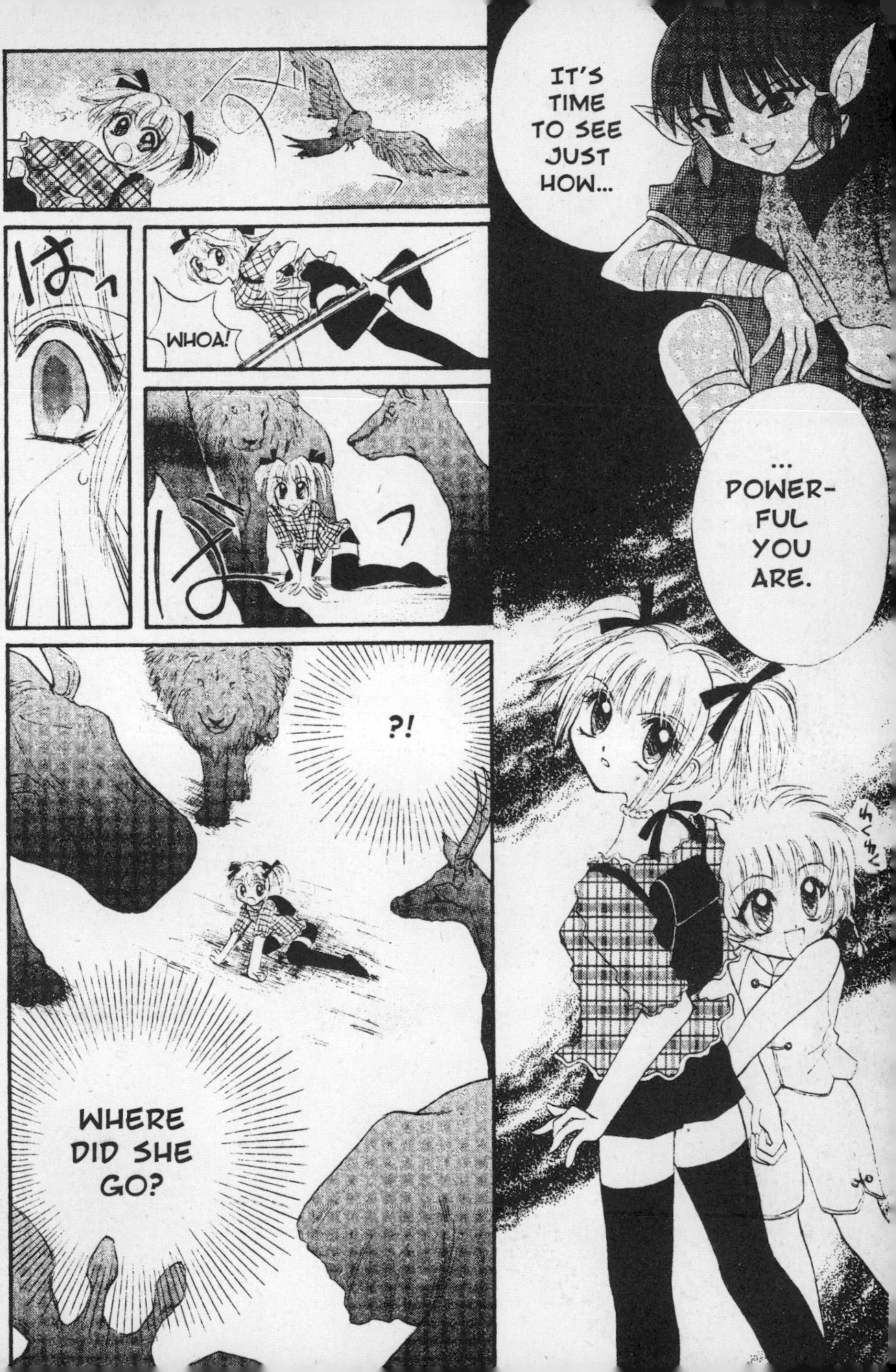
IT'S TIME TO SEE JUST HOW...
... POWERFUL YOU ARE.
WHOA!
はっ
はっ
?!
WHERE DID SHE GO?

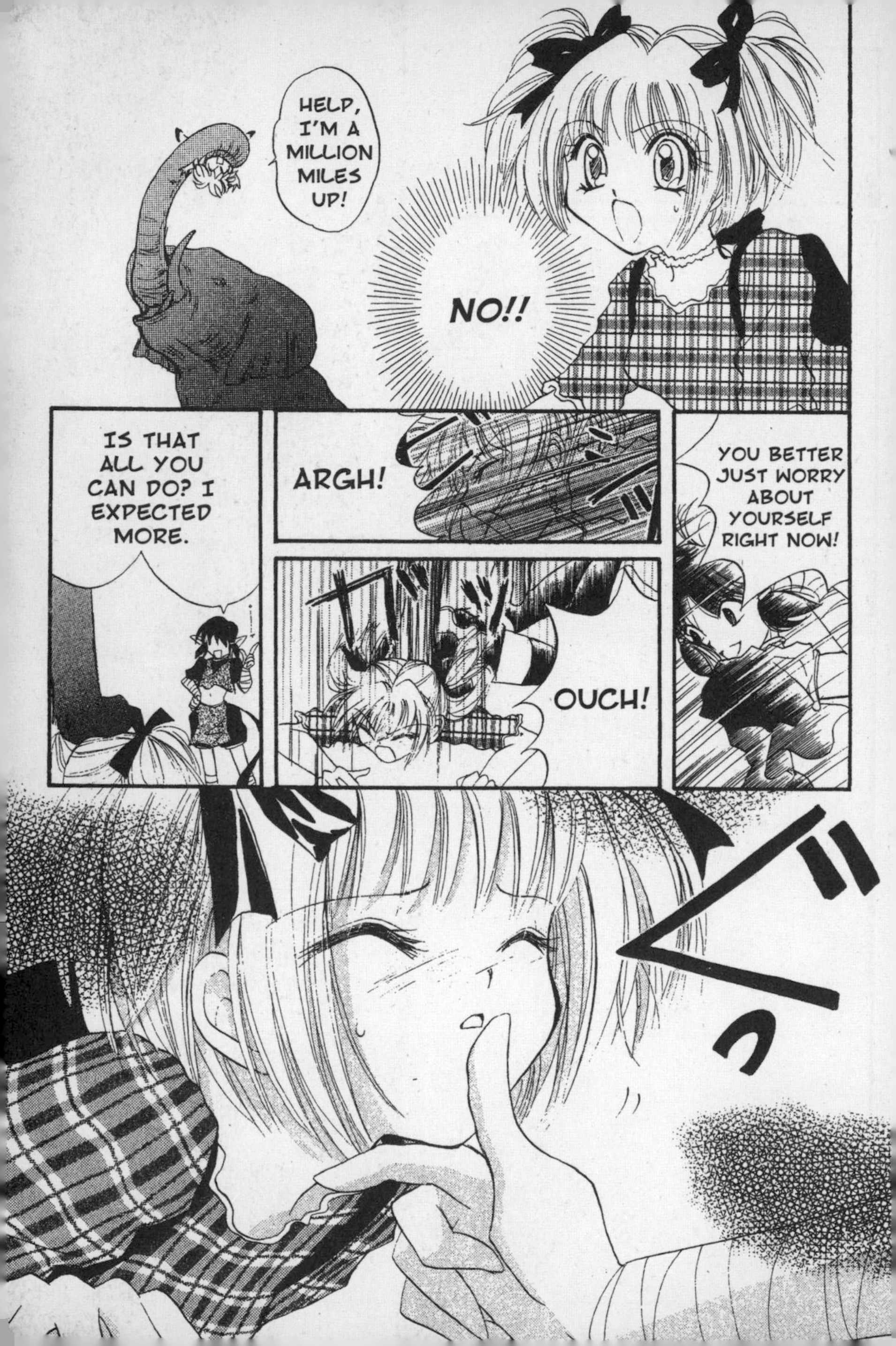
HELP, I'M A MILLION MILES UP!
NO!!
YOU BETTER JUST WORRY ABOUT YOURSELF RIGHT NOW!
ARGH!
OUCH!
IS THAT ALL YOU CAN DO? I EXPECTED MORE.

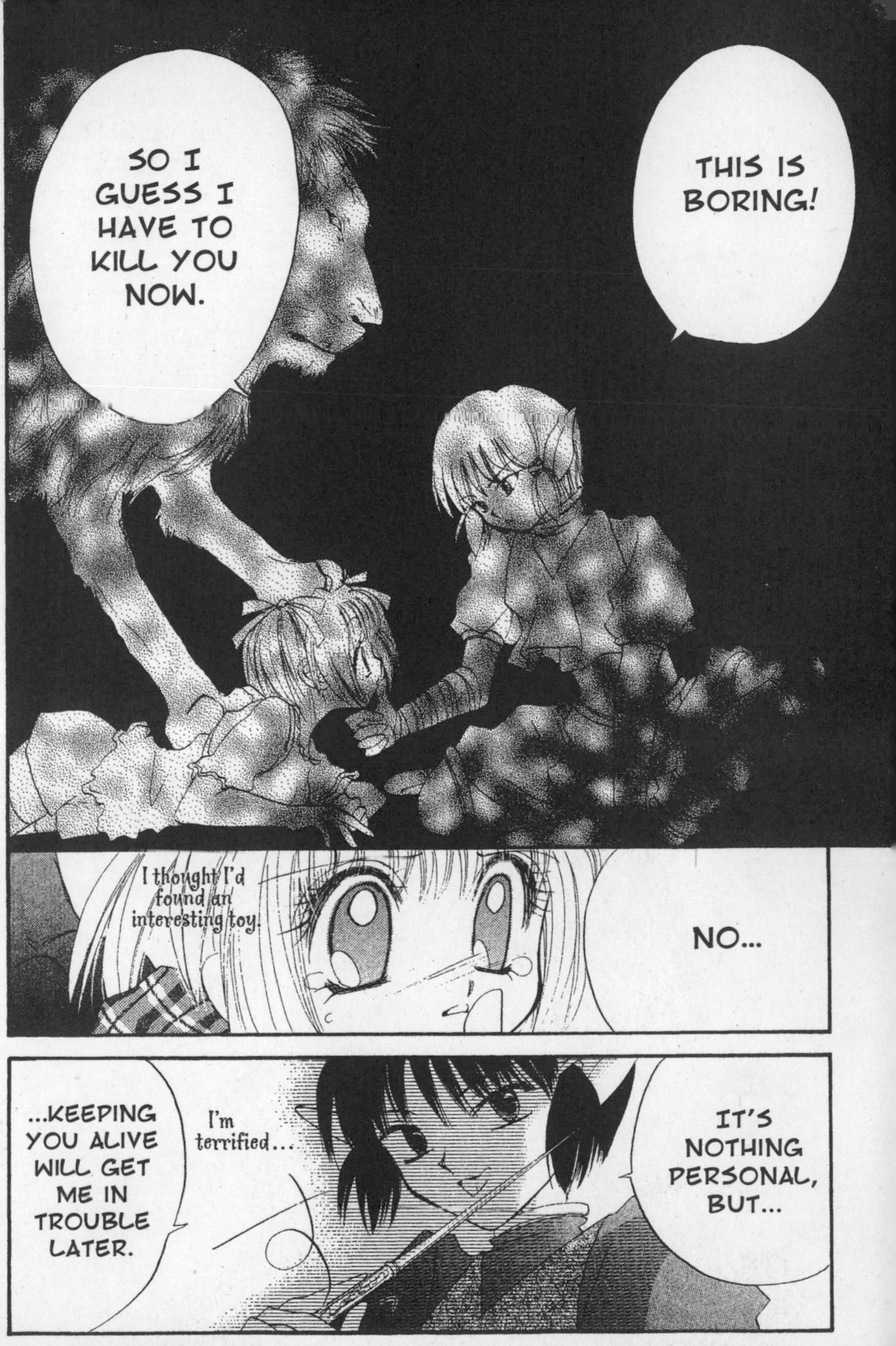
THIS IS BORING!
SO I GUESS I HAVE TO KILL YOU NOW.
NO...
I thought I'd found an interesting toy.
IT'S NOTHING PERSONAL, BUT...
I'm terrified...
...KEEPING YOU ALIVE WILL GET ME IN TROUBLE LATER.

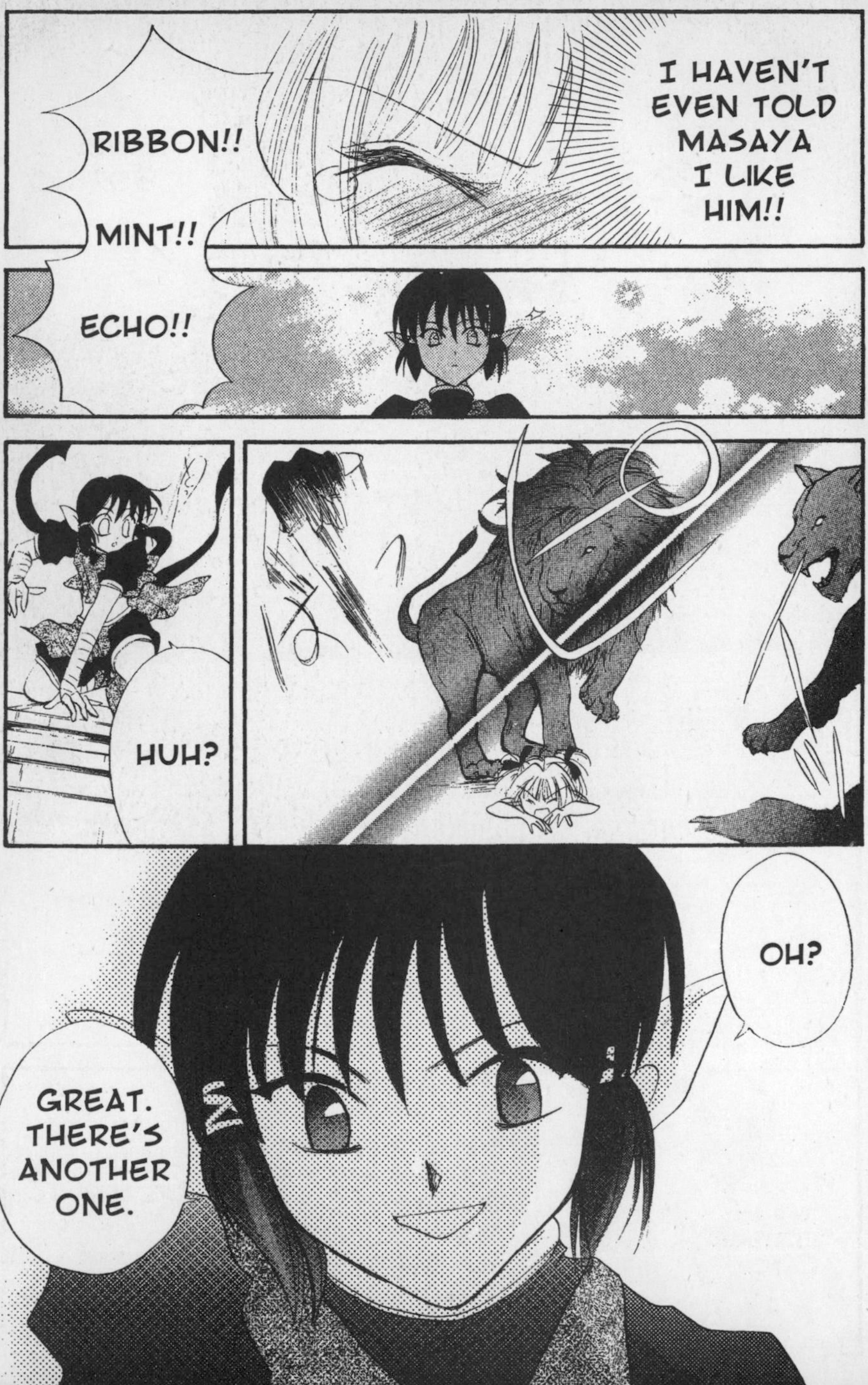
I HAVEN'T EVEN TOLD MASAYA I LIKE HIM!!
RIBBON!! MINT!! ECHO!!
HUH?
OH?
GREAT. THERE'S ANOTHER ONE.

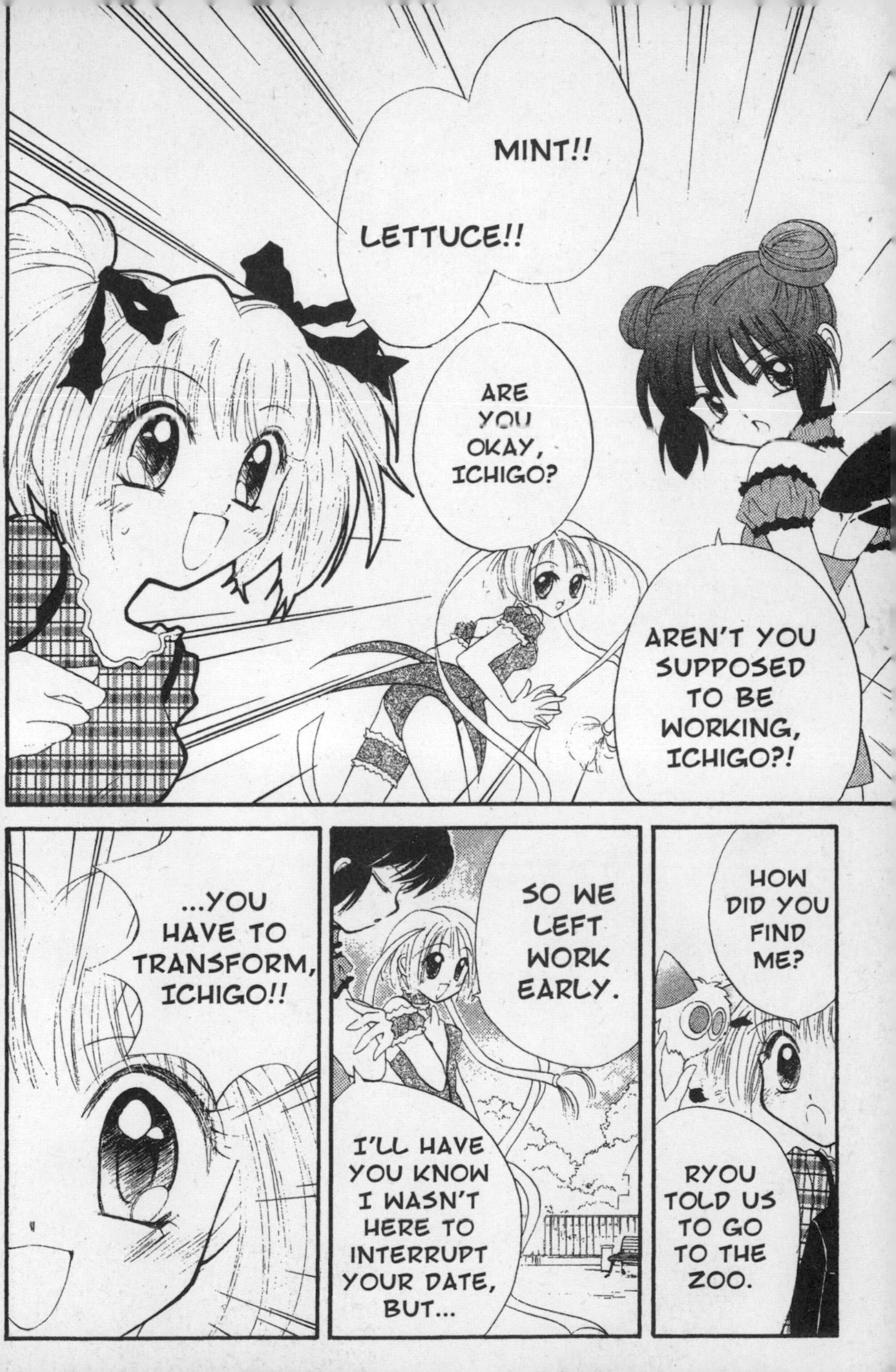
MINT!! LETTUCE!!
ARE YOU OKAY, ICHIGO?
AREN'T YOU SUPPOSED TO BE WORKING, ICHIGO?!
HOW DID YOU FIND ME?
RYOU TOLD US TO GO TO THE ZOO.
SO WE LEFT WORK EARLY.
I'LL HAVE YOU KNOW I WASN'T HERE TO INTERRUPT YOUR DATE, BUT...
...YOU HAVE TO TRANSFORM, ICHIGO!!

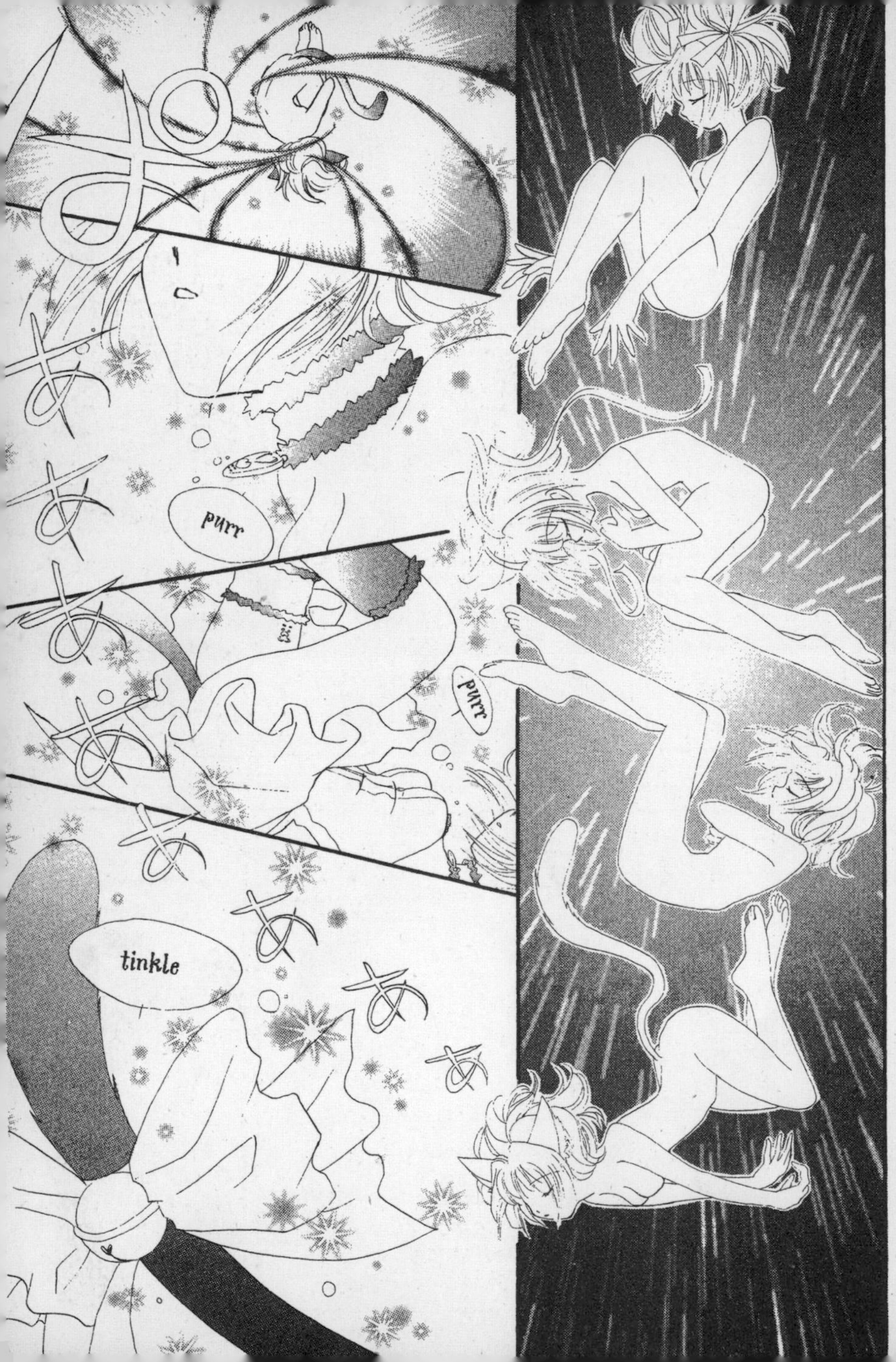

あ
あ
あ
あ
あ
あ
あ
あ
purr
purr
tinkle

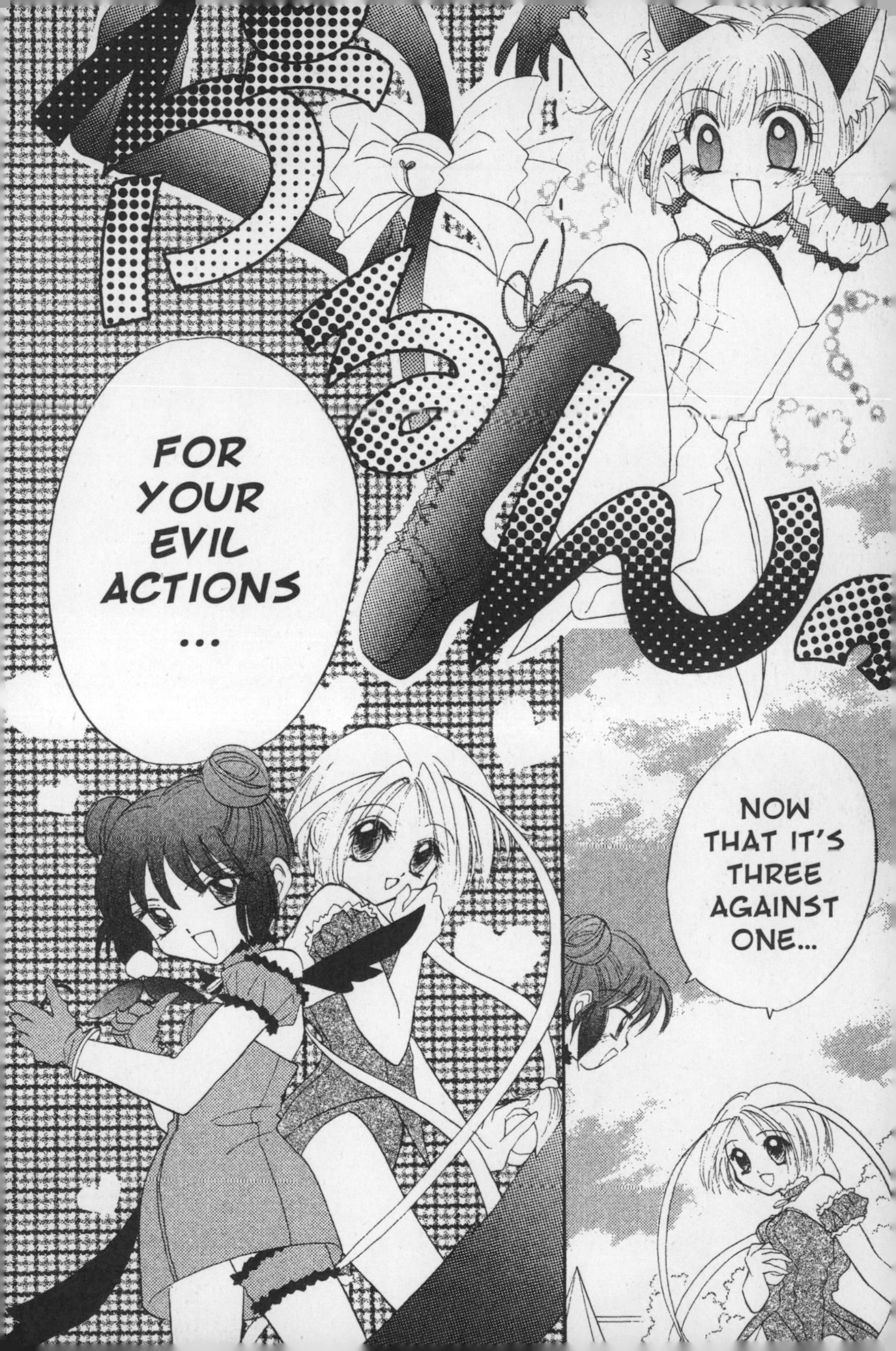
FOR YOUR EVIL ACTIONS ...
NOW THAT IT'S THREE AGAINST ONE...

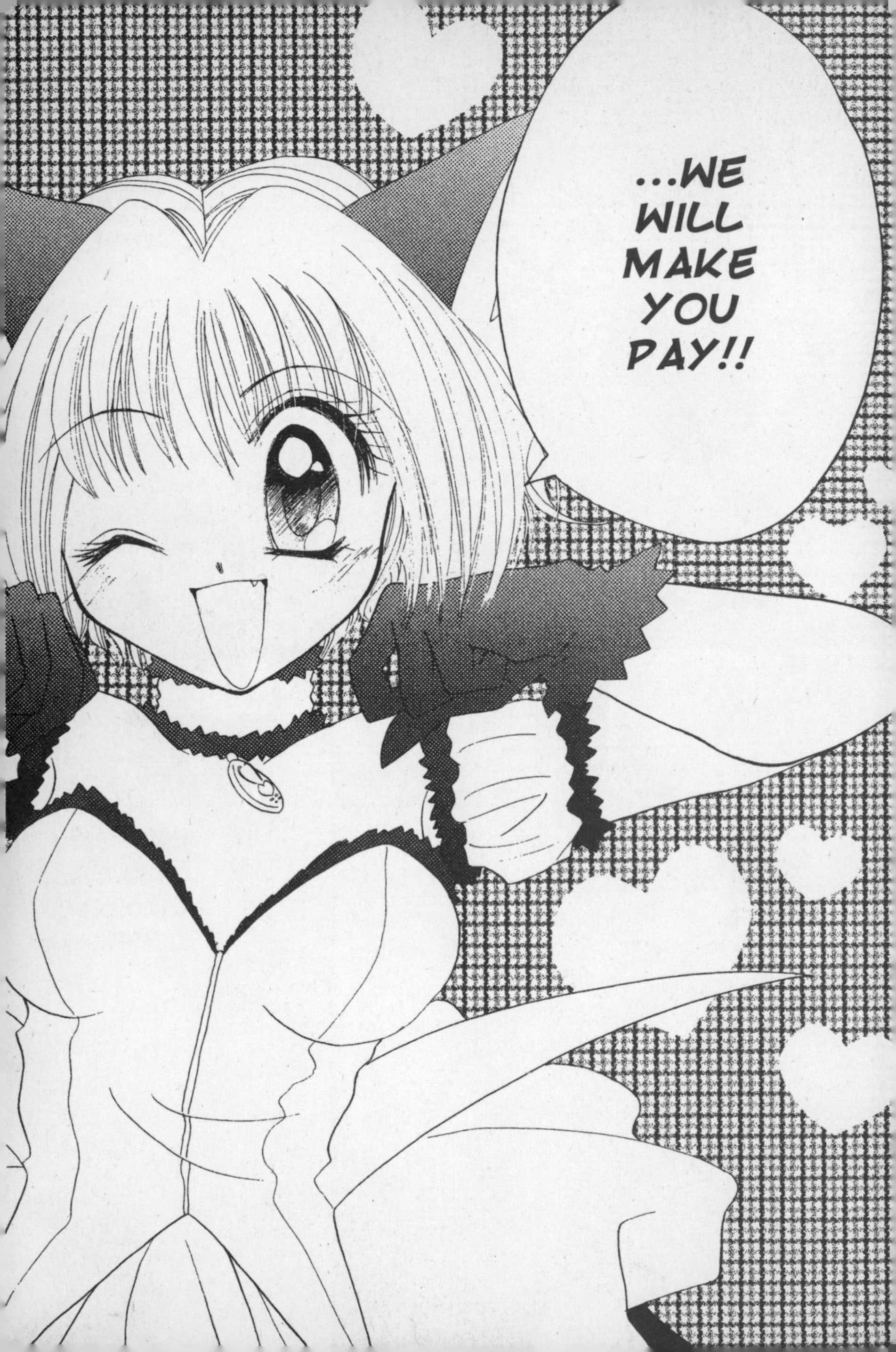
...WE WILL MAKE YOU PAY!!

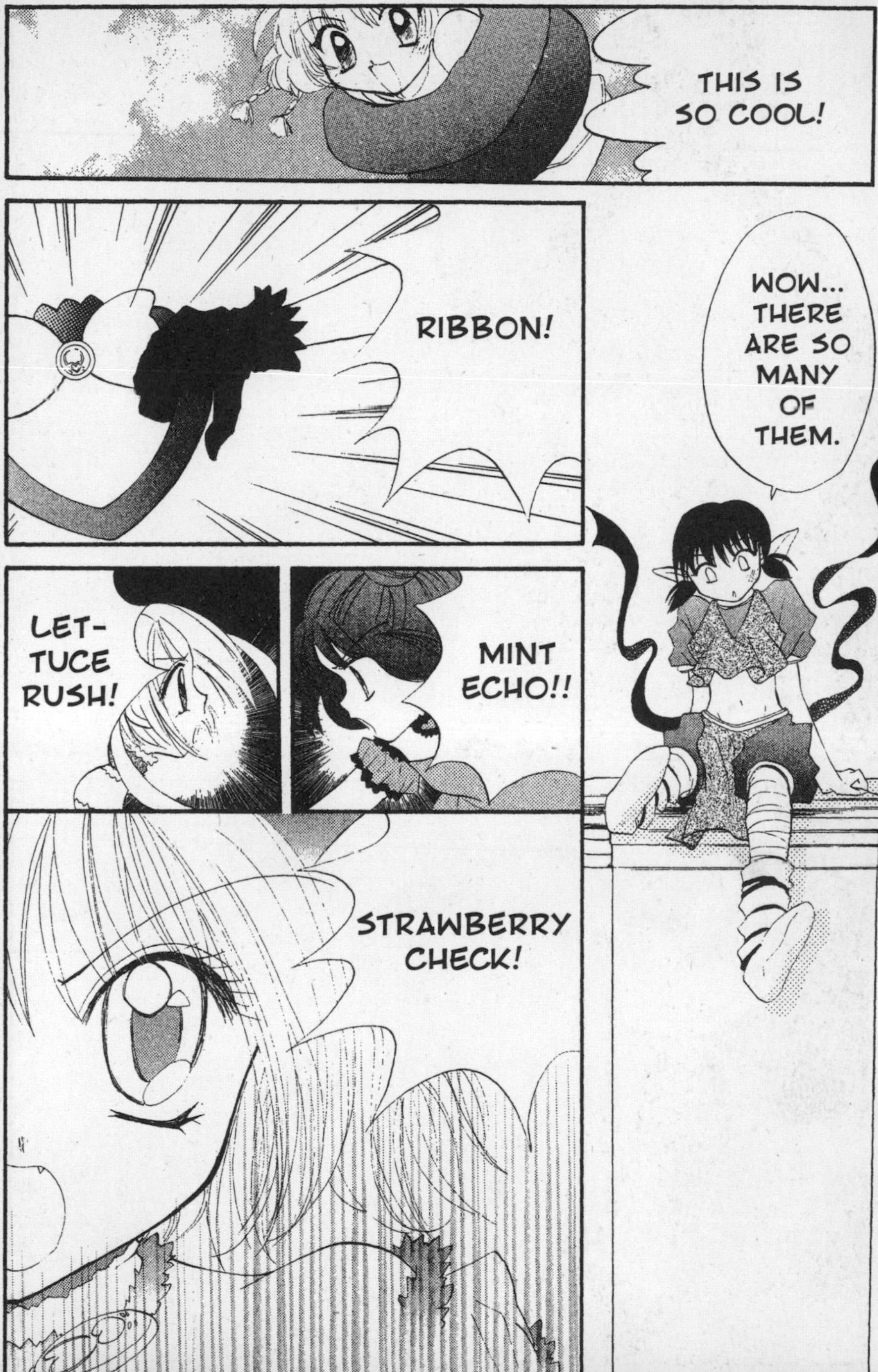
THIS IS SO COOL!
WOW... THERE ARE SO MANY OF THEM.
RIBBON!
MINT ECHO!!
LET-TUCE RUSH!
STRAWBERRY CHECK!

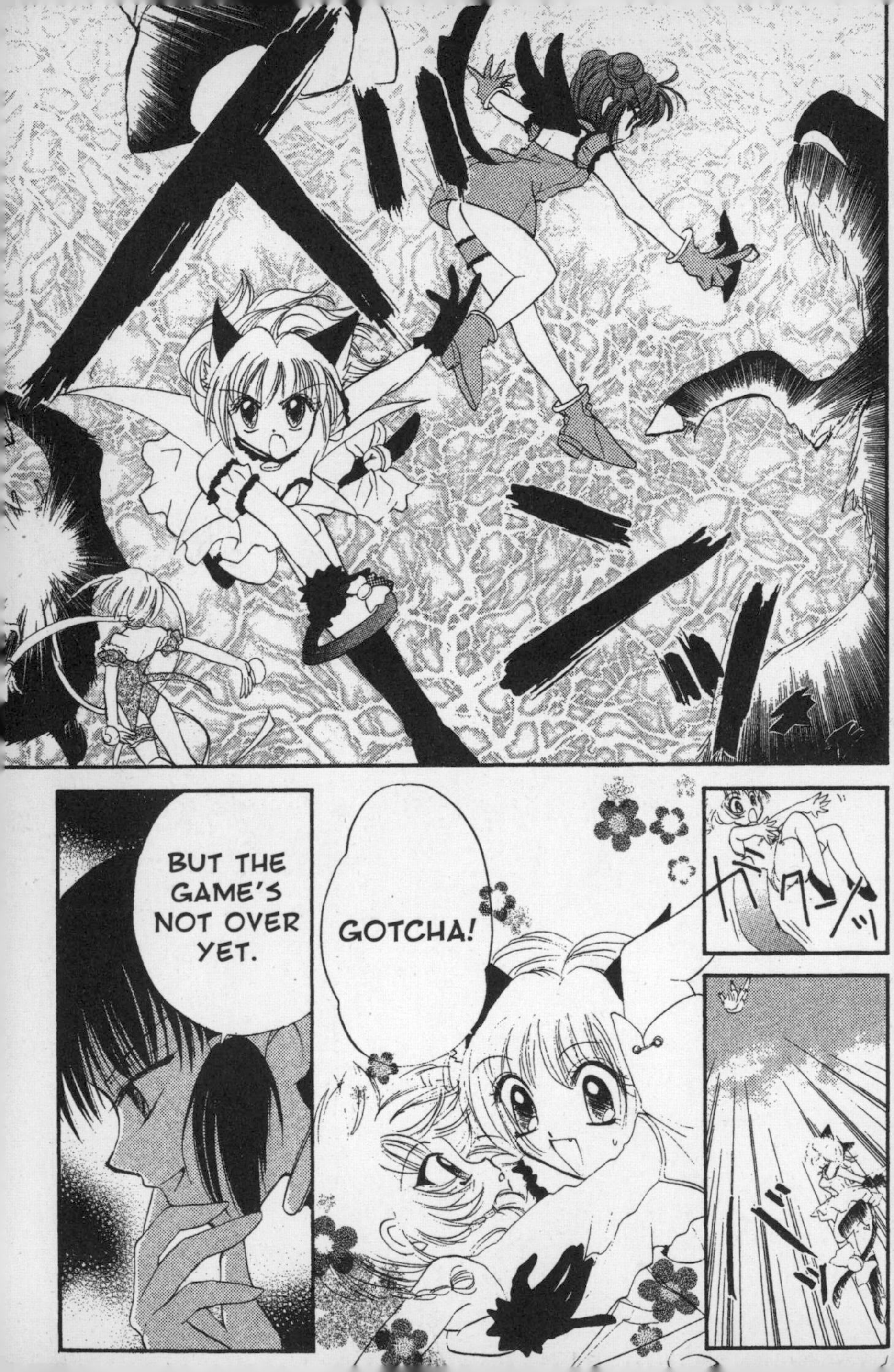
GOTCHA!
BUT THE GAME'S NOT OVER YET.

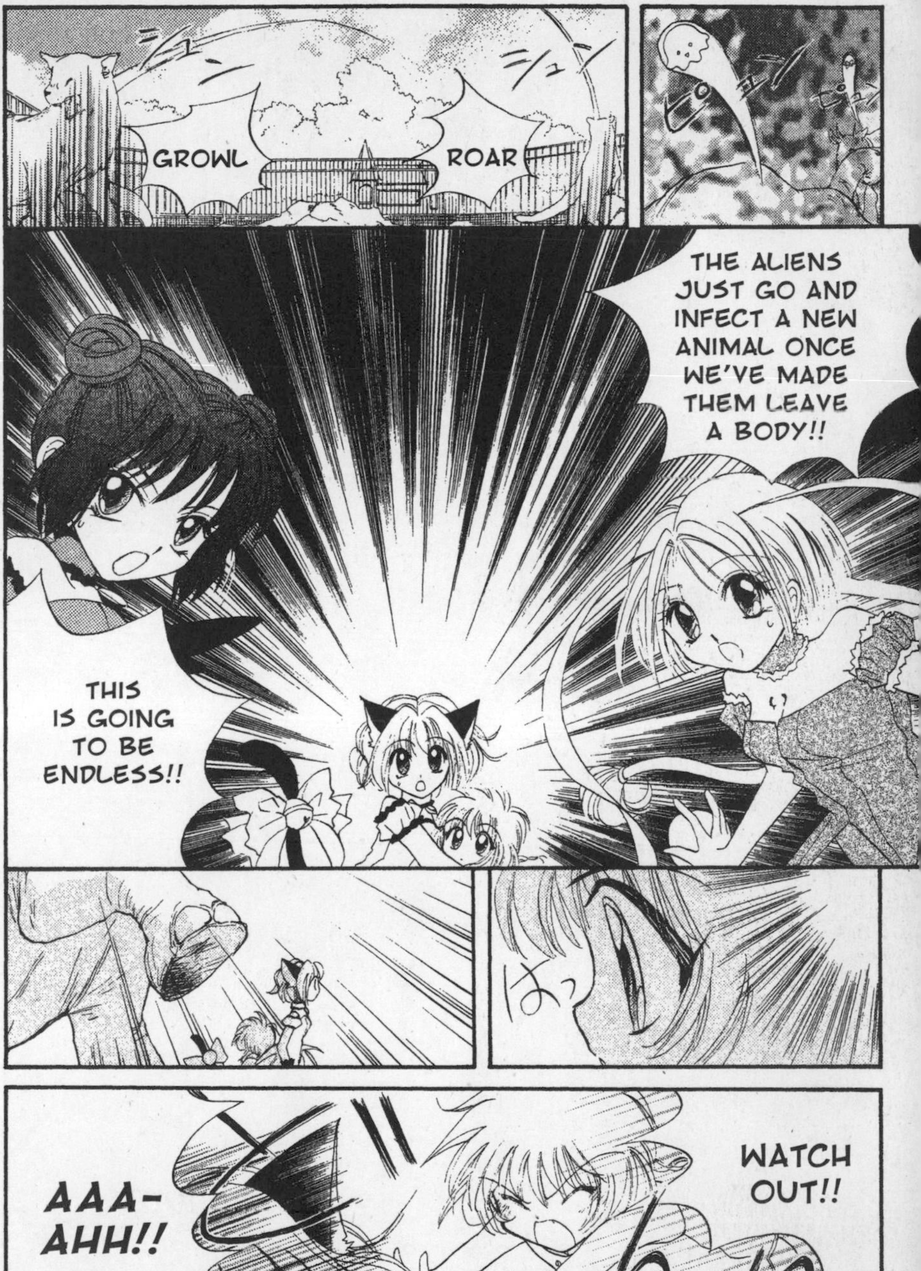
ROAR
GROWL
THE ALIENS JUST GO AND INFECT A NEW ANIMAL ONCE WE'VE MADE THEM LEAVE A BODY!!
THIS IS GOING TO BE ENDLESS!!
はっ
WATCH OUT!!
AAA-AHH!!

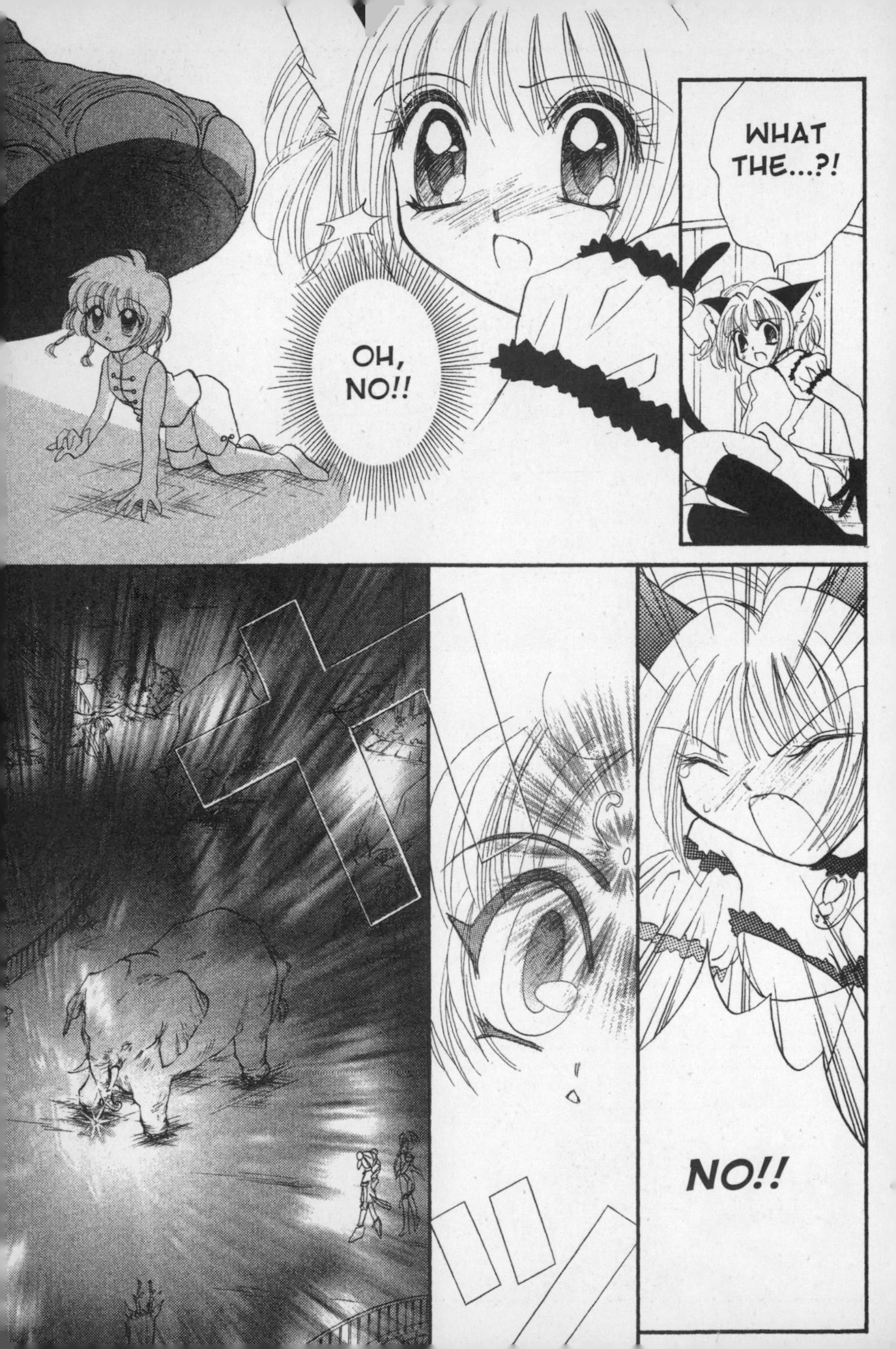
WHAT THE...?!
OH, NO!!
NO!!

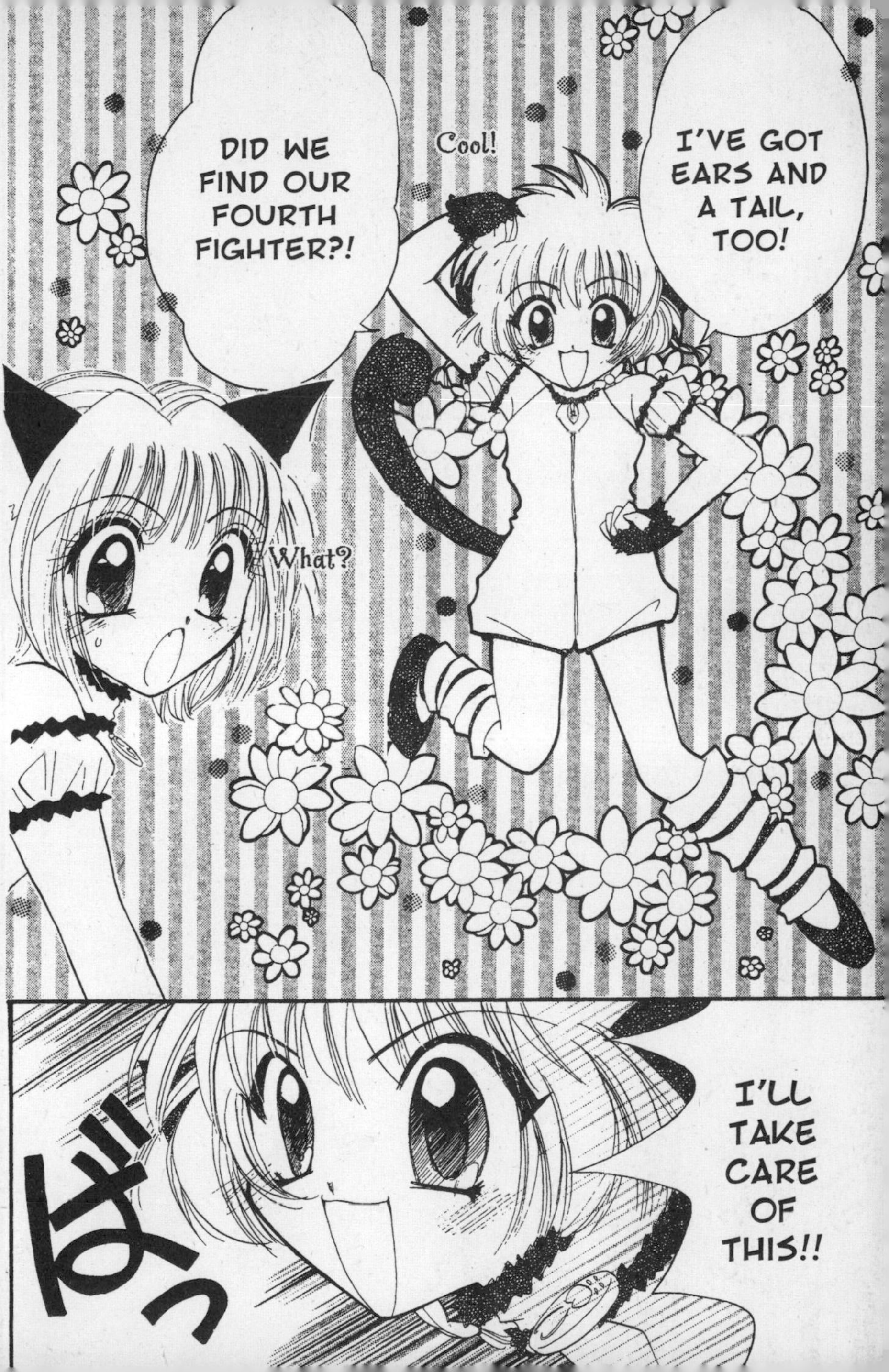
I'VE GOT EARS AND A TAIL, TOO!
Cool!
DID WE FIND OUR FOURTH FIGHTER?!
What?
I'LL TAKE CARE OF THIS!!

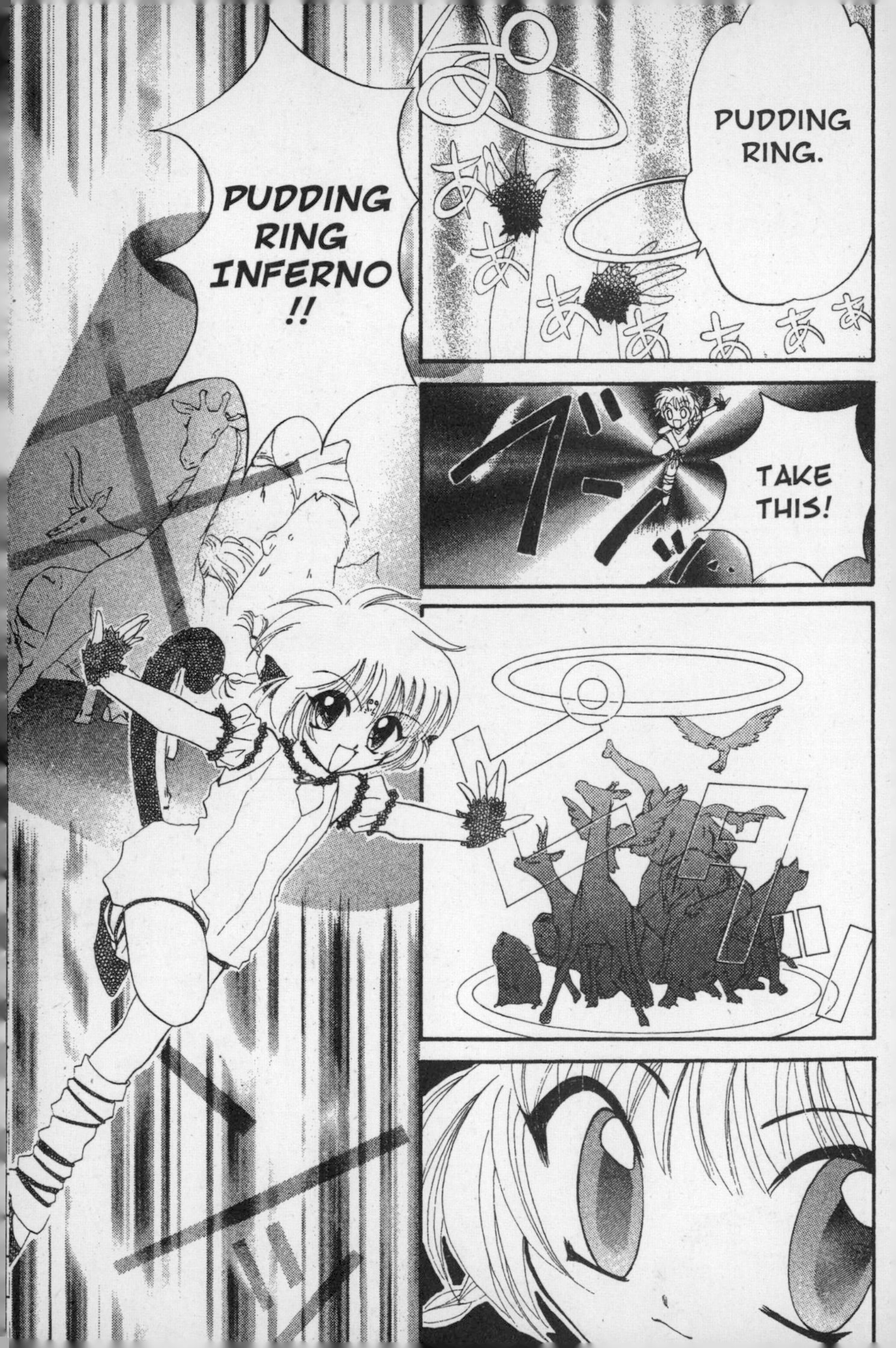
PUDDING RING.
TAKE THIS!
PUDDING RING INFERNO !!

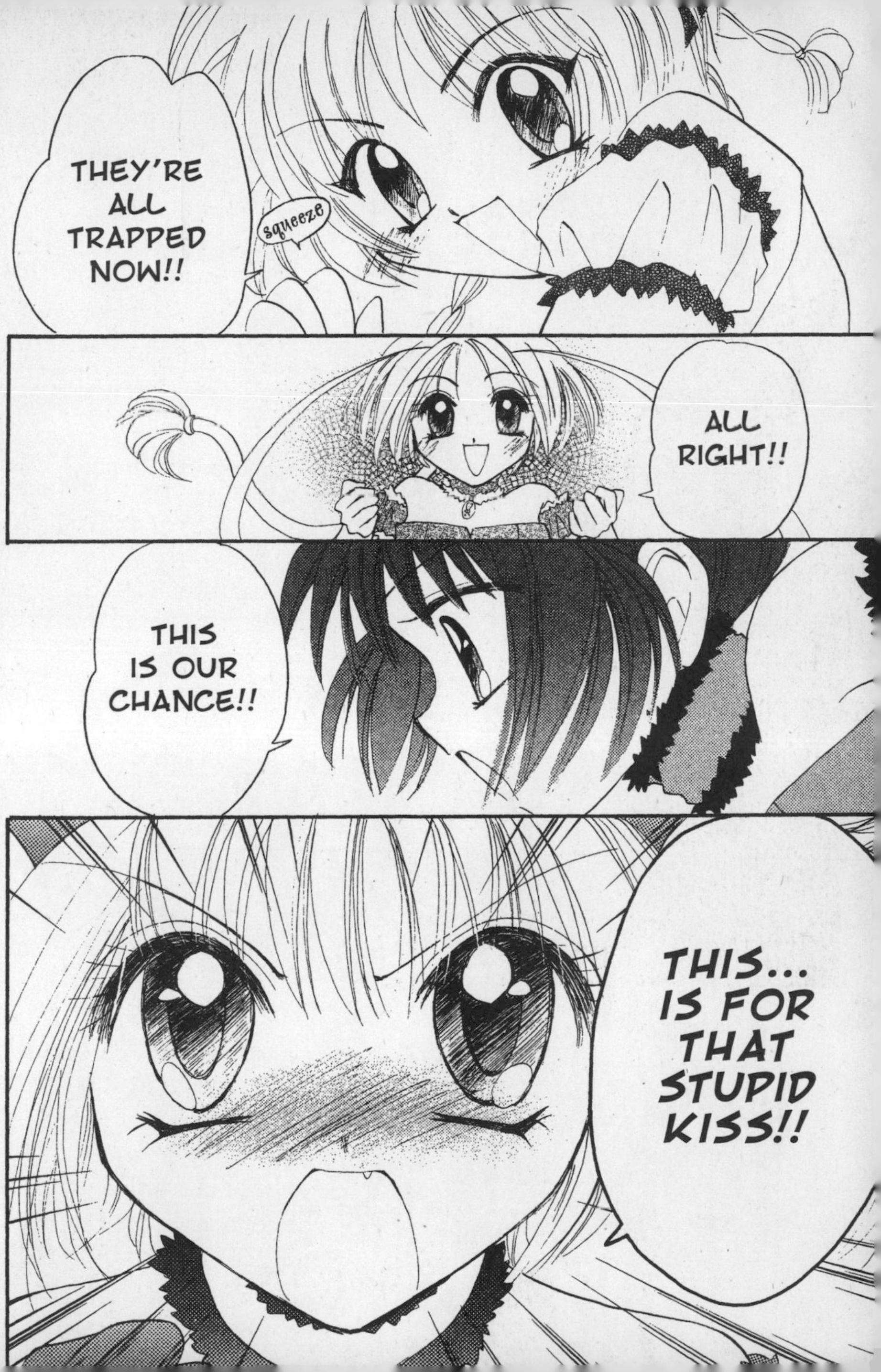
THEY'RE ALL TRAPPED NOW!!
squeeze
ALL RIGHT!!
THIS IS OUR CHANCE!!
THIS... IS FOR THAT STUPID KISS!!

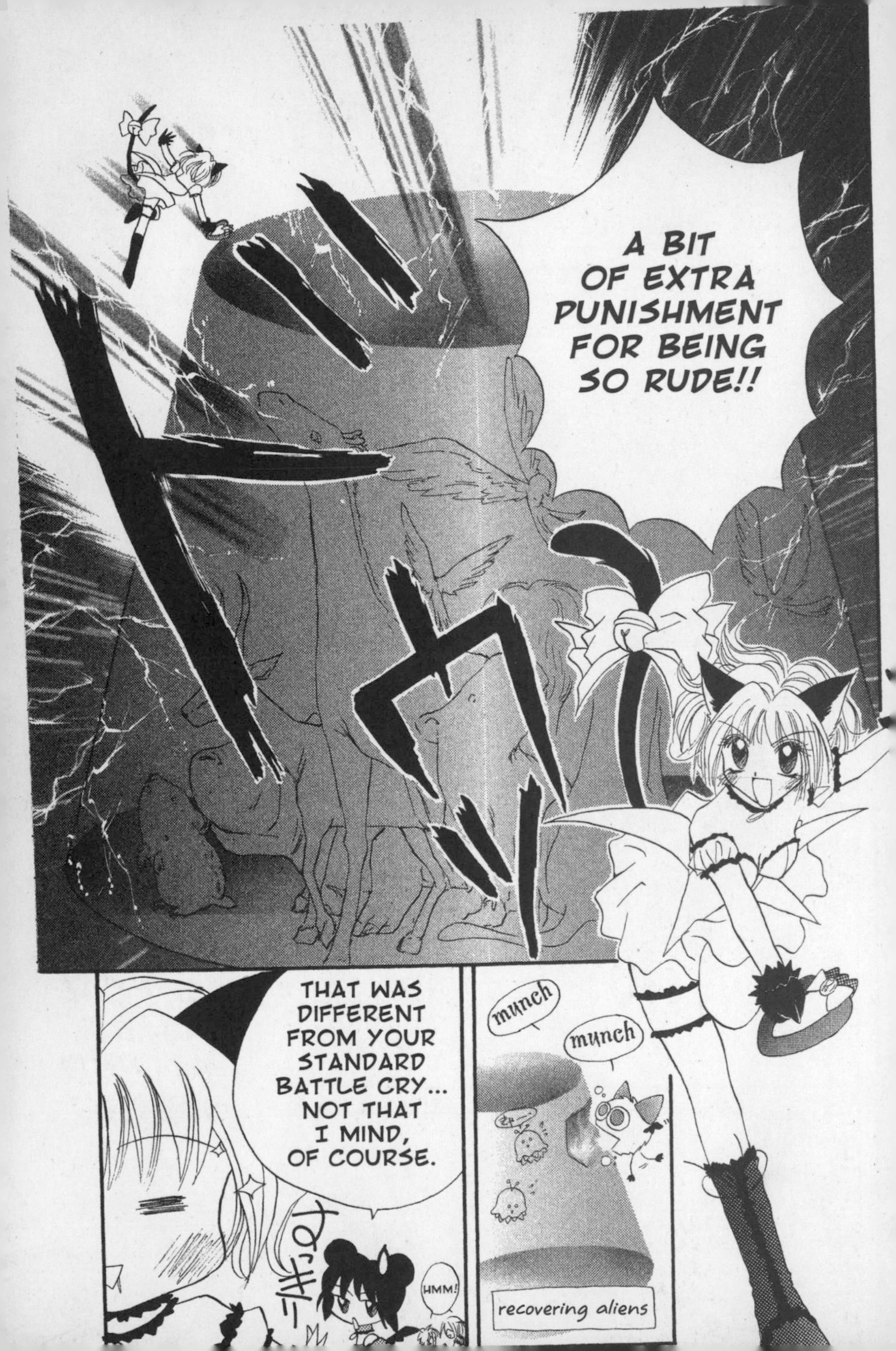
A BIT OF EXTRA PUNISHMENT FOR BEING SO RUDE!!
munch
munch
recovering aliens
THAT WAS DIFFERENT FROM YOUR STANDARD BATTLE CRY... NOT THAT I MIND, OF COURSE.
HMM!

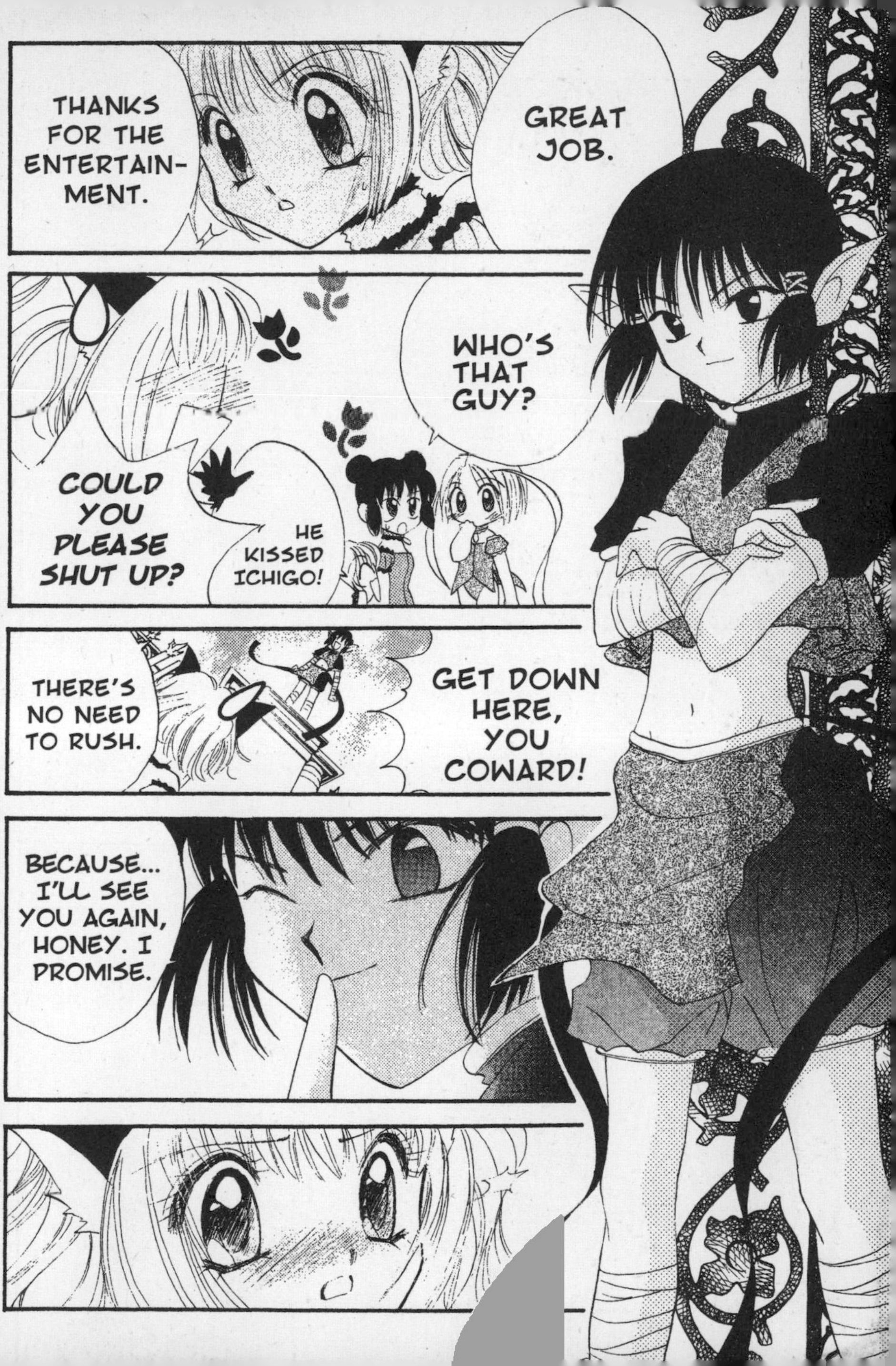
GREAT JOB.
THANKS FOR THE ENTERTAIN-MENT.
WHO'S THAT GUY?
HE KISSED ICHIGO!
COULD YOU PLEASE SHUT UP?
GET DOWN HERE, YOU COWARD!
THERE'S NO NEED TO RUSH.
BECAUSE... I'LL SEE YOU AGAIN, HONEY. I PROMISE.

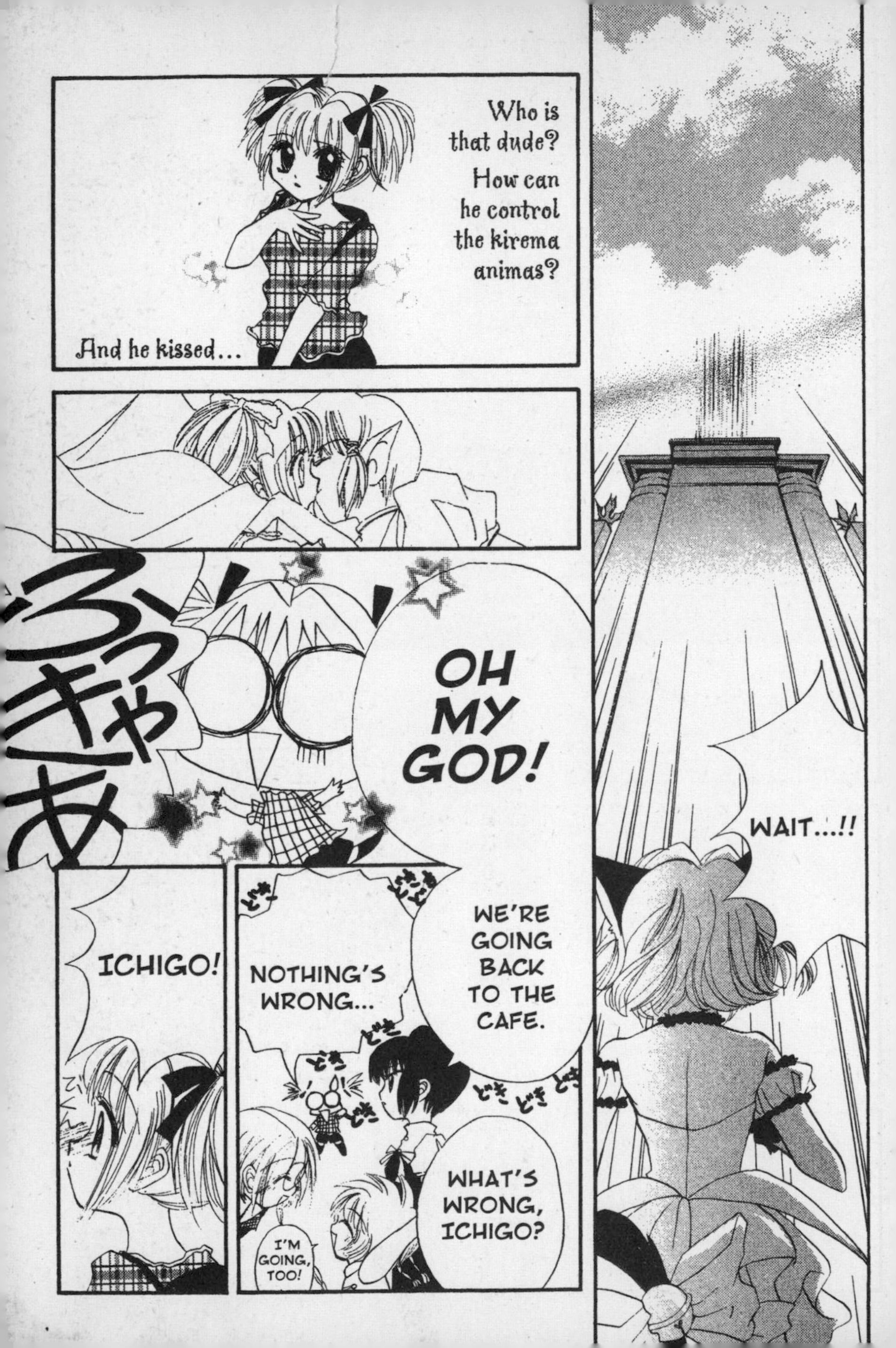
WAIT...!!
Who is that dude? How can he control the kirema animas?
And he kissed...
OH MY GOD!
WE'RE GOING BACK TO THE CAFE.
NOTHING'S WRONG...
どき どき どき
WHAT'S WRONG, ICHIGO?
I'M GOING, TOO!
ICHIGO!

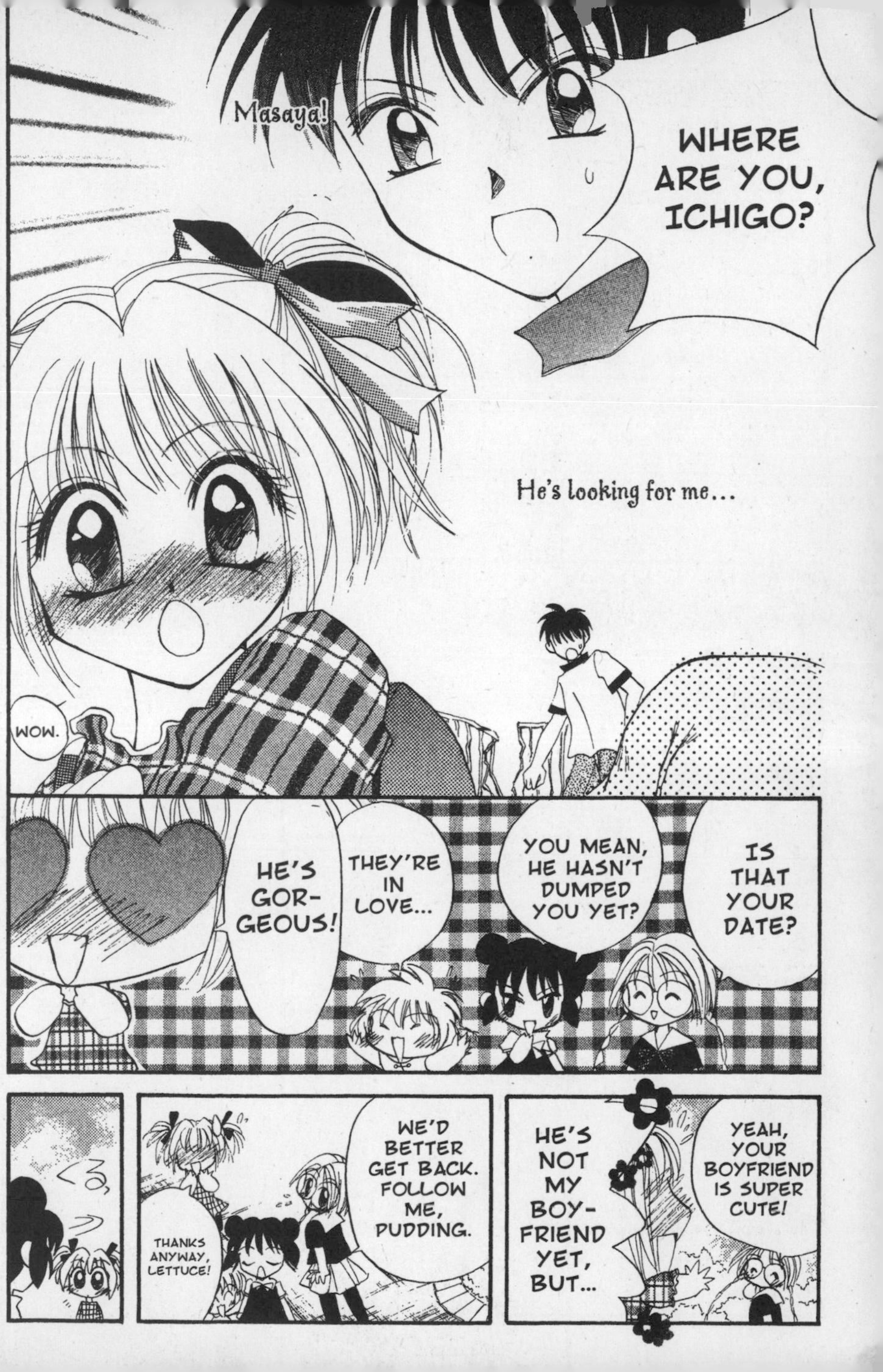
WHERE ARE YOU, ICHIGO?
Masaya!
He's looking for me...
WOW.
IS THAT YOUR DATE?
YOU MEAN, HE HASN'T DUMPED YOU YET?
THEY'RE IN LOVE...
HE'S GORGEOUS!
YEAH, YOUR BOYFRIEND IS SUPER CUTE!
HE'S NOT MY BOYFRIEND YET, BUT...
WE'D BETTER GET BACK. FOLLOW ME, PUDDING.
THANKS ANYWAY, LETTUCE!
くる

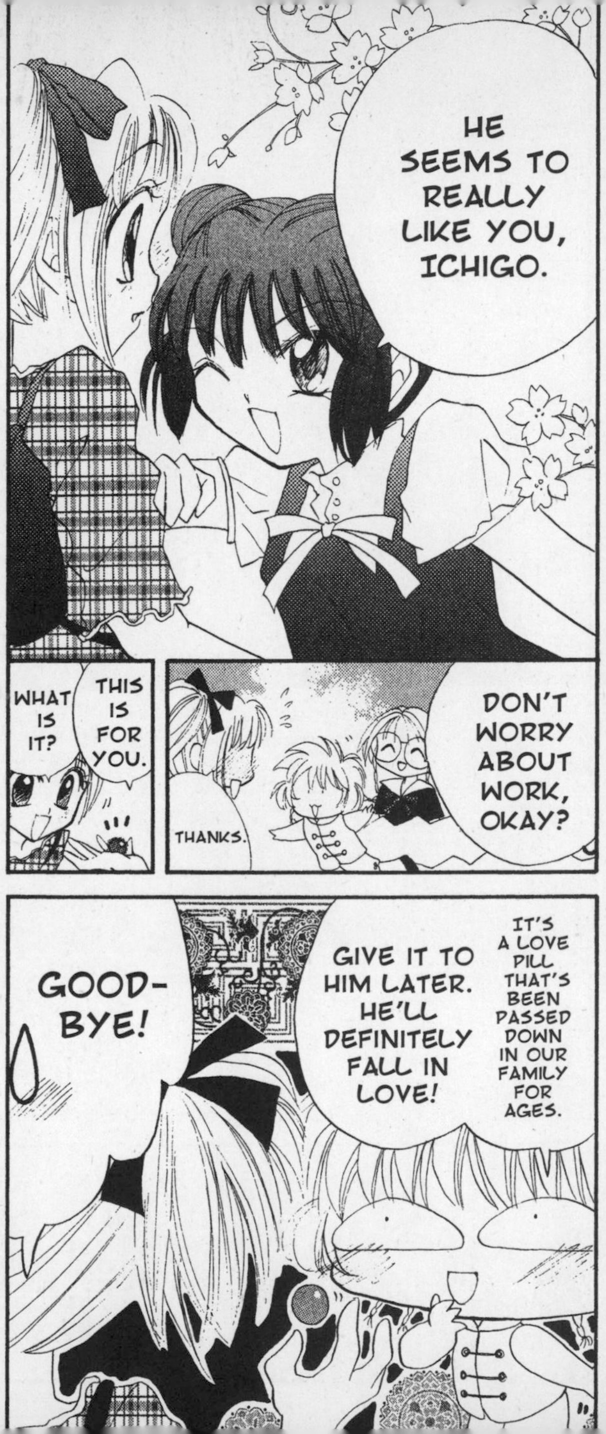

HE SEEMS TO REALLY LIKE YOU, ICHIGO.
DON'T WORRY ABOUT WORK, OKAY?
THANKS.
THIS IS FOR YOU.
WHAT IS IT?
IT'S A LOVE PILL THAT'S BEEN PASSED DOWN IN OUR FAMILY FOR AGES.
GIVE IT TO HIM LATER. HE'LL DEFINITELY FALL IN LOVE!
GOOD-BYE!

Business Meeting 1

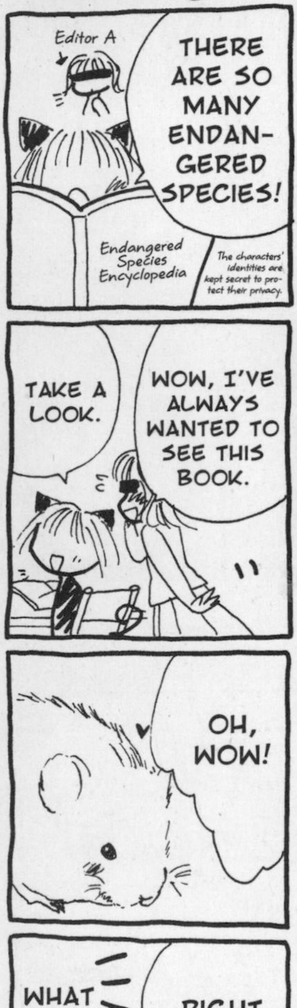

Editor A
THERE ARE SO MANY ENDANGERED SPECIES!
Endangered Species Encyclopedia
The characters' identities are kept secret to protect their privacy.
WOW, I'VE ALWAYS WANTED TO SEE THIS BOOK.
TAKE A LOOK.
OH, WOW!
RIGHT ON!!
WHAT?!

I think she was trying to explain that it was small and furry, but that's not exactly what came out.

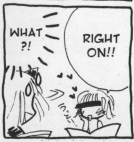

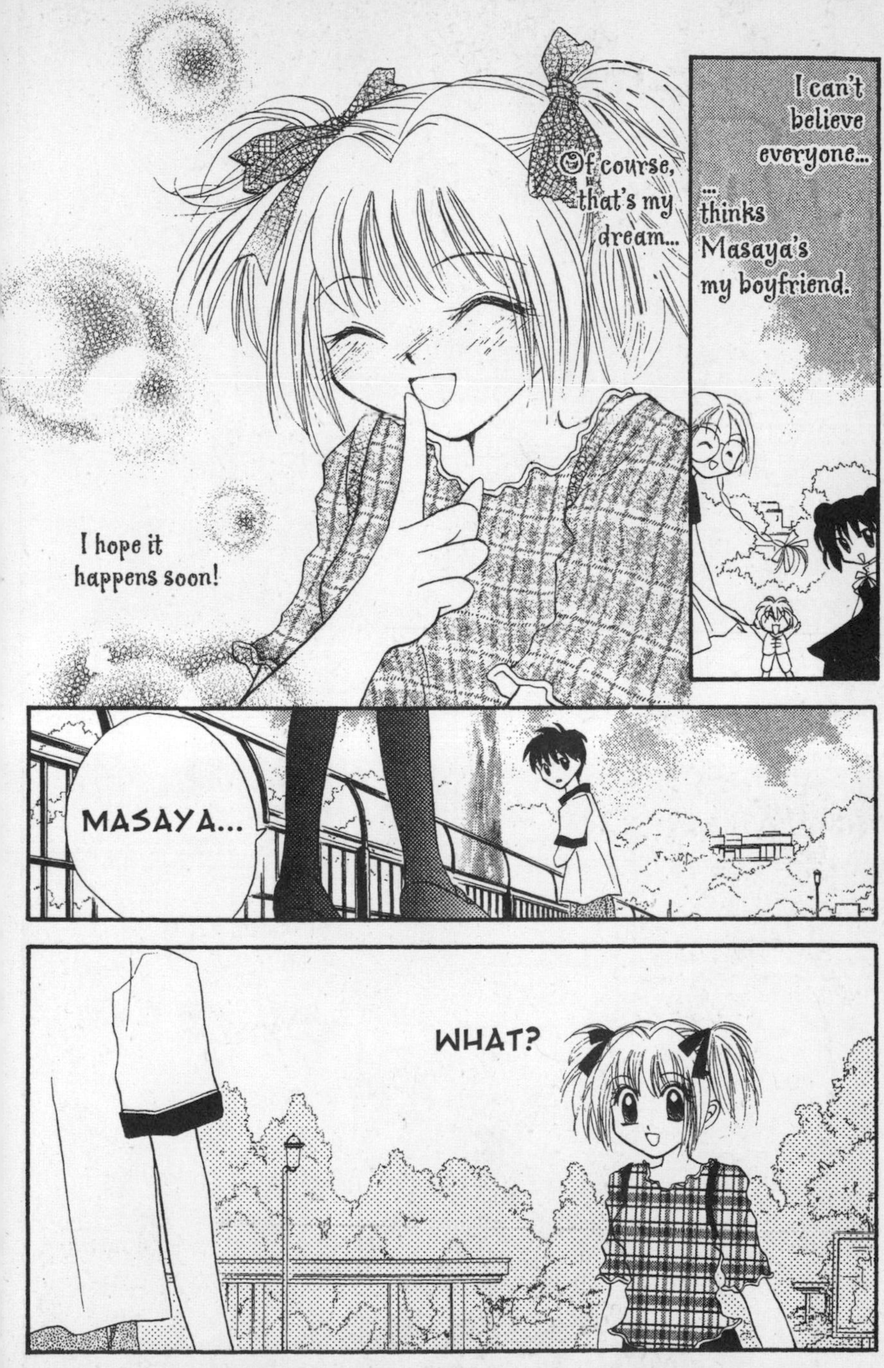
I can't believe everyone...
...thinks Masaya's my boyfriend.
Of course, that's my dream...
I hope it happens soon!
MASAYA...
WHAT?

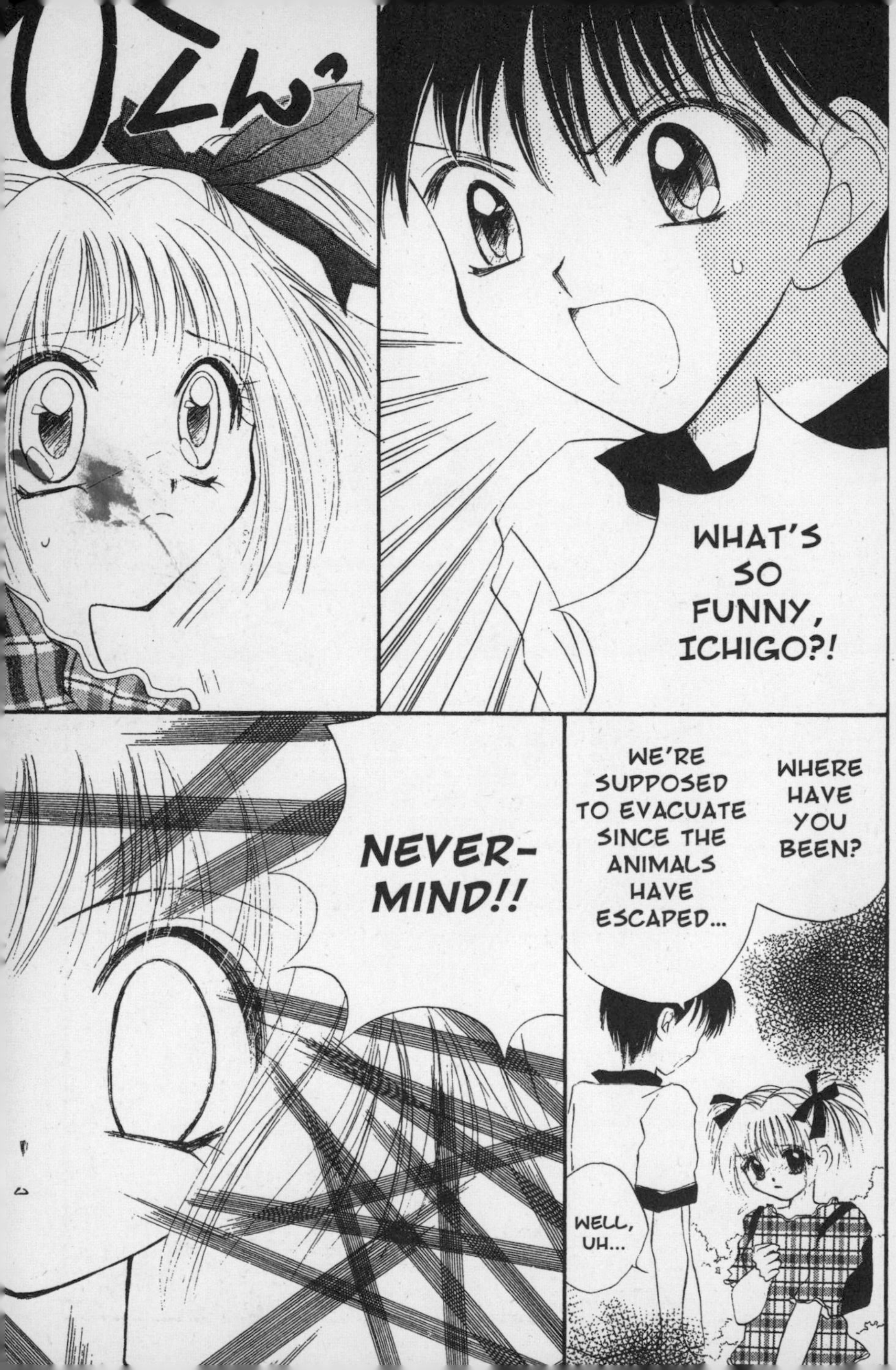
WHAT'S SO FUNNY, ICHIGO?!
WHERE HAVE YOU BEEN?
WE'RE SUPPOSED TO EVACUATE SINCE THE ANIMALS HAVE ESCAPED...
WELL, UH...
NEVER-MIND!!

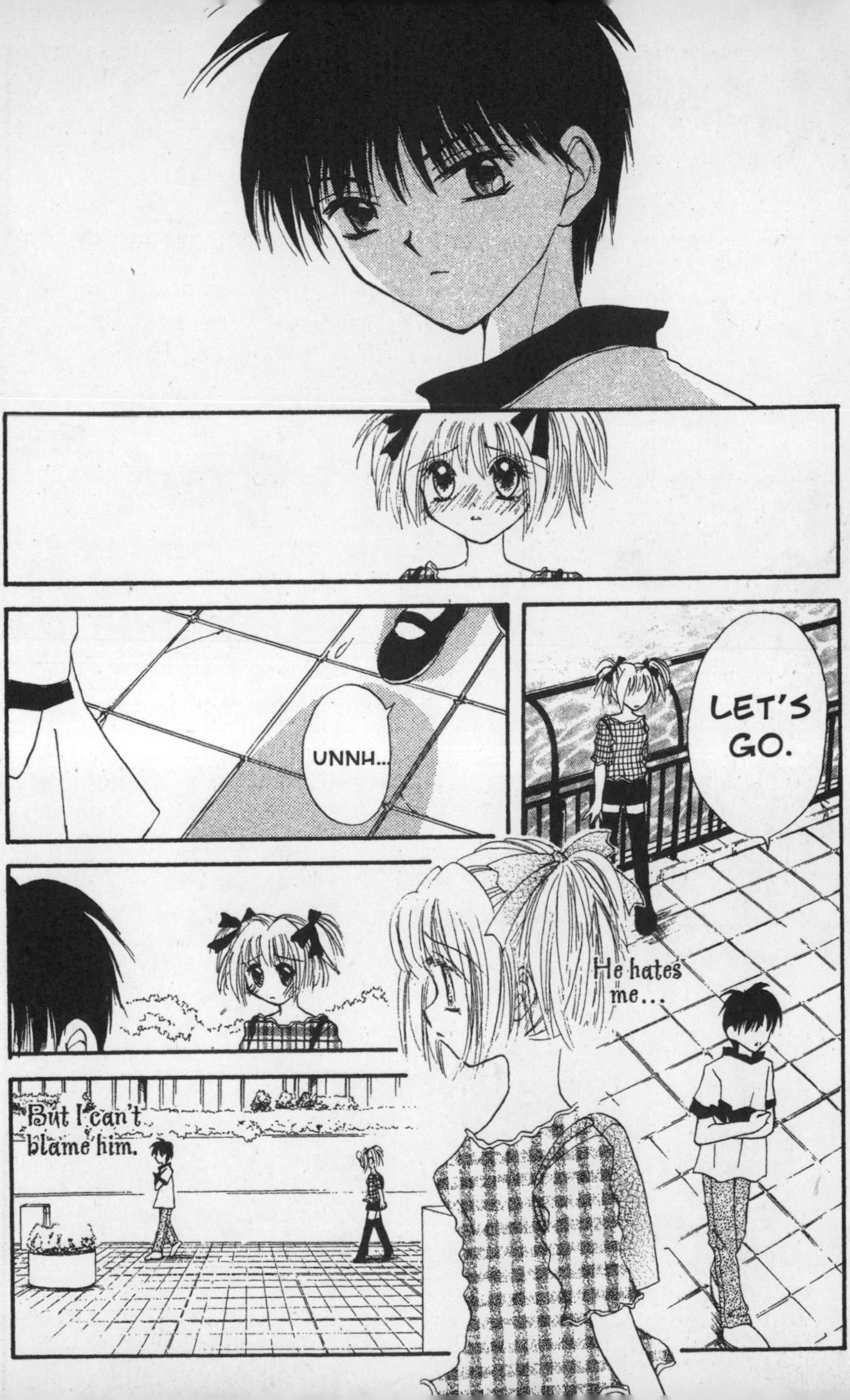
LET'S GO.
UNNH...
He hates me...
But I can't blame him.

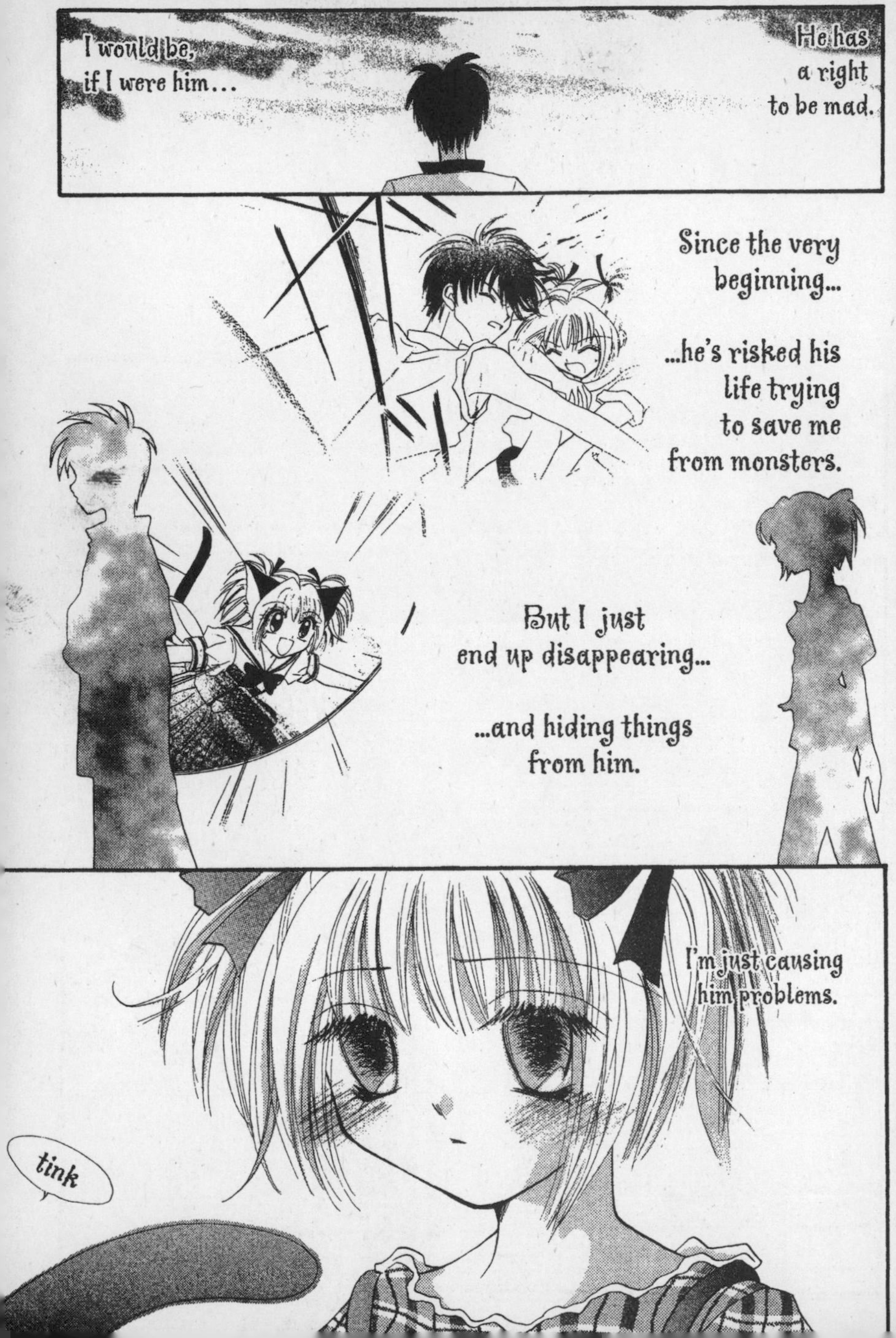
He has a right to be mad.
I would be, if I were him...
Since the very beginning...
...he's risked his life trying to save me from monsters.
But I just end up disappearing...
...and hiding things from him.
I'm just causing him problems.
tink

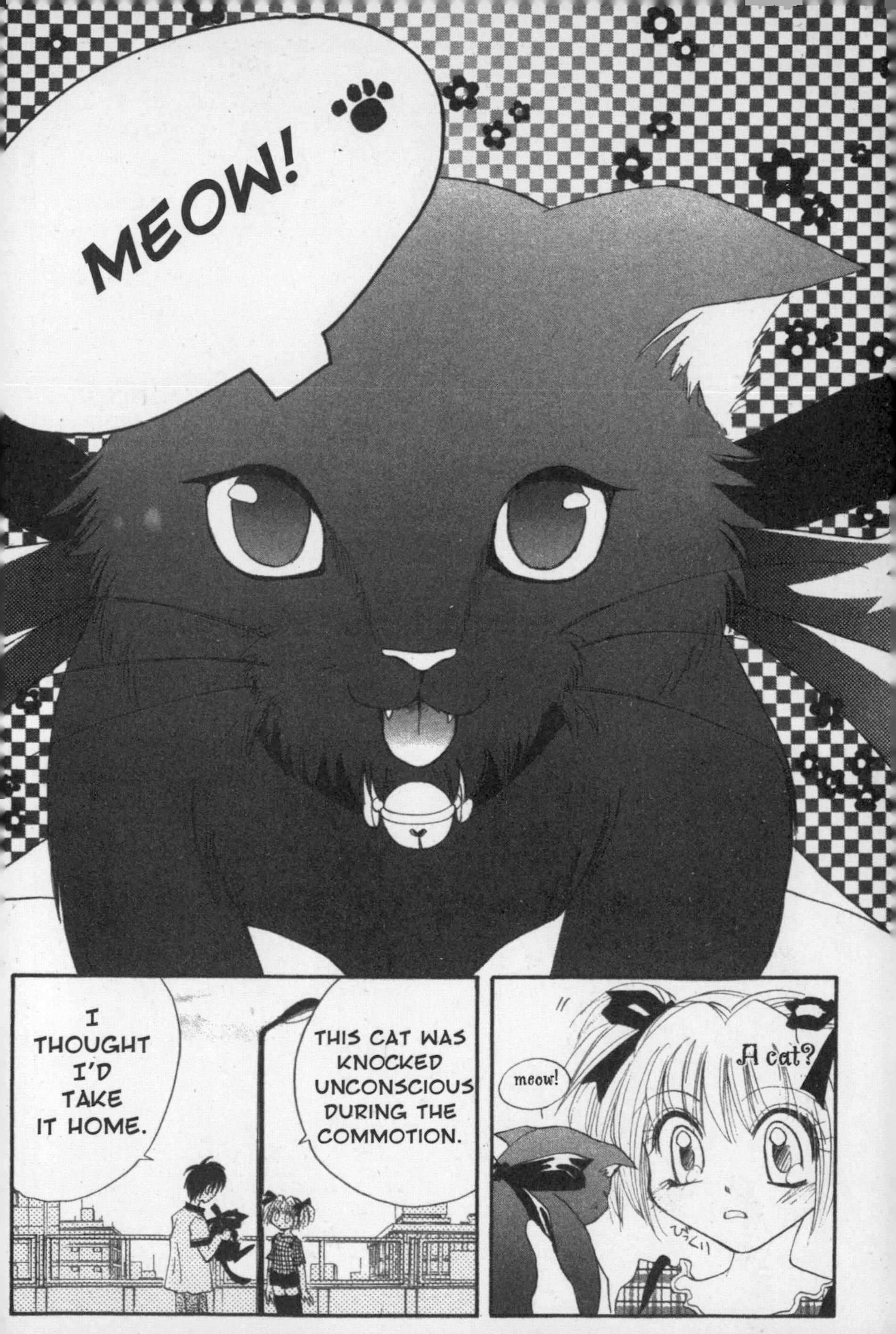
MEOW!
A cat?
meow!
THIS CAT WAS KNOCKED UNCONSCIOUS DURING THE COMMOTION.
I THOUGHT I'D TAKE IT HOME.

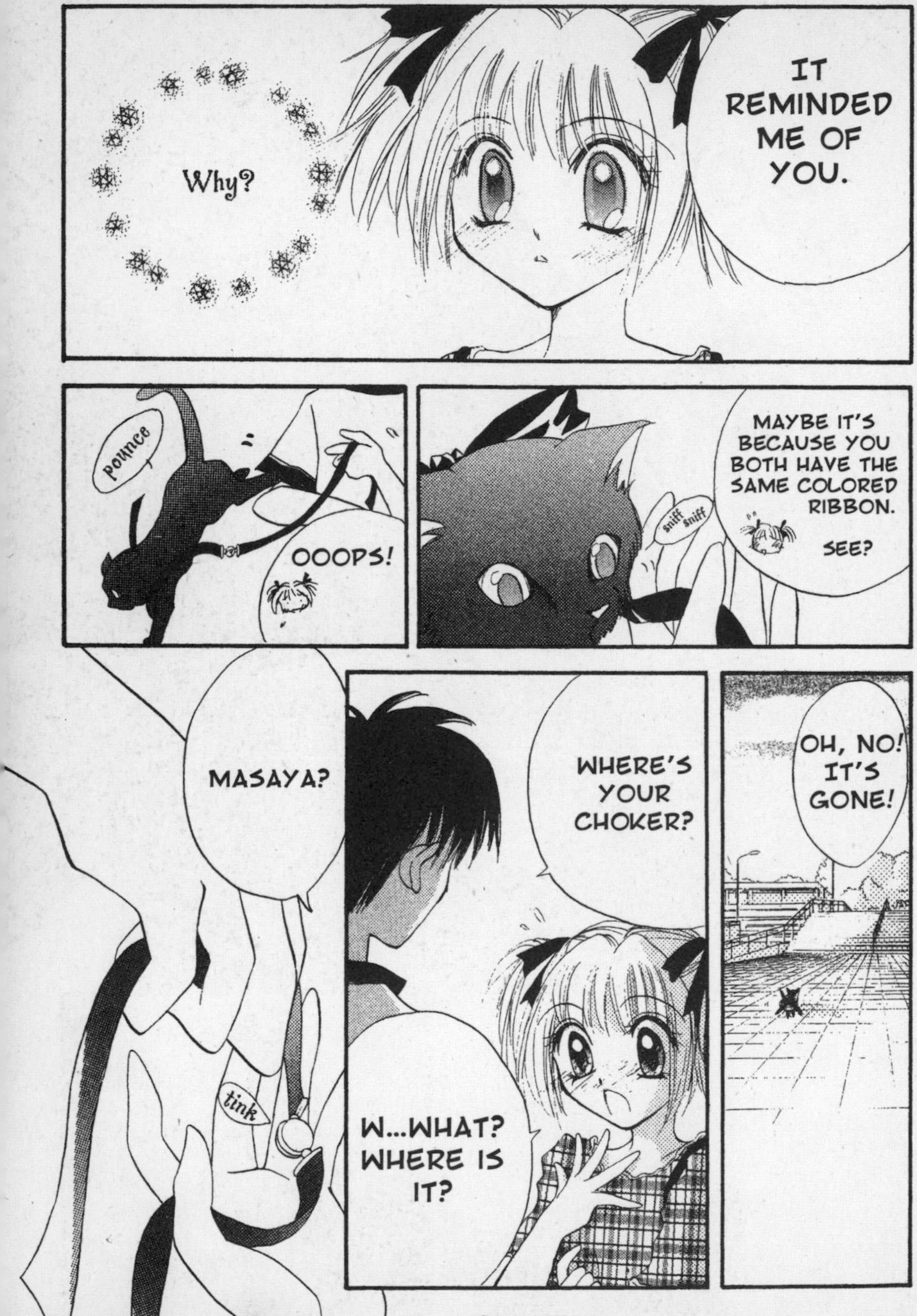
IT REMINDED ME OF YOU.
Why?
MAYBE IT'S BECAUSE YOU BOTH HAVE THE SAME COLORED RIBBON.
SEE?
sniff sniff
pounce
OOOPS!
OH, NO! IT'S GONE!
WHERE'S YOUR CHOKER?
W...WHAT? WHERE IS IT?
MASAYA?
tink

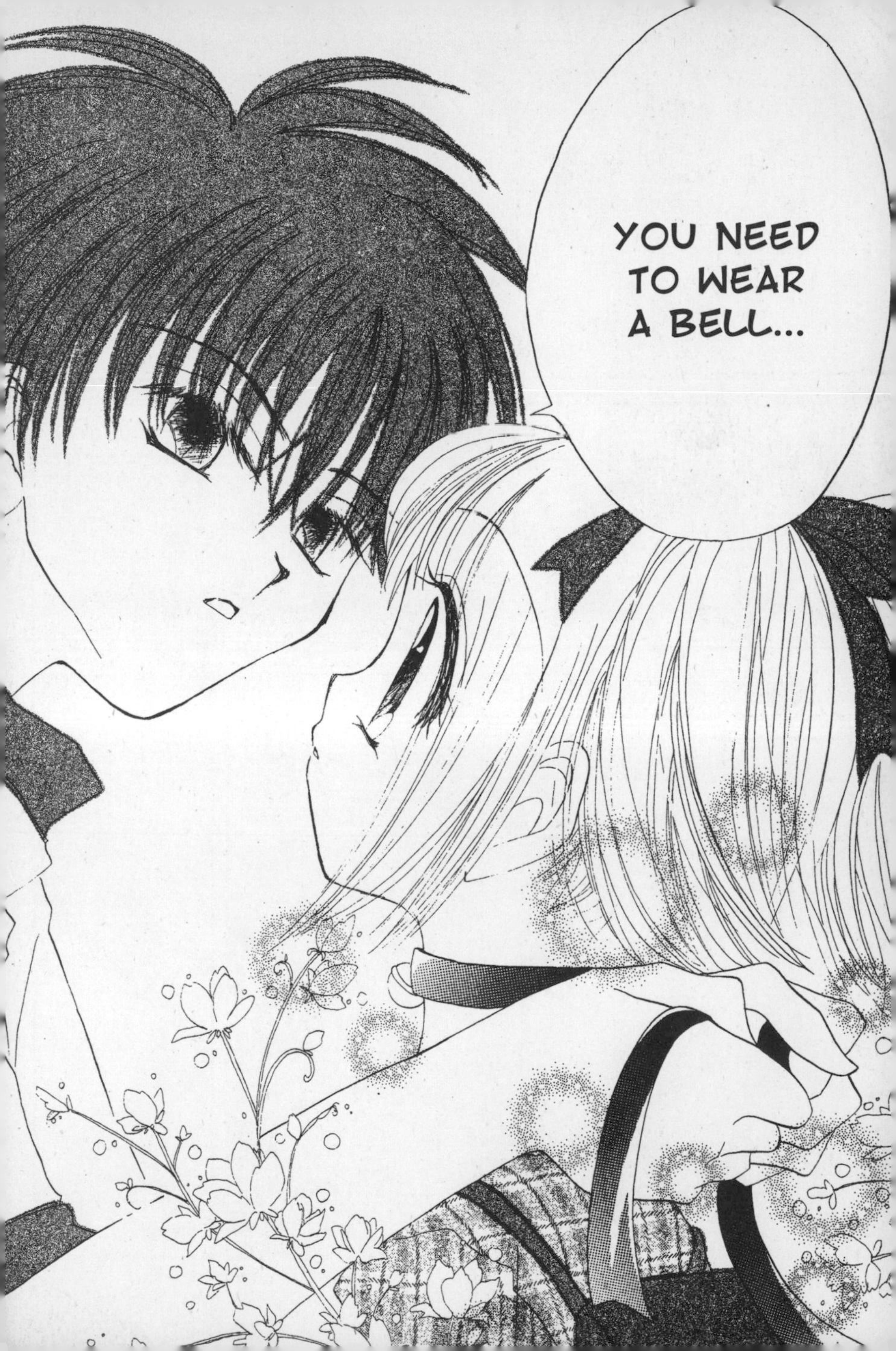
YOU NEED TO WEAR A BELL...

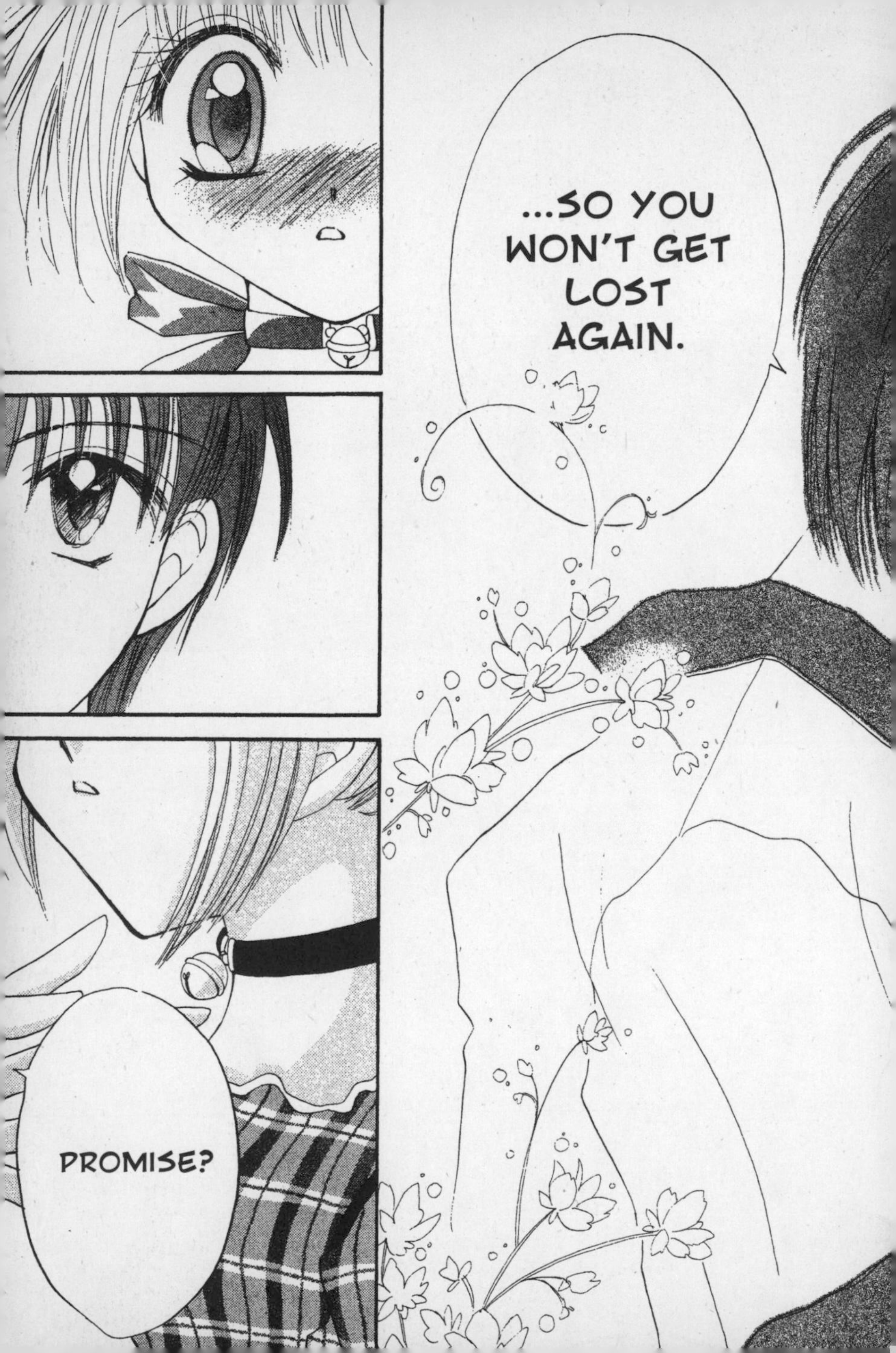
...SO YOU WON'T GET LOST AGAIN.
PROMISE?

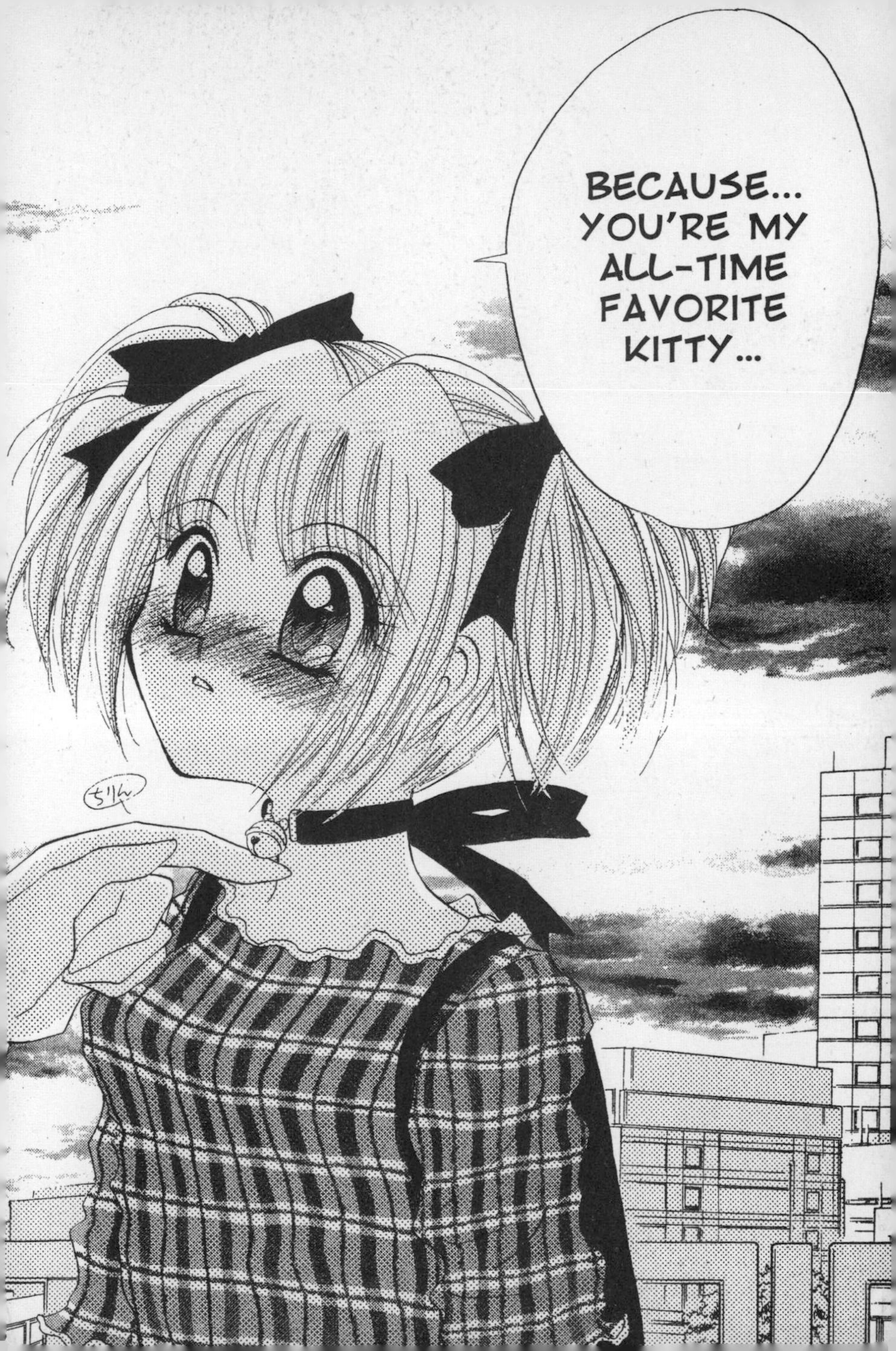
BECAUSE... YOU'RE MY ALL-TIME FAVORITE KITTY...
ちりん

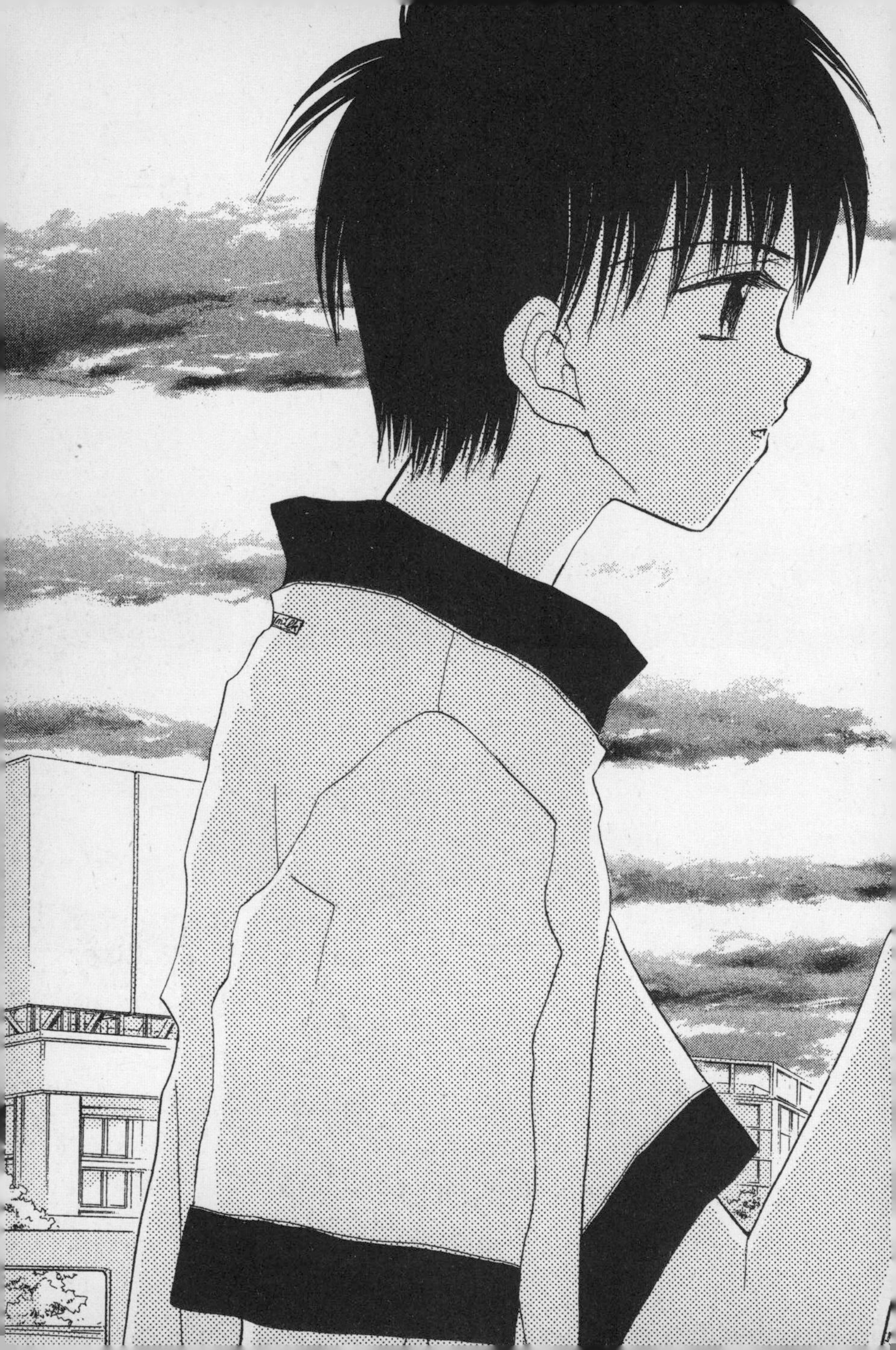

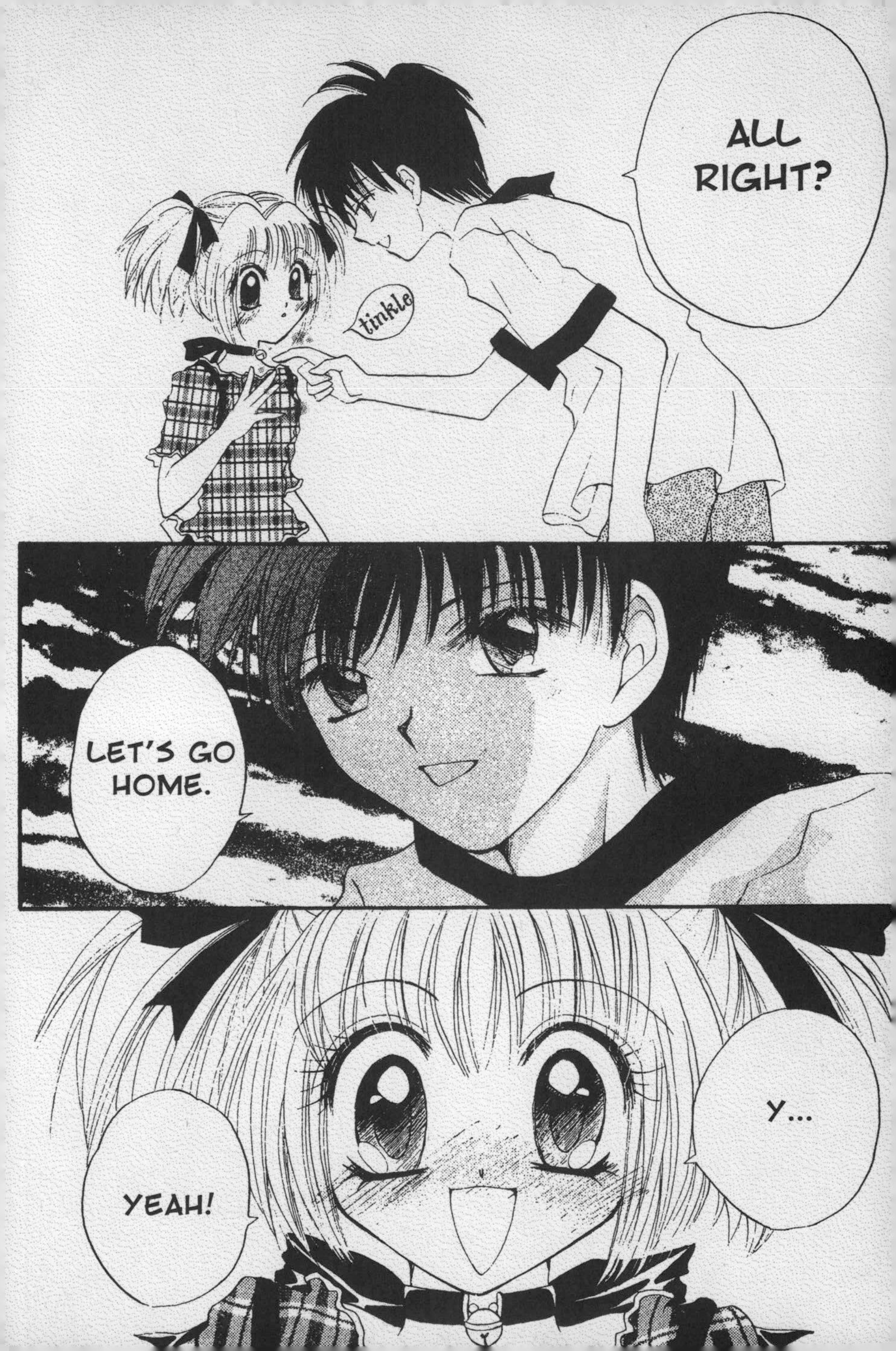
ALL RIGHT?
tinkle
LET'S GO HOME.
Y...
YEAH!

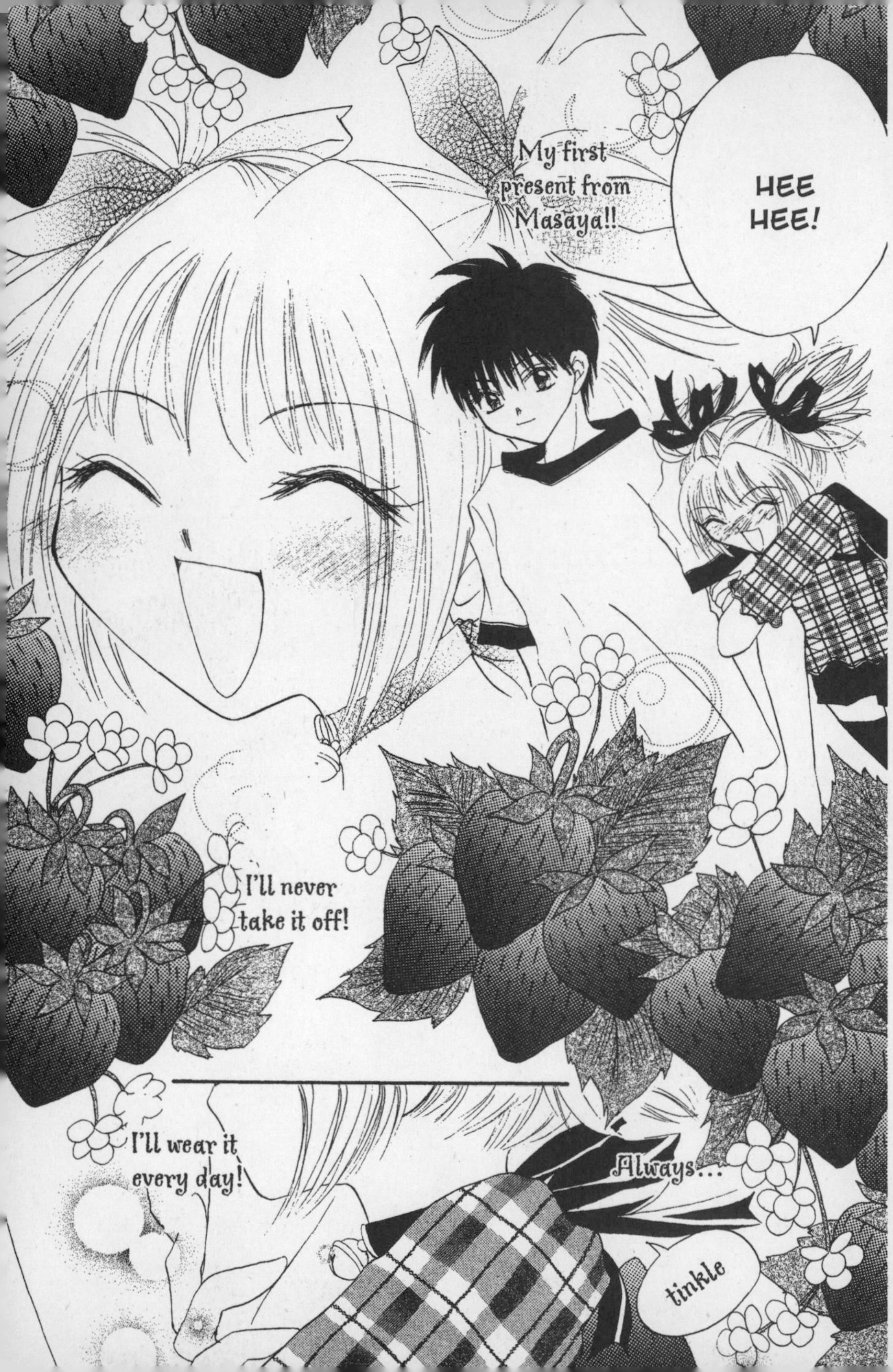
HEE HEE!
My first present from Masaya!!
I'll never take it off!
I'll wear it every day!
Always...
tinkle

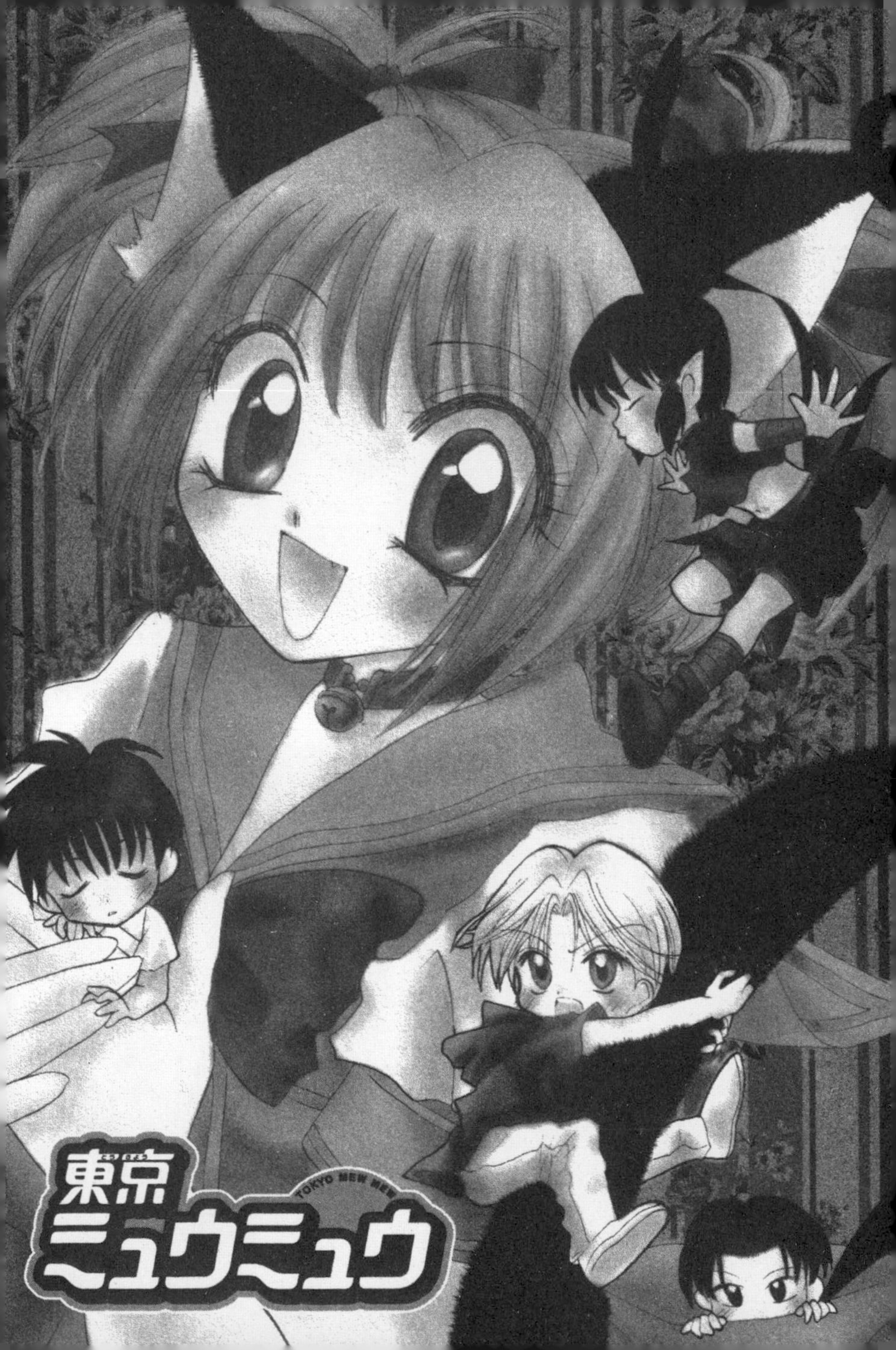
東京
ミュウミュウ
TOKYO MEW MEW

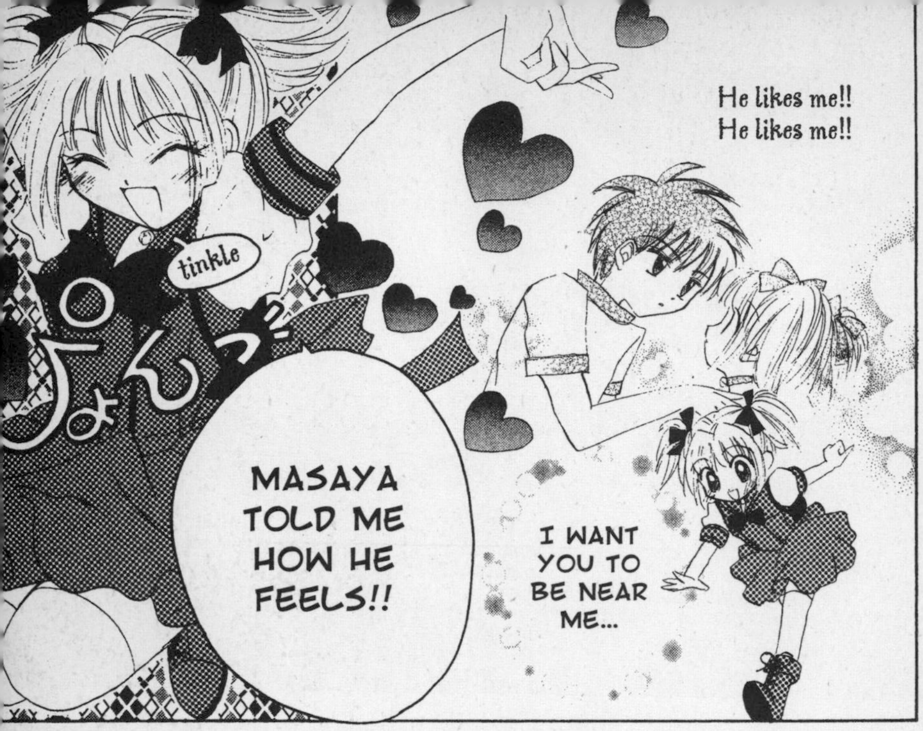
He likes me!!
He likes me!!
I WANT YOU TO BE NEAR ME...
MASAYA TOLD ME HOW HE FEELS!!
tinkle
ぴょんっ

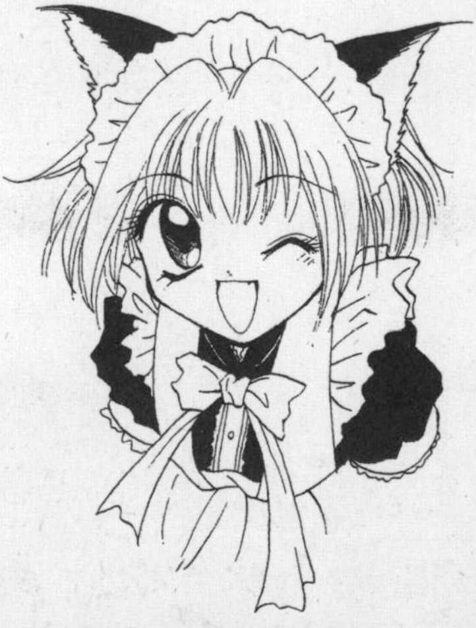

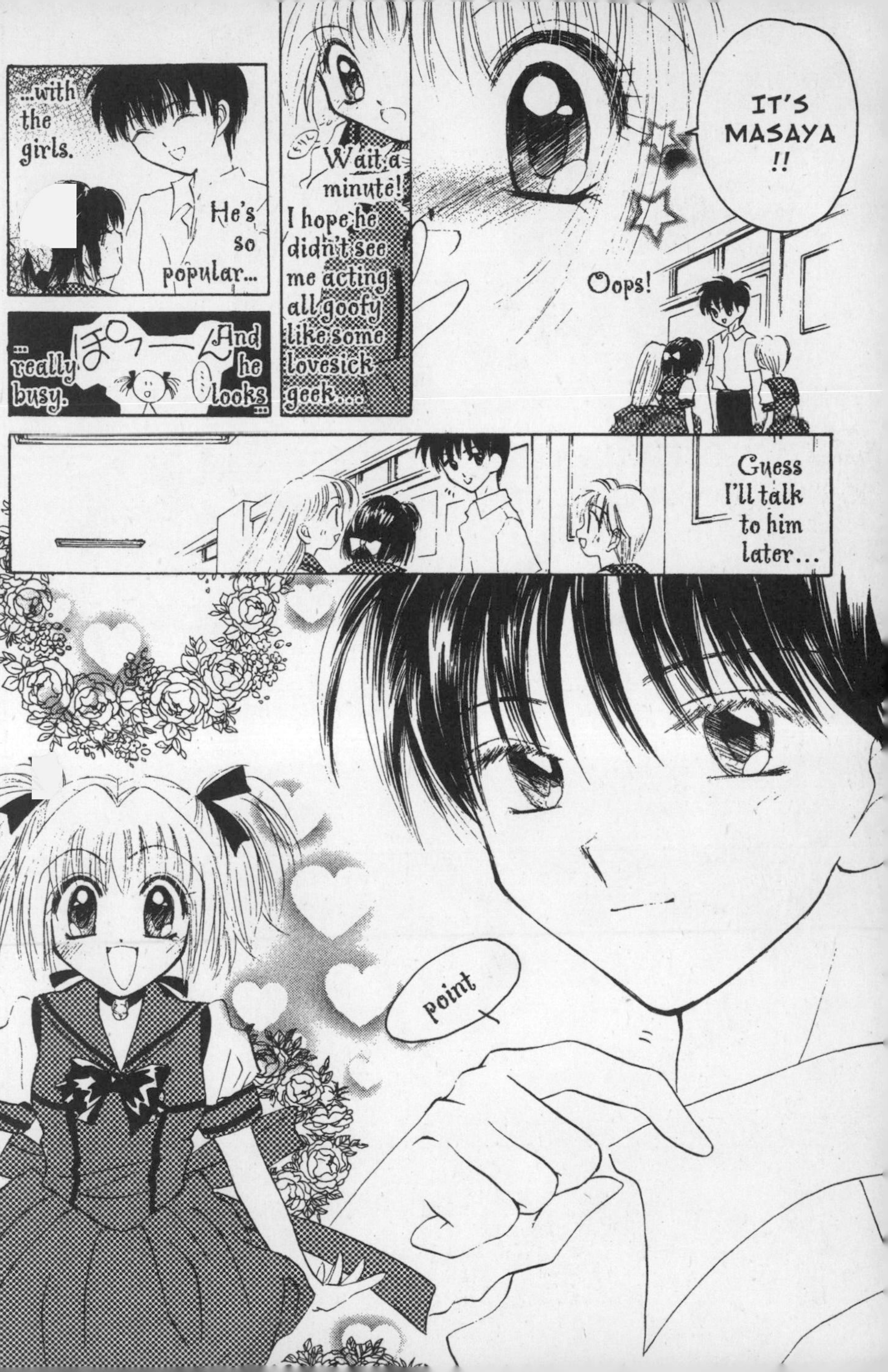
IT'S MASAYA !!
Oops!
Wait a minute! I hope he didn't see me acting all goofy like some lovesick geek...
...with the girls.
He's so popular...
And he looks...
...really busy.
Guess I'll talk to him later...
point

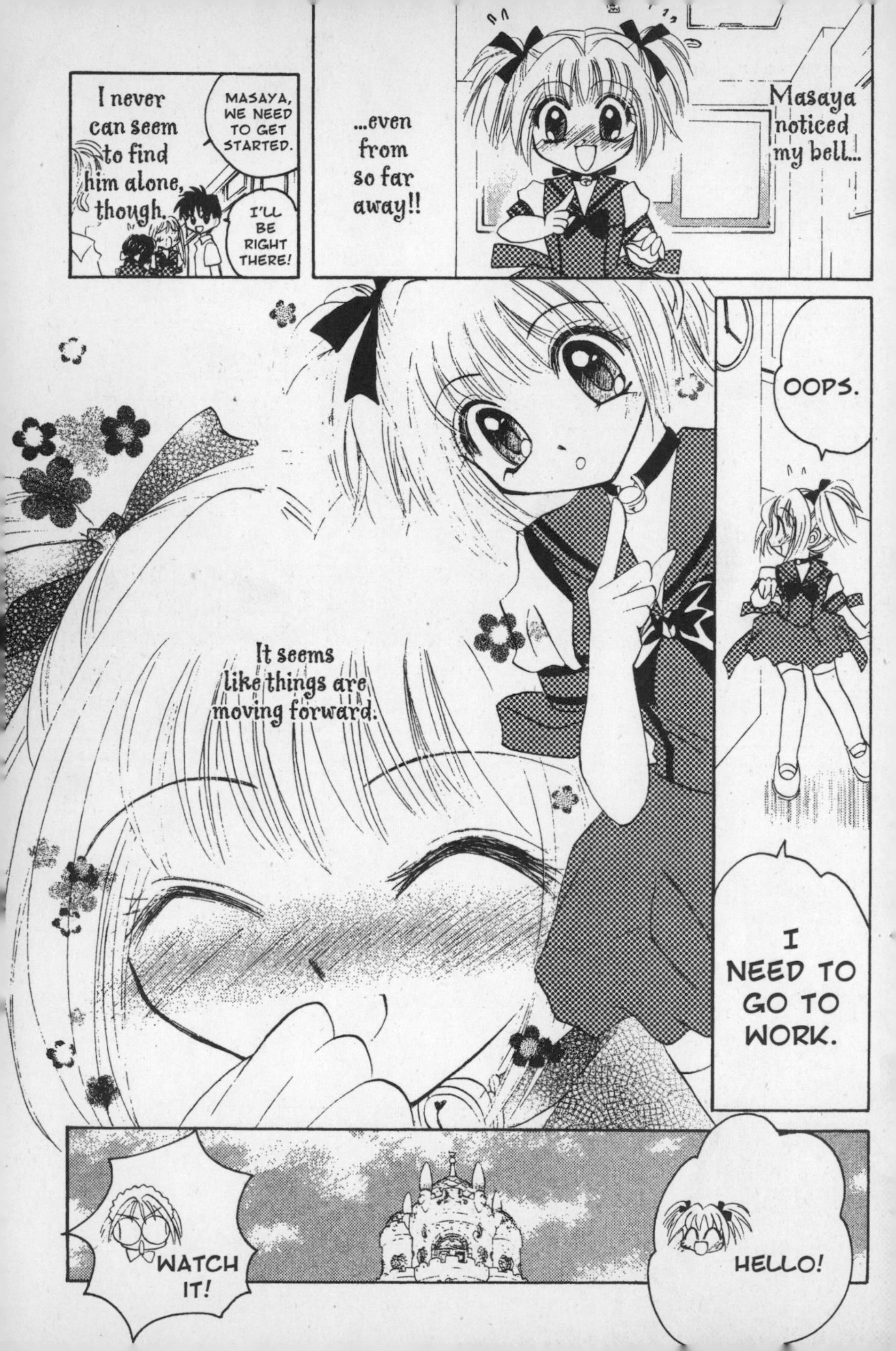

Masaya noticed my bell...
...even from so far away!!
MASAYA, WE NEED TO GET STARTED.
I never can seem to find him alone, though.
I'LL BE RIGHT THERE!
OOPS.
I NEED TO GO TO WORK.
It seems like things are moving forward.
HELLO!
WATCH IT!

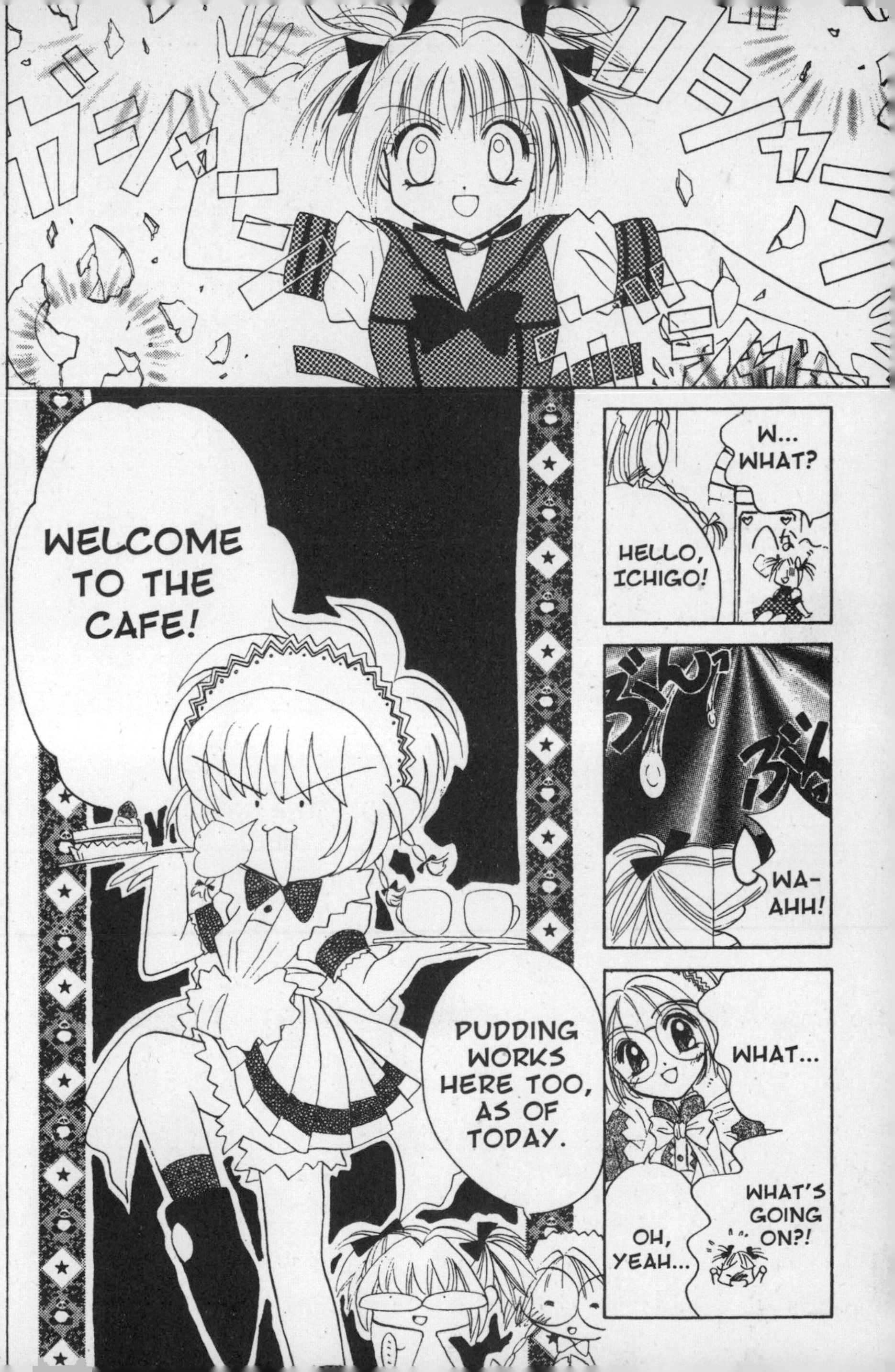
W... WHAT?
HELLO, ICHIGO!
WA-AHH!
WHAT...
WHAT'S GOING ON?!
OH, YEAH...
WELCOME TO THE CAFE!
PUDDING WORKS HERE TOO, AS OF TODAY.

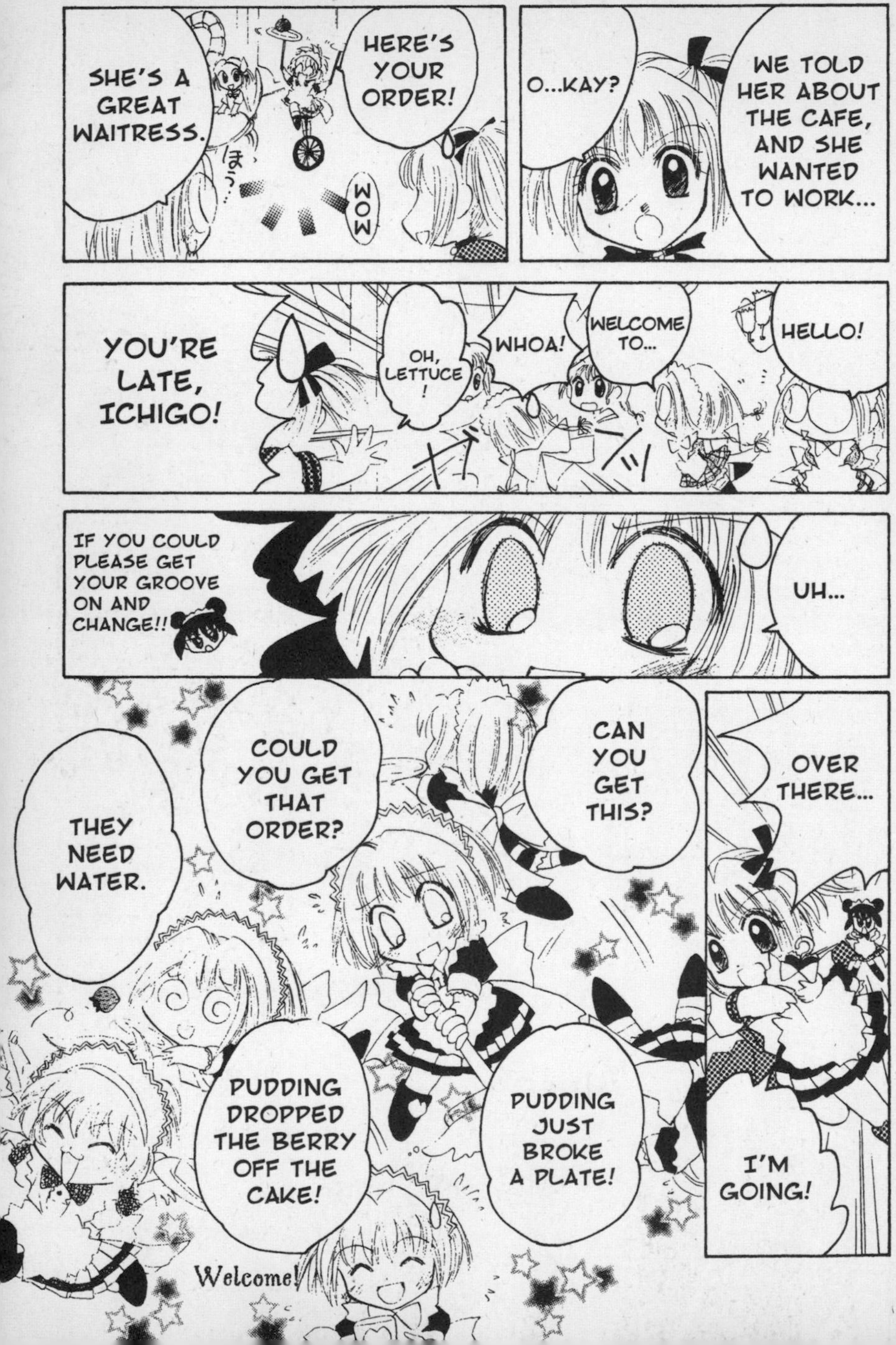
WE TOLD HER ABOUT THE CAFE, AND SHE WANTED TO WORK...
O...KAY?
HERE'S YOUR ORDER!
WOW
SHE'S A GREAT WAITRESS.
HELLO!
WELCOME TO...
WHOA!
OH, LETTUCE!
YOU'RE LATE, ICHIGO!
UH...
IF YOU COULD PLEASE GET YOUR GROOVE ON AND CHANGE!!
OVER THERE...
I'M GOING!
CAN YOU GET THIS?
COULD YOU GET THAT ORDER?
THEY NEED WATER.
PUDDING JUST BROKE A PLATE!
PUDDING DROPPED THE BERRY OFF THE CAKE!
Welcome!

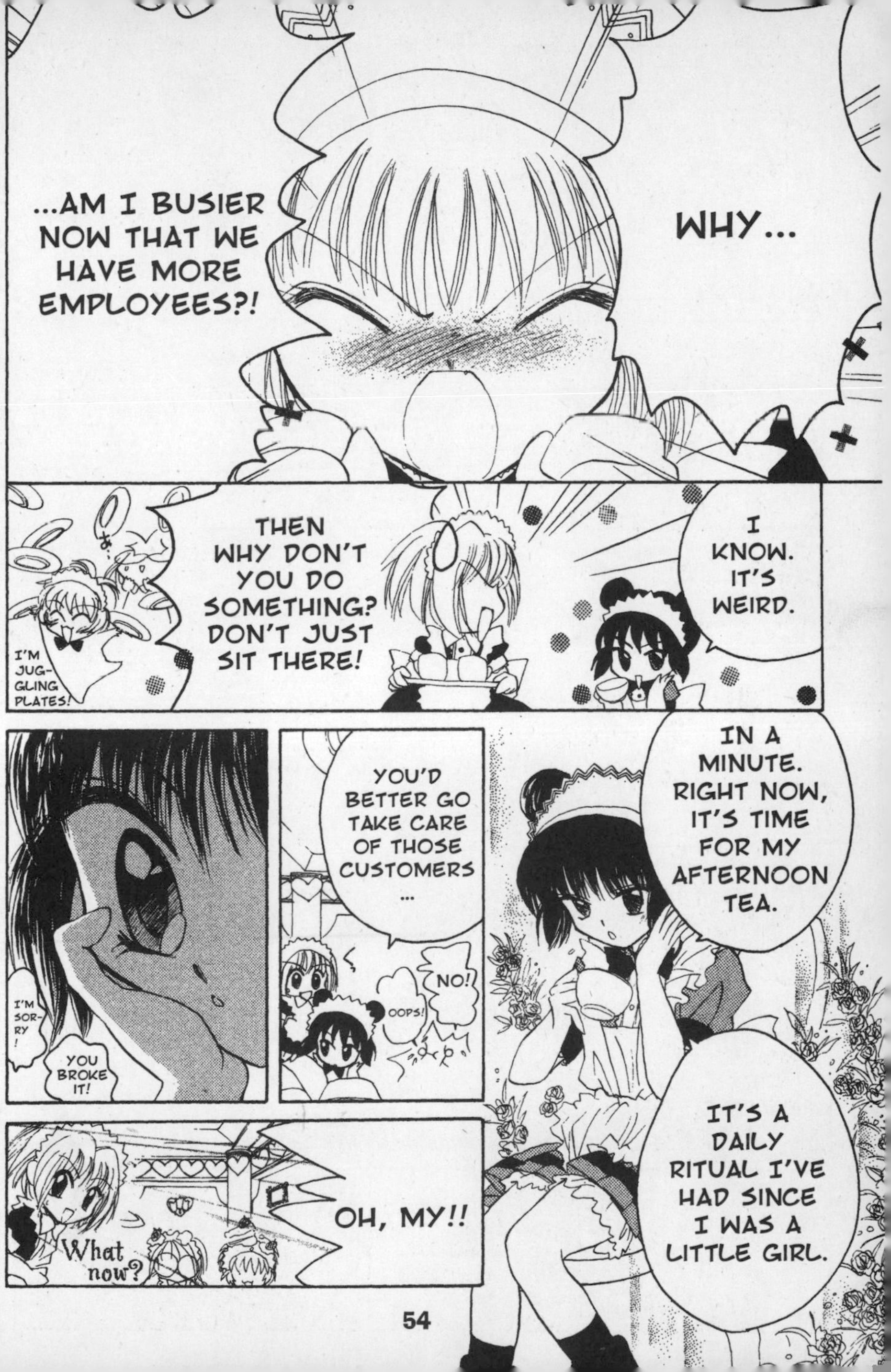

WHY...
...AM I BUSIER NOW THAT WE HAVE MORE EMPLOYEES?!
I KNOW. IT'S WEIRD.
THEN WHY DON'T YOU DO SOMETHING? DON'T JUST SIT THERE!
I'M JUG-GLING PLATES!
IN A MINUTE. RIGHT NOW, IT'S TIME FOR MY AFTERNOON TEA.
IT'S A DAILY RITUAL I'VE HAD SINCE I WAS A LITTLE GIRL.
YOU'D BETTER GO TAKE CARE OF THOSE CUSTOMERS ...
NO!
OOPS!
I'M SOR-RY!
YOU BROKE IT!
OH, MY!!
What now?

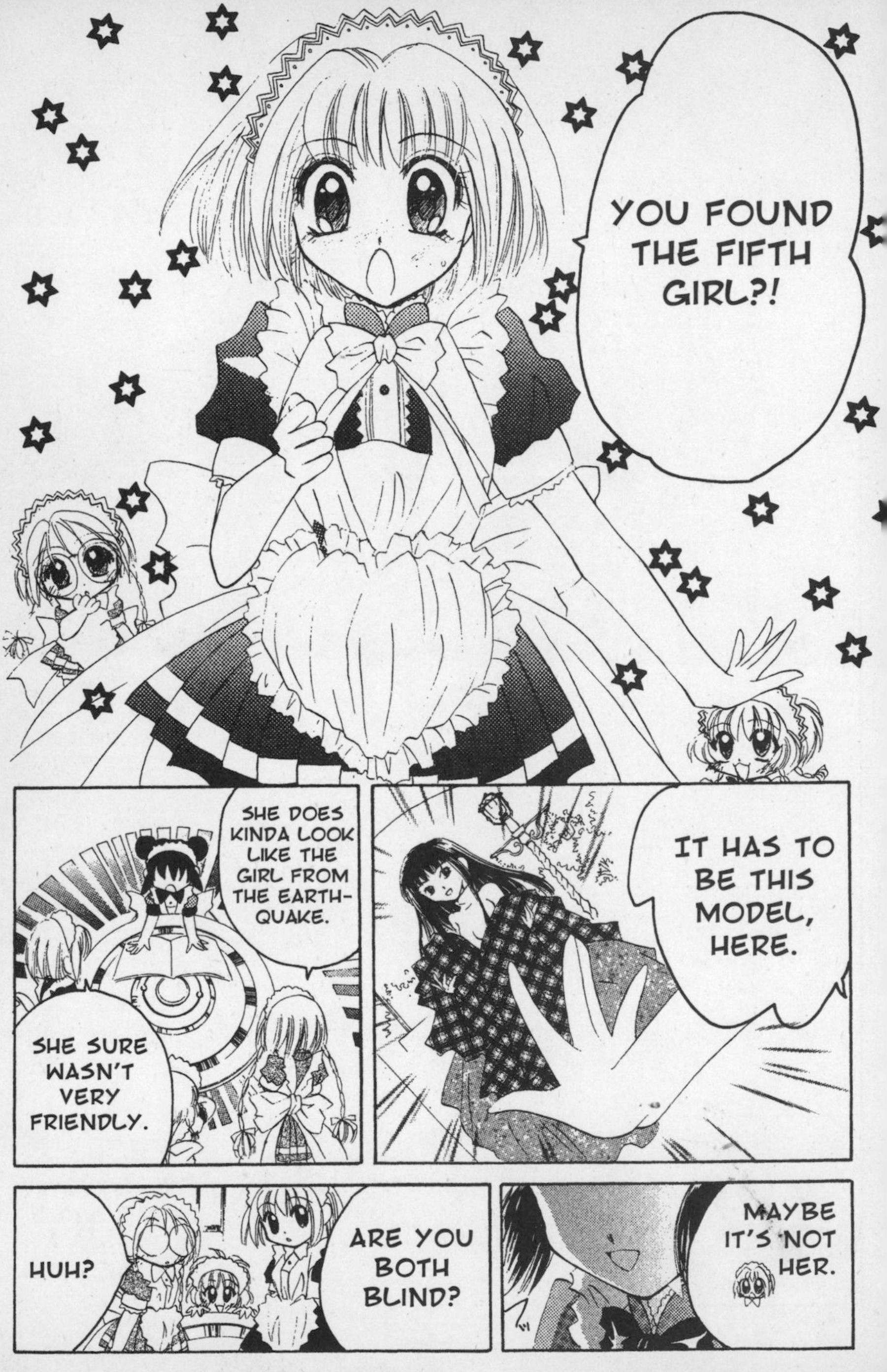
YOU FOUND THE FIFTH GIRL?!
IT HAS TO BE THIS MODEL, HERE.
SHE DOES KINDA LOOK LIKE THE GIRL FROM THE EARTH-QUAKE.
SHE SURE WASN'T VERY FRIENDLY.
MAYBE IT'S NOT HER.
ARE YOU BOTH BLIND?
HUH?

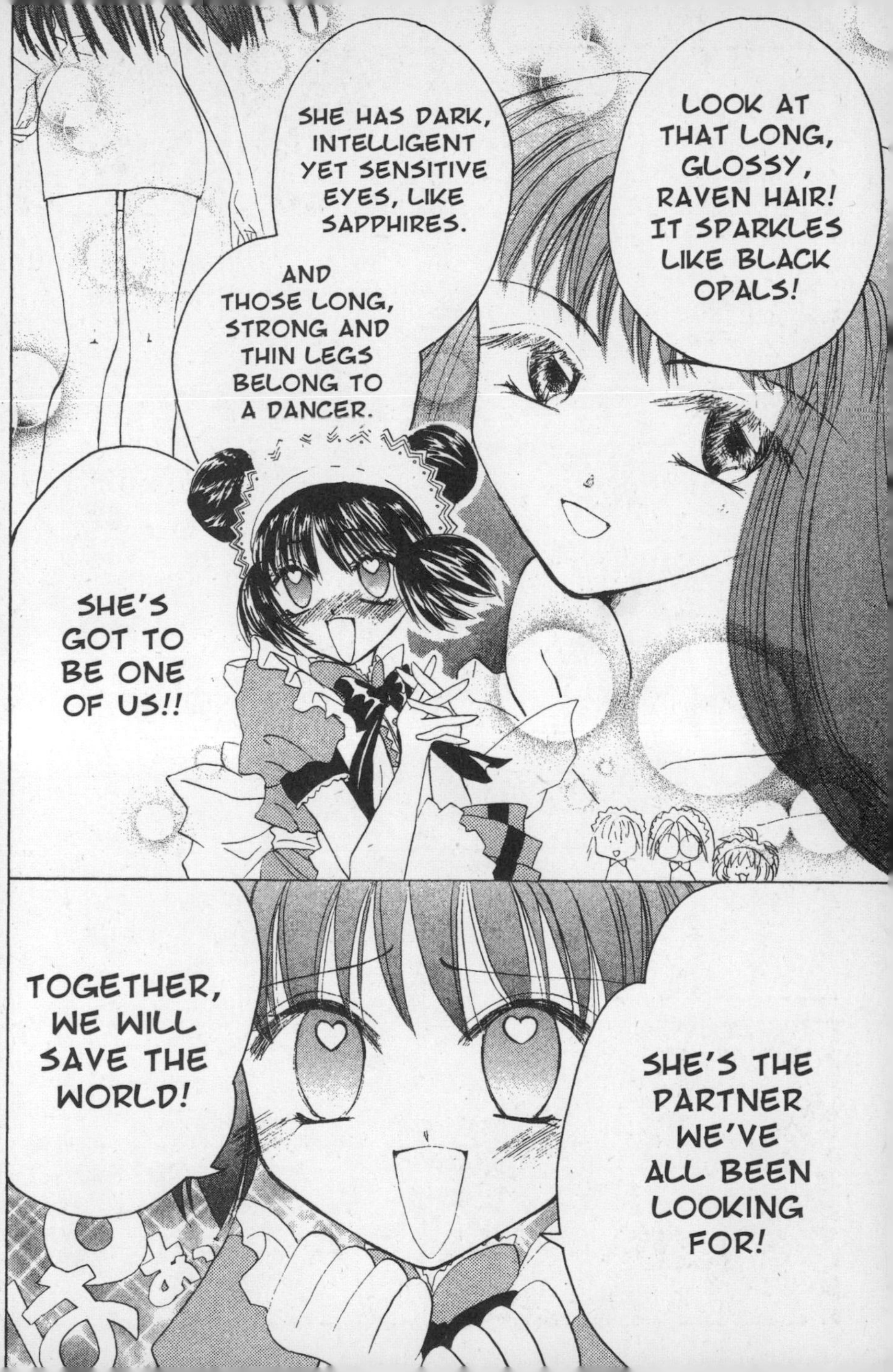
LOOK AT THAT LONG, GLOSSY, RAVEN HAIR! IT SPARKLES LIKE BLACK OPALS!
SHE HAS DARK, INTELLIGENT YET SENSITIVE EYES, LIKE SAPPHIRES.
AND THOSE LONG, STRONG AND THIN LEGS BELONG TO A DANCER.
SHE'S GOT TO BE ONE OF US!!
SHE'S THE PARTNER WE'VE ALL BEEN LOOKING FOR!
TOGETHER, WE WILL SAVE THE WORLD!

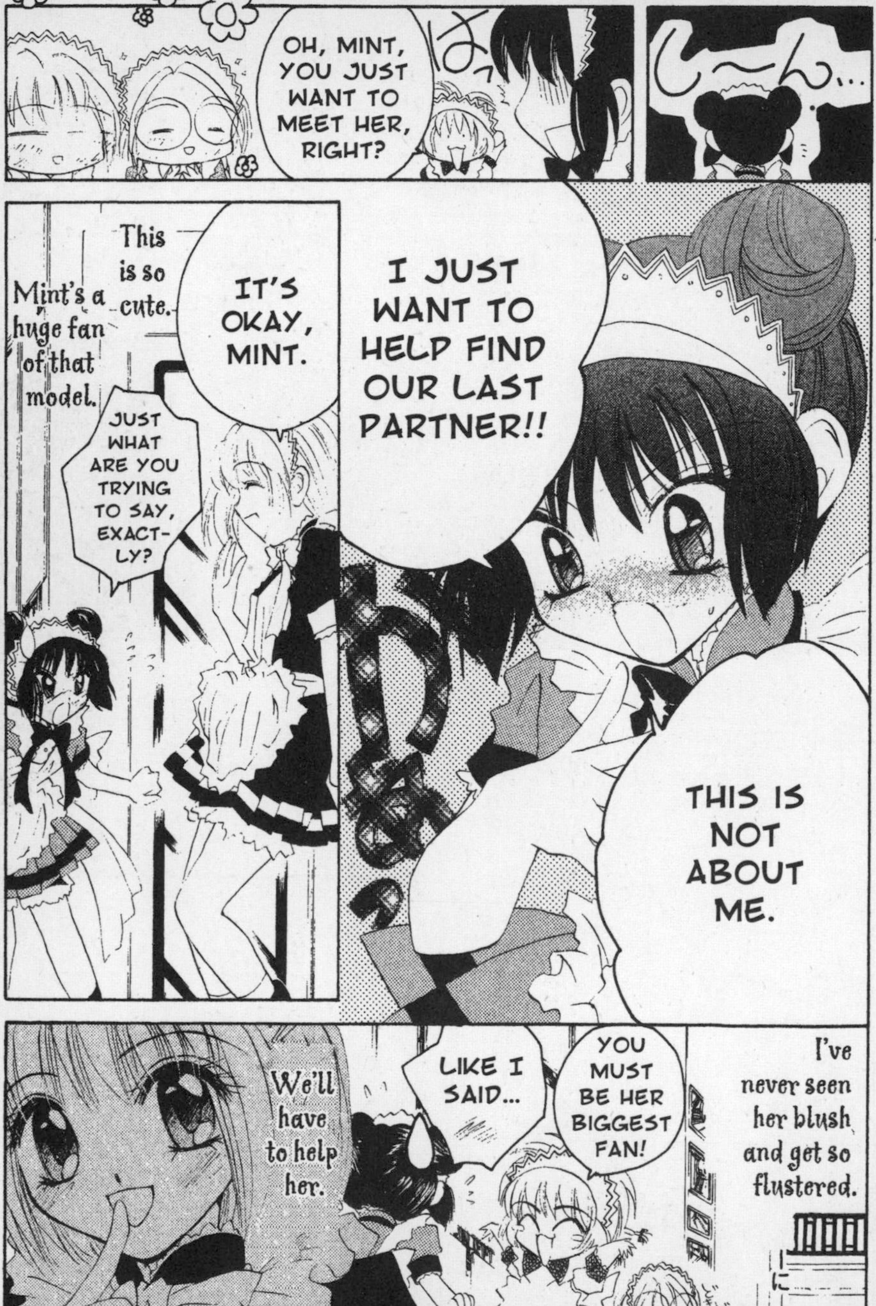

しーん…
は
OH, MINT, YOU JUST WANT TO MEET HER, RIGHT?
I JUST WANT TO HELP FIND OUR LAST PARTNER!!
THIS IS NOT ABOUT ME.
IT'S OKAY, MINT.
This is so cute.
Mint's a huge fan of that model.
JUST WHAT ARE YOU TRYING TO SAY, EXACTLY?
I've never seen her blush and get so flustered.
YOU MUST BE HER BIGGEST FAN!
LIKE I SAID...
We'll have to help her.

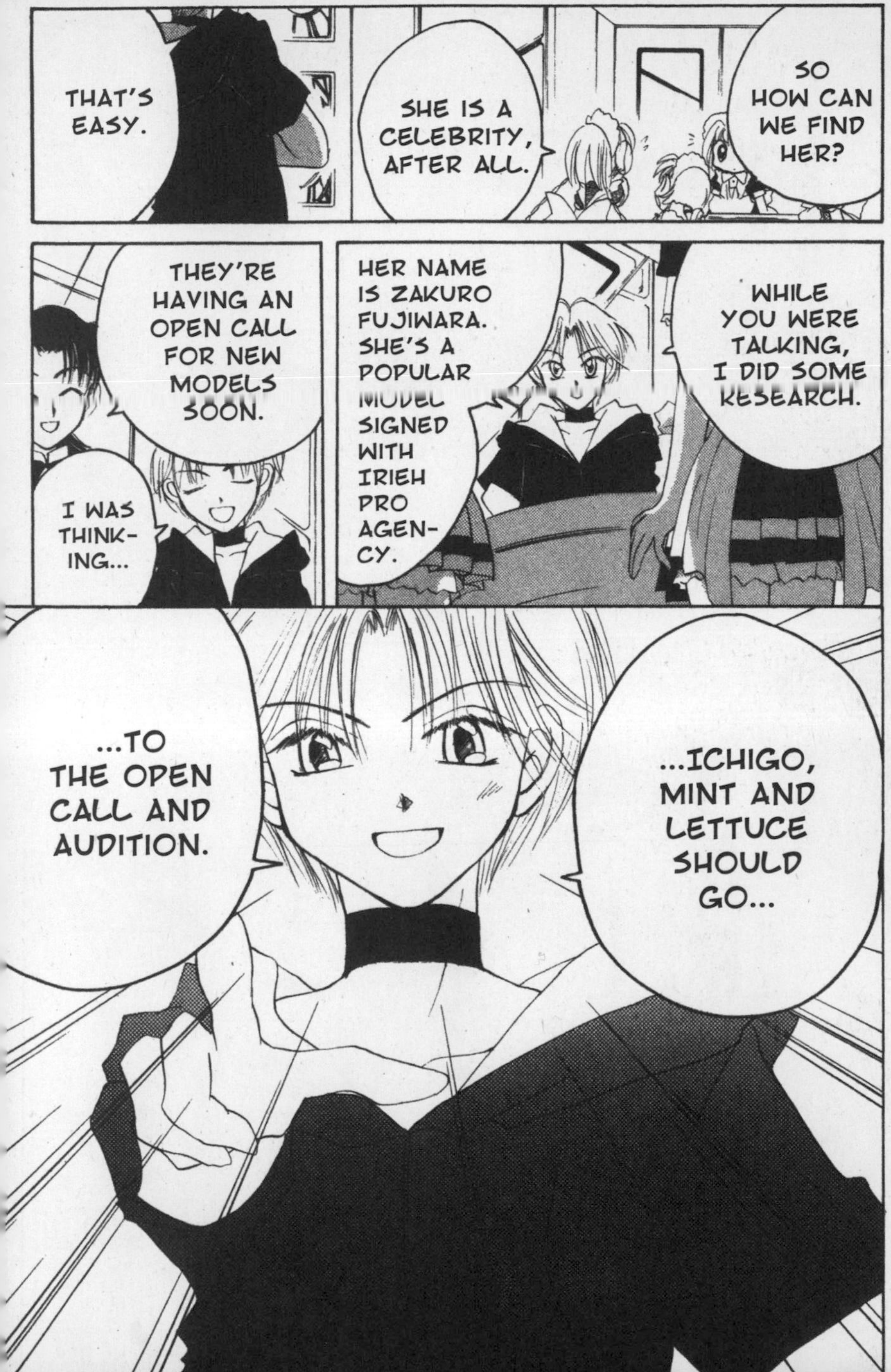
SO HOW CAN WE FIND HER?
SHE IS A CELEBRITY, AFTER ALL.
THAT'S EASY.
WHILE YOU WERE TALKING, I DID SOME RESEARCH.
HER NAME IS ZAKURO FUJIWARA. SHE'S A POPULAR MODEL SIGNED WITH IRIEH PRO AGEN-CY.
THEY'RE HAVING AN OPEN CALL FOR NEW MODELS SOON.
I WAS THINK-ING...
...ICHIGO, MINT AND LETTUCE SHOULD GO...
...TO THE OPEN CALL AND AUDITION.

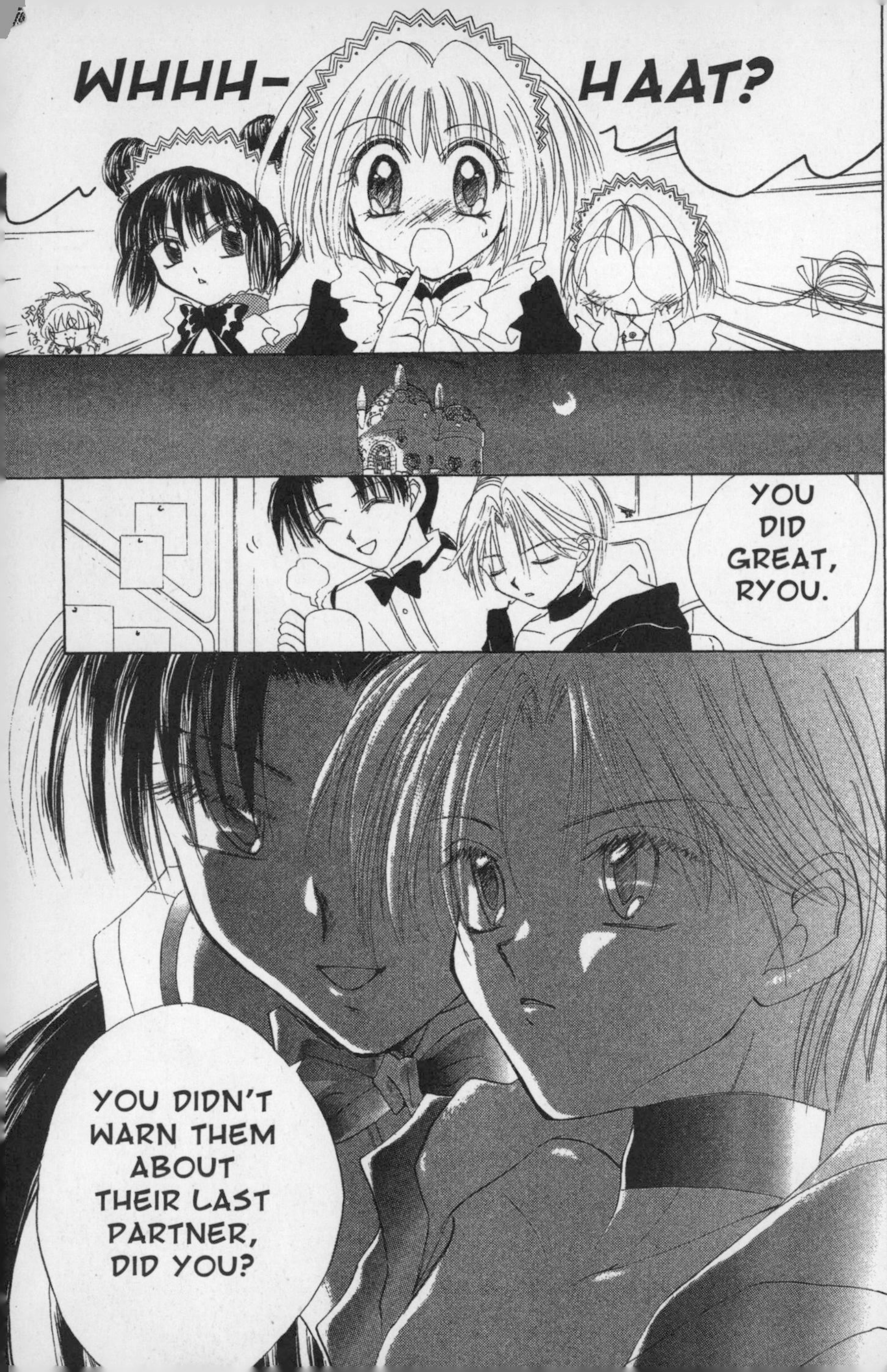
WHHH-HAAT?
YOU DID GREAT, RYOU.
YOU DIDN'T WARN THEM ABOUT THEIR LAST PARTNER, DID YOU?

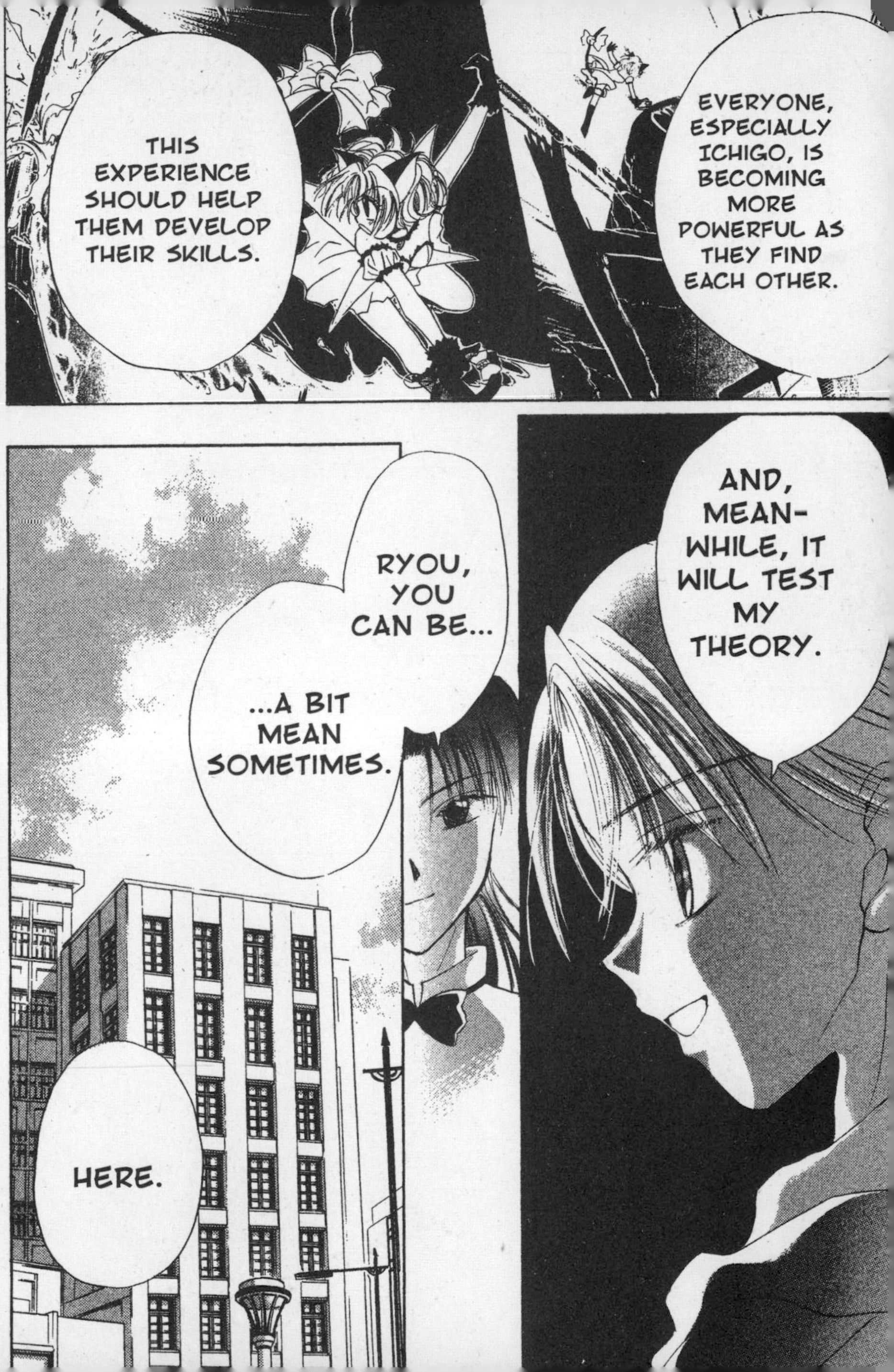
EVERYONE, ESPECIALLY ICHIGO, IS BECOMING MORE POWERFUL AS THEY FIND EACH OTHER.
THIS EXPERIENCE SHOULD HELP THEM DEVELOP THEIR SKILLS.
AND, MEAN-WHILE, IT WILL TEST MY THEORY.
RYOU, YOU CAN BE...
...A BIT MEAN SOMETIMES.
HERE.

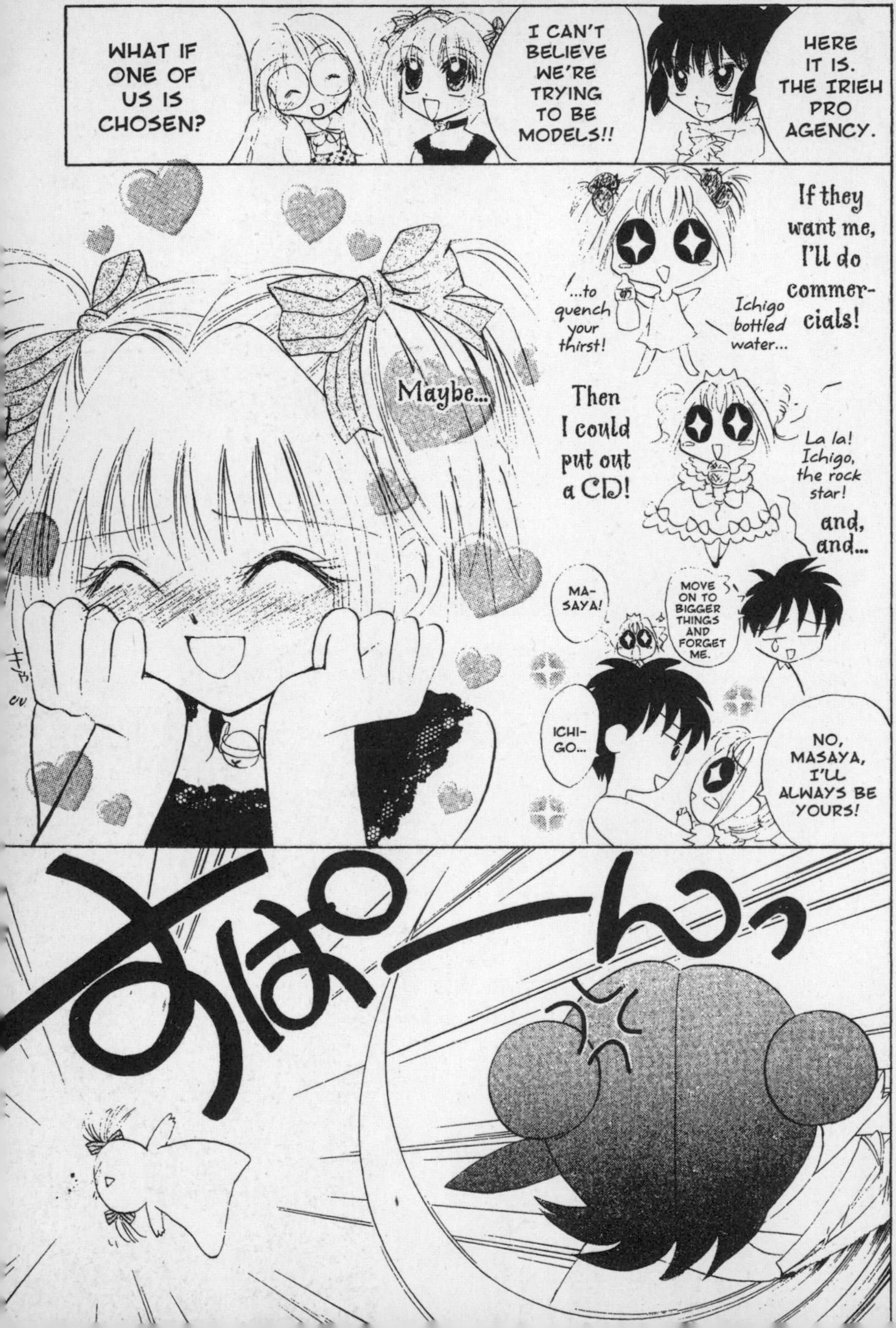
HERE IT IS. THE IRIEH PRO AGENCY.
I CAN'T BELIEVE WE'RE TRYING TO BE MODELS!!
WHAT IF ONE OF US IS CHOSEN?
If they want me, I'll do commercials!
Ichigo bottled water...
...to quench your thirst!
Then I could put out a CD!
La la! Ichigo, the rock star!
Maybe...
and, and...
MOVE ON TO BIGGER THINGS AND FORGET ME.
MA-SAYA!
NO, MASAYA, I'LL ALWAYS BE YOURS!
ICHI-GO...
すぱーんっ

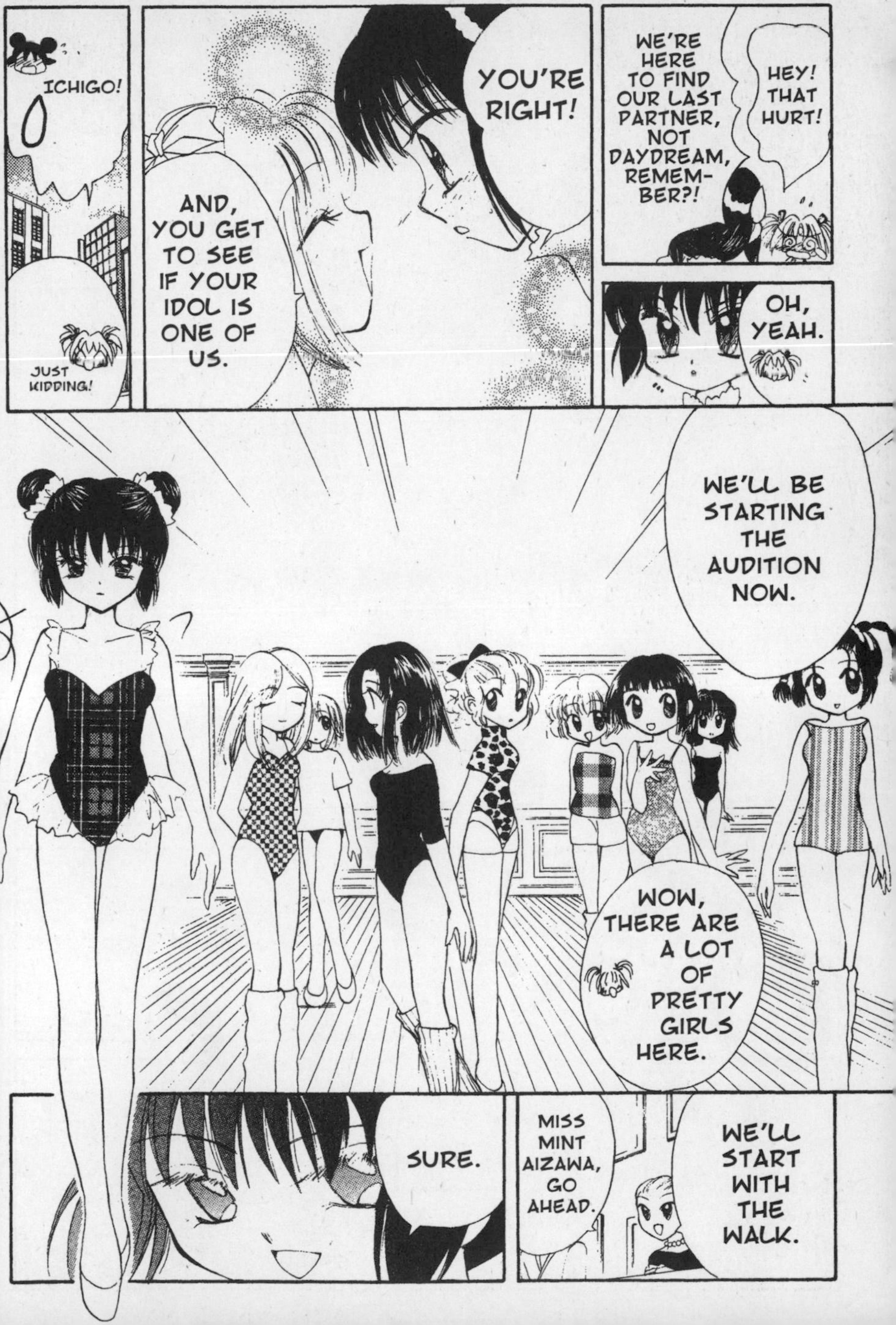
HEY! THAT HURT!
WE'RE HERE TO FIND OUR LAST PARTNER, NOT DAYDREAM, REMEMBER?!
OH, YEAH.
YOU'RE RIGHT!
AND, YOU GET TO SEE IF YOUR IDOL IS ONE OF US.
ICHIGO!
JUST KIDDING!
WE'LL BE STARTING THE AUDITION NOW.
WOW, THERE ARE A LOT OF PRETTY GIRLS HERE.
WE'LL START WITH THE WALK.
MISS MINT AIZAWA, GO AHEAD.
SURE.

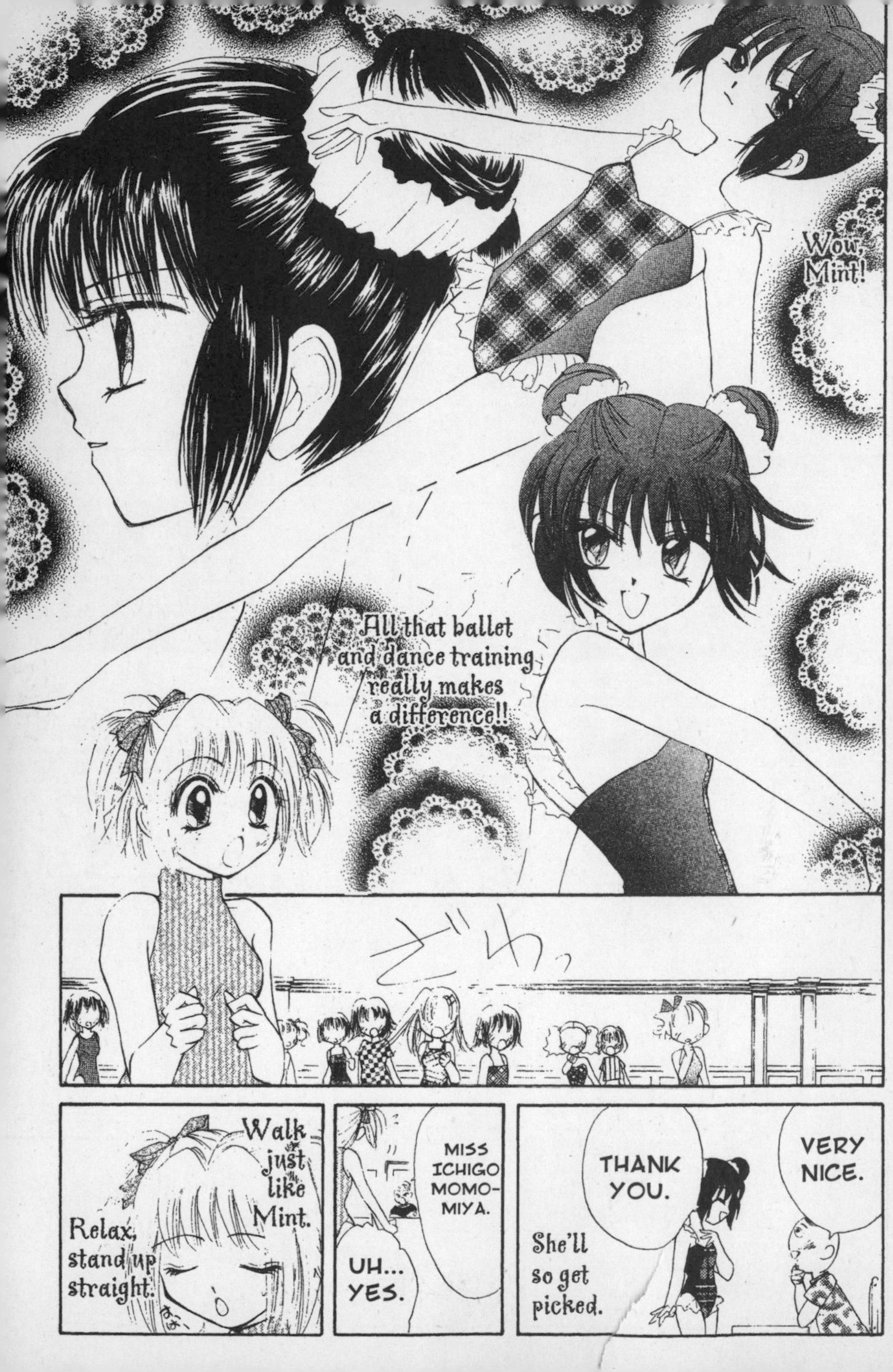
Wow, Mint!
All that ballet and dance training really makes a difference!!
ざわっ
VERY NICE.
THANK YOU.
She'll so get picked.
MISS ICHIGO MOMOMIYA.
UH... YES.
Walk just like Mint.
Relax, stand up straight.

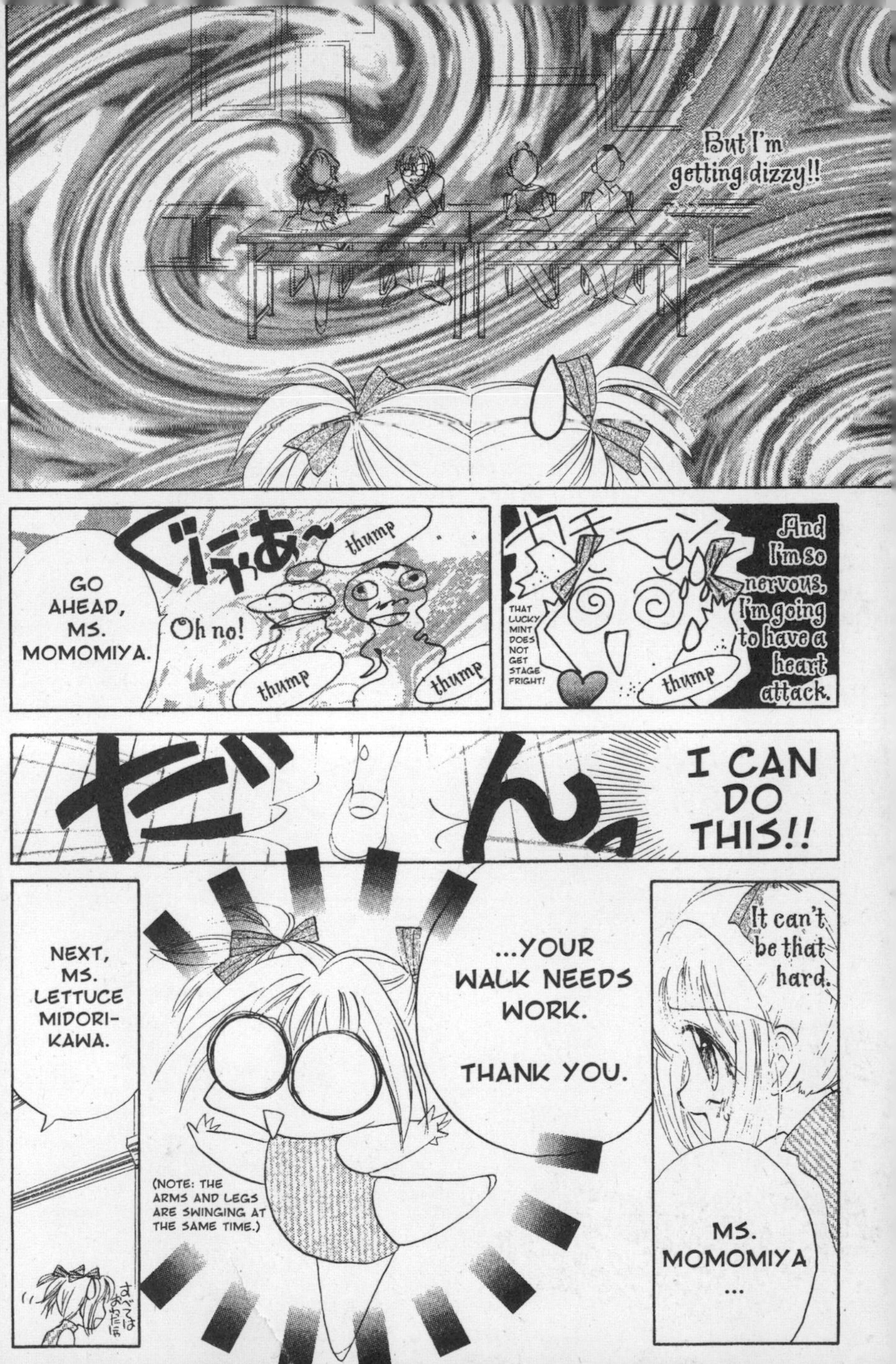
But I'm getting dizzy!!
And I'm so nervous, I'm going to have a heart attack.
thump
THAT LUCKY MINT DOES NOT GET STAGE FRIGHT!
thump
thump
thump
Oh no!
GO AHEAD, MS. MOMOMIYA.
I CAN DO THIS!!
It can't be that hard.
MS. MOMOMIYA ...
...YOUR WALK NEEDS WORK.
THANK YOU.
NEXT, MS. LETTUCE MIDORI-KAWA.
(NOTE: THE ARMS AND LEGS ARE SWINGING AT THE SAME TIME.)

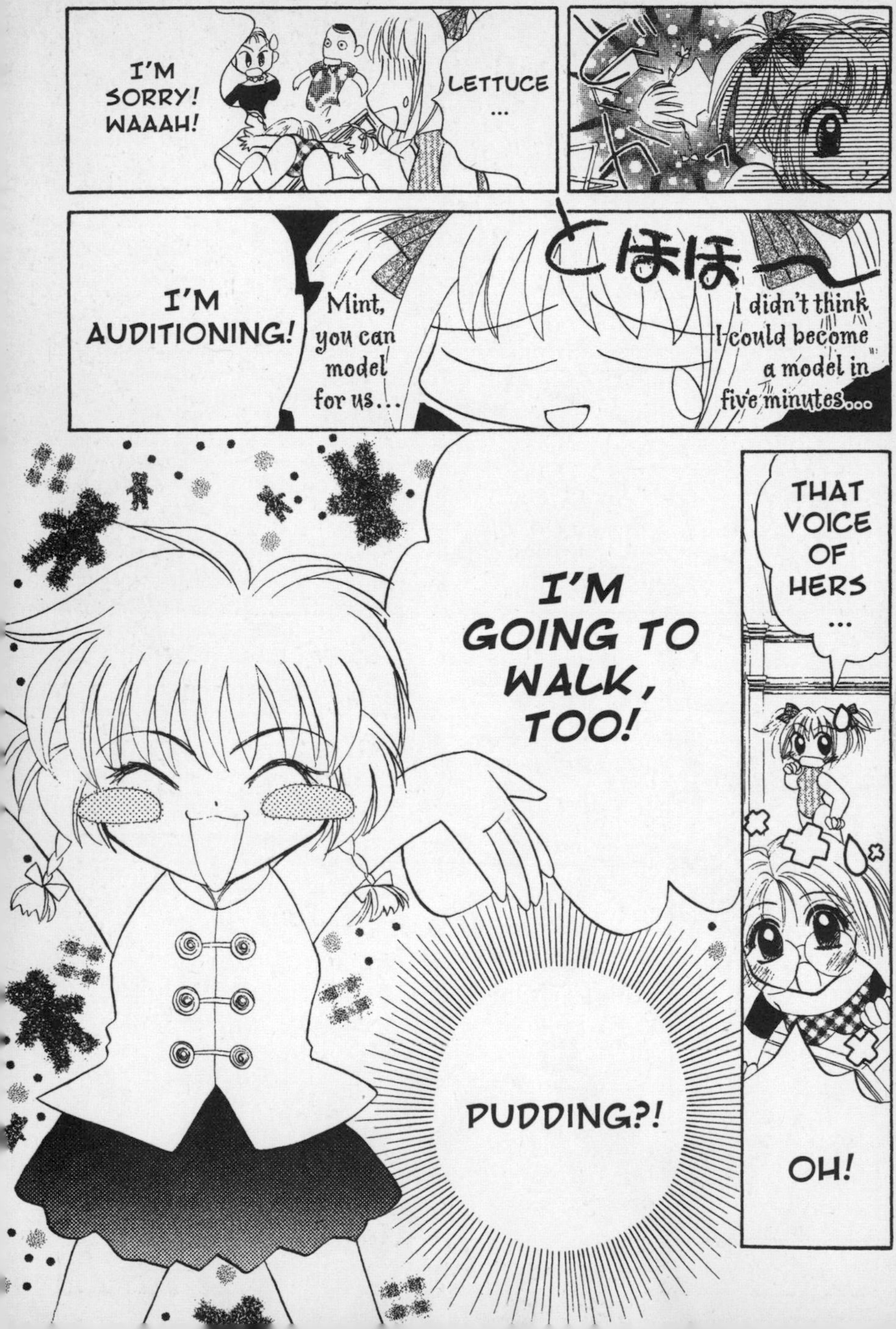

LETTUCE ...
I'M SORRY! WAAAH!
とほほ〜
I didn't think I could become a model in five minutes...
Mint, you can model for us...
I'M AUDITIONING!
THAT VOICE OF HERS ...
OH!
I'M GOING TO WALK, TOO!
PUDDING?!

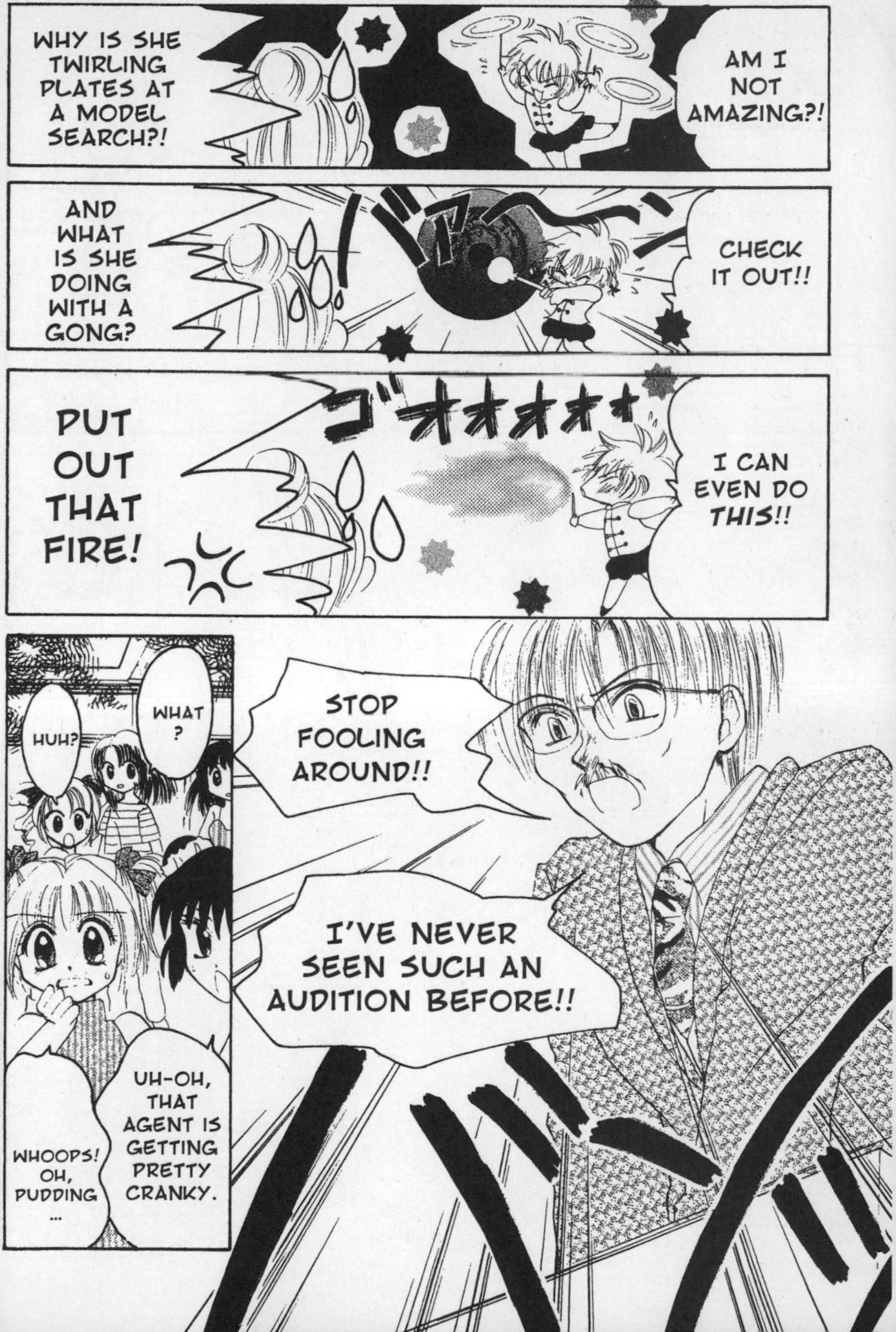
AM I NOT AMAZING?!
WHY IS SHE TWIRLING PLATES AT A MODEL SEARCH?!
CHECK IT OUT!!
AND WHAT IS SHE DOING WITH A GONG?
I CAN EVEN DO *THIS*!!
ゴオオオオオ
PUT OUT THAT FIRE!
STOP FOOLING AROUND!!
I'VE NEVER SEEN SUCH AN AUDITION BEFORE!!
WHAT?
HUH?
UH-OH, THAT AGENT IS GETTING PRETTY CRANKY.
WHOOPS! OH, PUDDING ...

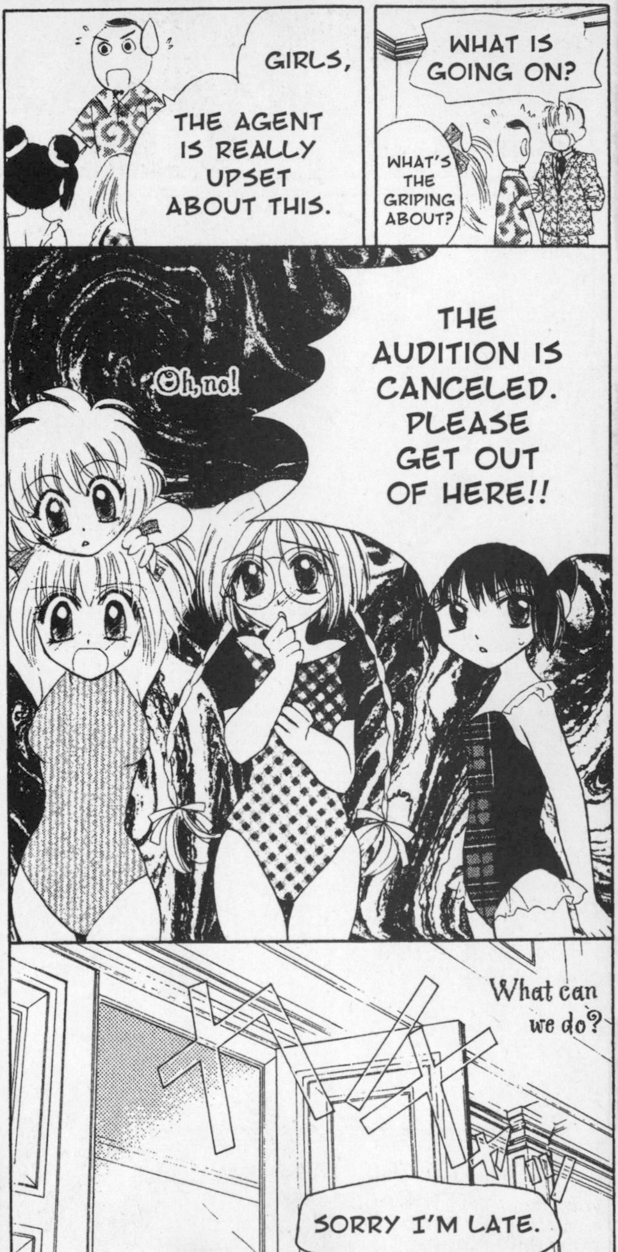
WHAT IS GOING ON?
WHAT'S THE GRIPING ABOUT?
GIRLS,
THE AGENT IS REALLY UPSET ABOUT THIS.
THE AUDITION IS CANCELED. PLEASE GET OUT OF HERE!!
Oh, no!
What can we do?
SORRY I'M LATE.

Ikumi's Train of Thought

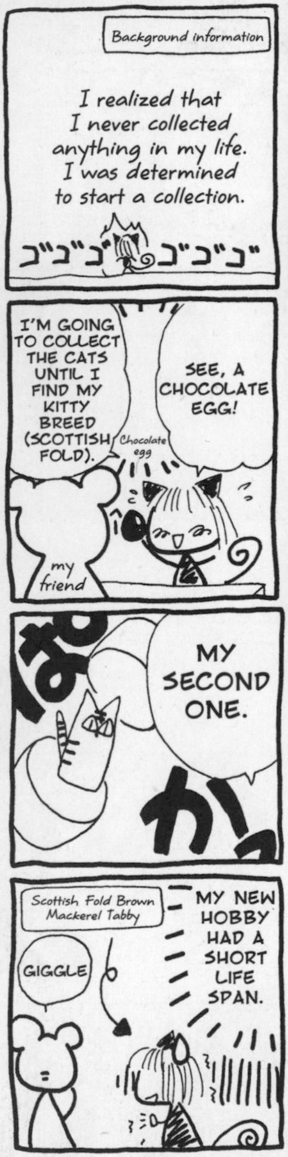
Background information
I realized that I never collected anything in my life. I was determined to start a collection.
I'M GOING TO COLLECT THE CATS UNTIL I FIND MY KITTY BREED (SCOTTISH FOLD).
SEE, A CHOCOLATE EGG!
Chocolate egg
my friend
MY SECOND ONE.
Scottish Fold Brown Mackerel Tabby
GIGGLE
MY NEW HOBBY HAD A SHORT LIFE SPAN.

I wanted my collection to grow first!

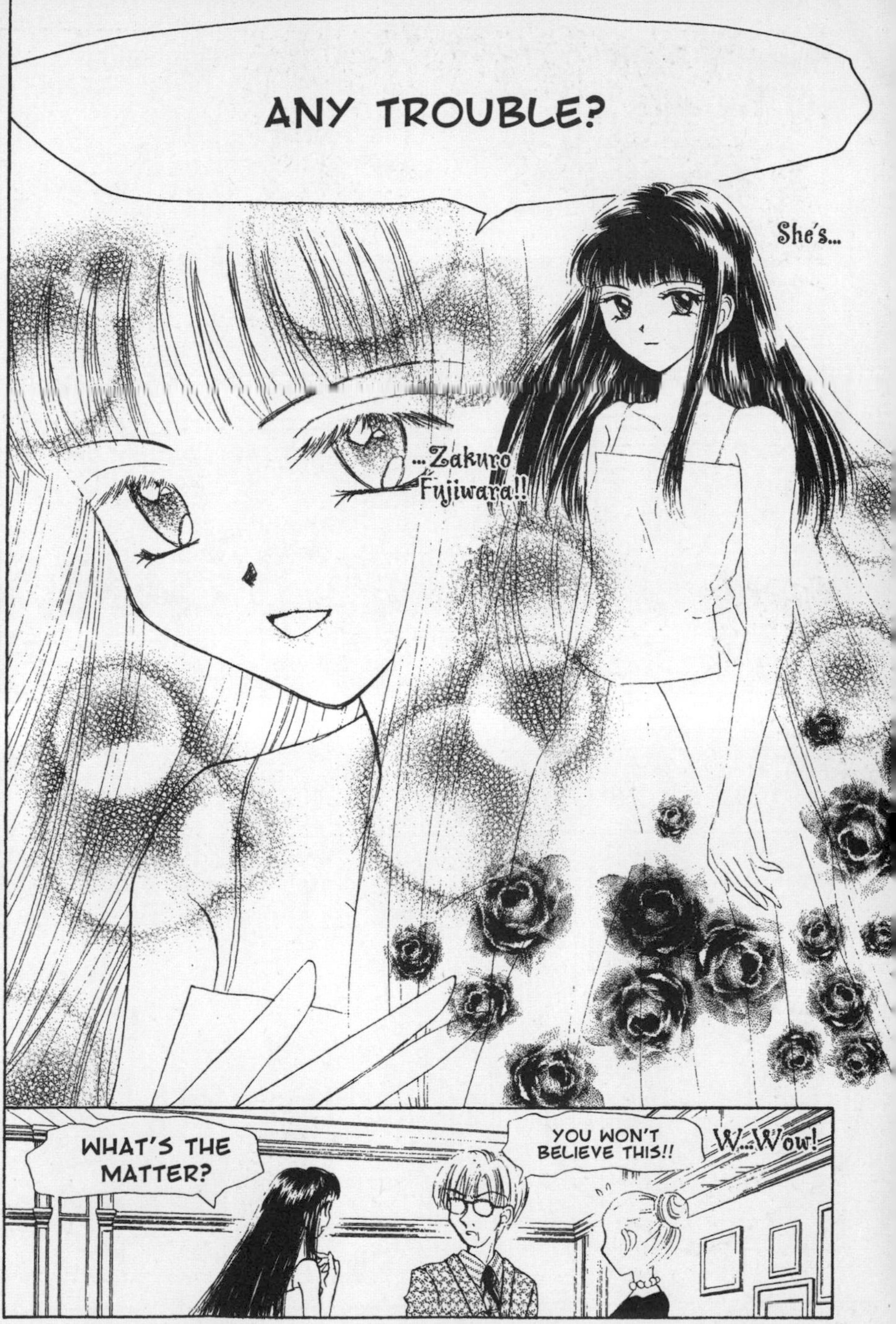
ANY TROUBLE?
She's...
...Zakuro Fujiwara!!
W...Wow!
YOU WON'T BELIEVE THIS!!
WHAT'S THE MATTER?

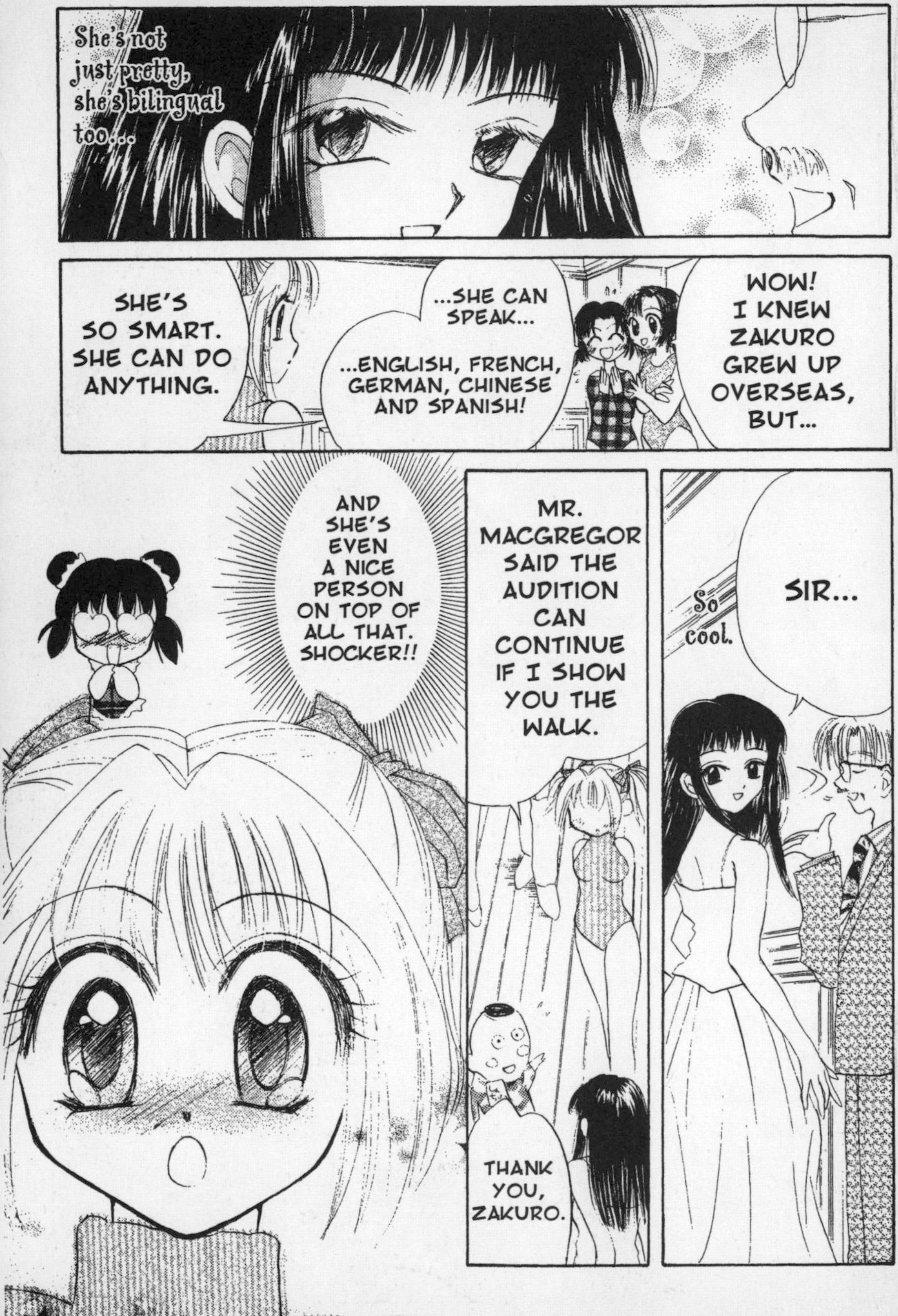
She's not just pretty, she's bilingual too...
WOW! I KNEW ZAKURO GREW UP OVERSEAS, BUT...
...SHE CAN SPEAK...
...ENGLISH, FRENCH, GERMAN, CHINESE AND SPANISH!
SHE'S SO SMART. SHE CAN DO ANYTHING.
SIR...
So cool.
MR. MACGREGOR SAID THE AUDITION CAN CONTINUE IF I SHOW YOU THE WALK.
THANK YOU, ZAKURO.
AND SHE'S EVEN A NICE PERSON ON TOP OF ALL THAT. SHOCKER!!

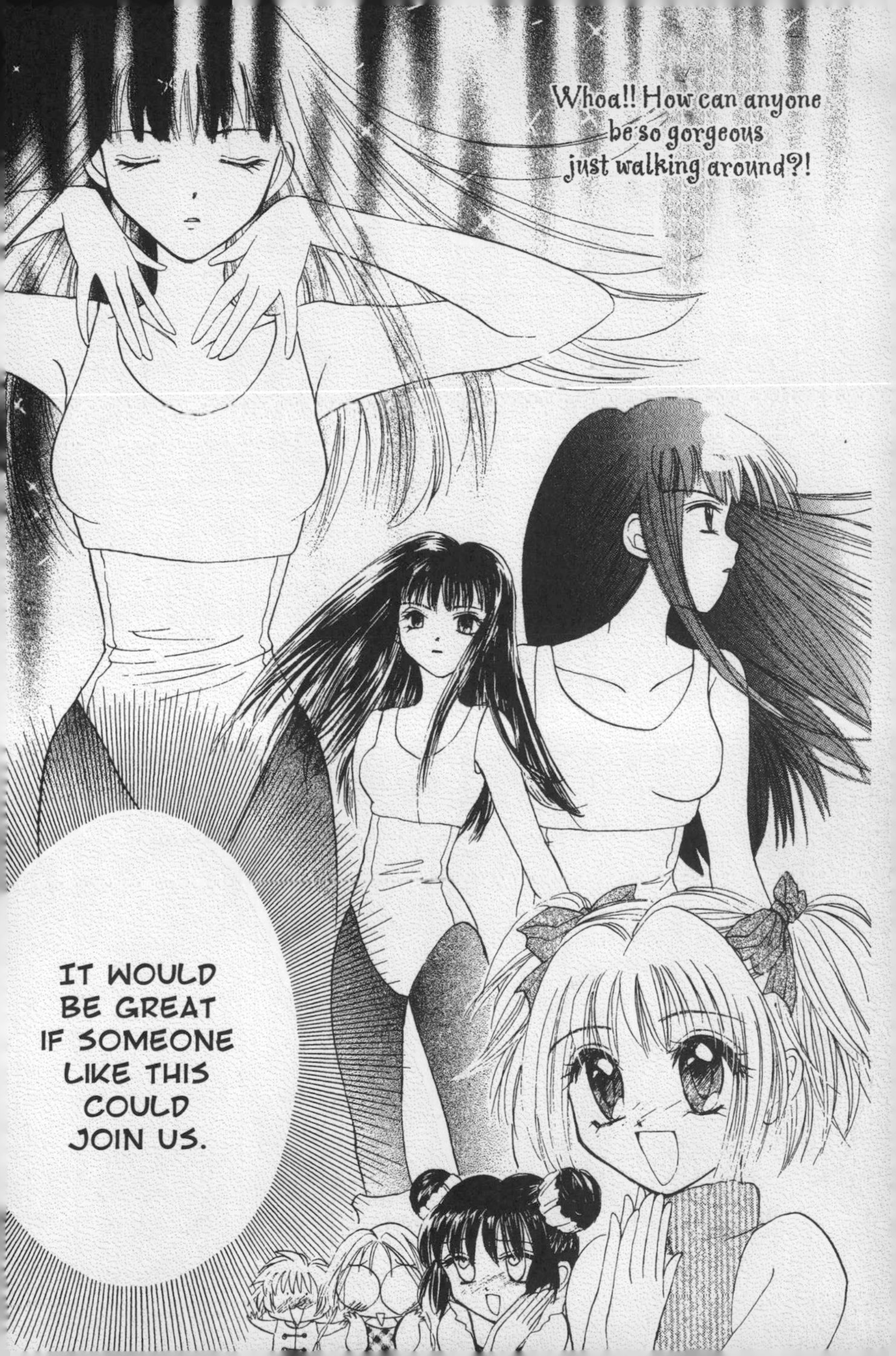
Whoa!! How can anyone be so gorgeous just walking around?!
IT WOULD BE GREAT IF SOMEONE LIKE THIS COULD JOIN US.

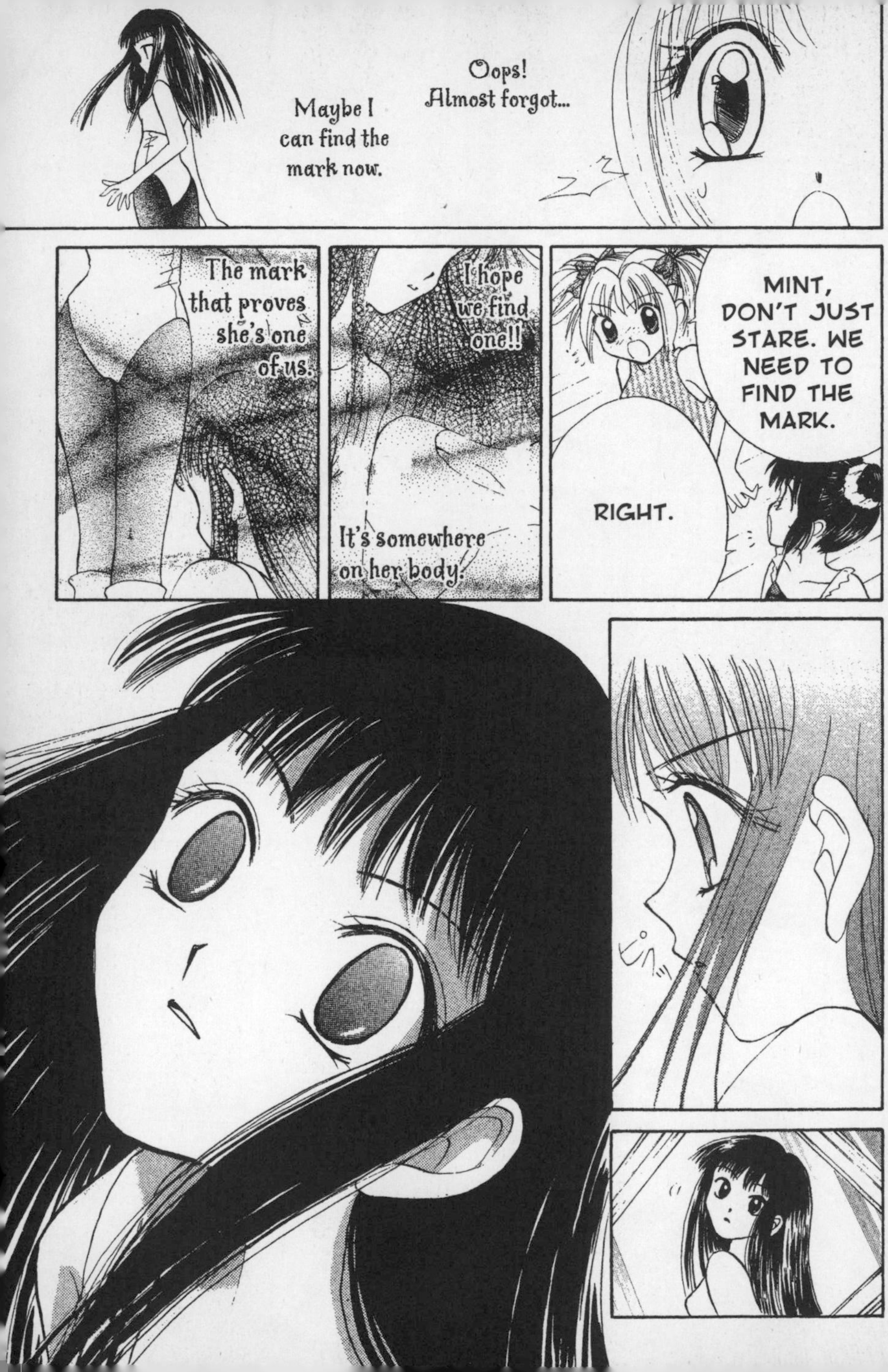
Oops! Almost forgot...
Maybe I can find the mark now.
MINT, DON'T JUST STARE. WE NEED TO FIND THE MARK.
RIGHT.
I hope we find one!!
It's somewhere on her body.
The mark that proves she's one of us.

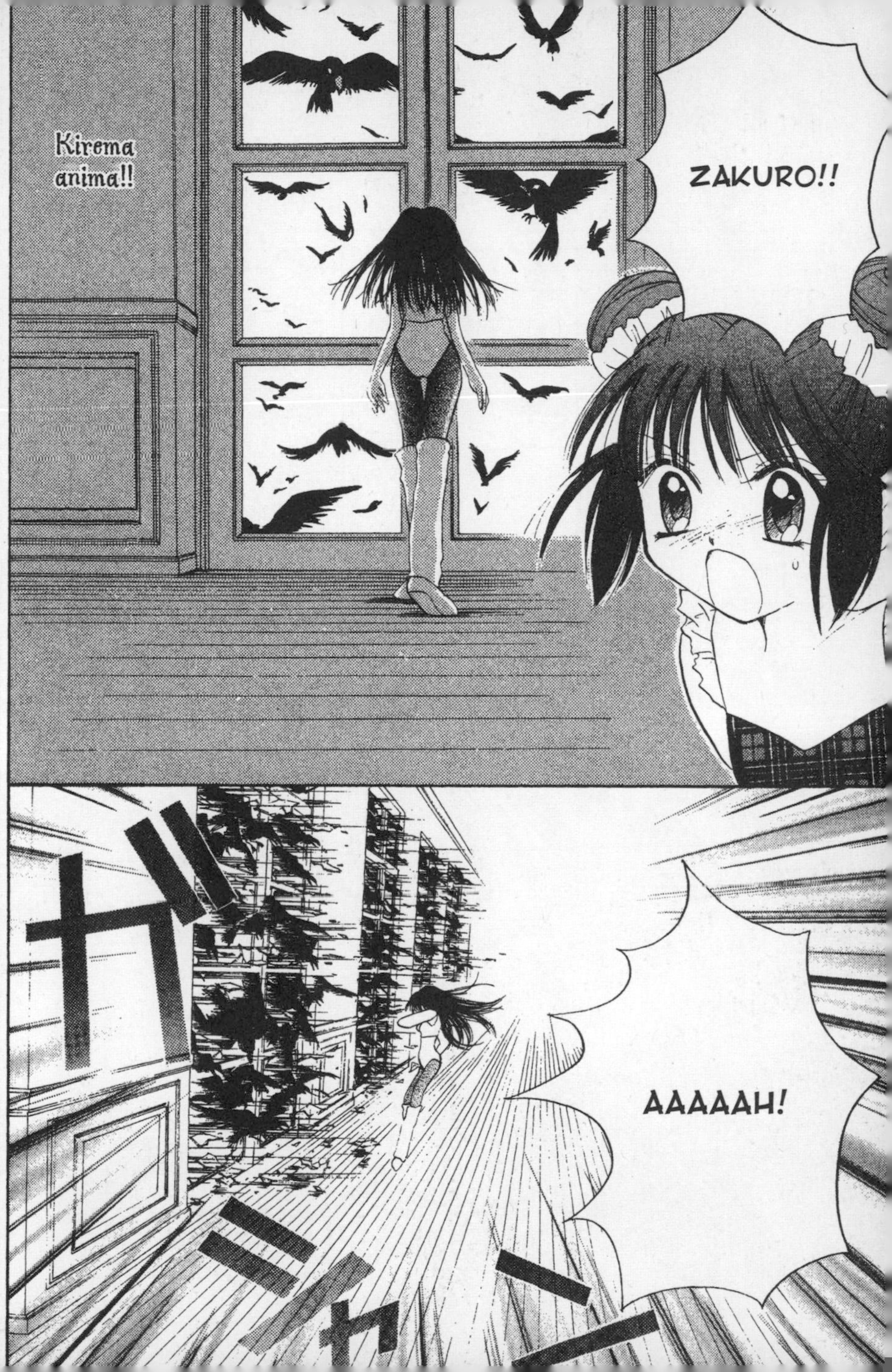
ZAKURO!!
Kirema anima!!
AAAAAH!

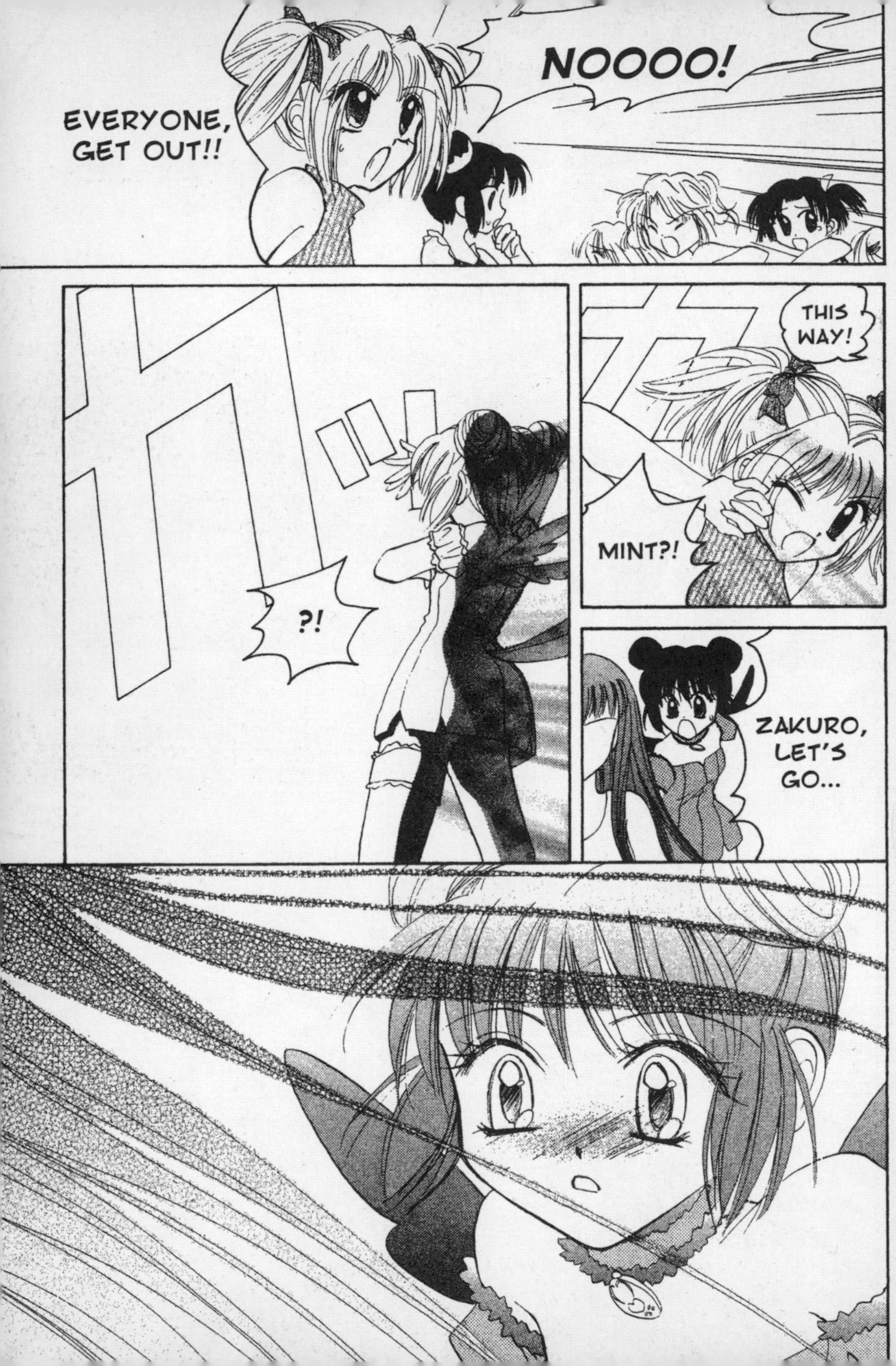
NOOOO!
EVERYONE, GET OUT!!
THIS WAY!
MINT?!
ZAKURO, LET'S GO...
?!

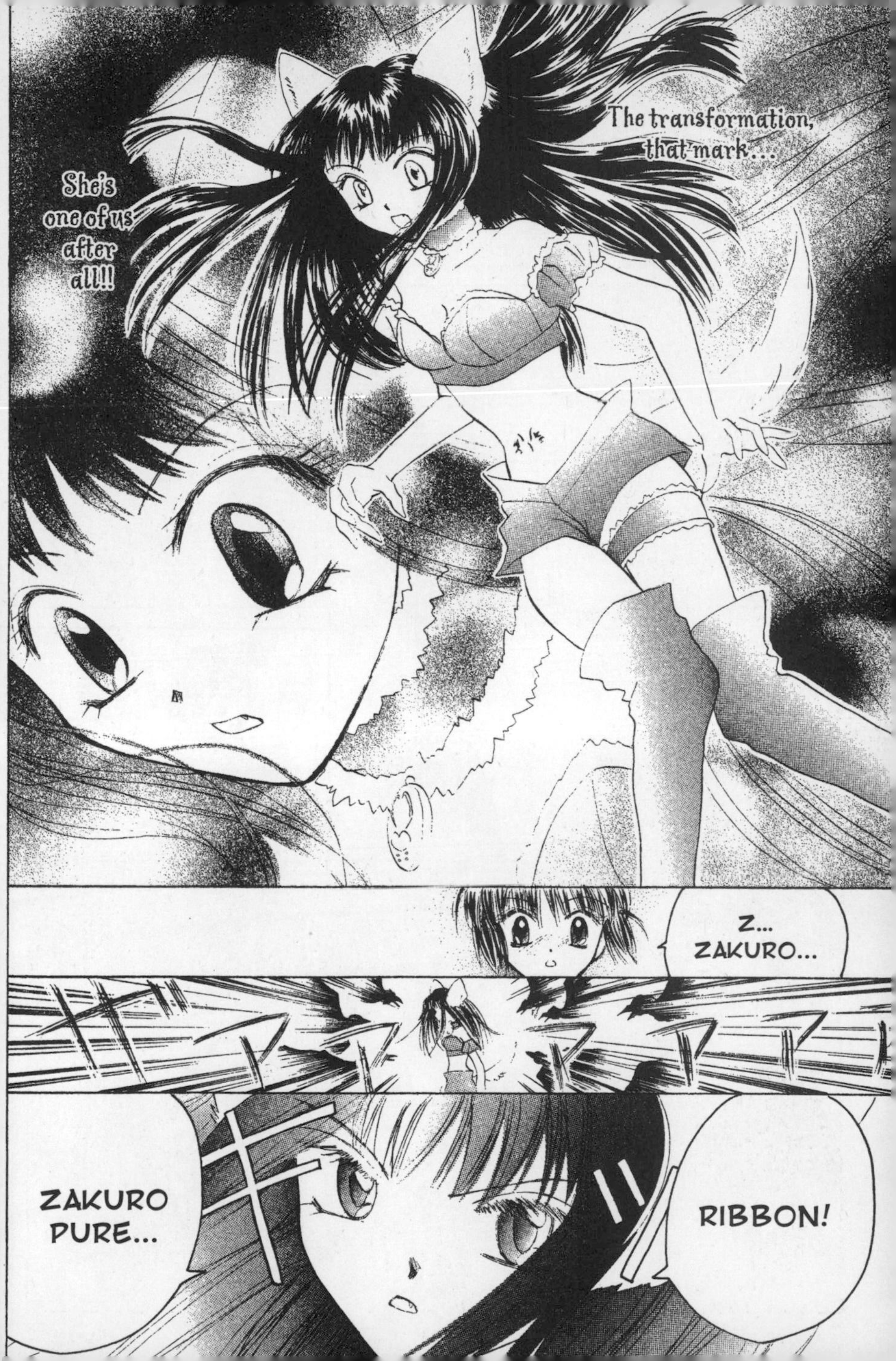
The transformation, that mark...
She's one of us after all!!
Z... ZAKURO...
ZAKURO PURE...
RIBBON!

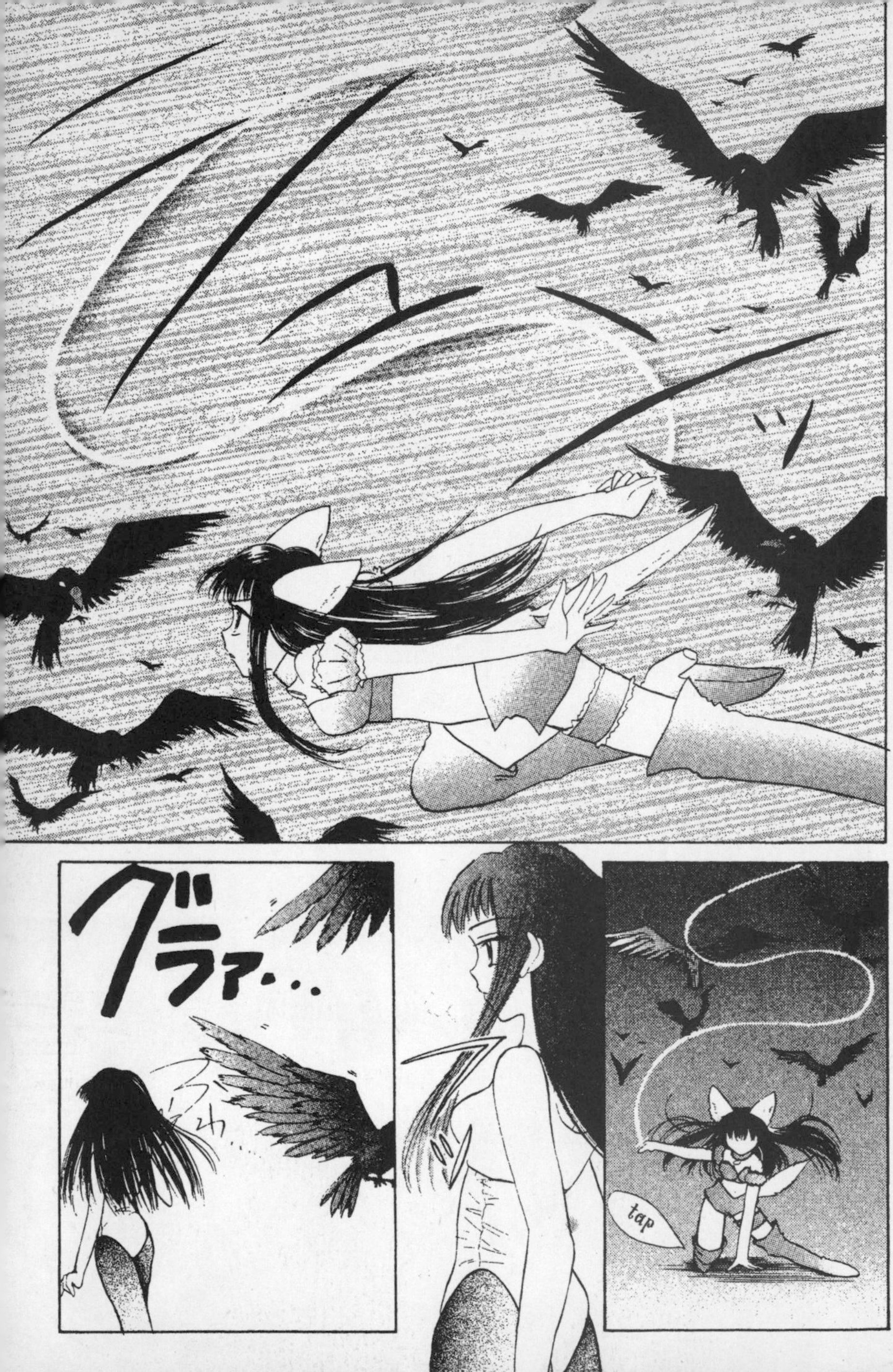
tap
グラァ...

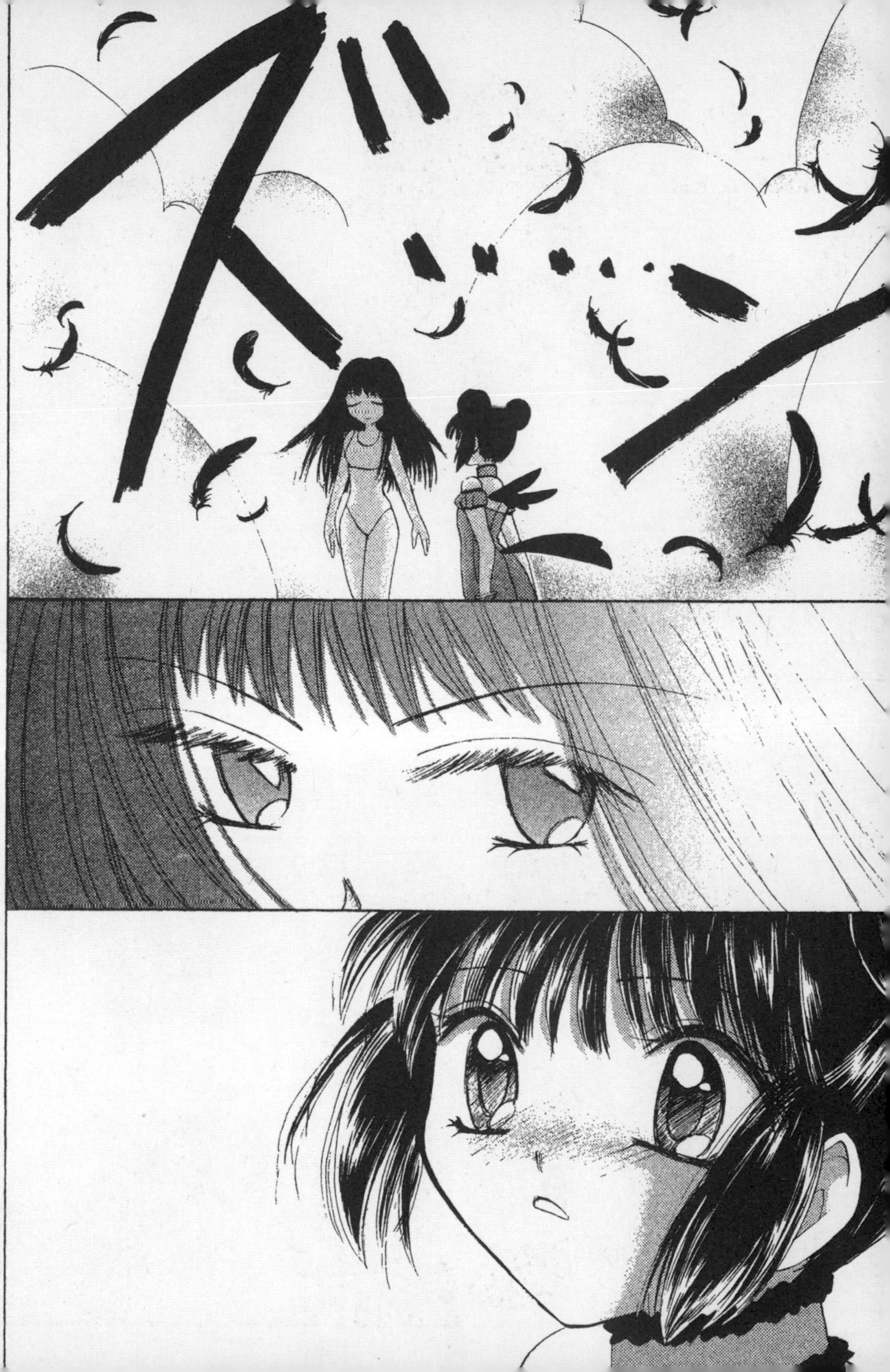

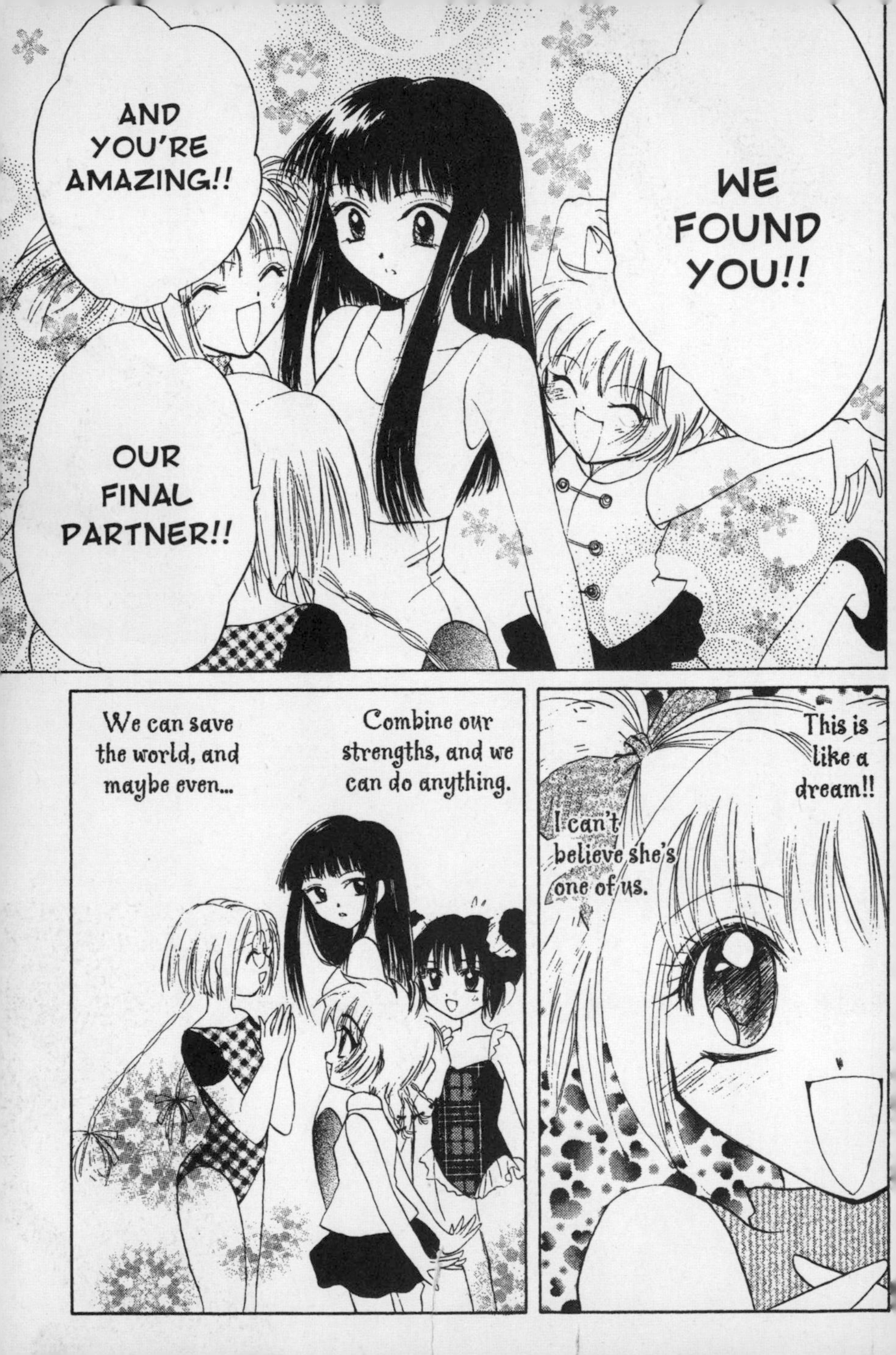
WE FOUND YOU!!
AND YOU'RE AMAZING!!
OUR FINAL PARTNER!!
This is like a dream!!
I can't believe she's one of us.
Combine our strengths, and we can do anything.
We can save the world, and maybe even...

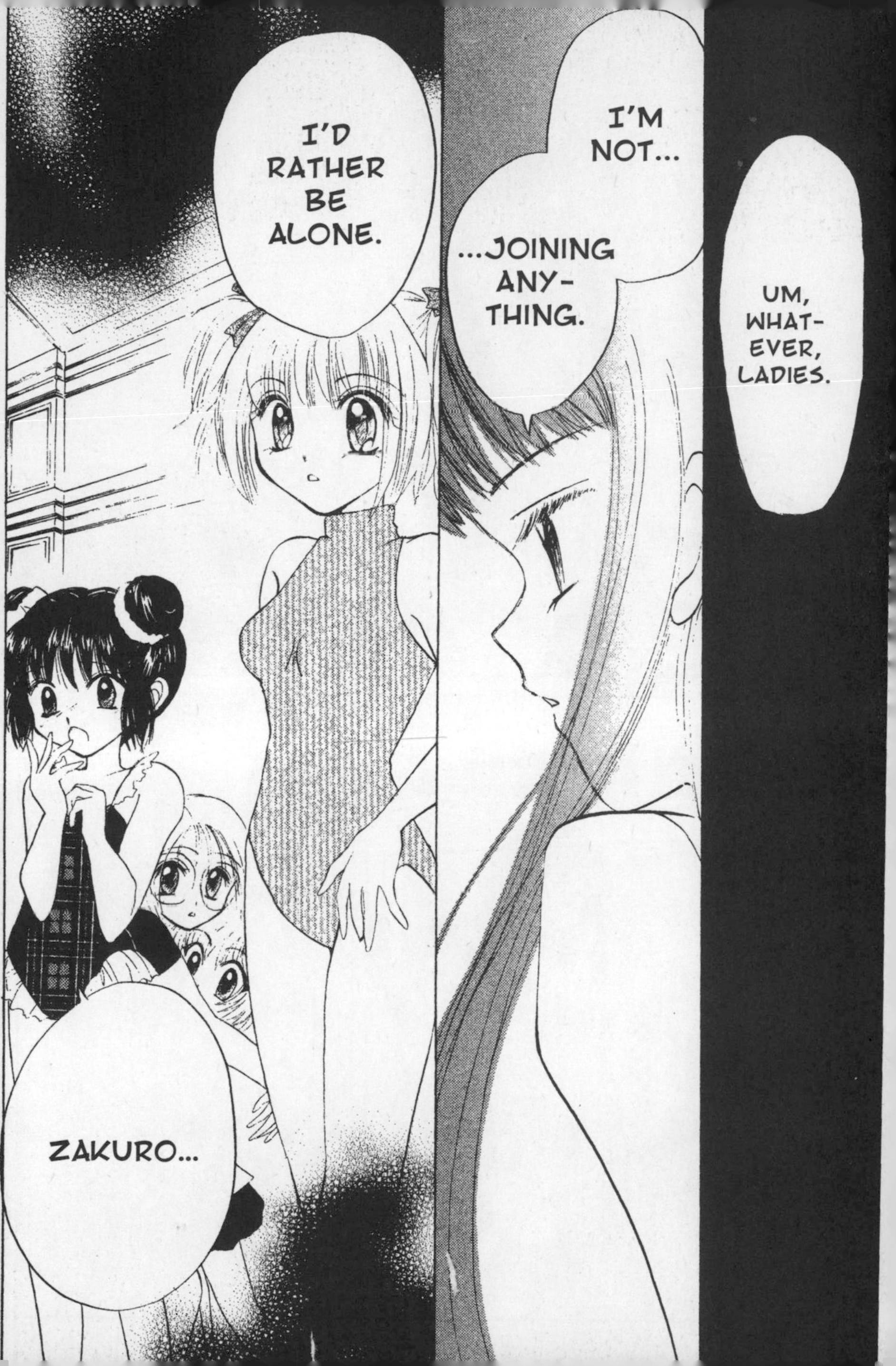
UM, WHAT-EVER, LADIES.
I'M NOT...
...JOINING ANY-THING.
I'D RATHER BE ALONE.
ZAKURO...

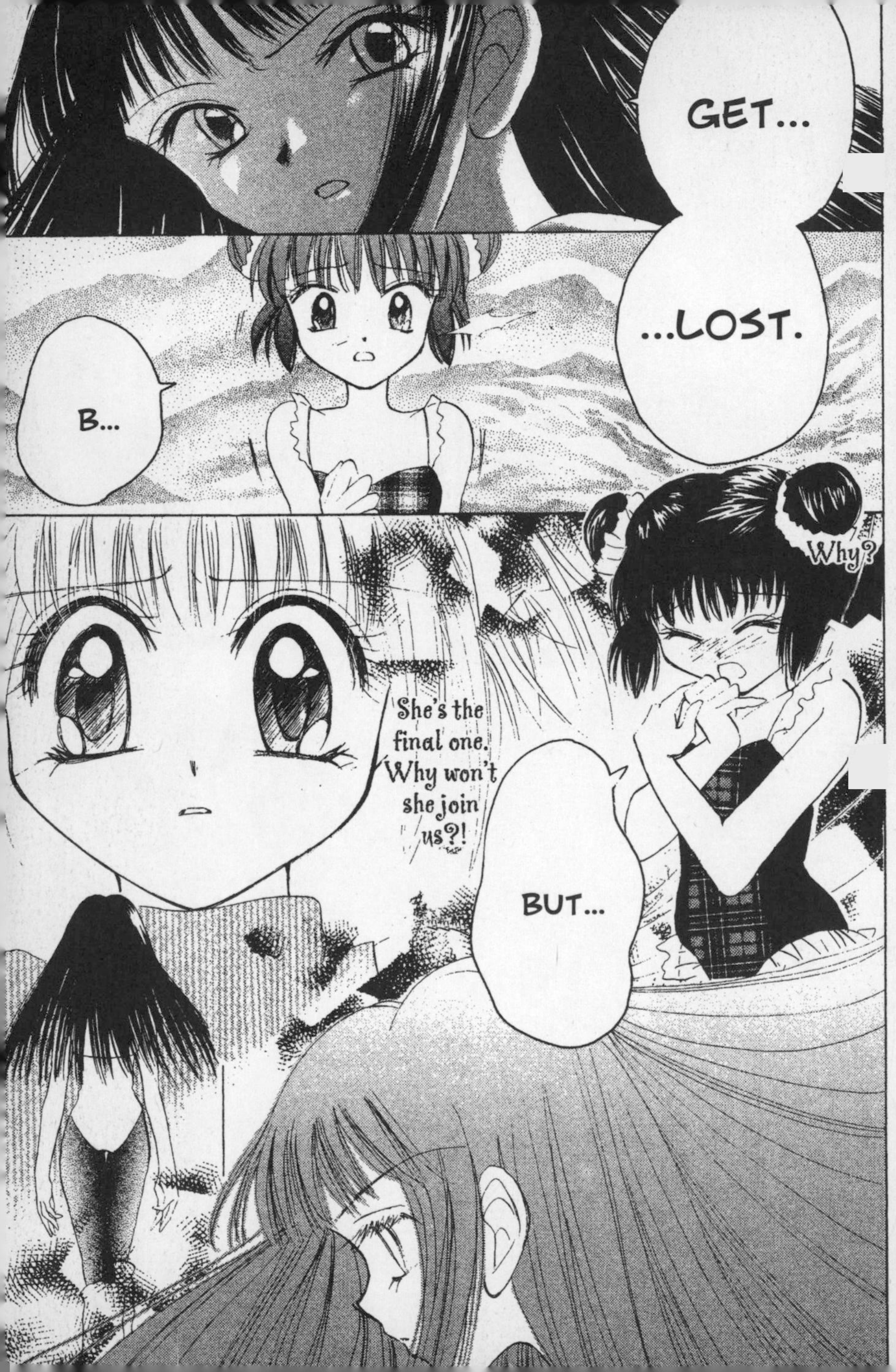
GET...
...LOST.
B...
Why?
She's the final one. Why won't she join us?!
BUT...

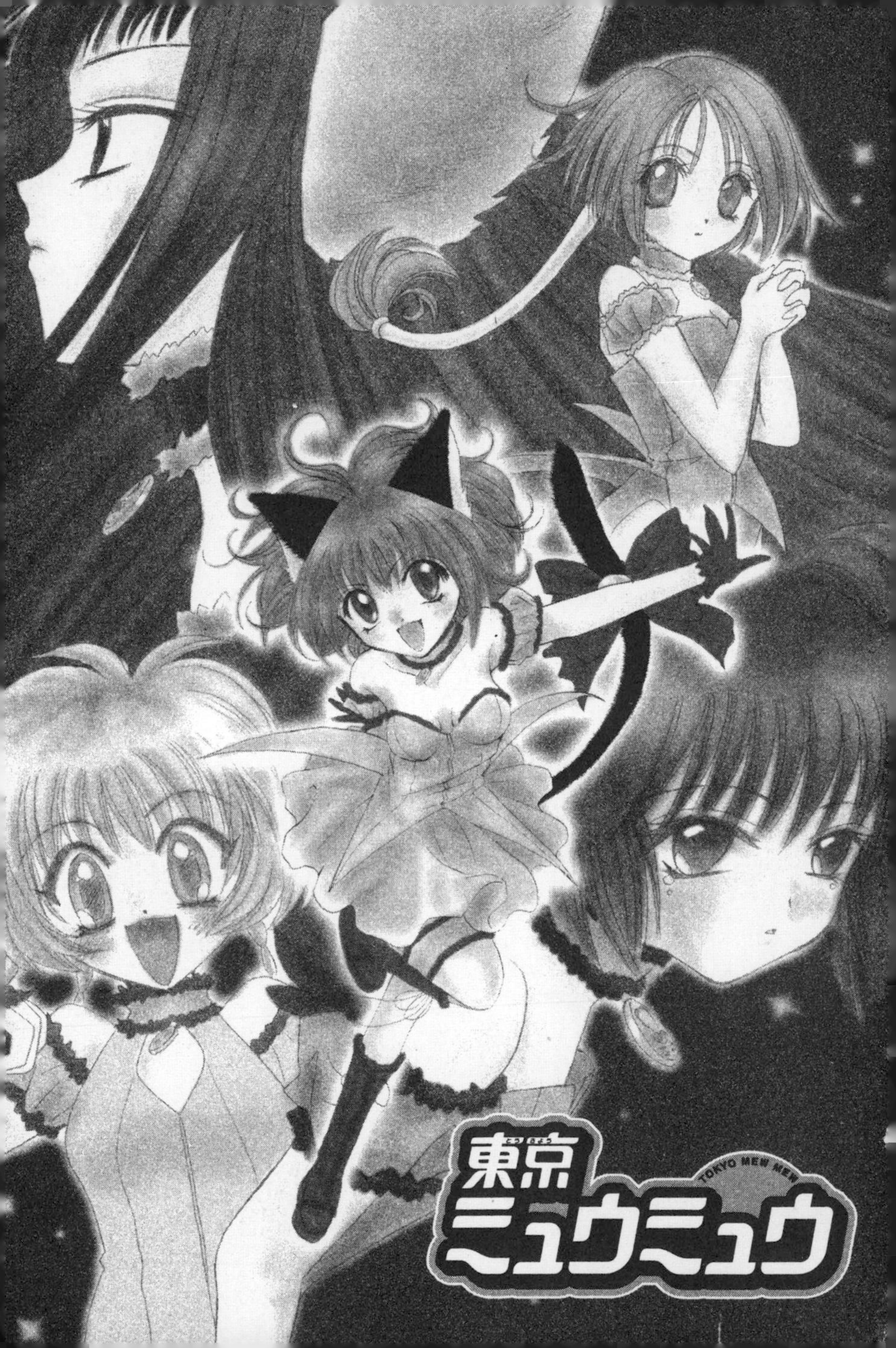
東京ミュウミュウ
TOKYO MEW MEW

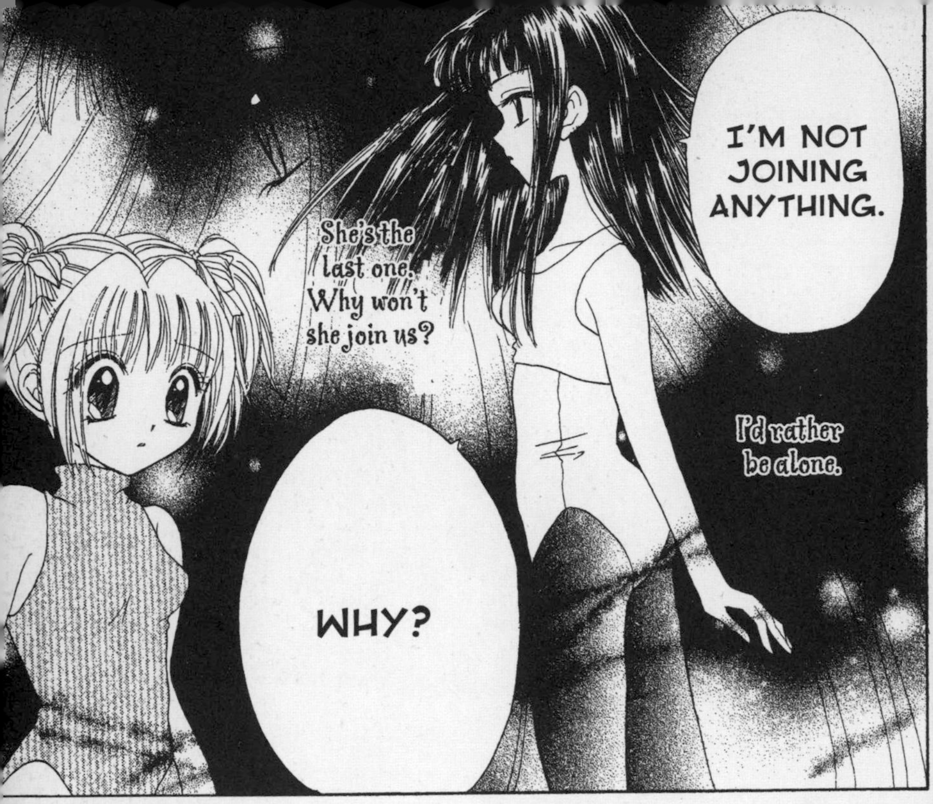
I'M NOT JOINING ANYTHING.
I'd rather be alone.
She's the last one. Why won't she join us?
WHY?

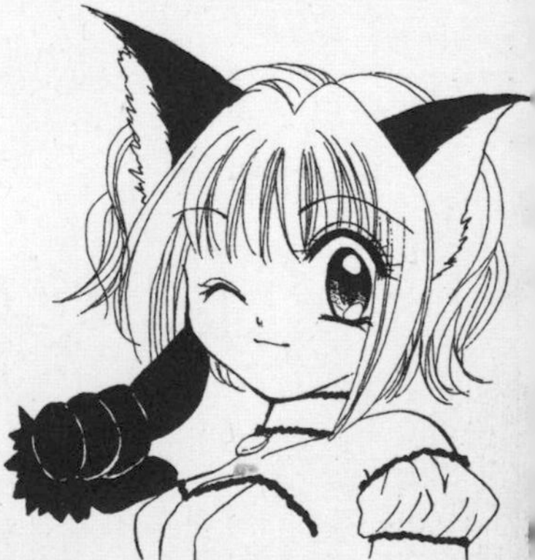

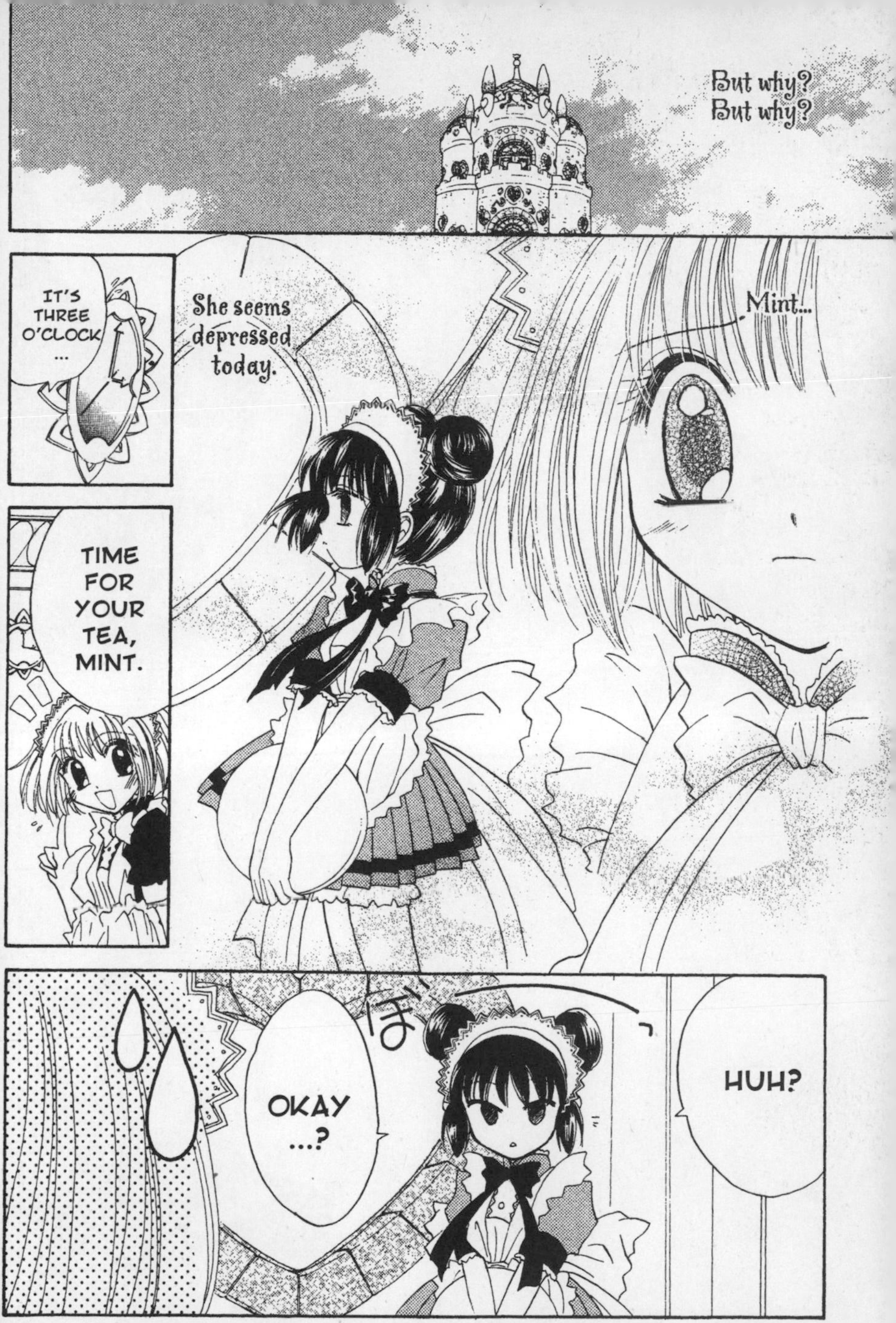
But why?
But why?
Mint...
She seems depressed today.
IT'S THREE O'CLOCK ...
TIME FOR YOUR TEA, MINT.
HUH?
ぼ
OKAY ...?

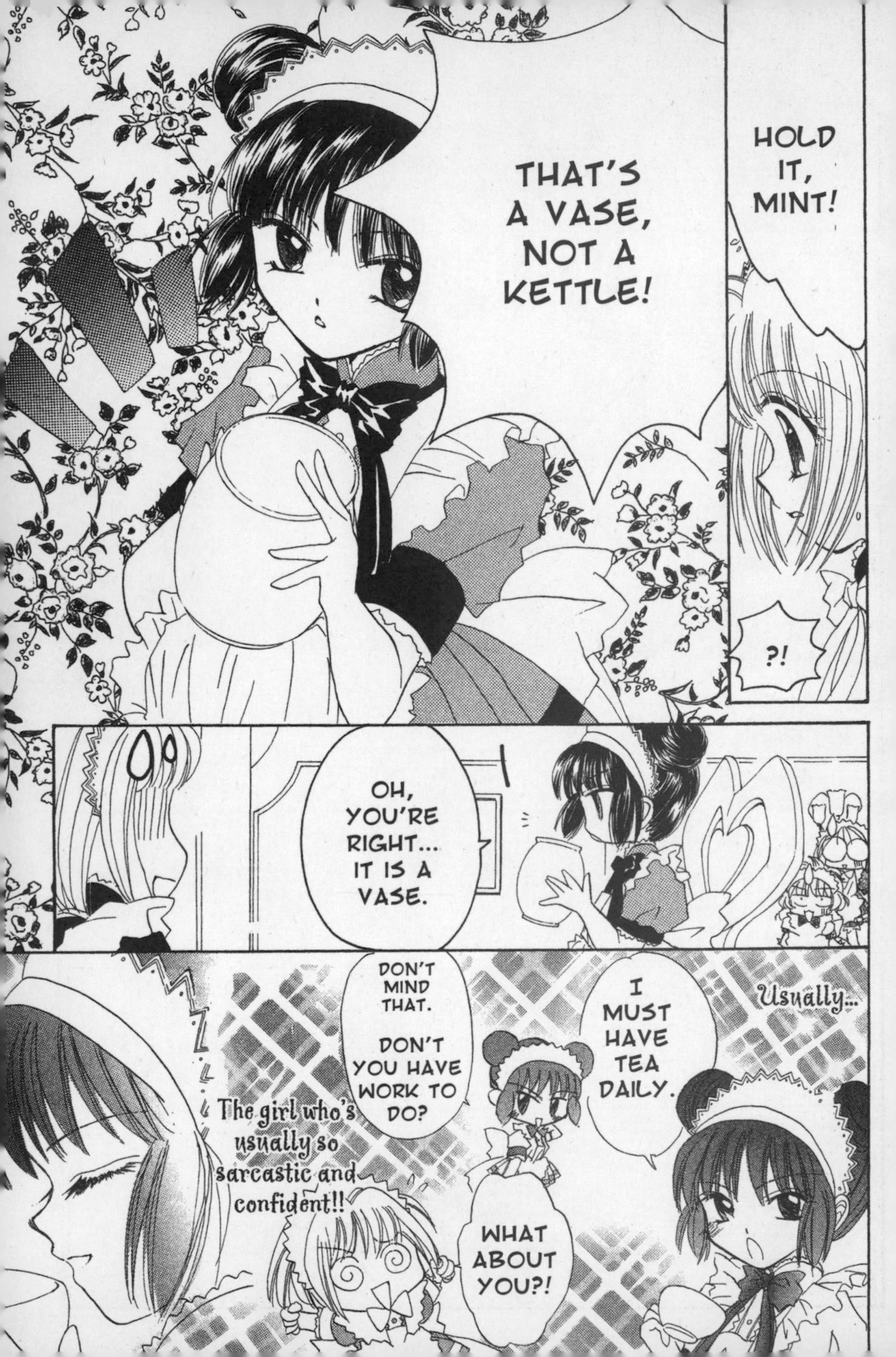
HOLD IT, MINT!
?!
THAT'S A VASE, NOT A KETTLE!
OH, YOU'RE RIGHT... IT IS A VASE.
Usually...
I MUST HAVE TEA DAILY.
DON'T MIND THAT.
DON'T YOU HAVE WORK TO DO?
WHAT ABOUT YOU?!
The girl who's usually so sarcastic and confident!!

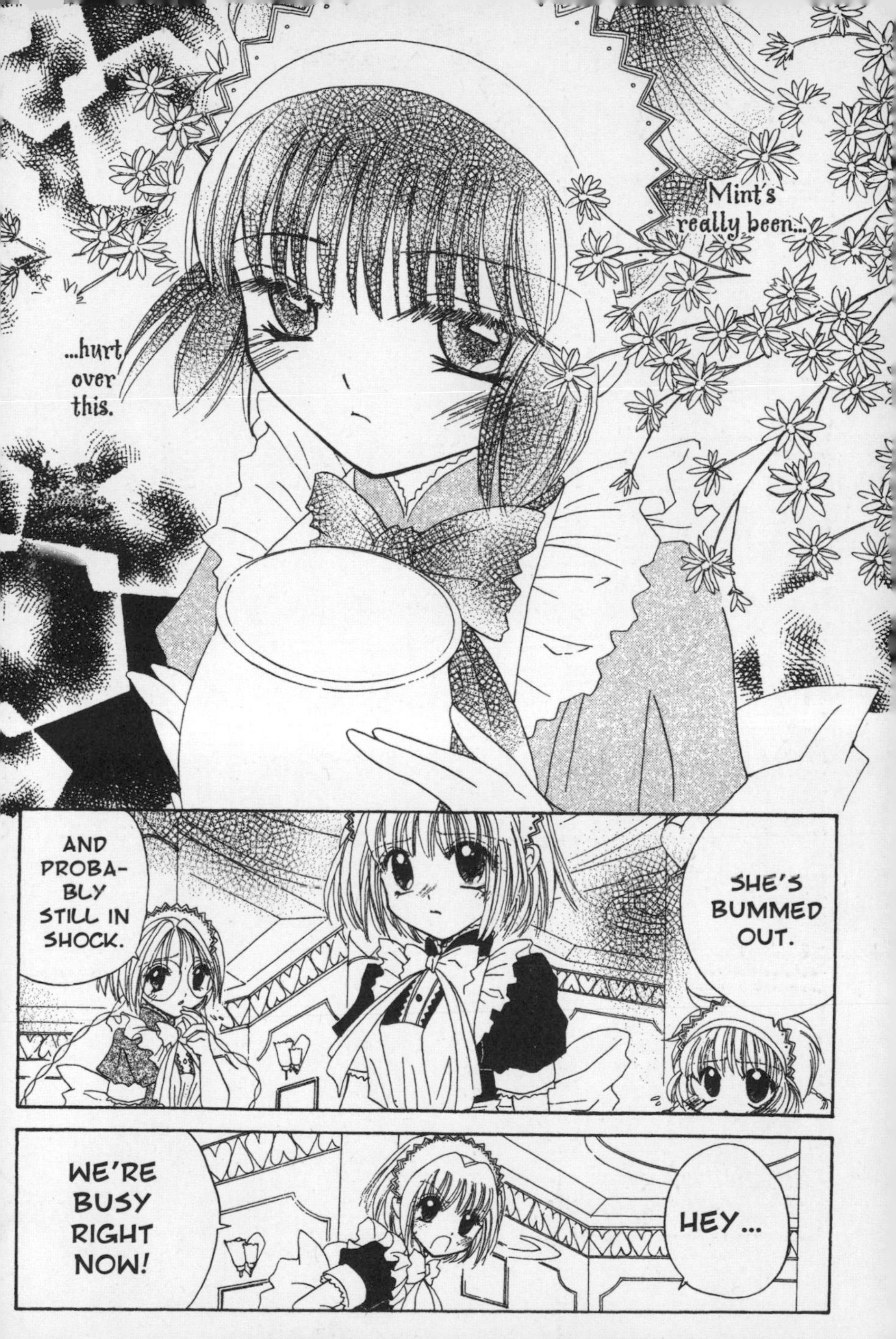
Mint's really been...
...hurt over this.
SHE'S BUMMED OUT.
AND PROBA-BLY STILL IN SHOCK.
HEY...
WE'RE BUSY RIGHT NOW!

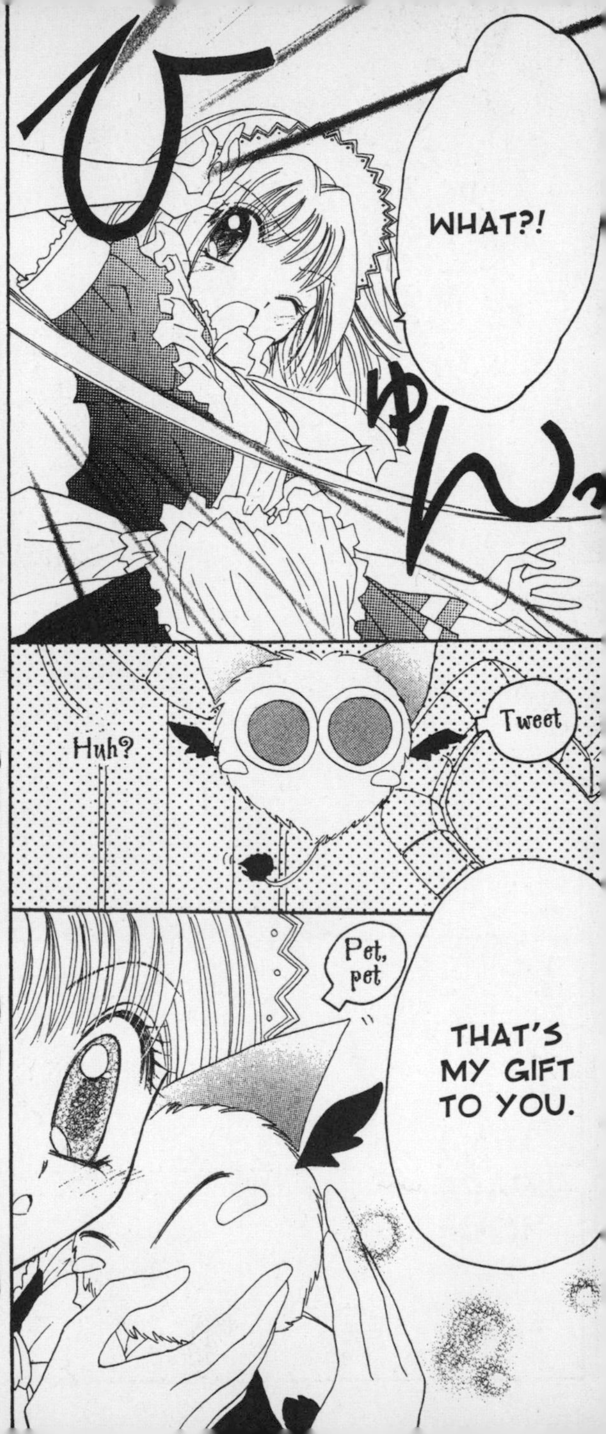
WHAT?!
Tweet
Huh?
THAT'S MY GIFT TO YOU.
Pet, pet

Business Meeting 2

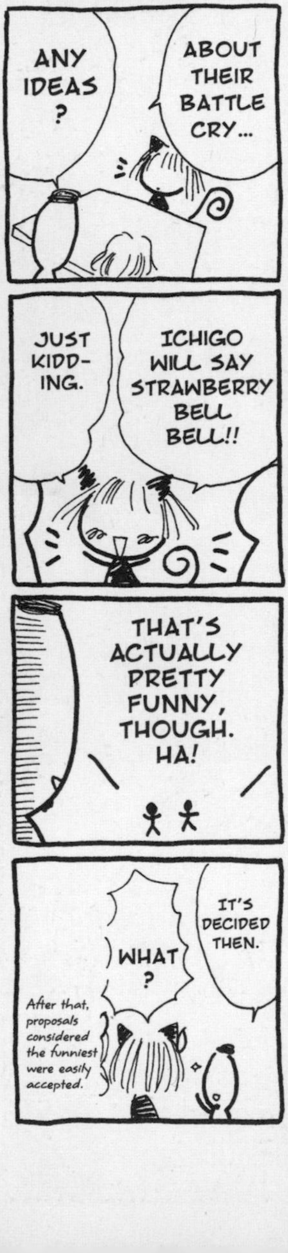
ABOUT THEIR BATTLE CRY...
ANY IDEAS?
ICHIGO WILL SAY STRAWBERRY BELL BELL!!
JUST KIDD-ING.
THAT'S ACTUALLY PRETTY FUNNY, THOUGH. HA!
IT'S DECIDED THEN.
WHAT?
After that, proposals considered the funniest were easily accepted.

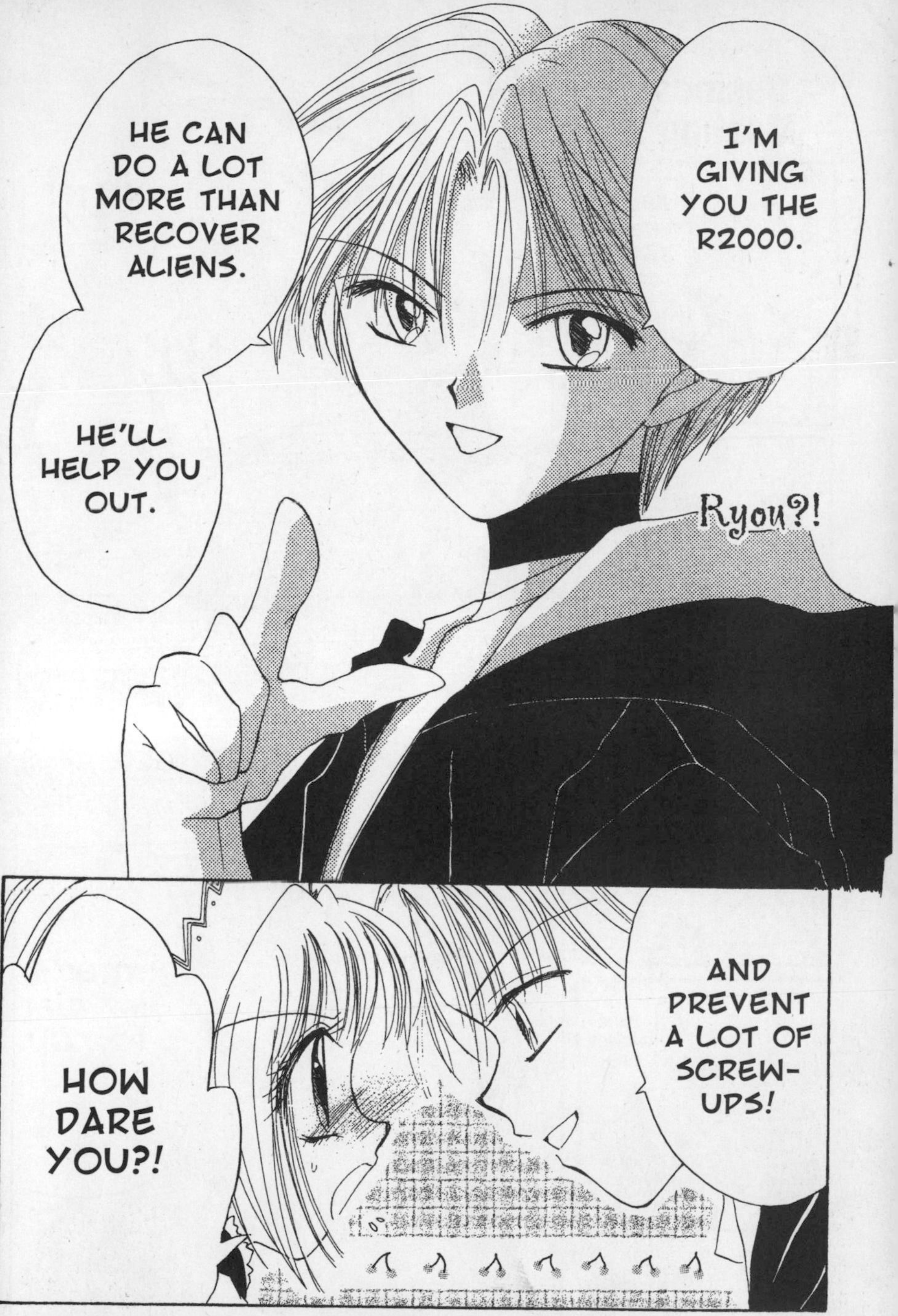
I'M GIVING YOU THE R2000.
HE CAN DO A LOT MORE THAN RECOVER ALIENS.
HE'LL HELP YOU OUT.
Ryou?!
AND PREVENT A LOT OF SCREW-UPS!
HOW DARE YOU?!

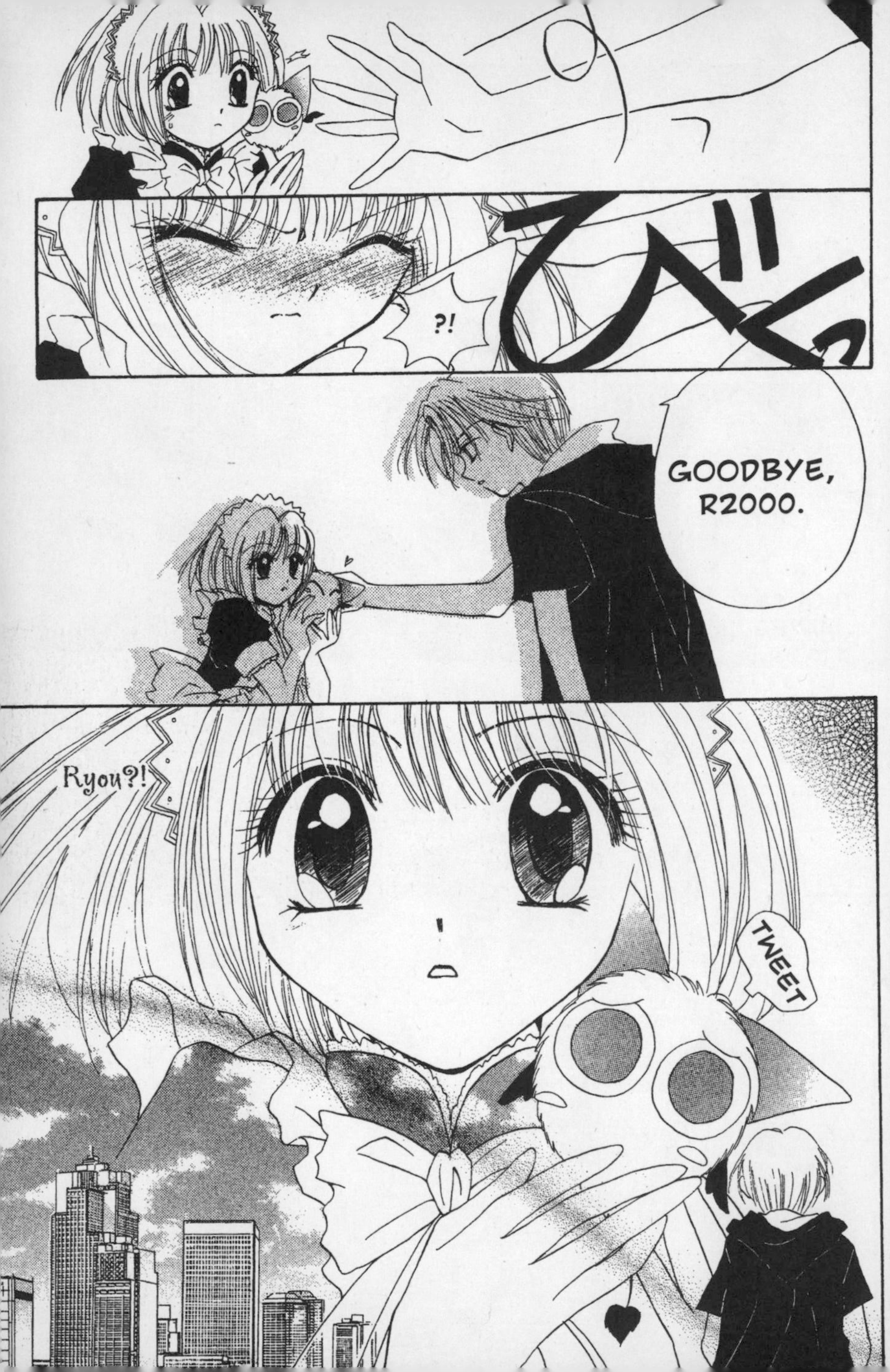
?!
GOODBYE, R2000.
Ryou?!
TWEET

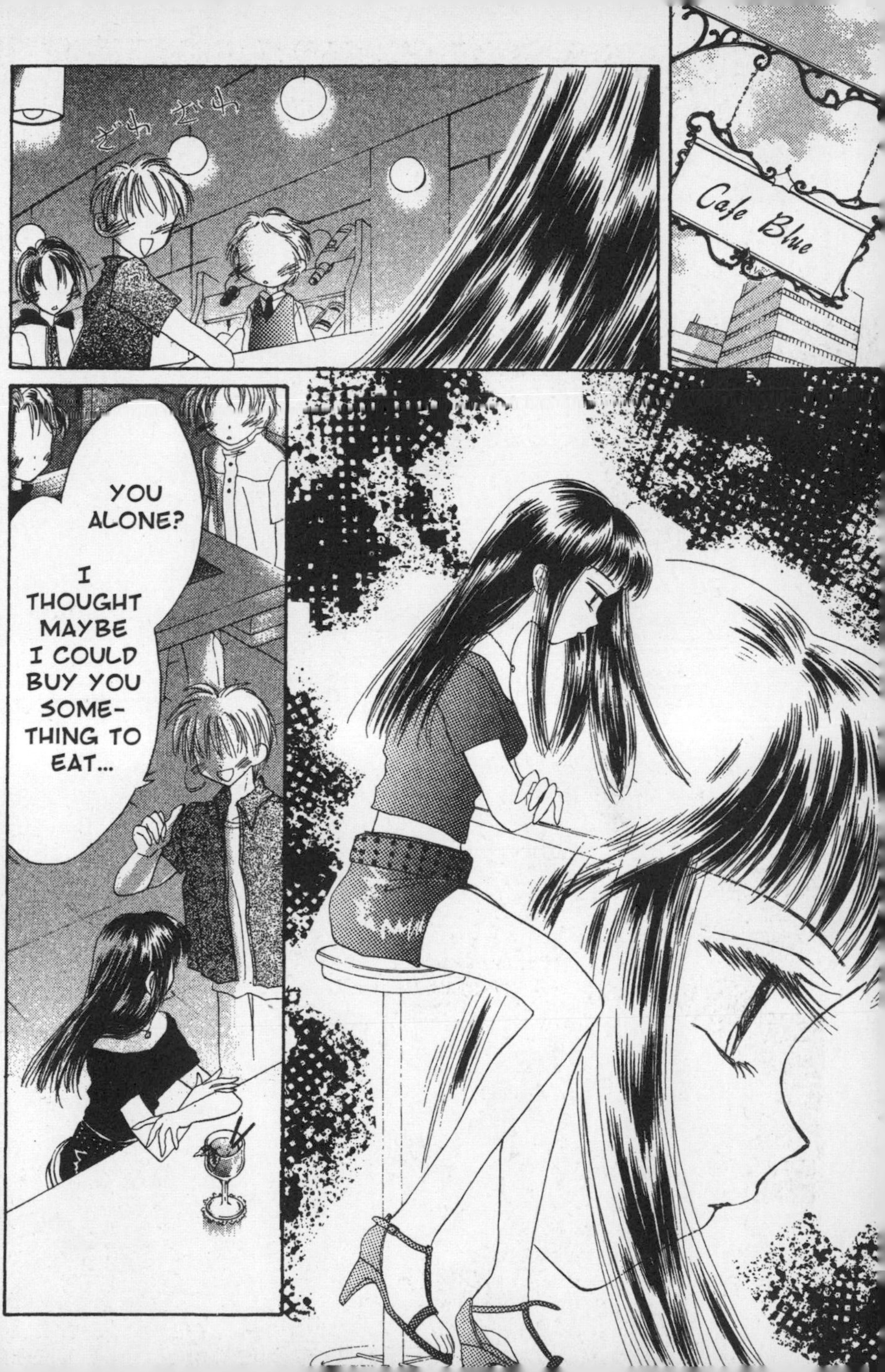
Cafe Blue
ざわざわ
YOU ALONE? I THOUGHT MAYBE I COULD BUY YOU SOME-THING TO EAT...

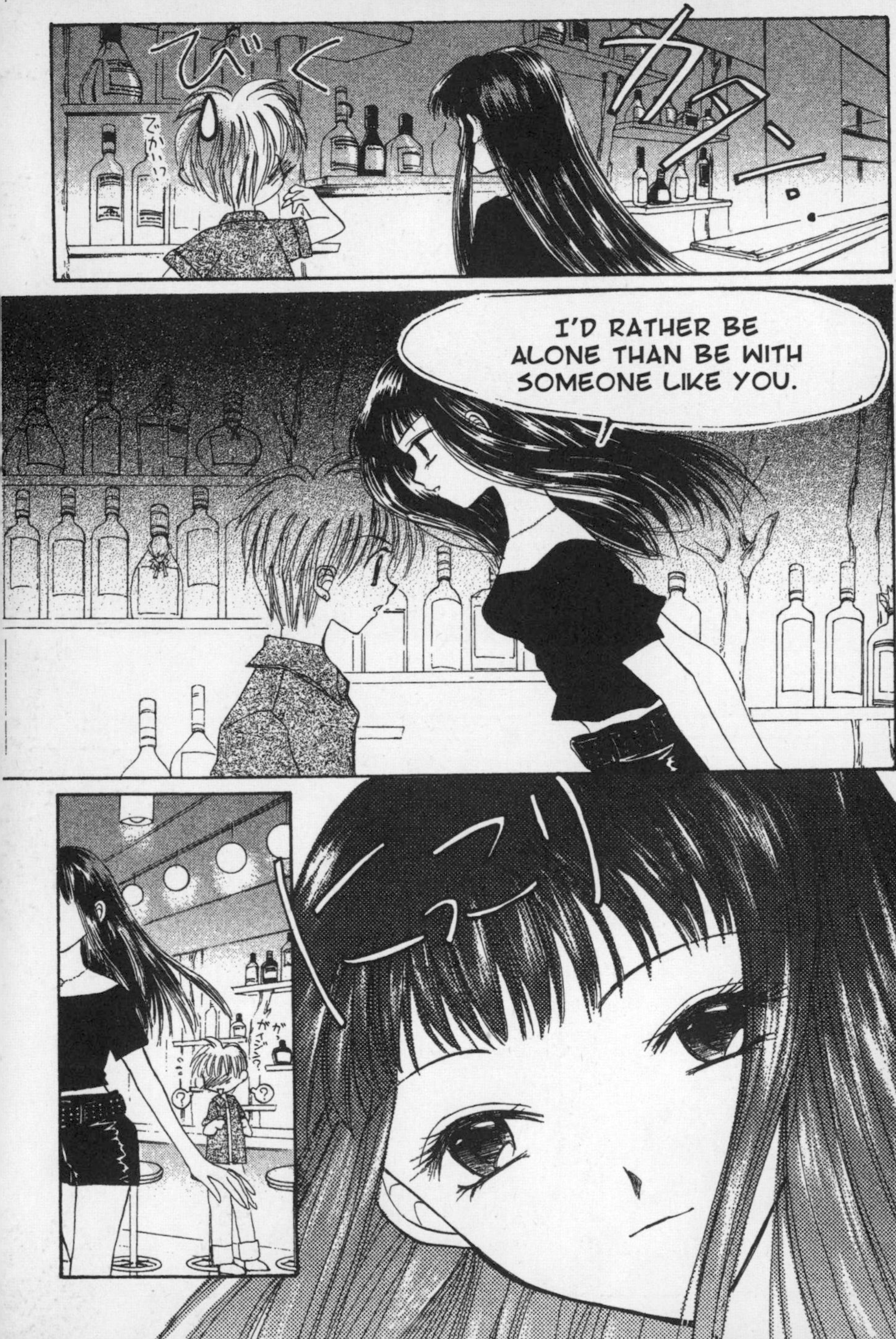

カターン
びく
でかいっ
I'D RATHER BE ALONE THAN BE WITH SOMEONE LIKE YOU.
ガッ ガイジン?

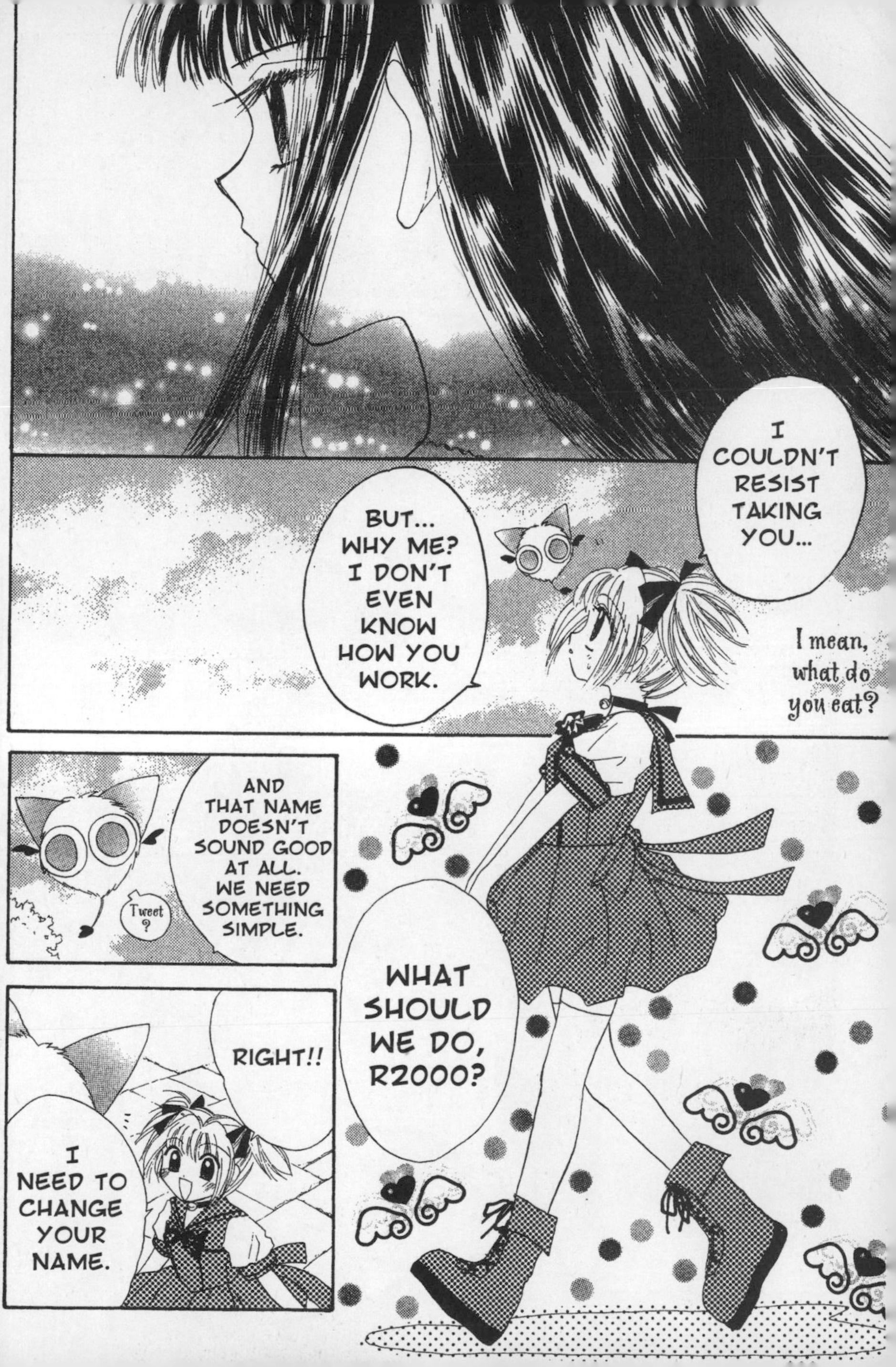
I COULDN'T RESIST TAKING YOU...
BUT... WHY ME? I DON'T EVEN KNOW HOW YOU WORK.
I mean, what do you eat?
WHAT SHOULD WE DO, R2000?
AND THAT NAME DOESN'T SOUND GOOD AT ALL. WE NEED SOMETHING SIMPLE.
Tweet ?
RIGHT!!
I NEED TO CHANGE YOUR NAME.

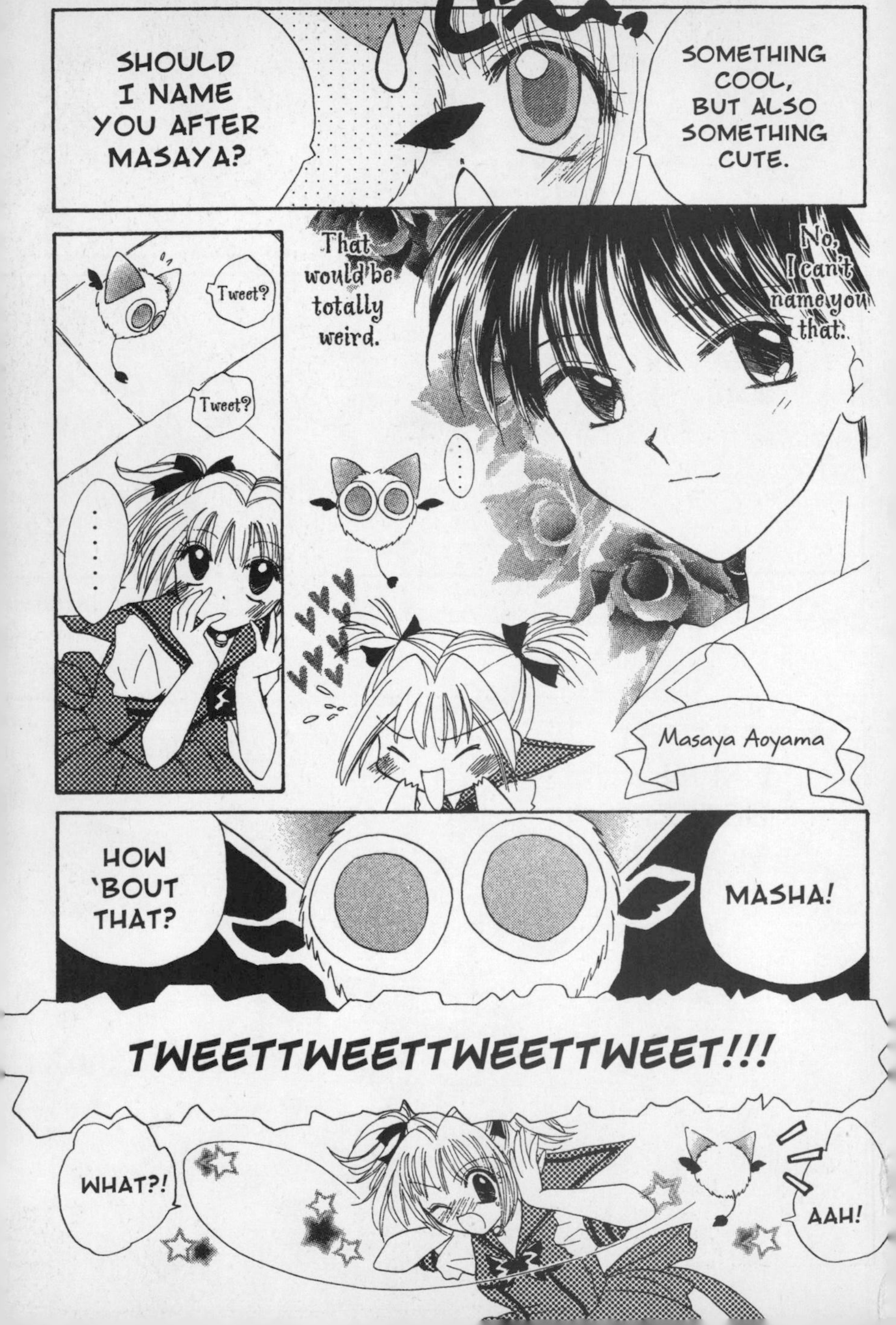
SOMETHING COOL, BUT ALSO SOMETHING CUTE.
SHOULD I NAME YOU AFTER MASAYA?
No, I can't name you that.
That would be totally weird.
...
Masaya Aoyama
Tweet?
Tweet?
......
MASHA!
HOW 'BOUT THAT?
TWEETTWEETTWEETTWEET!!!
AAH!
WHAT?!

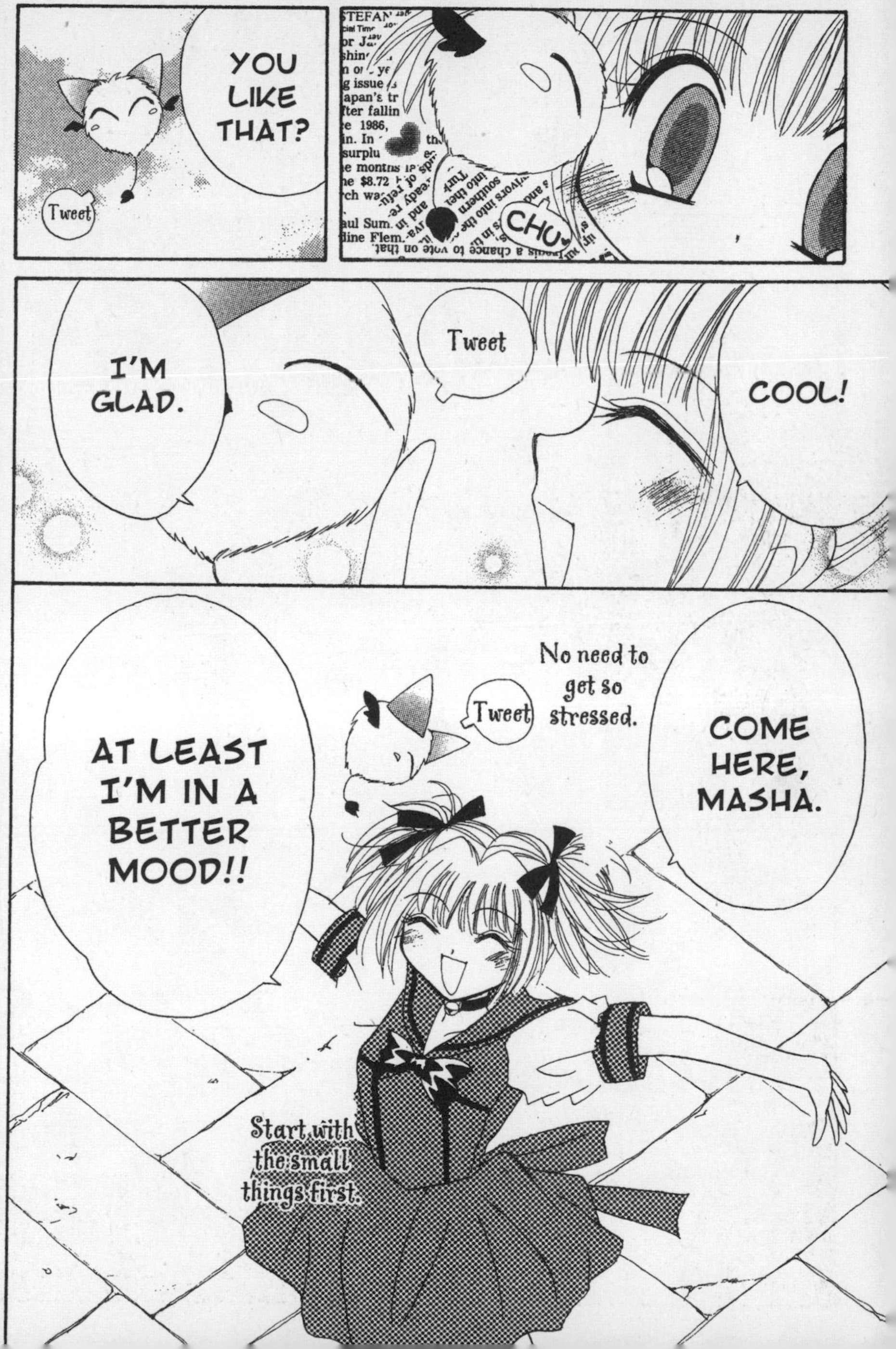
CHU
YOU LIKE THAT?
Tweet
COOL!
Tweet
I'M GLAD.
COME HERE, MASHA.
No need to get so stressed.
Tweet
AT LEAST I'M IN A BETTER MOOD!!
Start with the small things first.

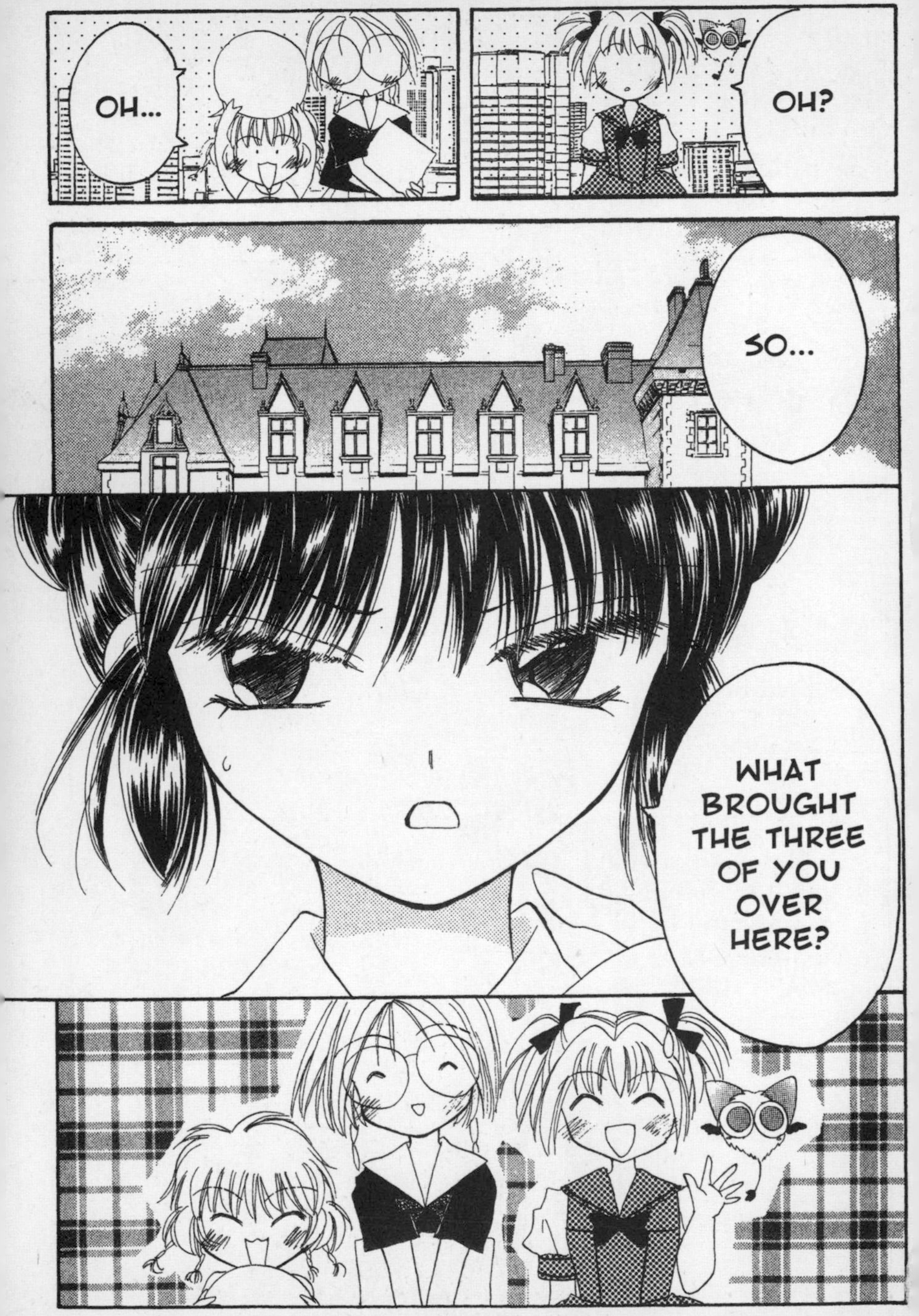
OH?
OH...
SO...
WHAT BROUGHT THE THREE OF YOU OVER HERE?

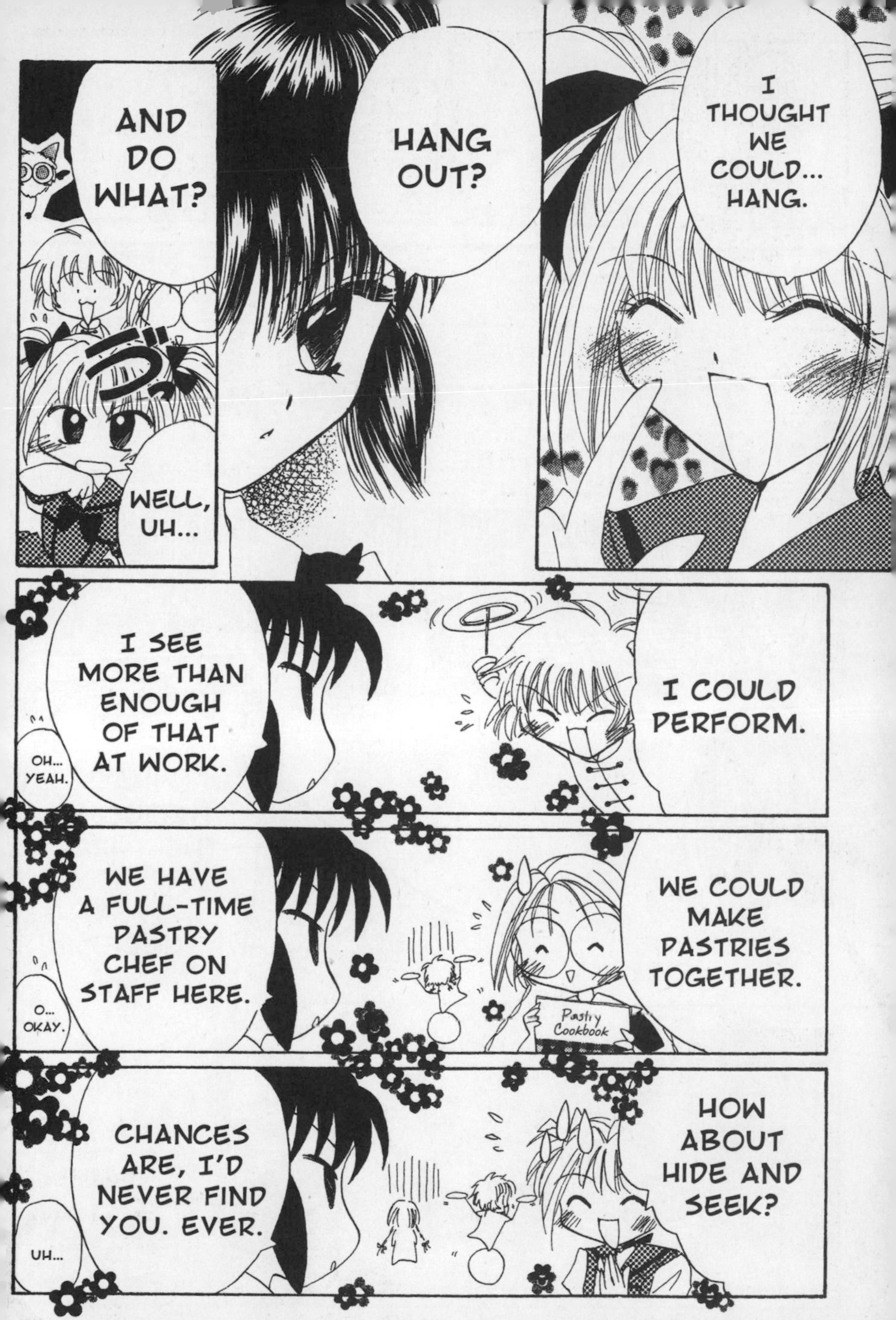
I THOUGHT WE COULD... HANG.
HANG OUT?
AND DO WHAT?
WELL, UH...
I COULD PERFORM.
I SEE MORE THAN ENOUGH OF THAT AT WORK.
OH... YEAH.
WE COULD MAKE PASTRIES TOGETHER.
Pastry Cookbook
WE HAVE A FULL-TIME PASTRY CHEF ON STAFF HERE.
O... OKAY.
HOW ABOUT HIDE AND SEEK?
CHANCES ARE, I'D NEVER FIND YOU. EVER.
UH...

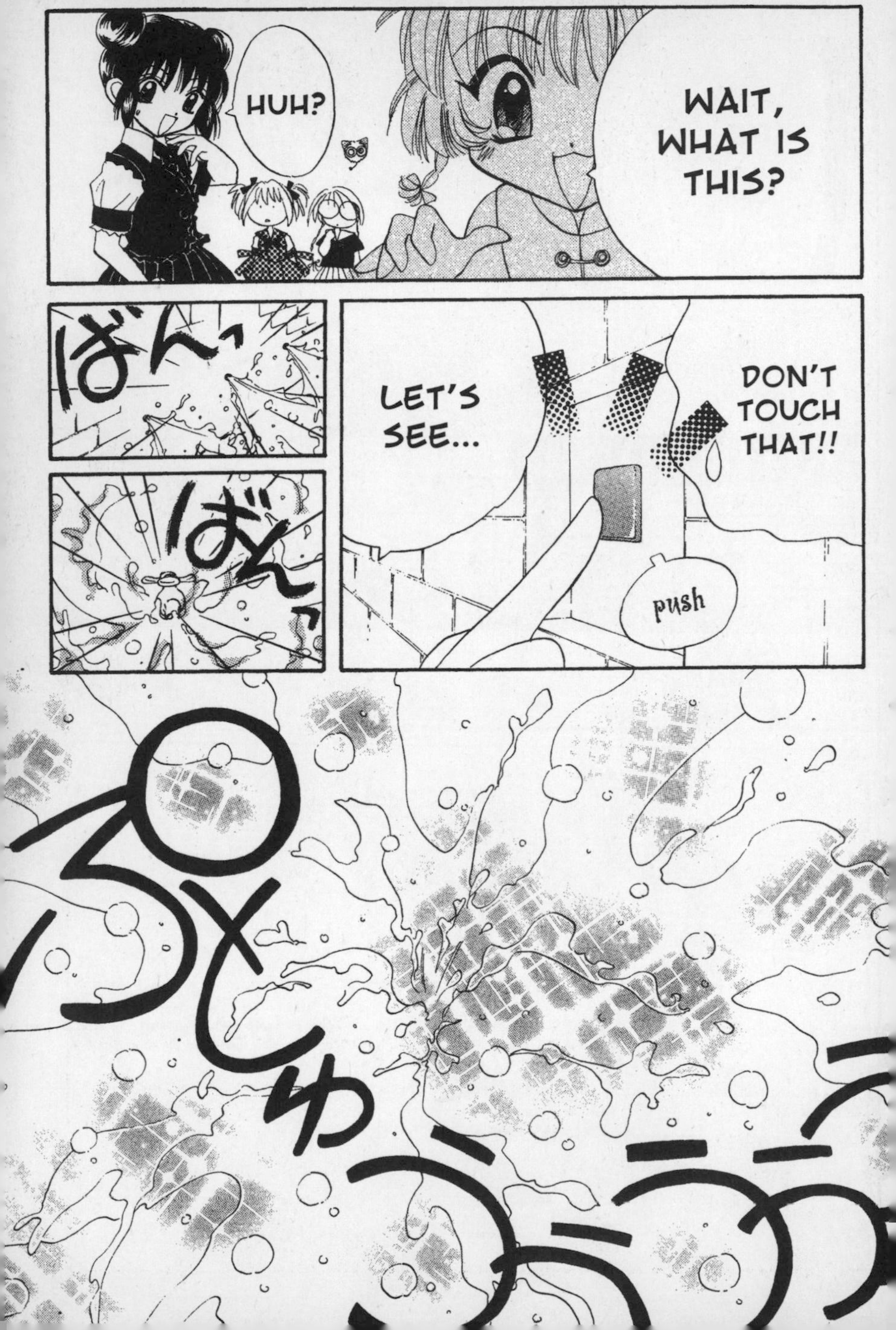
WAIT, WHAT IS THIS?
HUH?
DON'T TOUCH THAT!!
LET'S SEE...
push
ばんっ
ばんっ
ぷしゅうううう

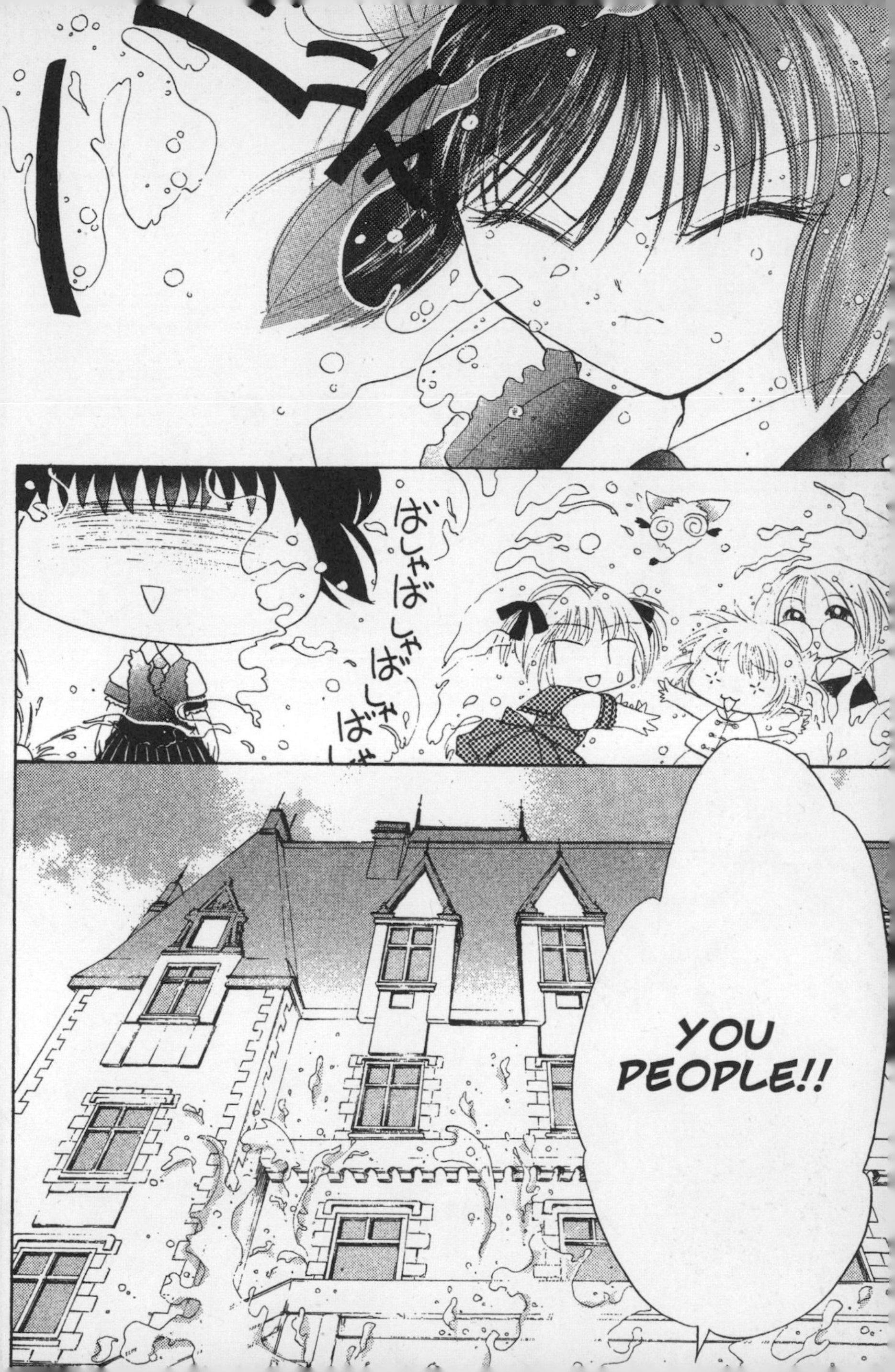
ばしゃばしゃばしゃ
YOU PEOPLE!!

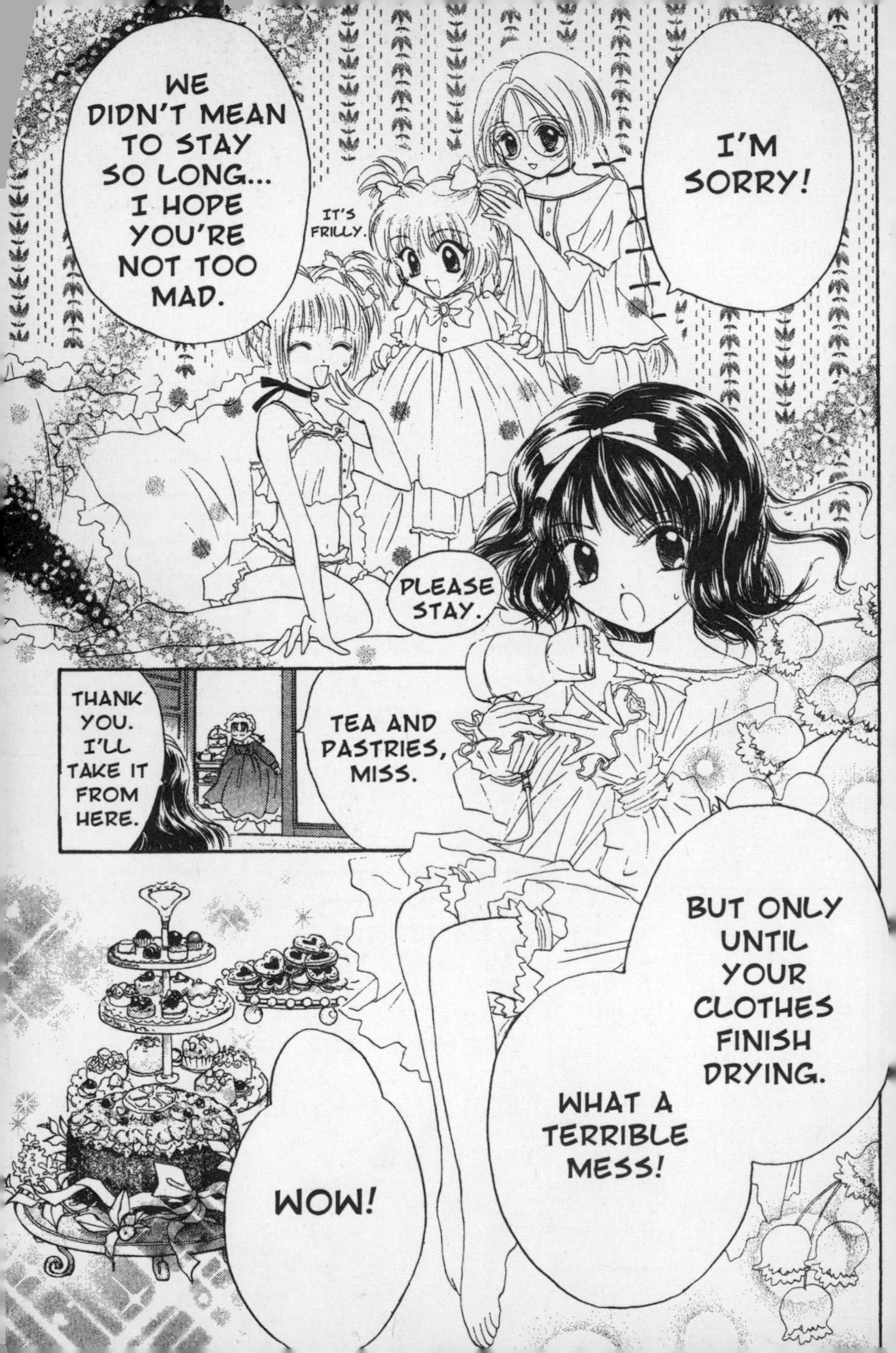

I'M SORRY!
WE DIDN'T MEAN TO STAY SO LONG... I HOPE YOU'RE NOT TOO MAD.
IT'S FRILLY.
PLEASE STAY.
BUT ONLY UNTIL YOUR CLOTHES FINISH DRYING.
WHAT A TERRIBLE MESS!
TEA AND PASTRIES, MISS.
THANK YOU. I'LL TAKE IT FROM HERE.
WOW!

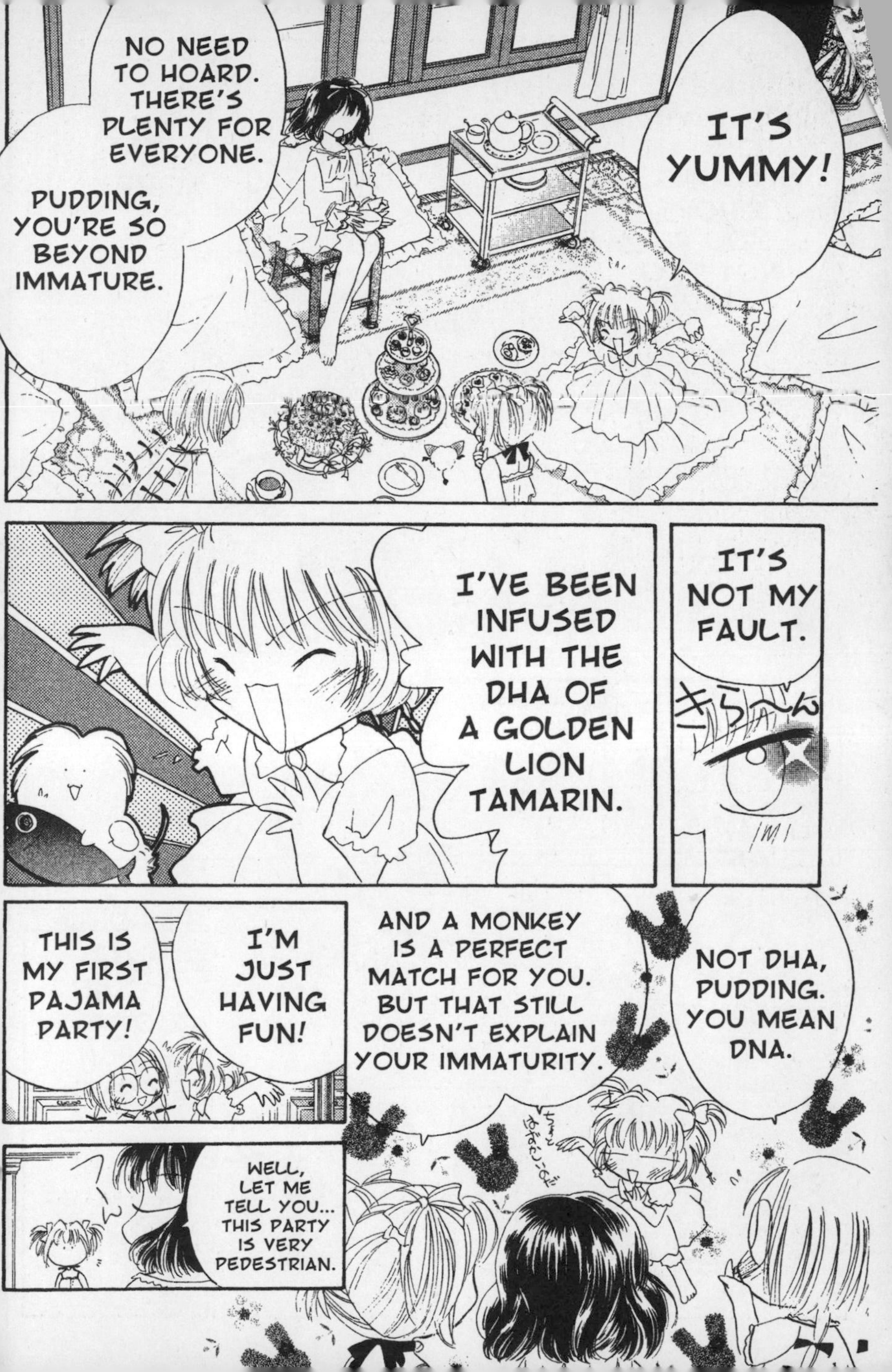
IT'S YUMMY!
NO NEED TO HOARD. THERE'S PLENTY FOR EVERYONE.
PUDDING, YOU'RE SO BEYOND IMMATURE.
IT'S NOT MY FAULT.
きら〜ん
I'VE BEEN INFUSED WITH THE DHA OF A GOLDEN LION TAMARIN.
NOT DHA, PUDDING. YOU MEAN DNA.
AND A MONKEY IS A PERFECT MATCH FOR YOU. BUT THAT STILL DOESN'T EXPLAIN YOUR IMMATURITY.
I'M JUST HAVING FUN!
THIS IS MY FIRST PAJAMA PARTY!
ちょっとはずかしいのだ
WELL, LET ME TELL YOU... THIS PARTY IS VERY PEDESTRIAN.

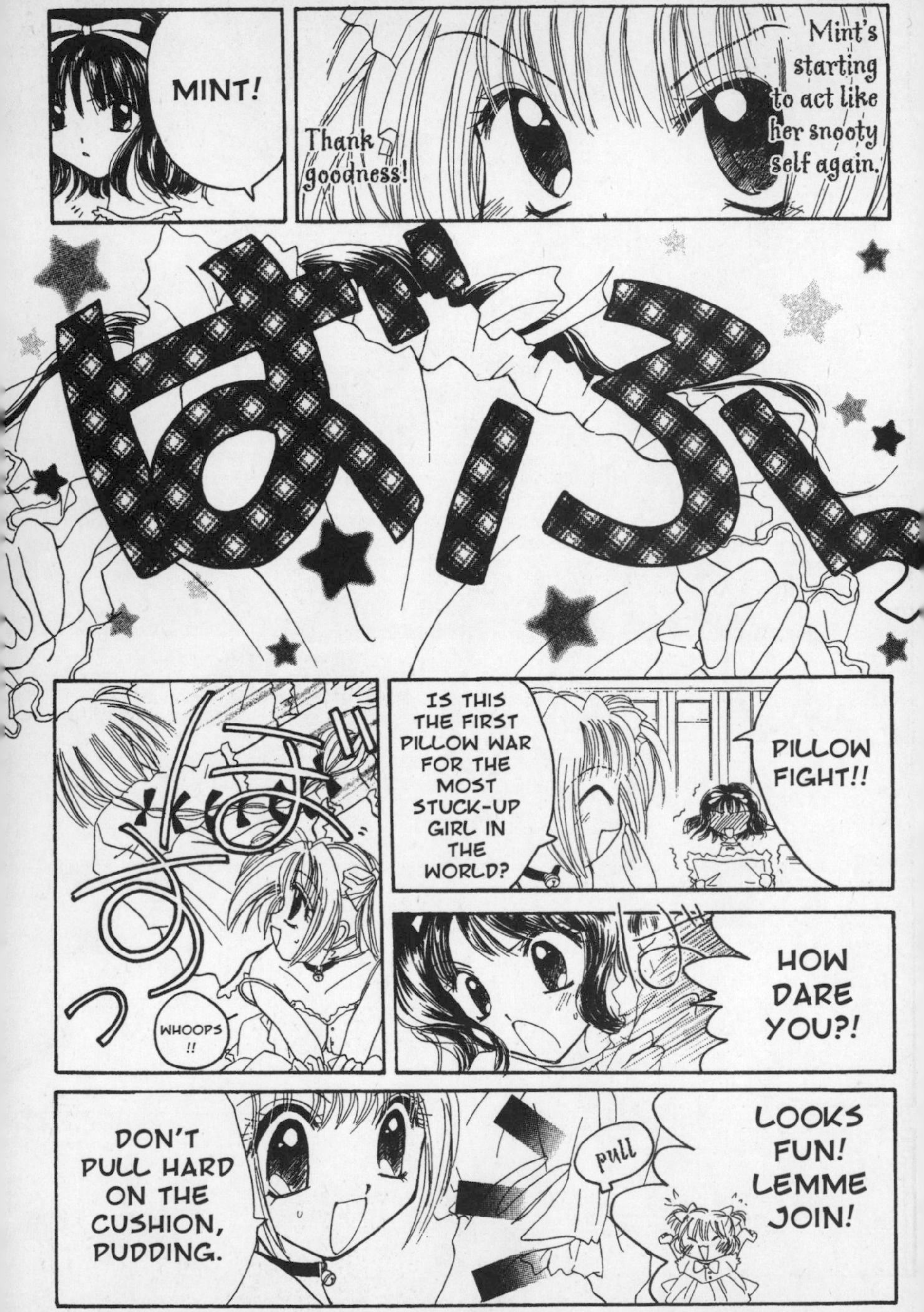

Mint's starting to act like her snooty self again.
Thank goodness!
MINT!
PILLOW FIGHT!!
IS THIS THE FIRST PILLOW WAR FOR THE MOST STUCK-UP GIRL IN THE WORLD?
HOW DARE YOU?!
WHOOPS !!
LOOKS FUN! LEMME JOIN!
pull
DON'T PULL HARD ON THE CUSHION, PUDDING.

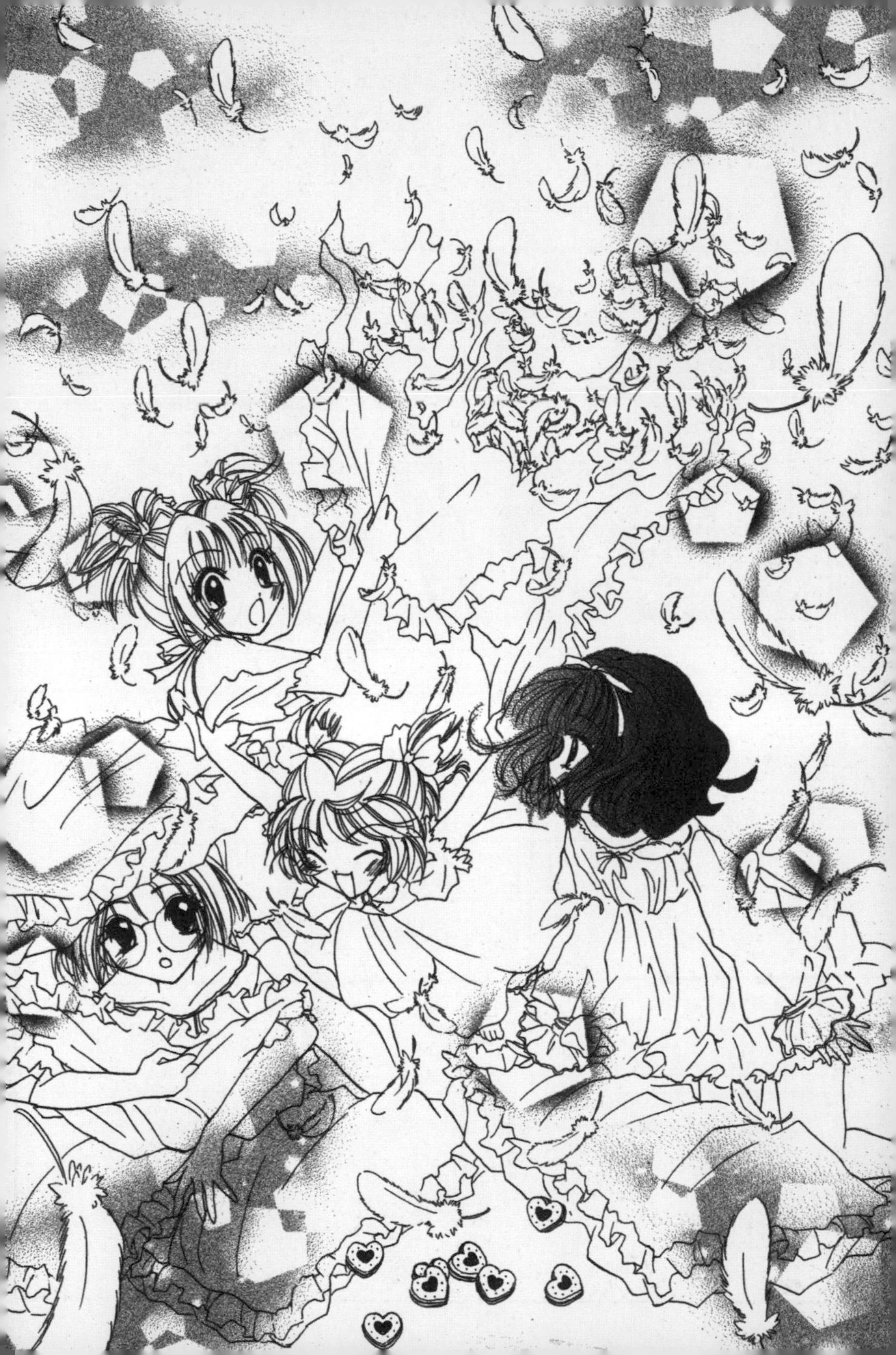

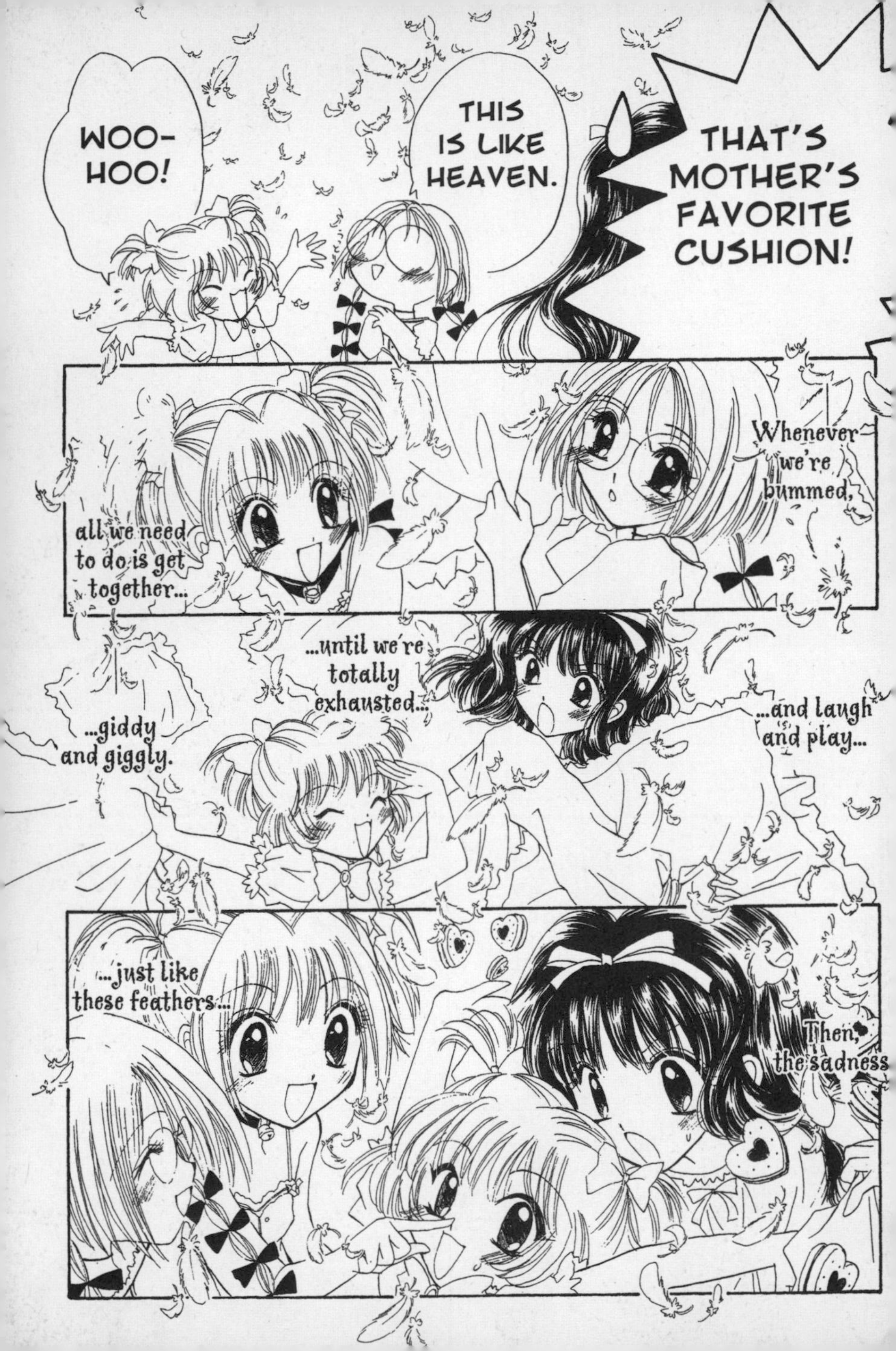
THAT'S MOTHER'S FAVORITE CUSHION!
THIS IS LIKE HEAVEN.
WOO-HOO!
Whenever we're bummed,
all we need to do is get together...
...and laugh and play...
...until we're totally exhausted...
...giddy and giggly.
Then, the sadness
...just like these feathers...

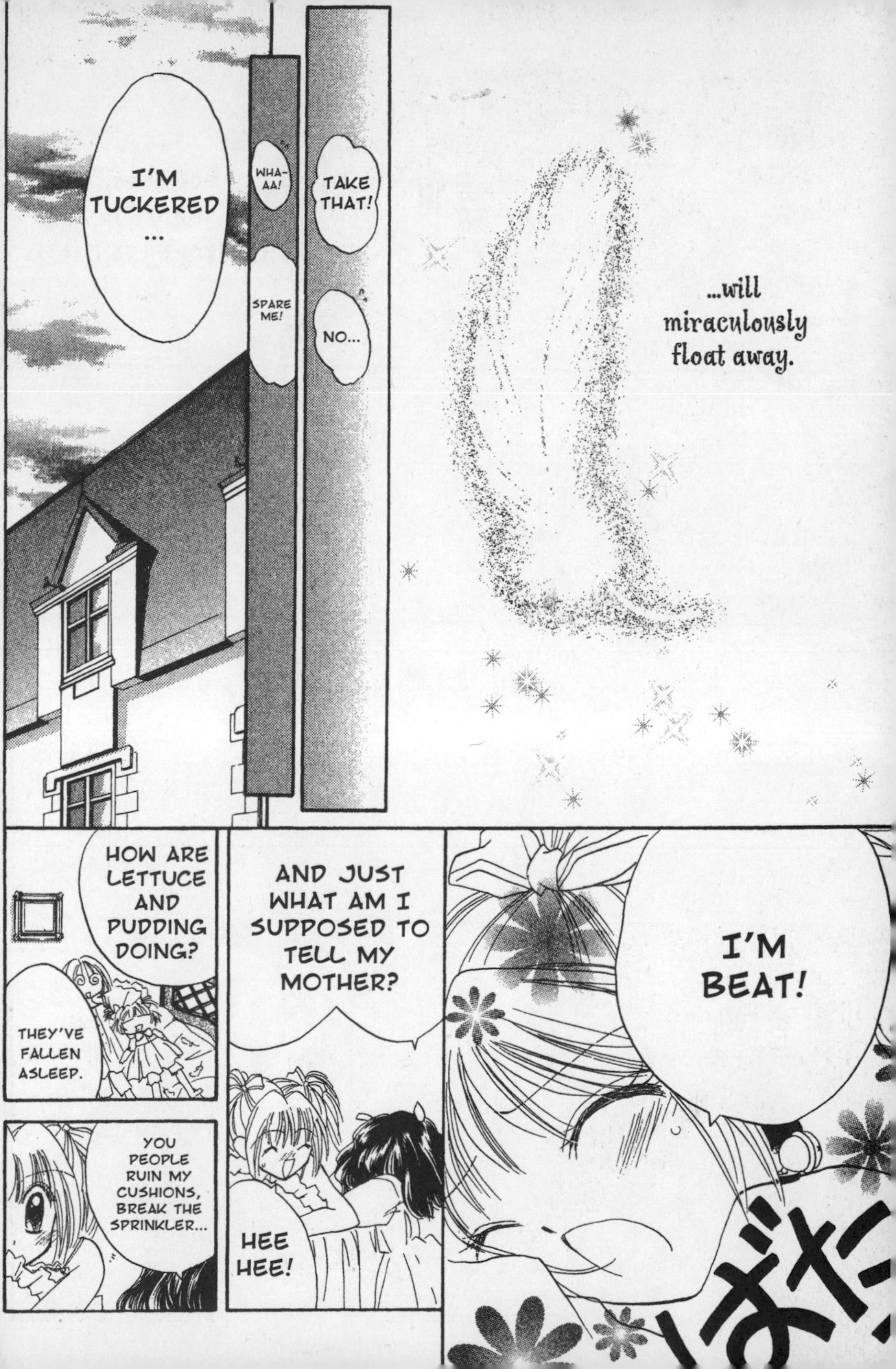
...will miraculously float away.
TAKE THAT!
NO...
WHA-AA!
SPARE ME!
I'M TUCKERED ...
I'M BEAT!
AND JUST WHAT AM I SUPPOSED TO TELL MY MOTHER?
HEE HEE!
HOW ARE LETTUCE AND PUDDING DOING?
THEY'VE FALLEN ASLEEP.
YOU PEOPLE RUIN MY CUSHIONS, BREAK THE SPRINKLER...

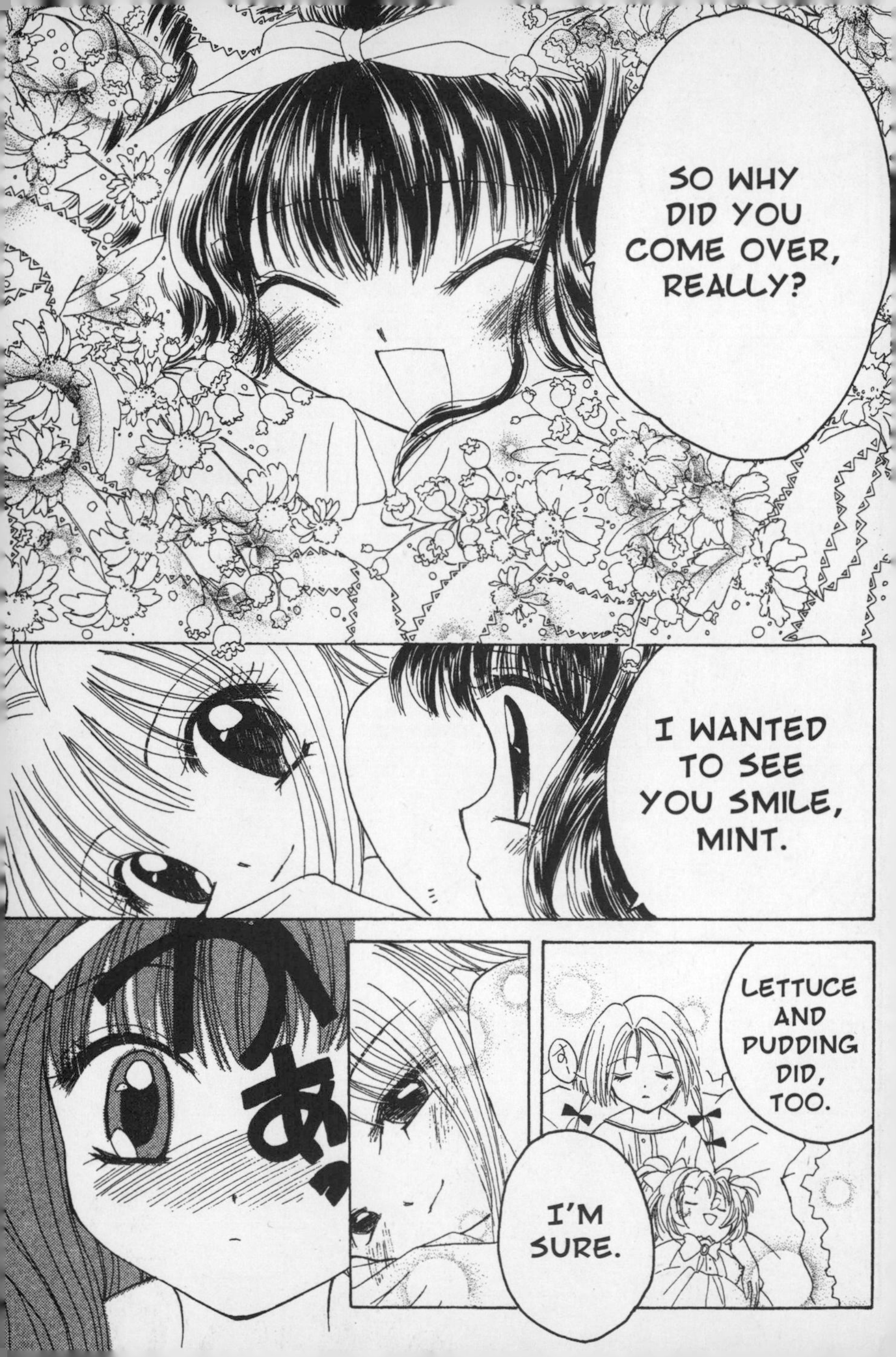
SO WHY DID YOU COME OVER, REALLY?
I WANTED TO SEE YOU SMILE, MINT.
LETTUCE AND PUDDING DID, TOO.
I'M SURE.

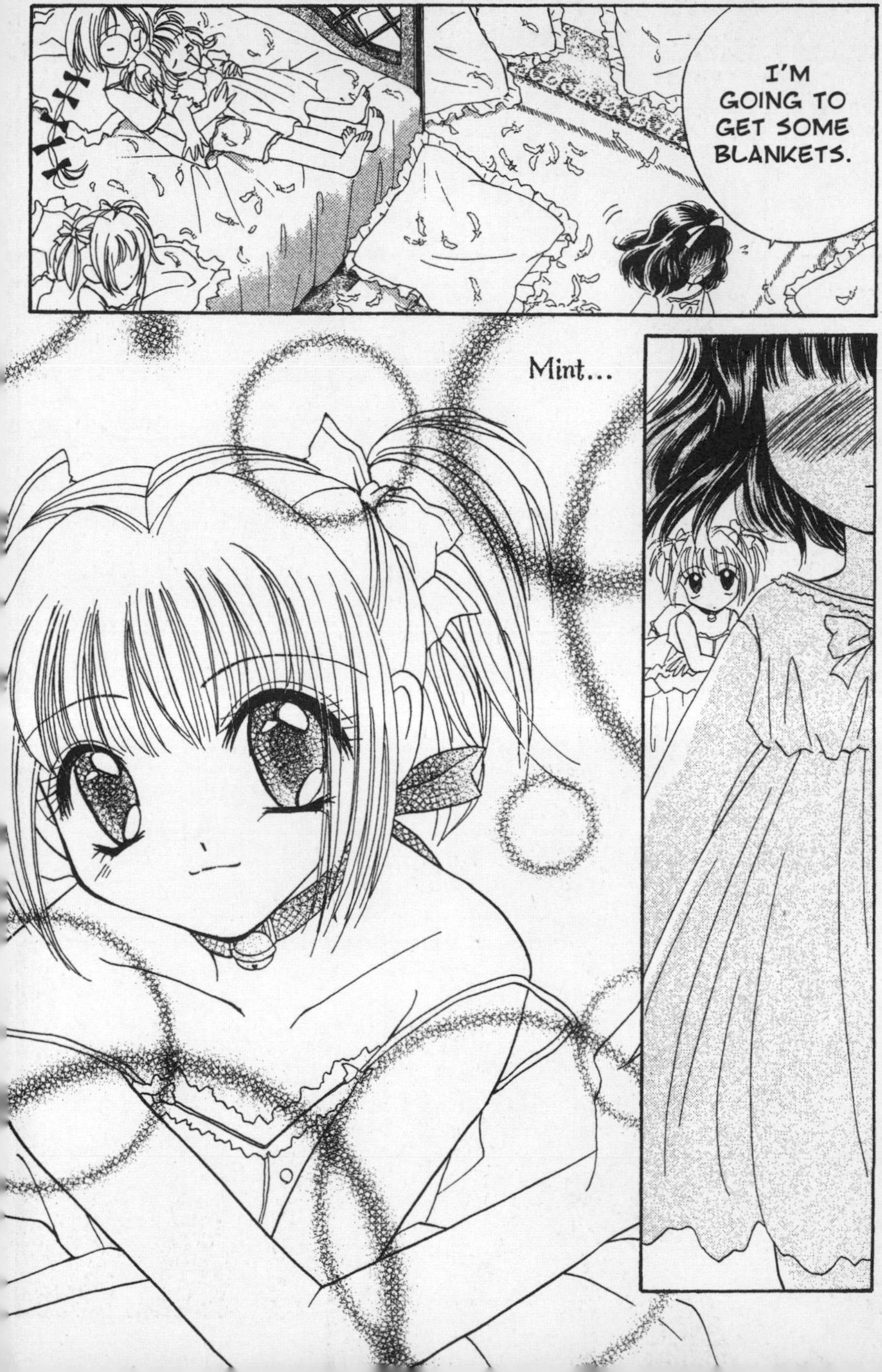
I'M GOING TO GET SOME BLANKETS.
Mint...

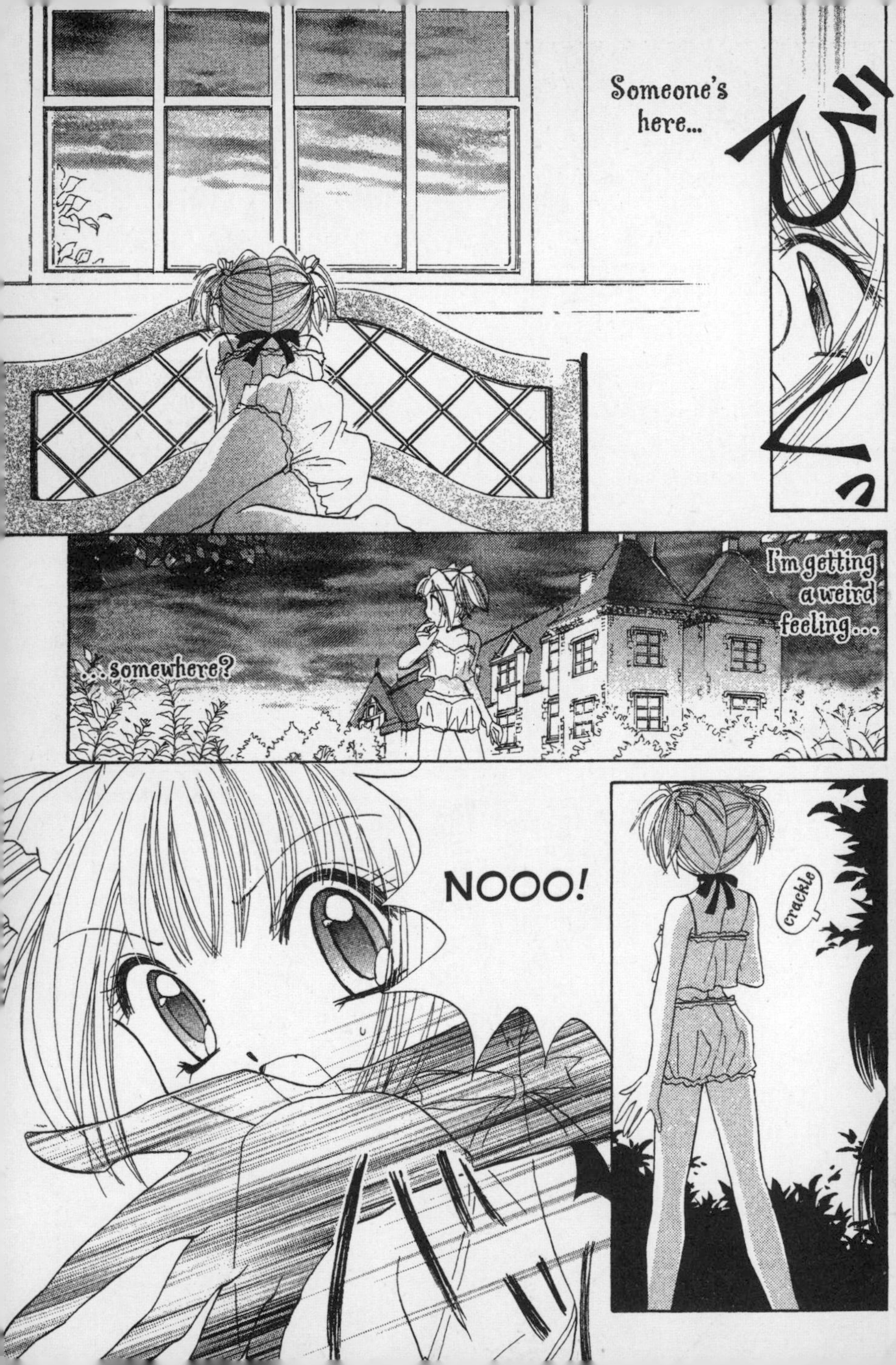
びくっ
Someone's here...
I'm getting a weird feeling...
...somewhere?
crackle
NOOO!

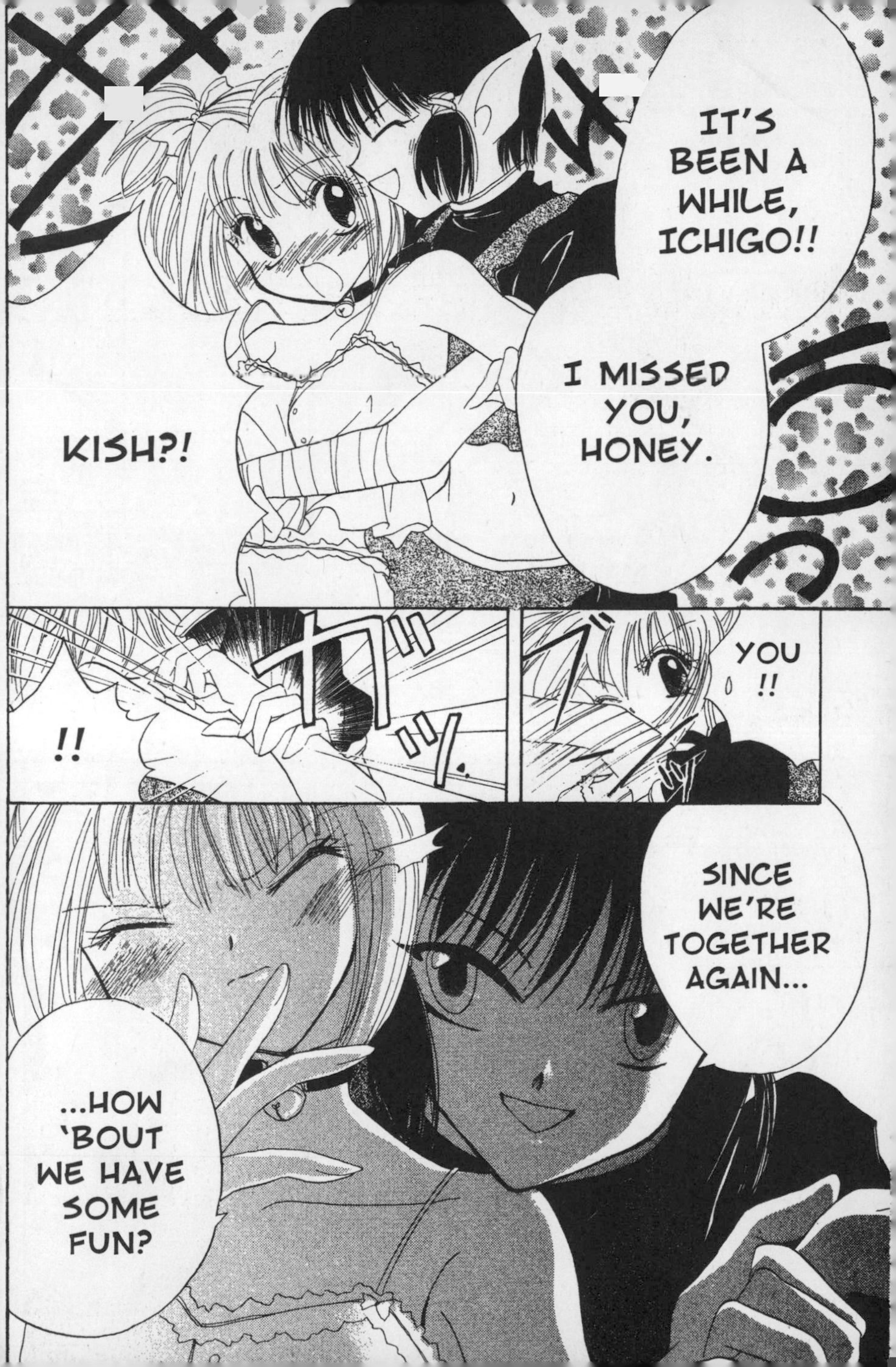
IT'S BEEN A WHILE, ICHIGO!!
I MISSED YOU, HONEY.
KISH?!
YOU !!
!!
SINCE WE'RE TOGETHER AGAIN...
...HOW 'BOUT WE HAVE SOME FUN?

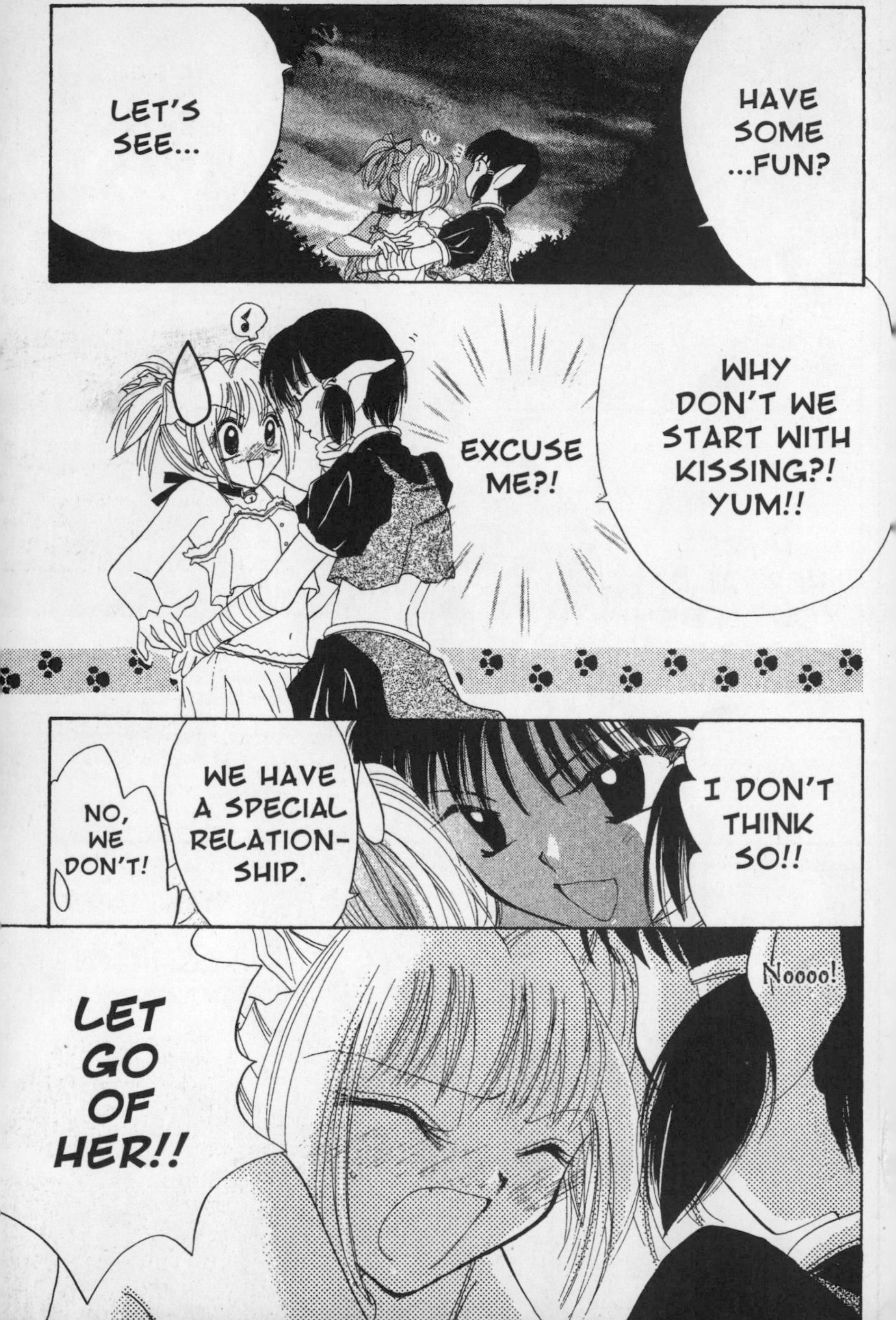
HAVE SOME ...FUN?
LET'S SEE...
WHY DON'T WE START WITH KISSING?! YUM!!
EXCUSE ME?!
I DON'T THINK SO!!
WE HAVE A SPECIAL RELATION-SHIP.
NO, WE DON'T!
Noooo!
LET GO OF HER!!

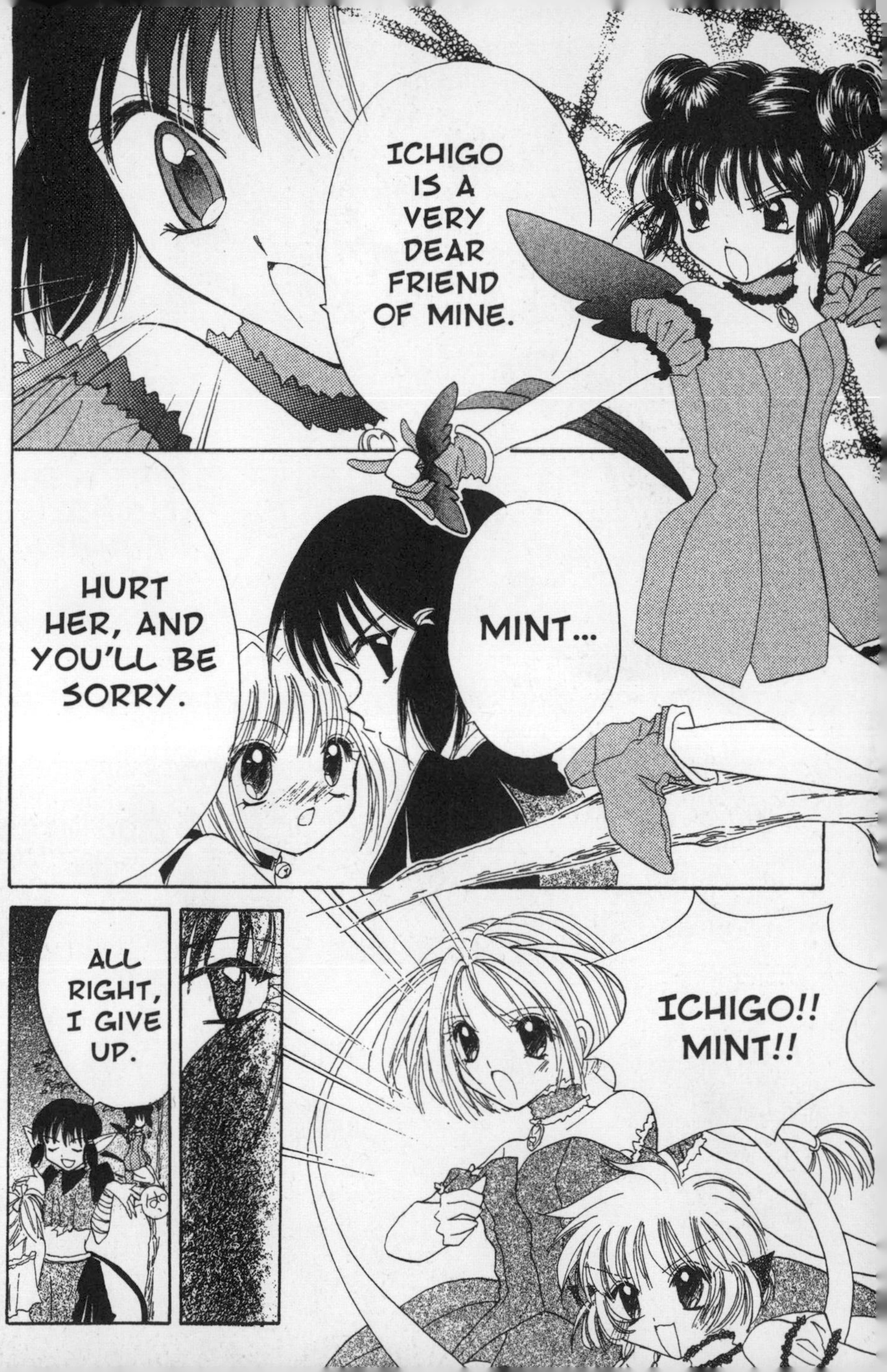

ICHIGO IS A VERY DEAR FRIEND OF MINE.
HURT HER, AND YOU'LL BE SORRY.
MINT...
ICHIGO!! MINT!!
ALL RIGHT, I GIVE UP.

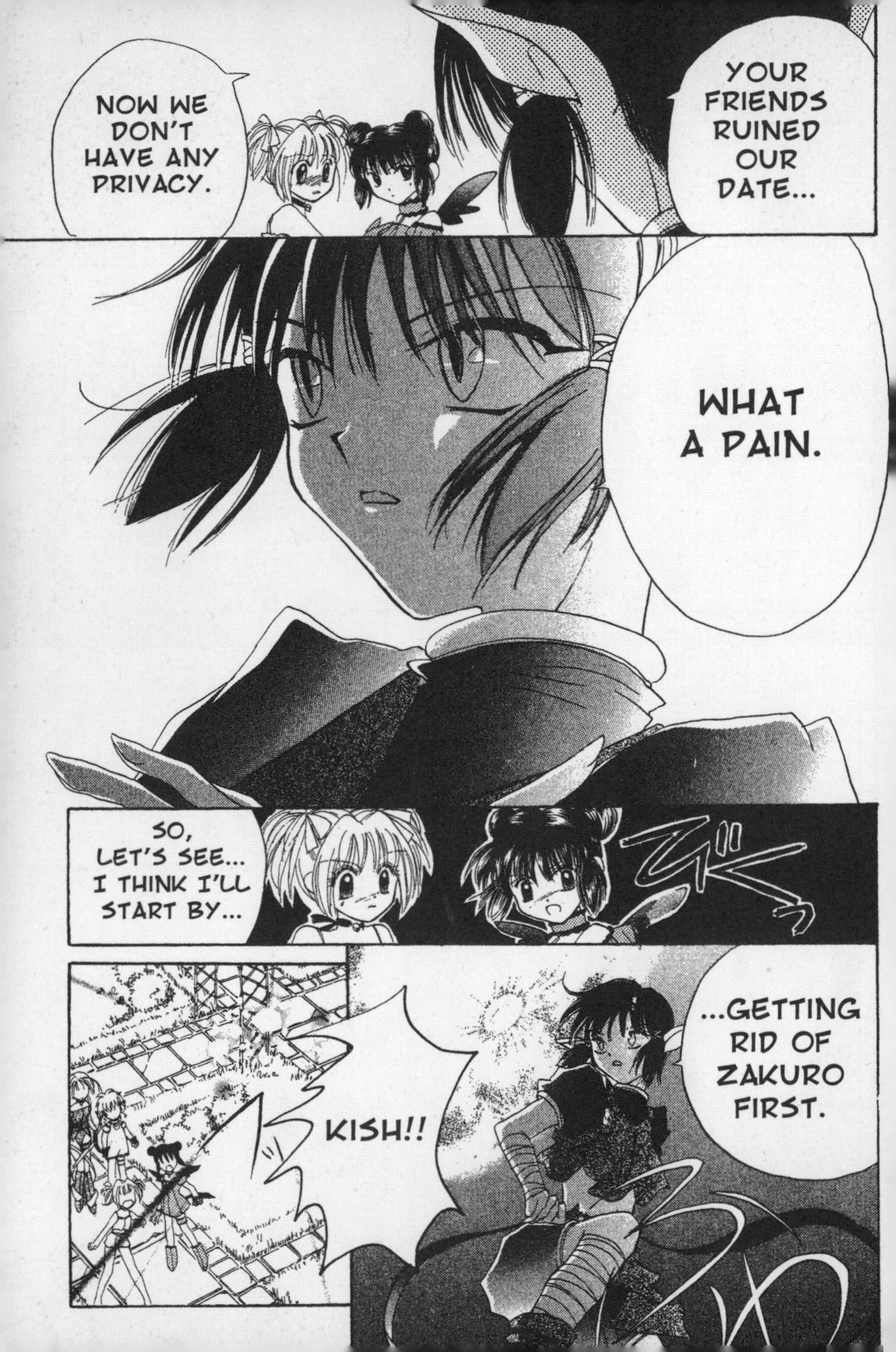
YOUR FRIENDS RUINED OUR DATE...
NOW WE DON'T HAVE ANY PRIVACY.
WHAT A PAIN.
SO, LET'S SEE... I THINK I'LL START BY...
...GETTING RID OF ZAKURO FIRST.
KISH!!

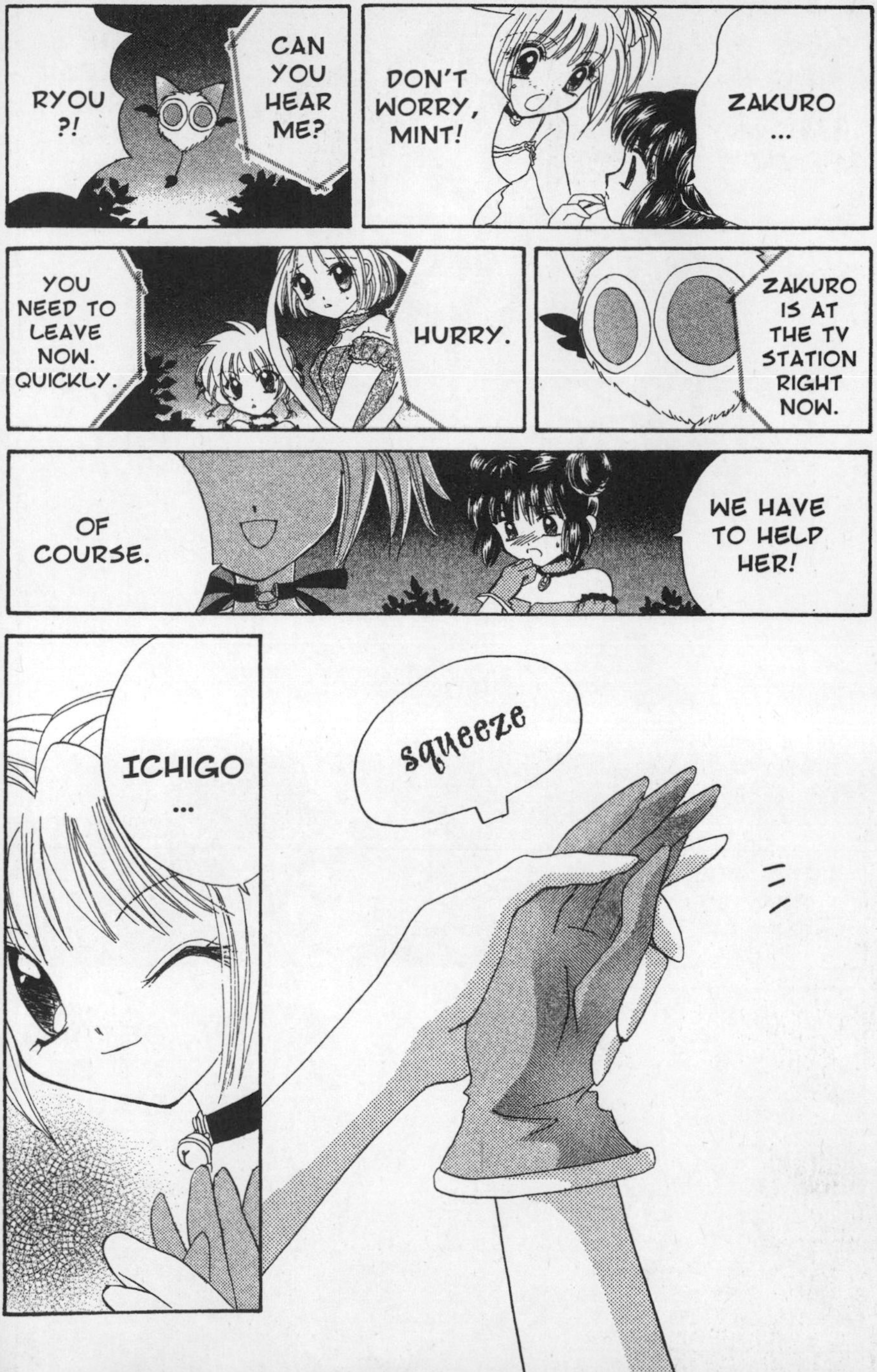
ZAKURO ...
DON'T WORRY, MINT!
CAN YOU HEAR ME?
RYOU ?!
ZAKURO IS AT THE TV STATION RIGHT NOW.
HURRY.
YOU NEED TO LEAVE NOW. QUICKLY.
WE HAVE TO HELP HER!
OF COURSE.
squeeze
ICHIGO ...

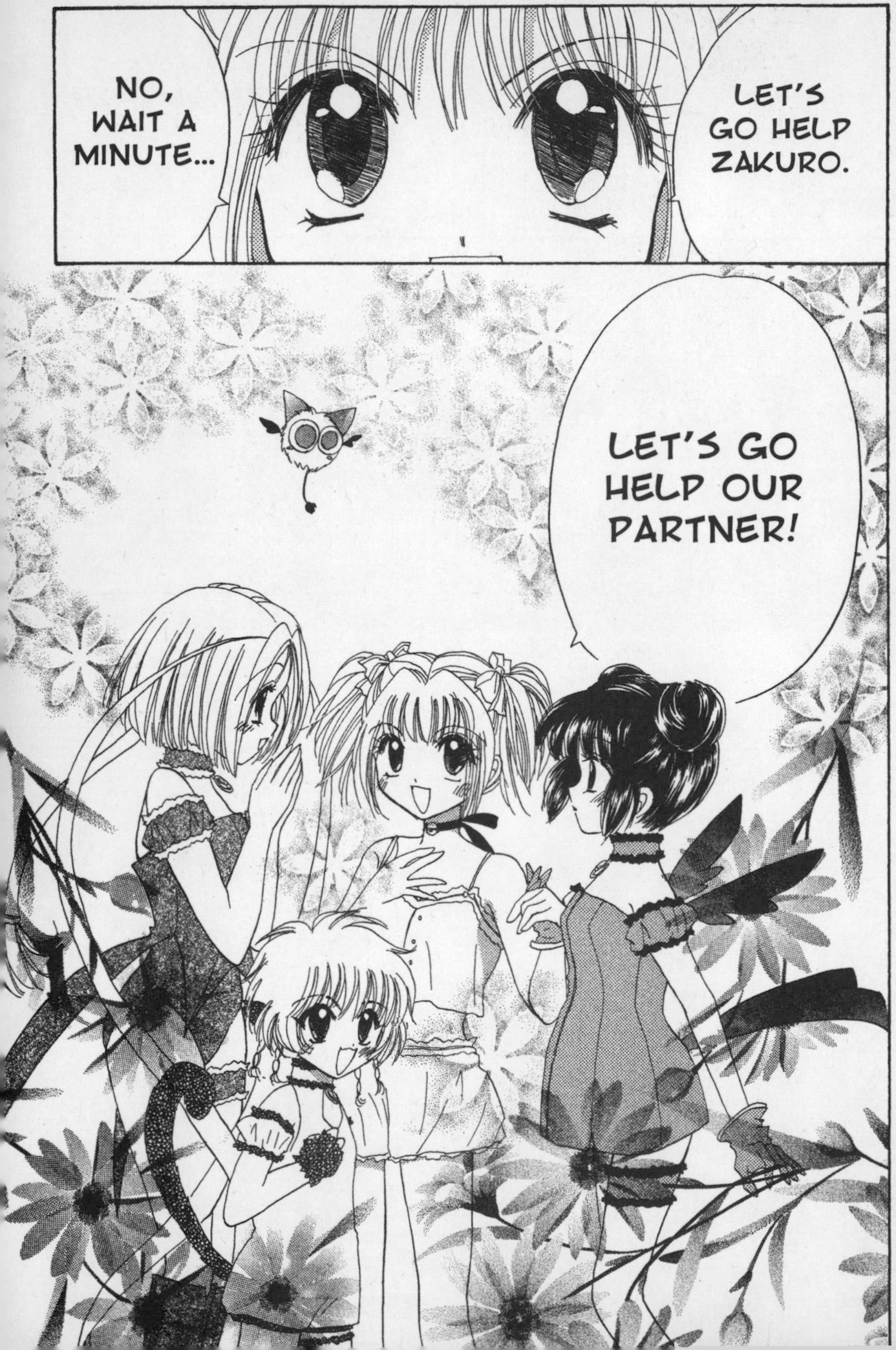
LET'S GO HELP ZAKURO.
NO, WAIT A MINUTE...
LET'S GO HELP OUR PARTNER!

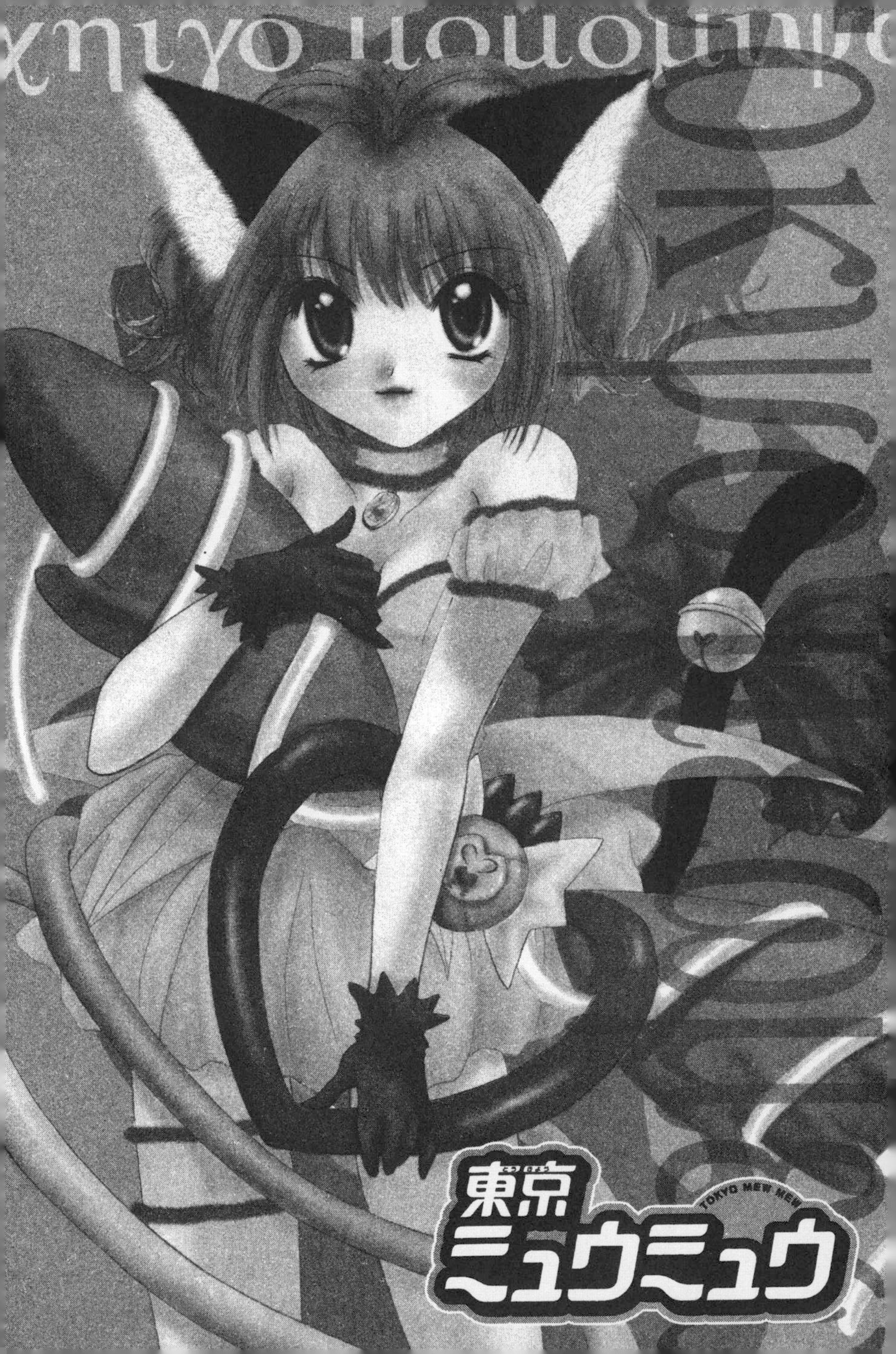
東京ミュウミュウ
TOKYO MEW MEW

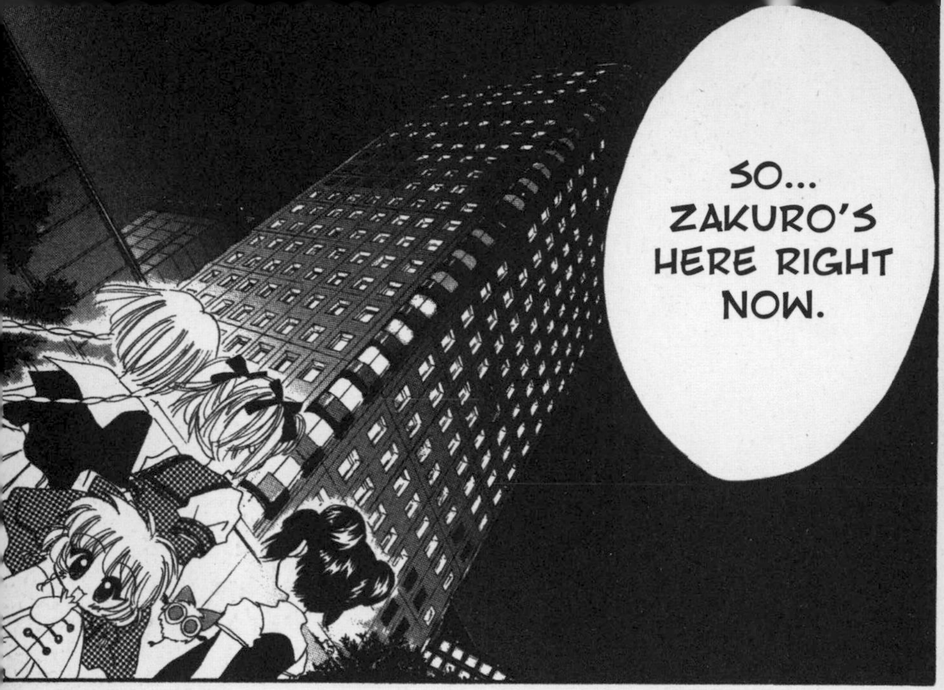
SO... ZAKURO'S HERE RIGHT NOW.

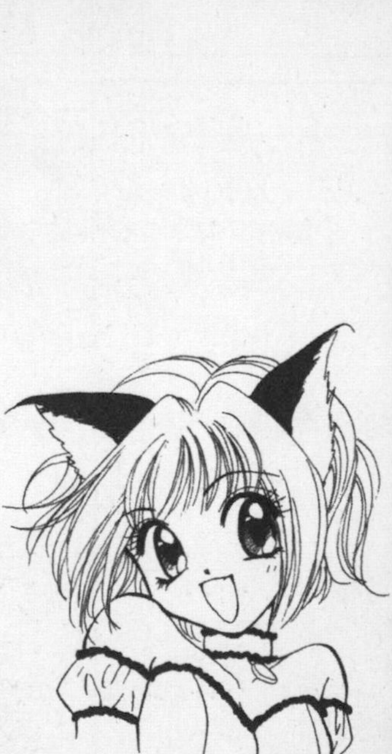

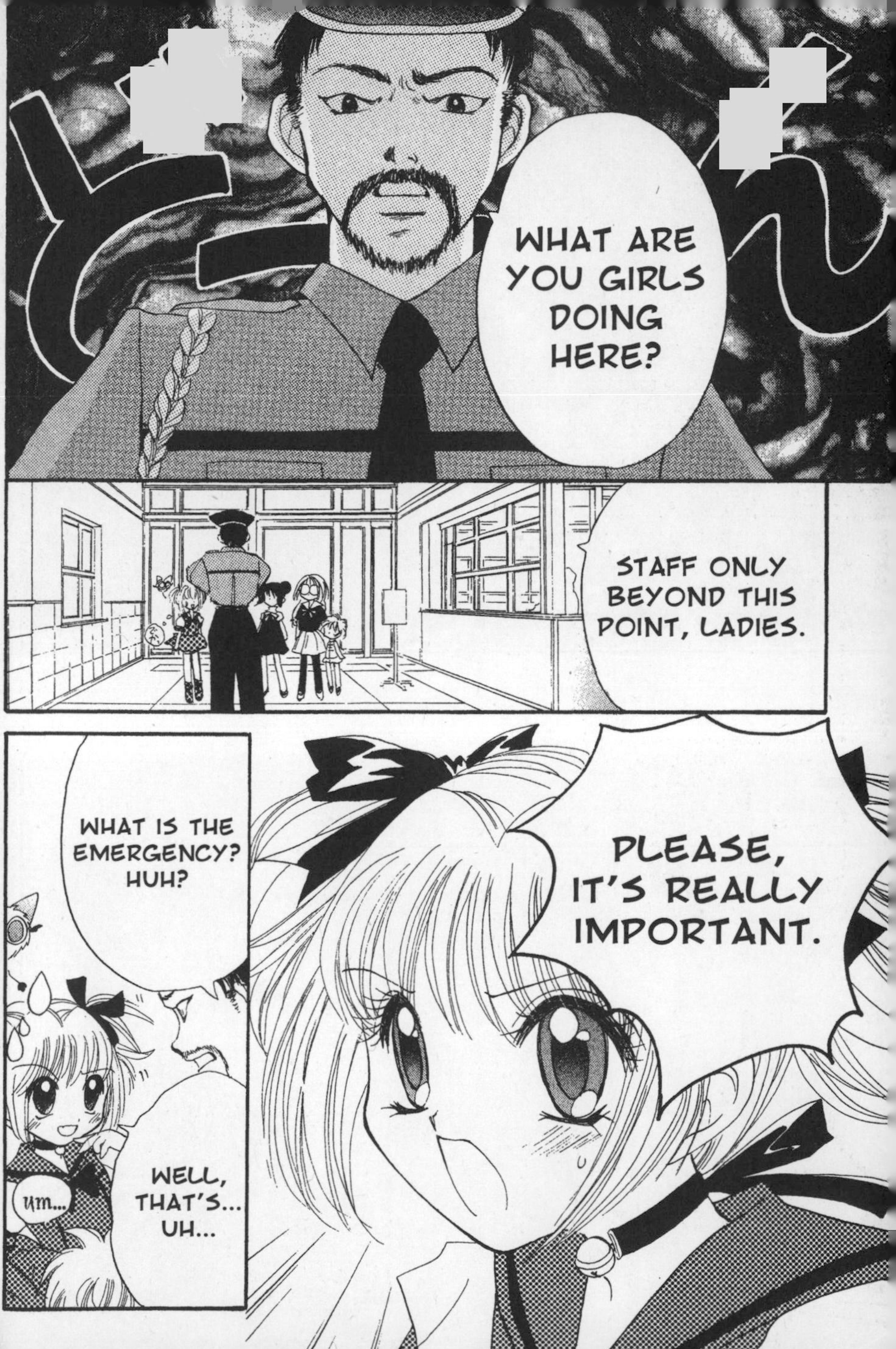
WHAT ARE YOU GIRLS DOING HERE?
STAFF ONLY BEYOND THIS POINT, LADIES.
PLEASE, IT'S REALLY IMPORTANT.
WHAT IS THE EMERGENCY? HUH?
WELL, THAT'S... UH...
um...

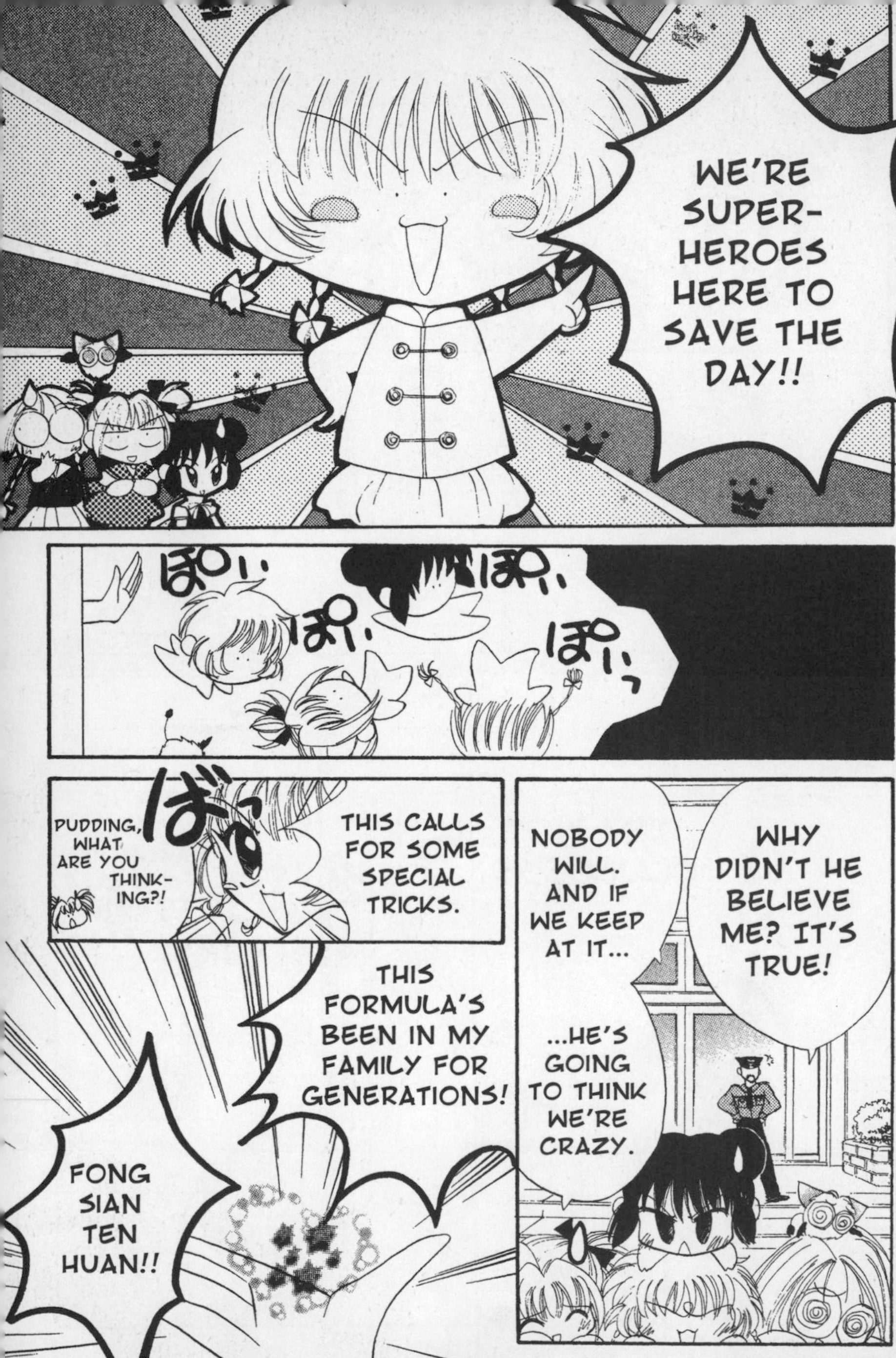
WE'RE SUPER-HEROES HERE TO SAVE THE DAY!!
ぽいっ
ぽい
ぽい
ぽい
WHY DIDN'T HE BELIEVE ME? IT'S TRUE!
NOBODY WILL. AND IF WE KEEP AT IT...
...HE'S GOING TO THINK WE'RE CRAZY.
ばっ
THIS CALLS FOR SOME SPECIAL TRICKS.
PUDDING, WHAT ARE YOU THINKING?!
THIS FORMULA'S BEEN IN MY FAMILY FOR GENERATIONS!
FONG SIAN TEN HUAN!!

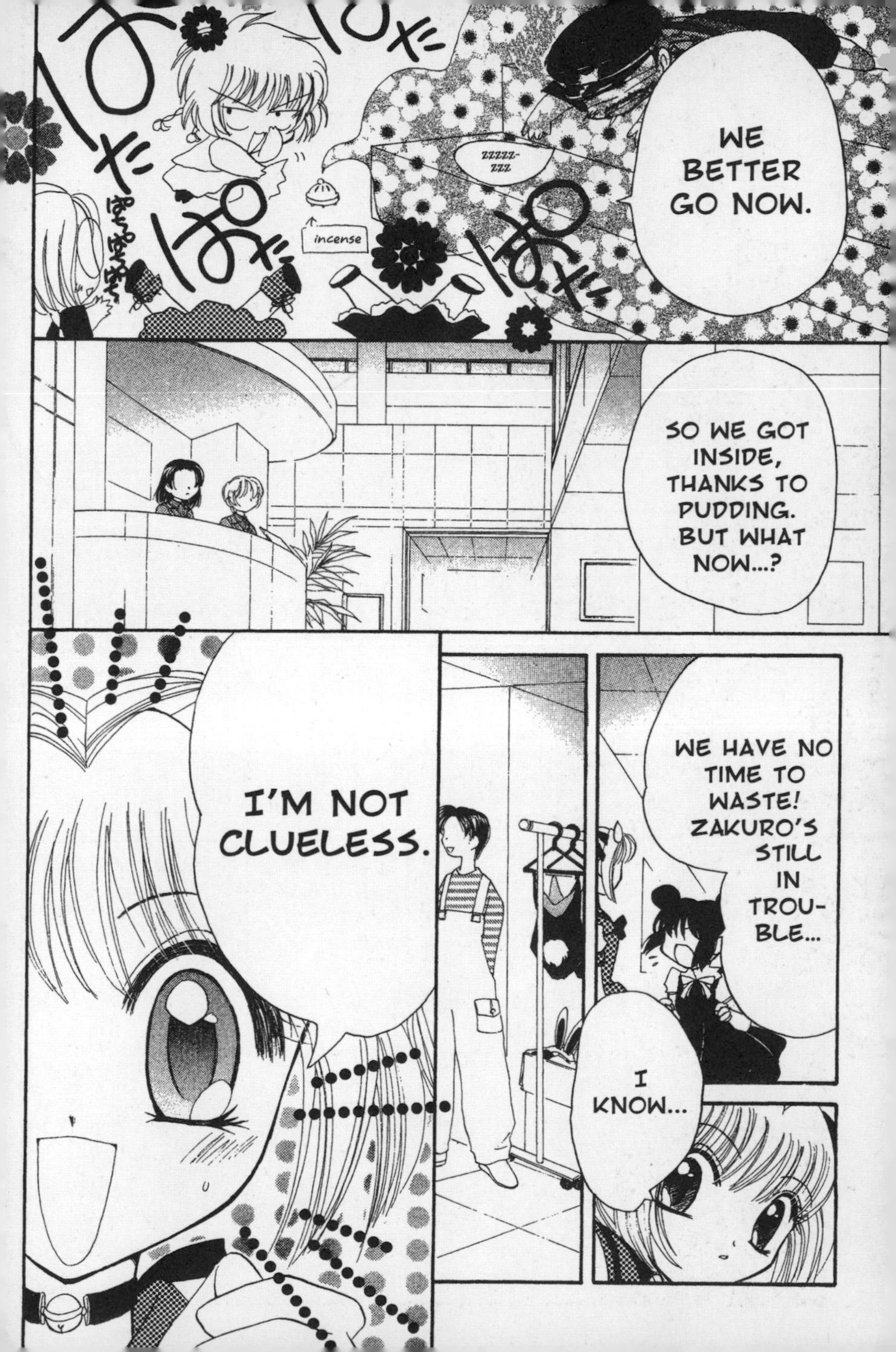
WE BETTER GO NOW.
zzzzz-zzz
incense
SO WE GOT INSIDE, THANKS TO PUDDING. BUT WHAT NOW...?
WE HAVE NO TIME TO WASTE! ZAKURO'S STILL IN TROU-BLE...
I KNOW...
I'M NOT CLUELESS.

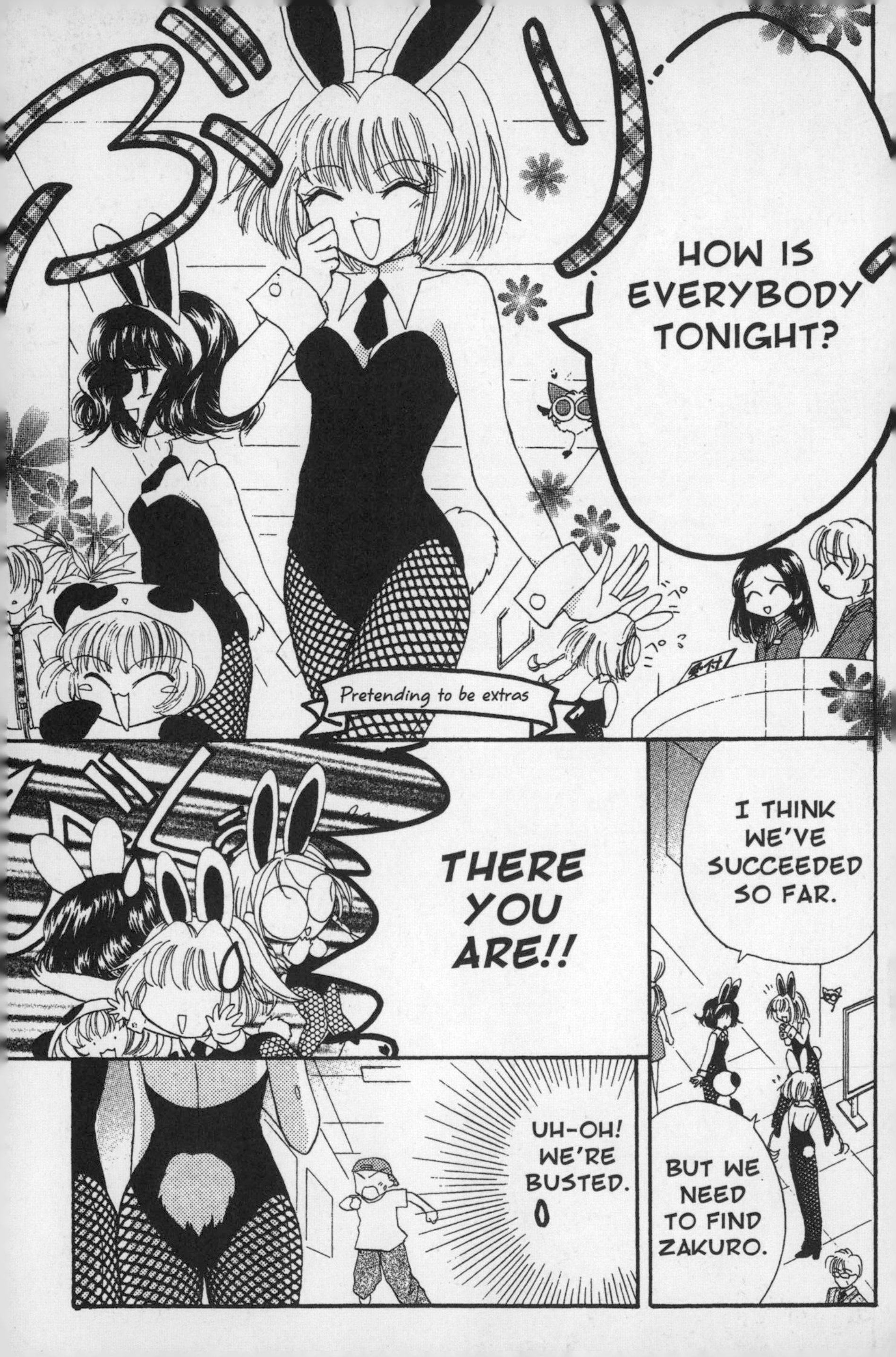
HOW IS EVERYBODY TONIGHT?
Pretending to be extras
I THINK WE'VE SUCCEEDED SO FAR.
BUT WE NEED TO FIND ZAKURO.
THERE YOU ARE!!
UH-OH! WE'RE BUSTED.

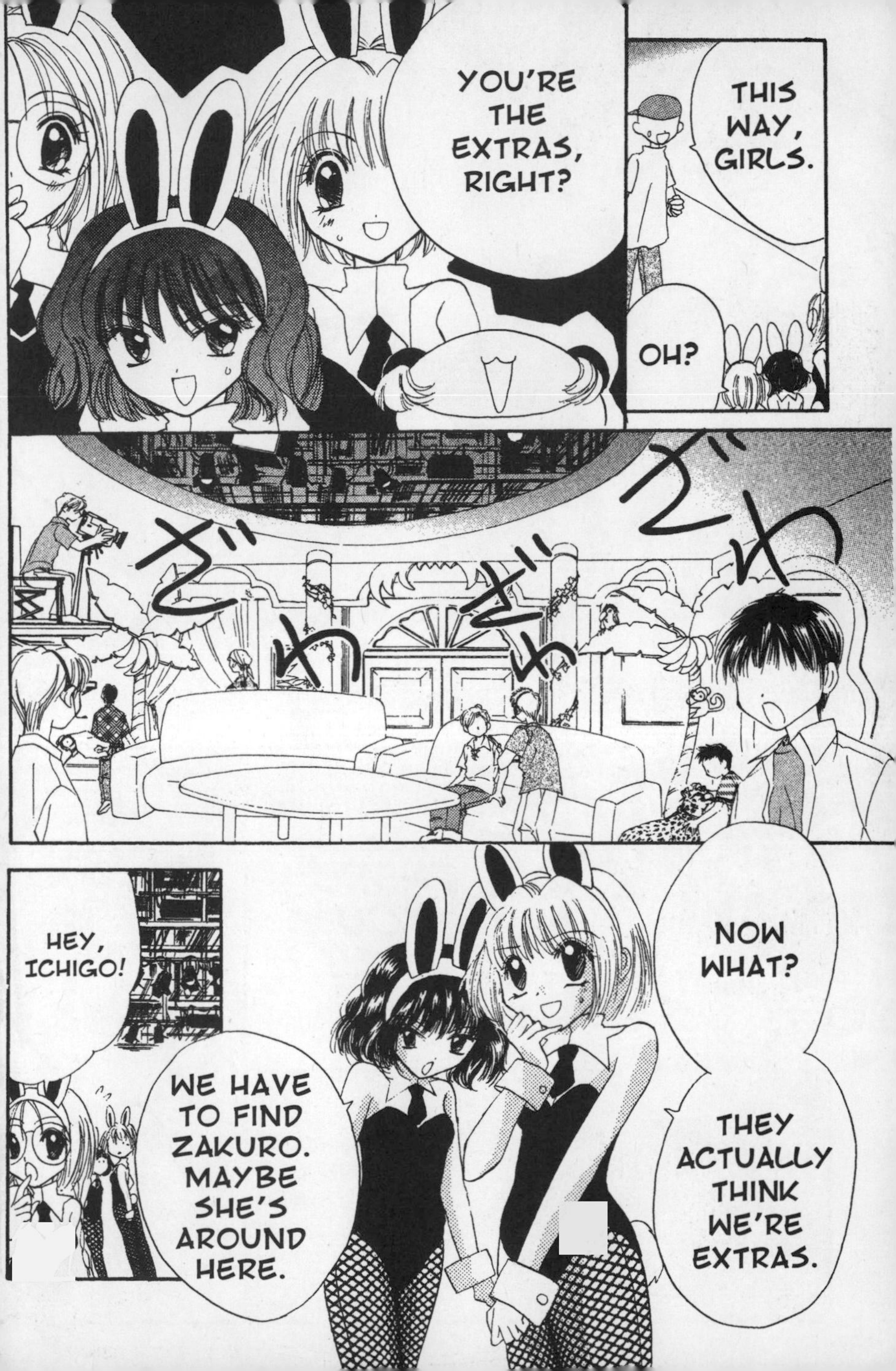
THIS WAY, GIRLS.
OH?
YOU'RE THE EXTRAS, RIGHT?
ざわ
ざわ
ざわ
NOW WHAT?
THEY ACTUALLY THINK WE'RE EXTRAS.
WE HAVE TO FIND ZAKURO. MAYBE SHE'S AROUND HERE.
HEY, ICHIGO!

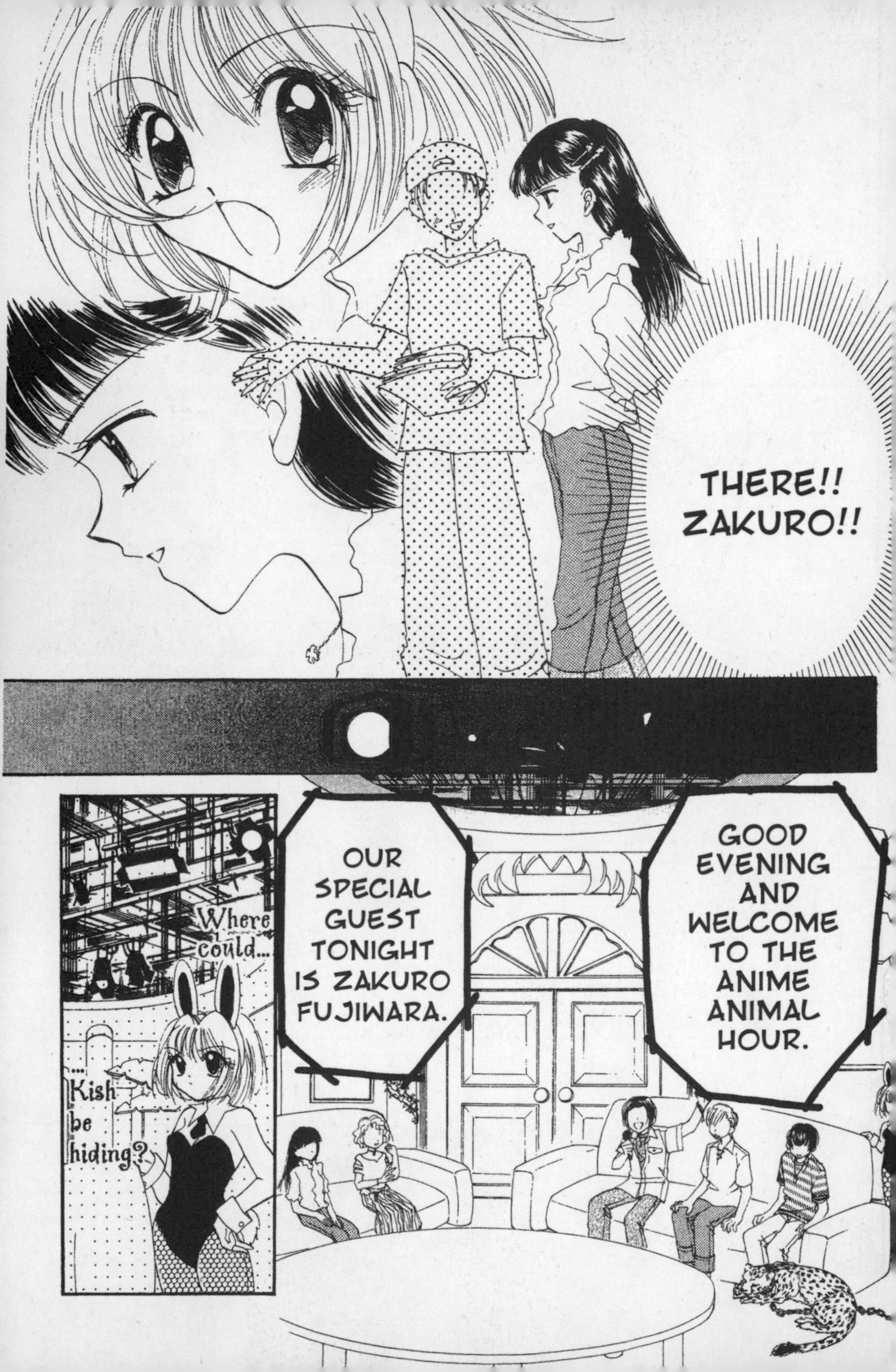
THERE!! ZAKURO!!
GOOD EVENING AND WELCOME TO THE ANIME ANIMAL HOUR.
OUR SPECIAL GUEST TONIGHT IS ZAKURO FUJIWARA.
Where could...
...Kish be hiding?

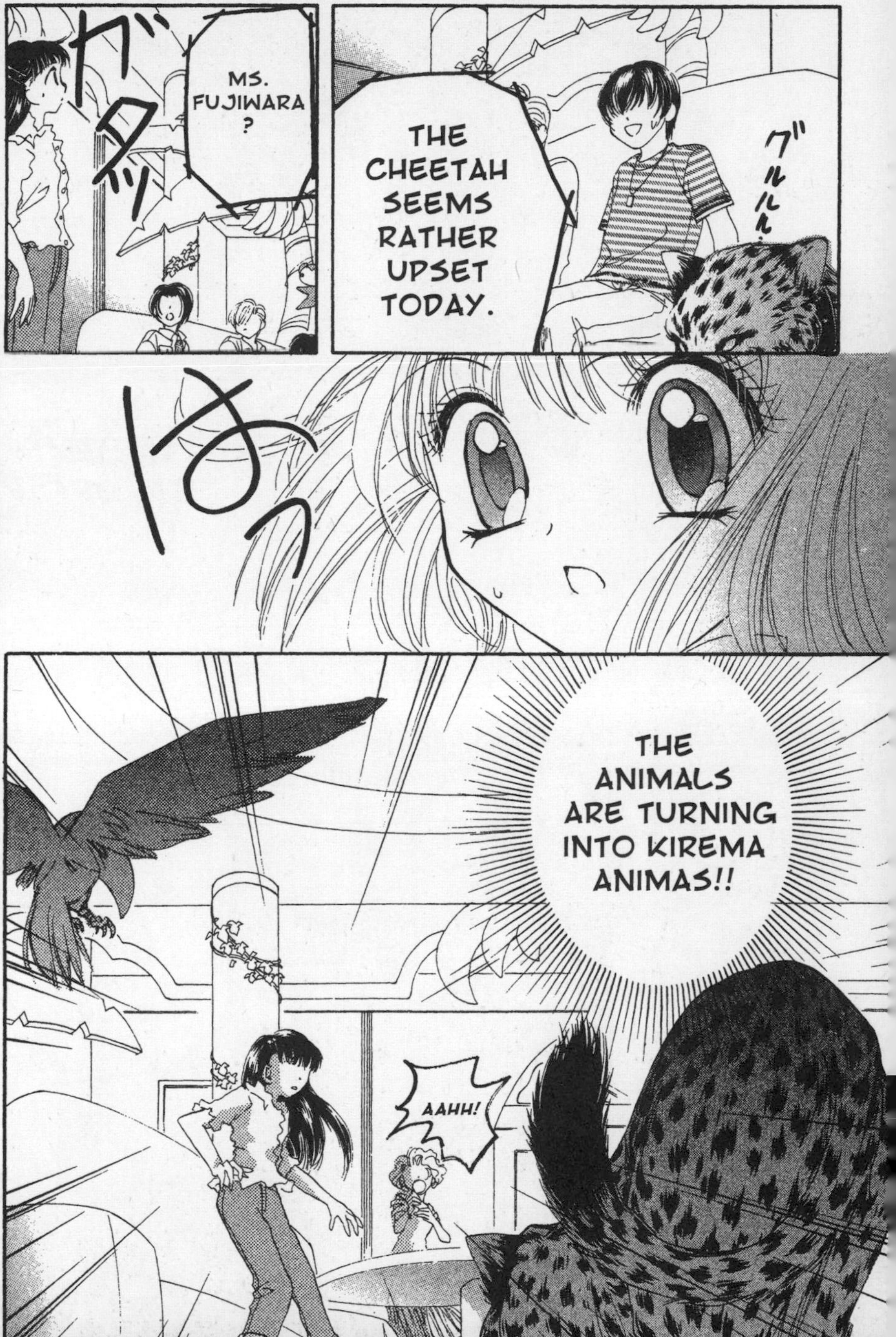
グルルル…
THE CHEETAH SEEMS RATHER UPSET TODAY.
ガタッ
MS. FUJIWARA ?
はっ
THE ANIMALS ARE TURNING INTO KIREMA ANIMAS!!
AAHH!

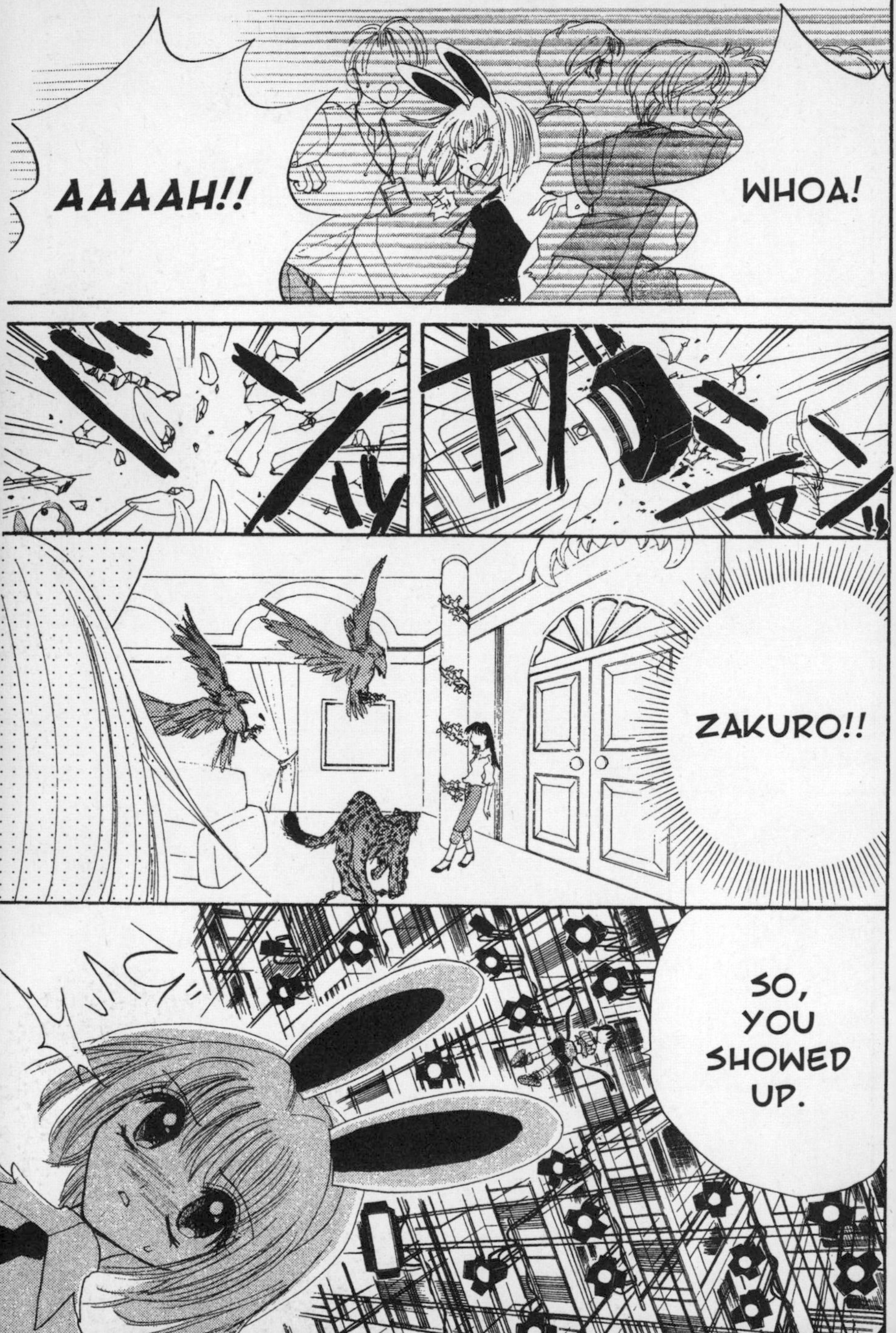
WHOA!
AAAAH!!
ZAKURO!!
SO, YOU SHOWED UP.

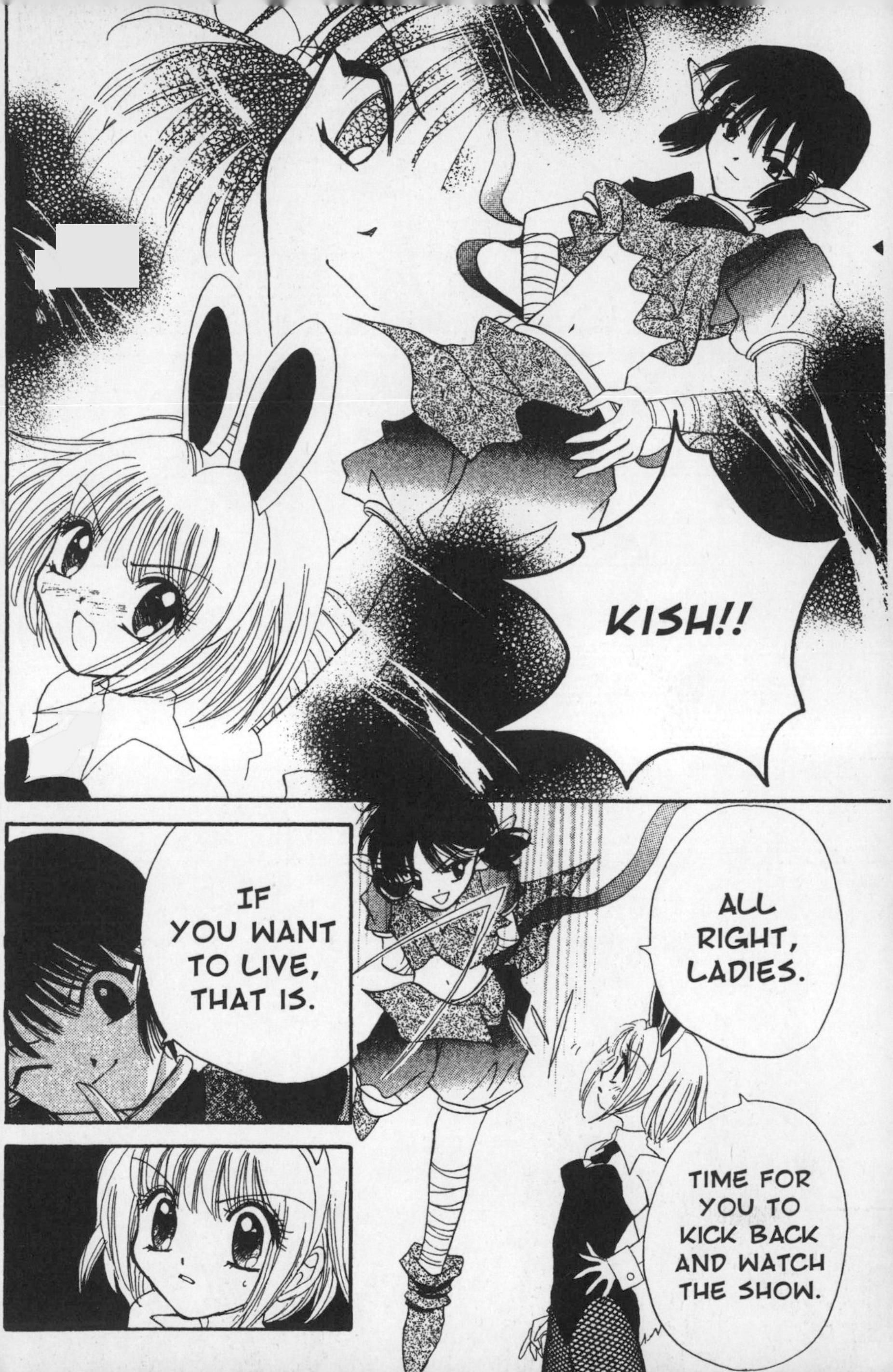
KISH!!
ALL RIGHT, LADIES.
TIME FOR YOU TO KICK BACK AND WATCH THE SHOW.
IF YOU WANT TO LIVE, THAT IS.

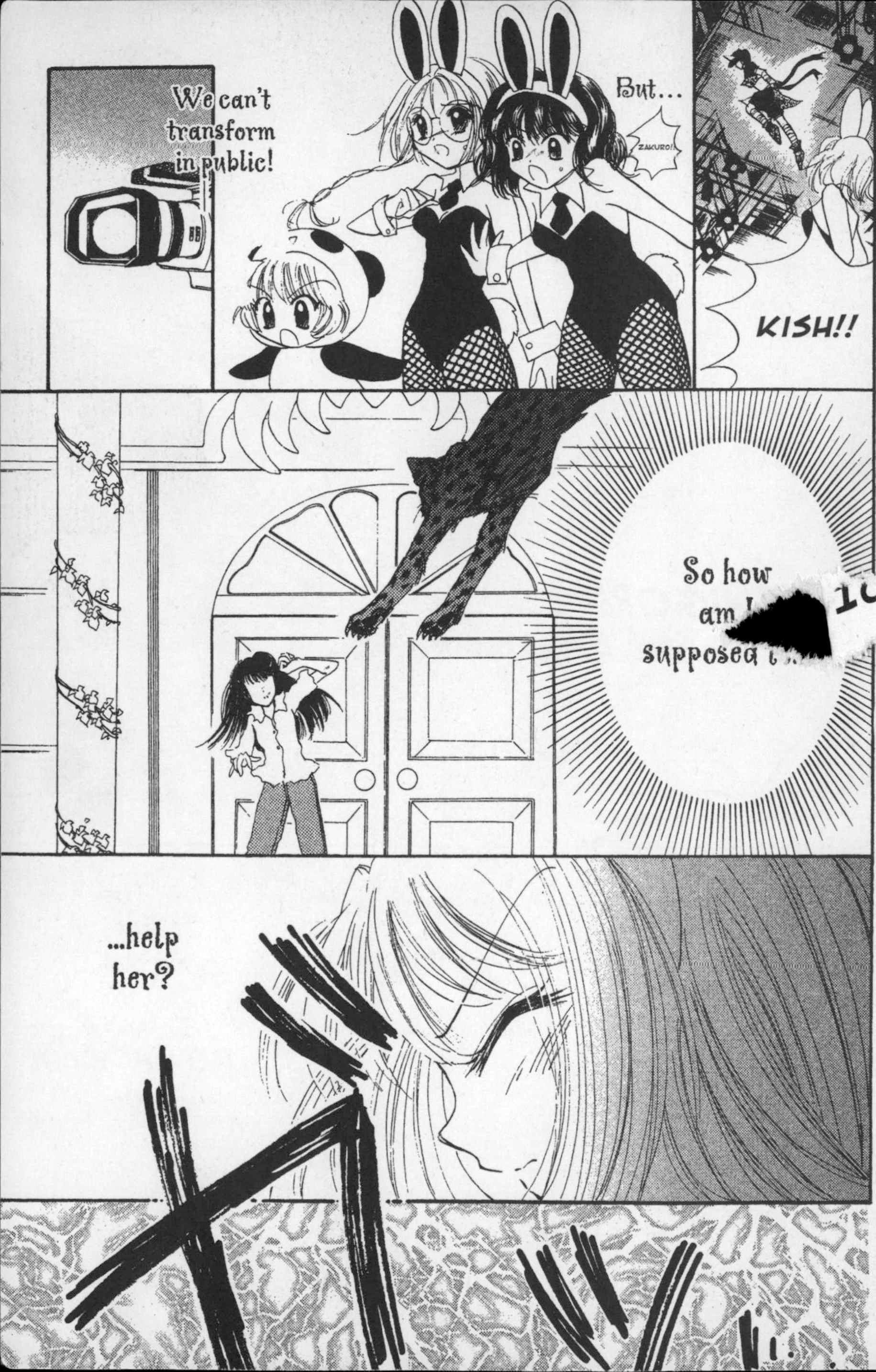
KISH!!
But...
ZAKURO!!
We can't transform in public!
So how am I supposed t
...help her?

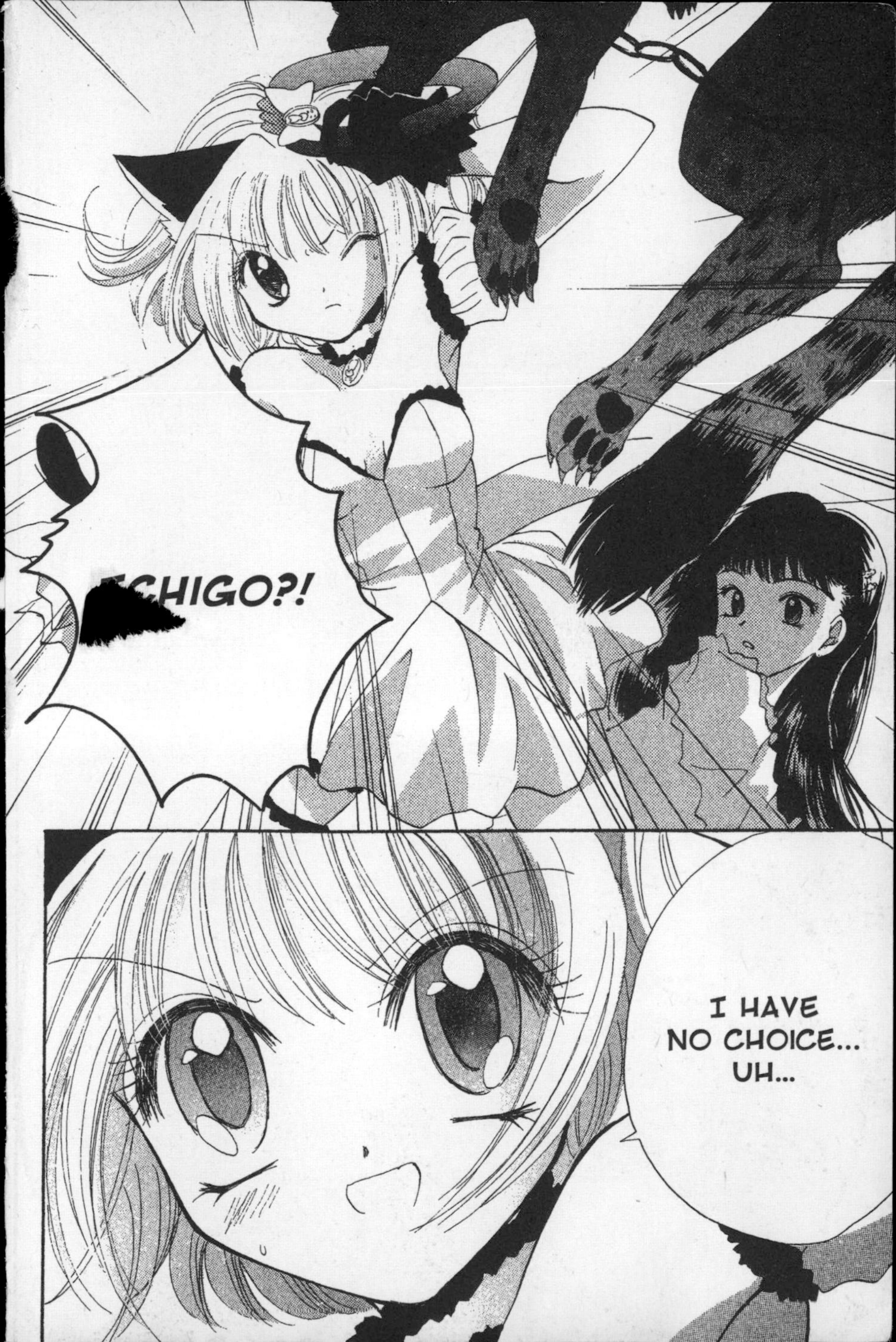
CHIGO?!
I HAVE NO CHOICE... UH...

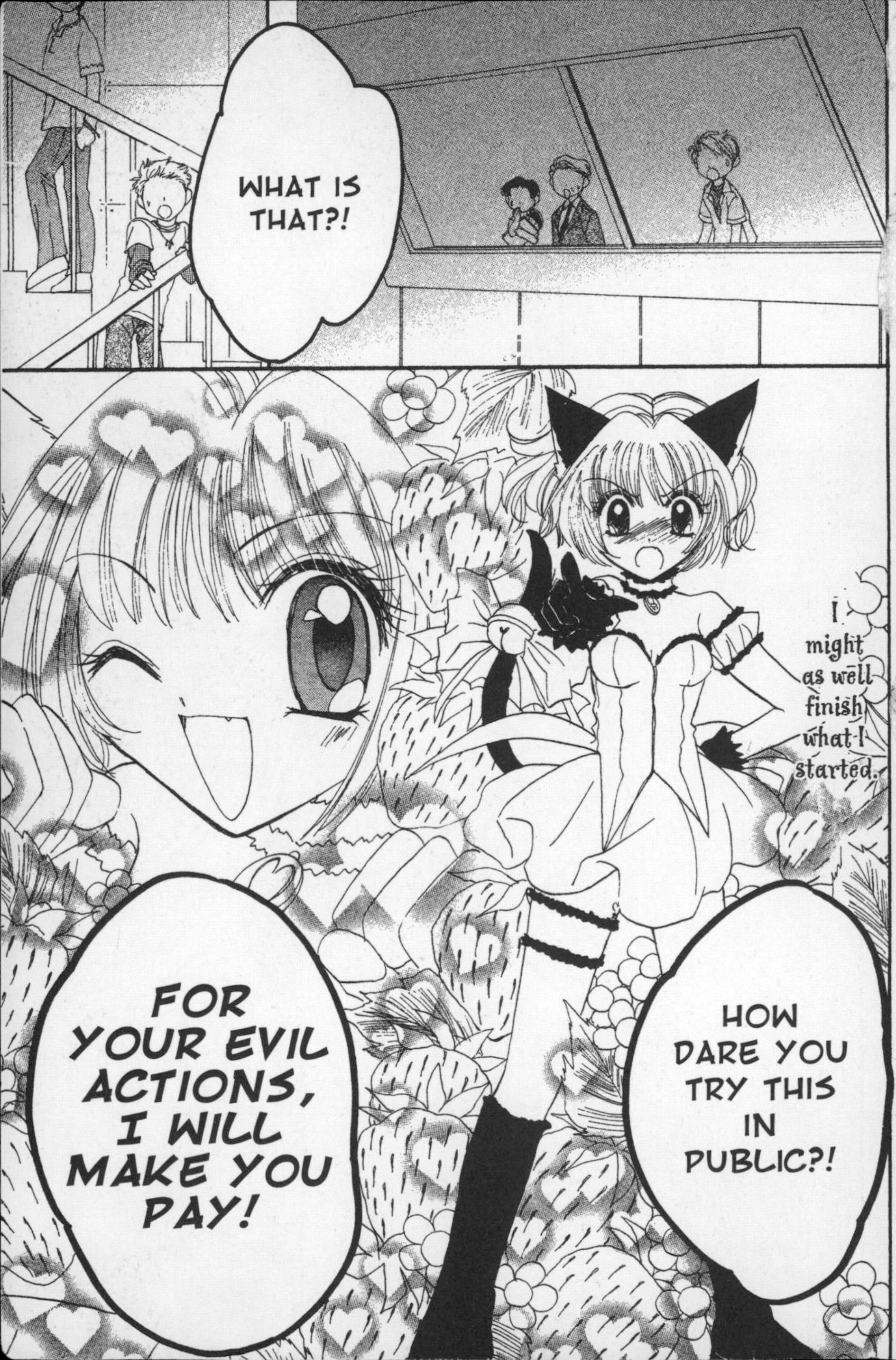
WHAT IS THAT?!
I might as well finish what I started.
HOW DARE YOU TRY THIS IN PUBLIC?!
FOR YOUR EVIL ACTIONS, I WILL MAKE YOU PAY!

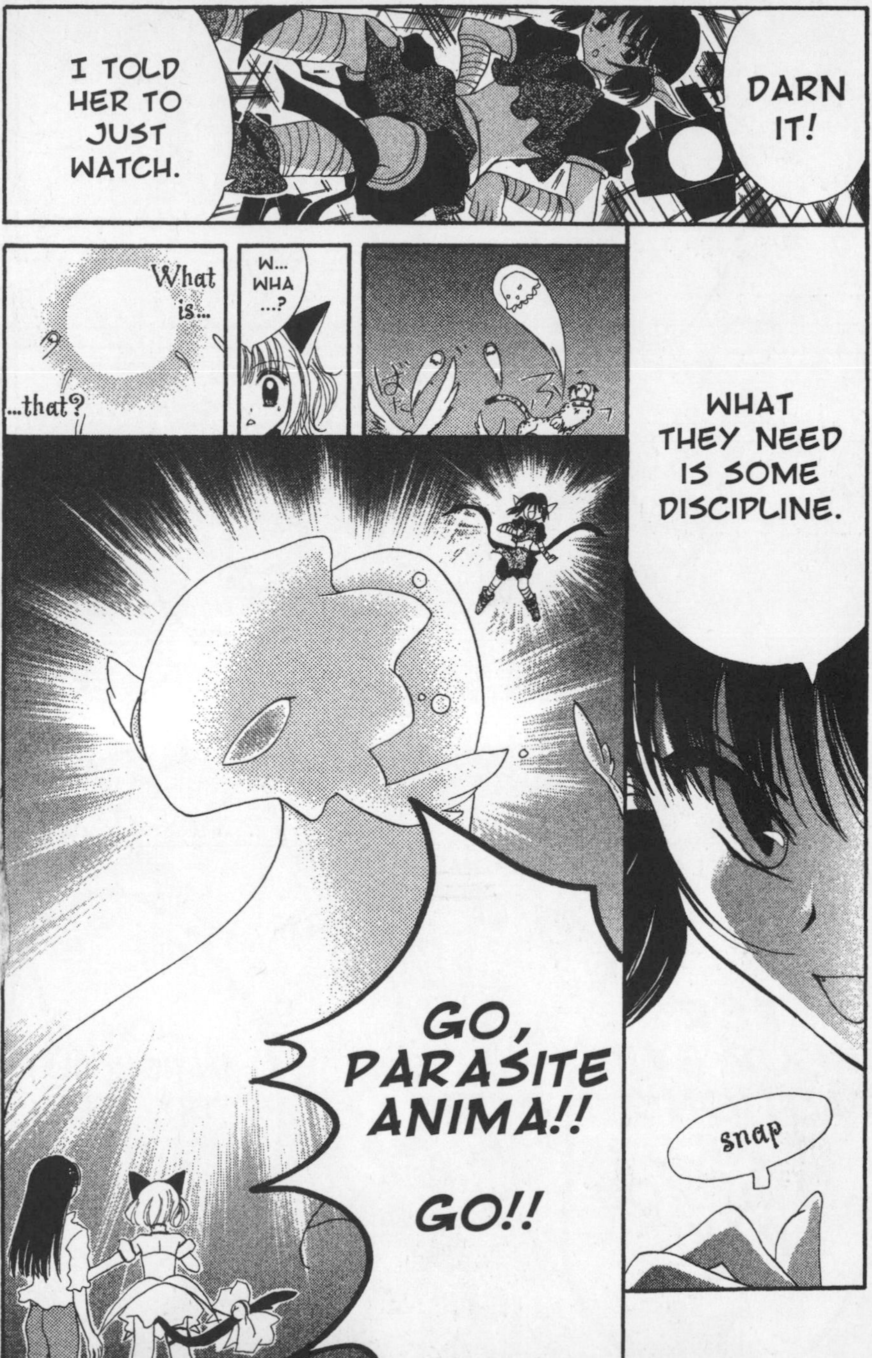
DARN IT!
I TOLD HER TO JUST WATCH.
WHAT THEY NEED IS SOME DISCIPLINE.
snap
W... WHA ...?
What is... ...that?
GO, PARASITE ANIMA!!
GO!!

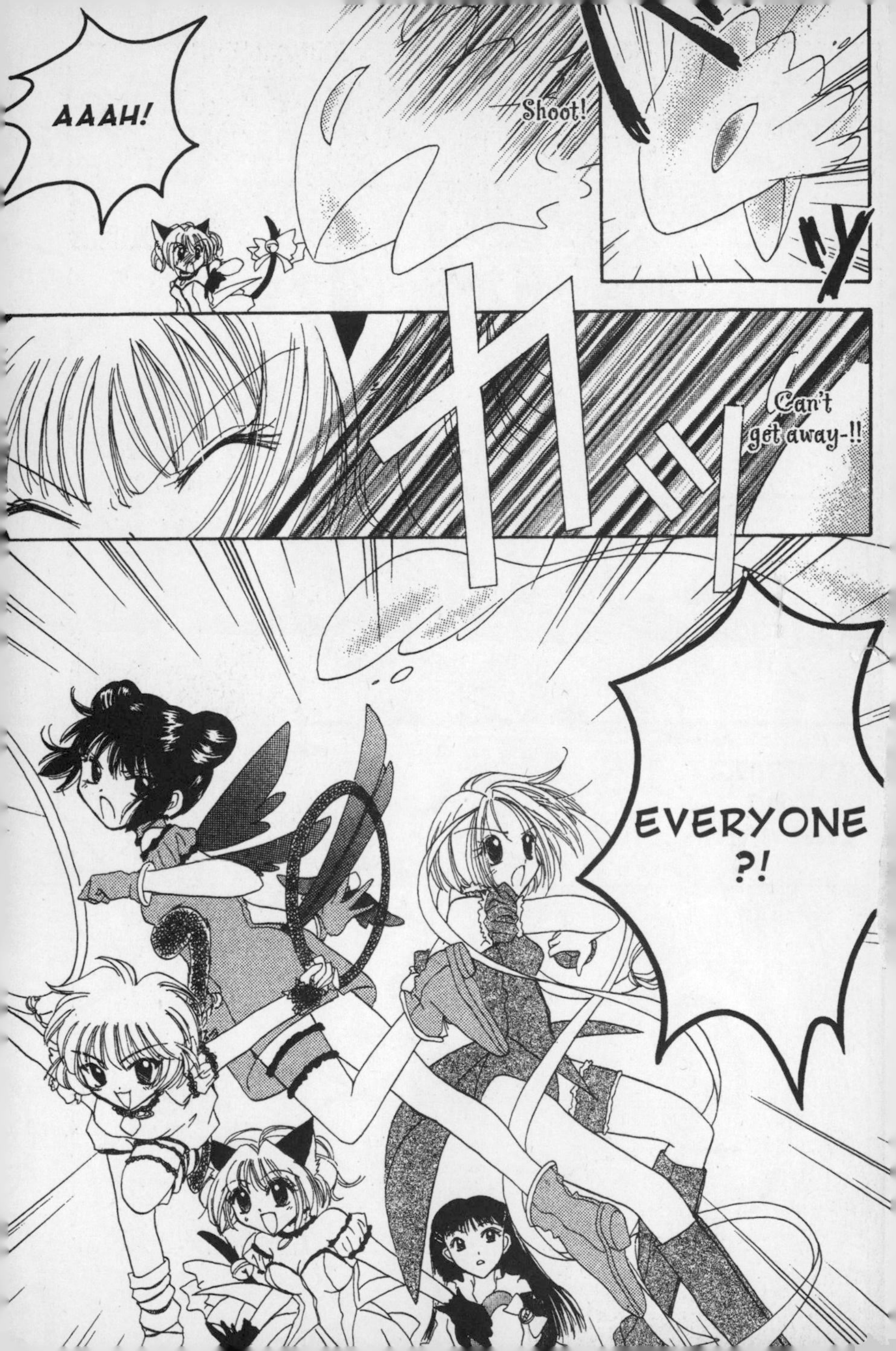
Shoot!
AAAH!
Can't get away-!!
EVERYONE ?!

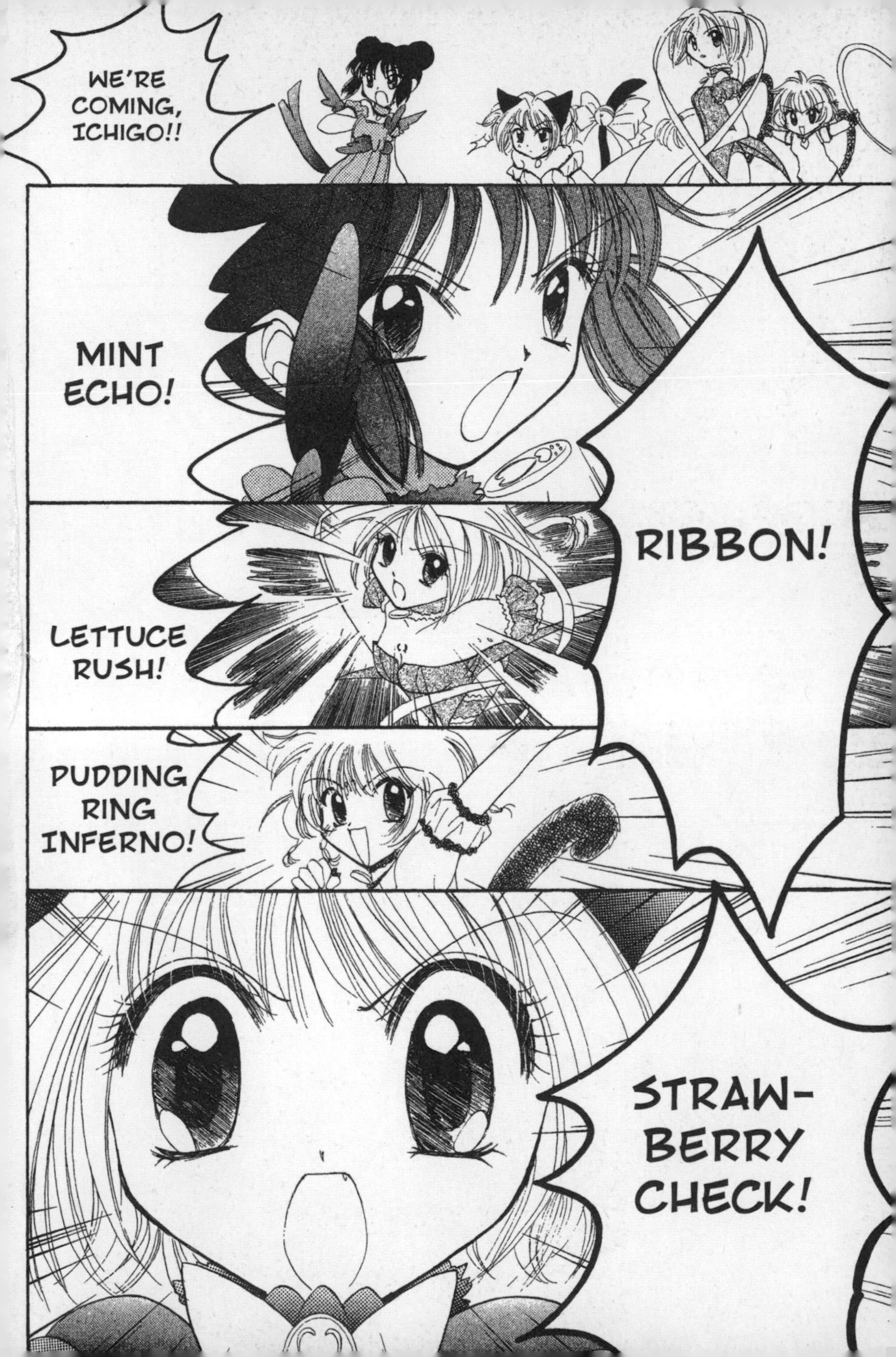
WE'RE COMING, ICHIGO!!
MINT ECHO!
LETTUCE RUSH!
PUDDING RING INFERNO!
RIBBON!
STRAW-BERRY CHECK!

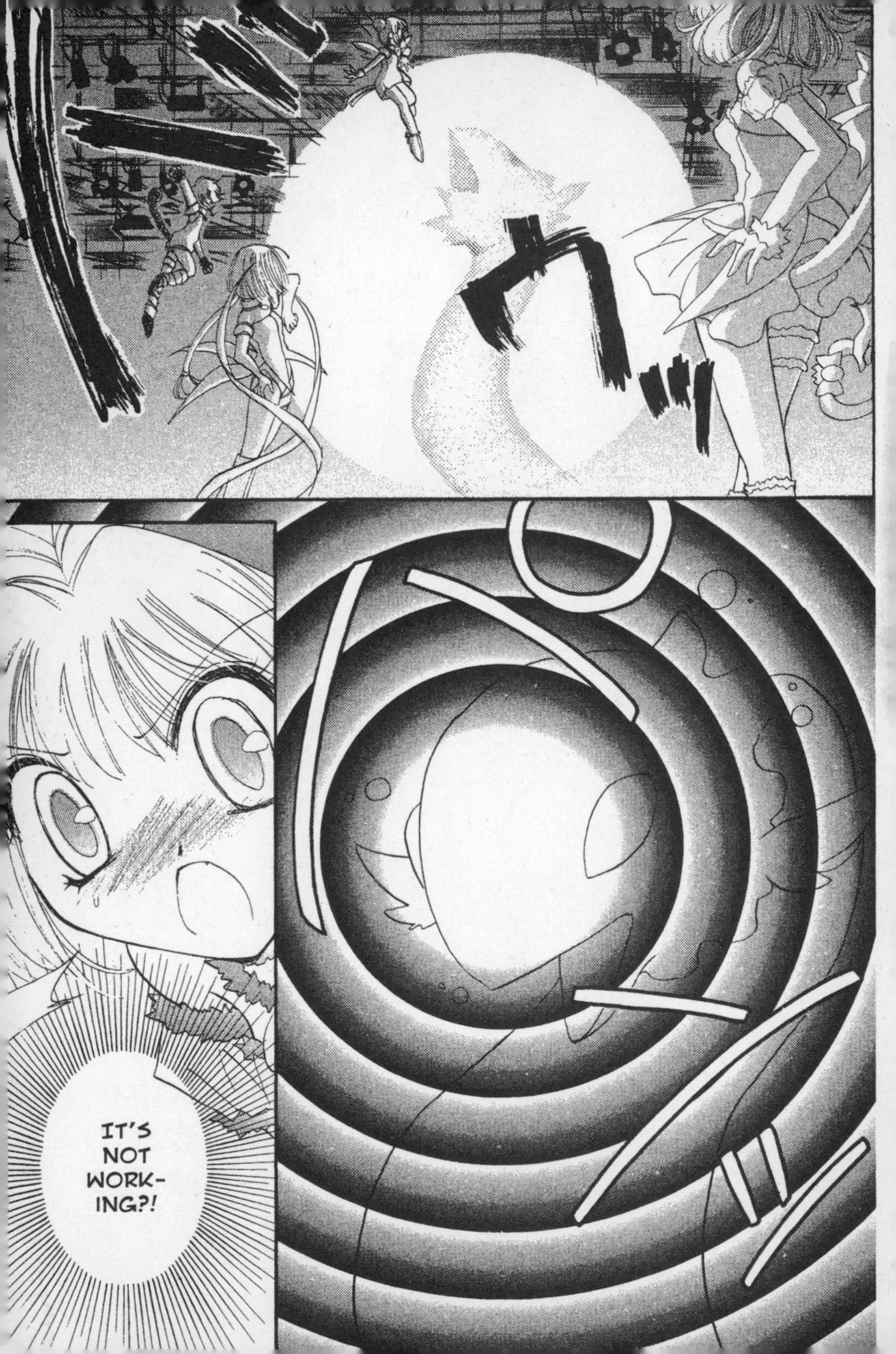
IT'S NOT WORKING?!

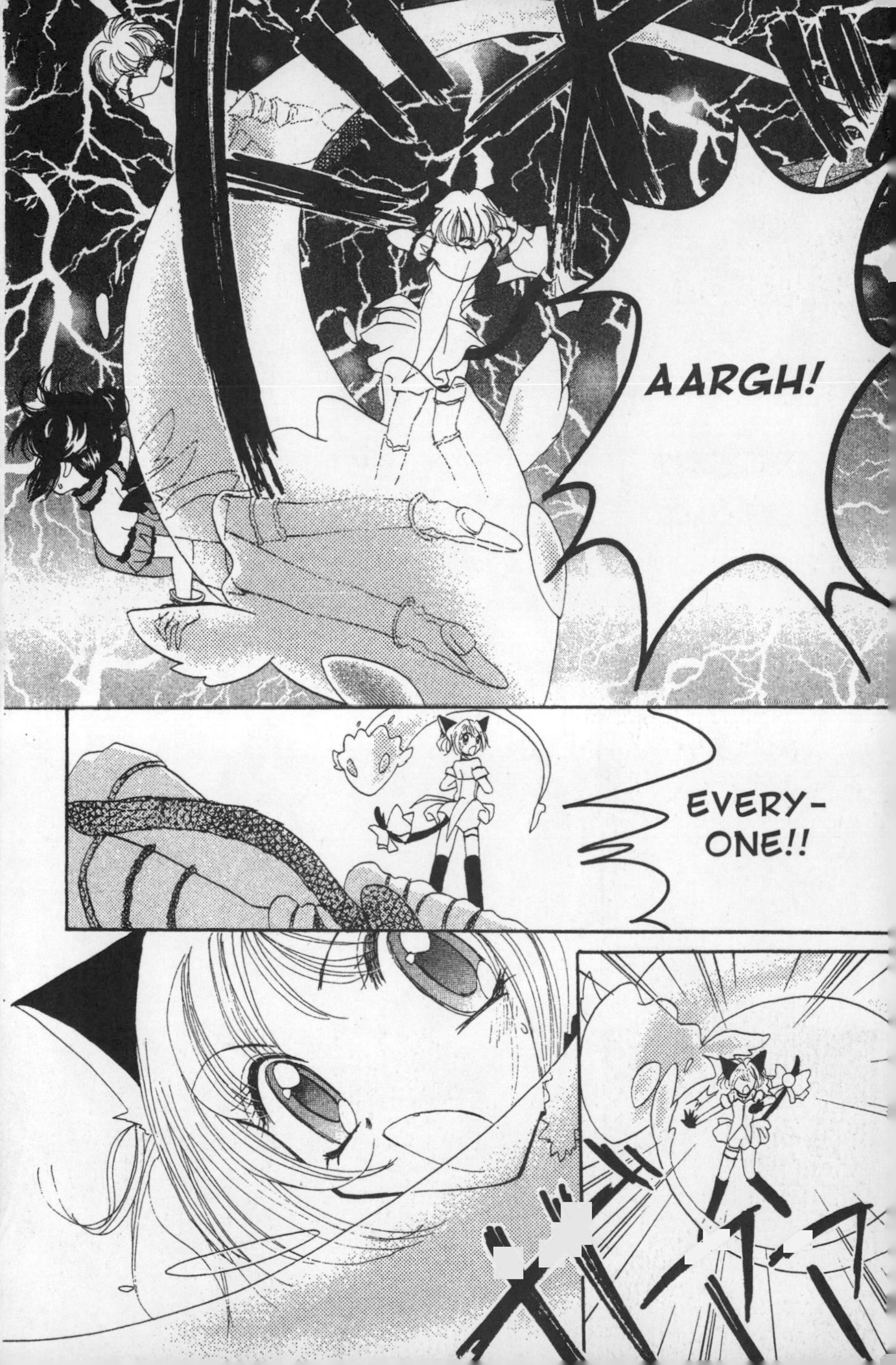
AARGH!
EVERY-ONE!!

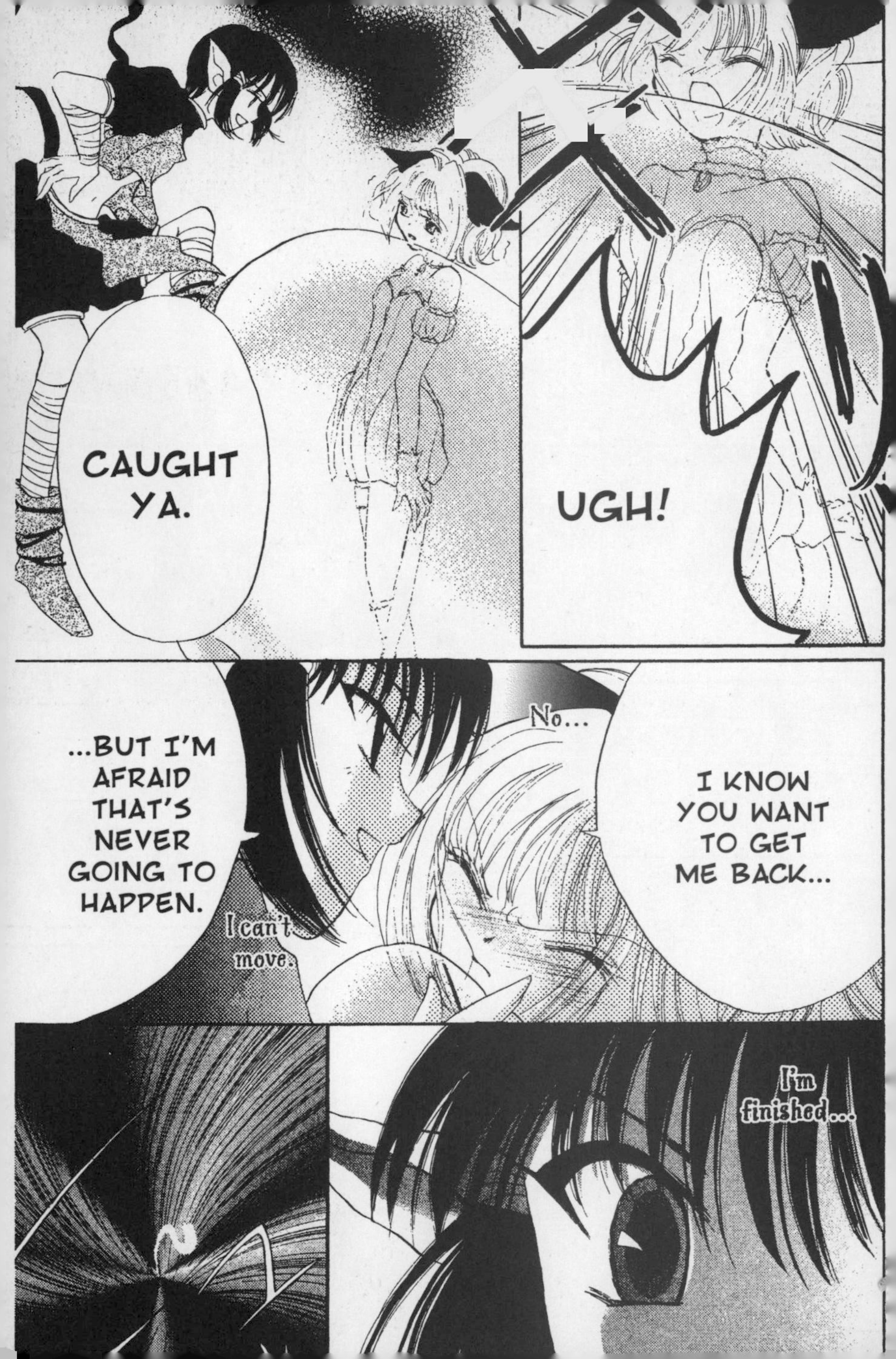
UGH!
CAUGHT YA.
I KNOW YOU WANT TO GET ME BACK...
No...
...BUT I'M AFRAID THAT'S NEVER GOING TO HAPPEN.
I can't move.
I'm finished...

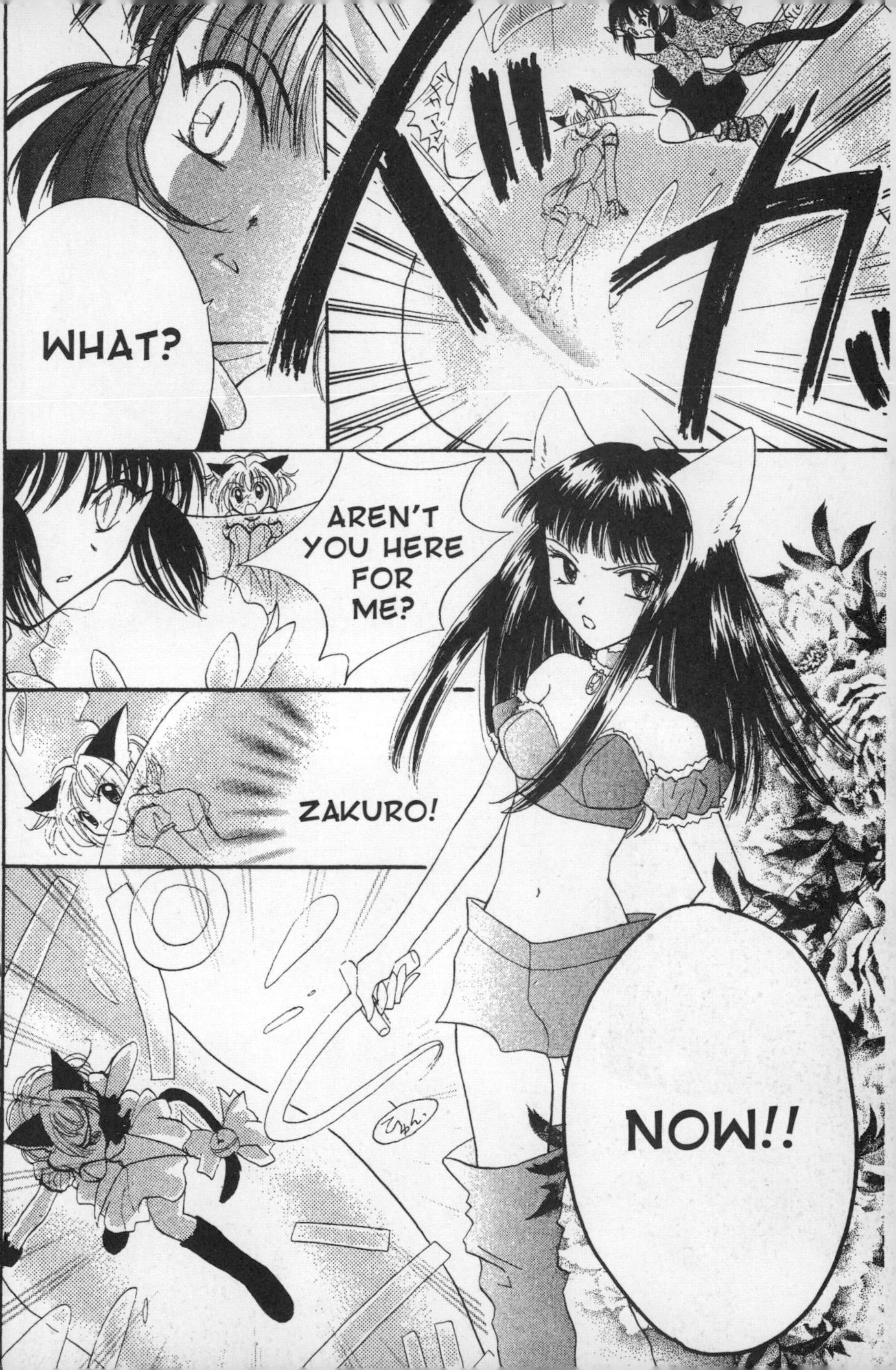
WHAT?
AREN'T YOU HERE FOR ME?
ZAKURO!
NOW!!

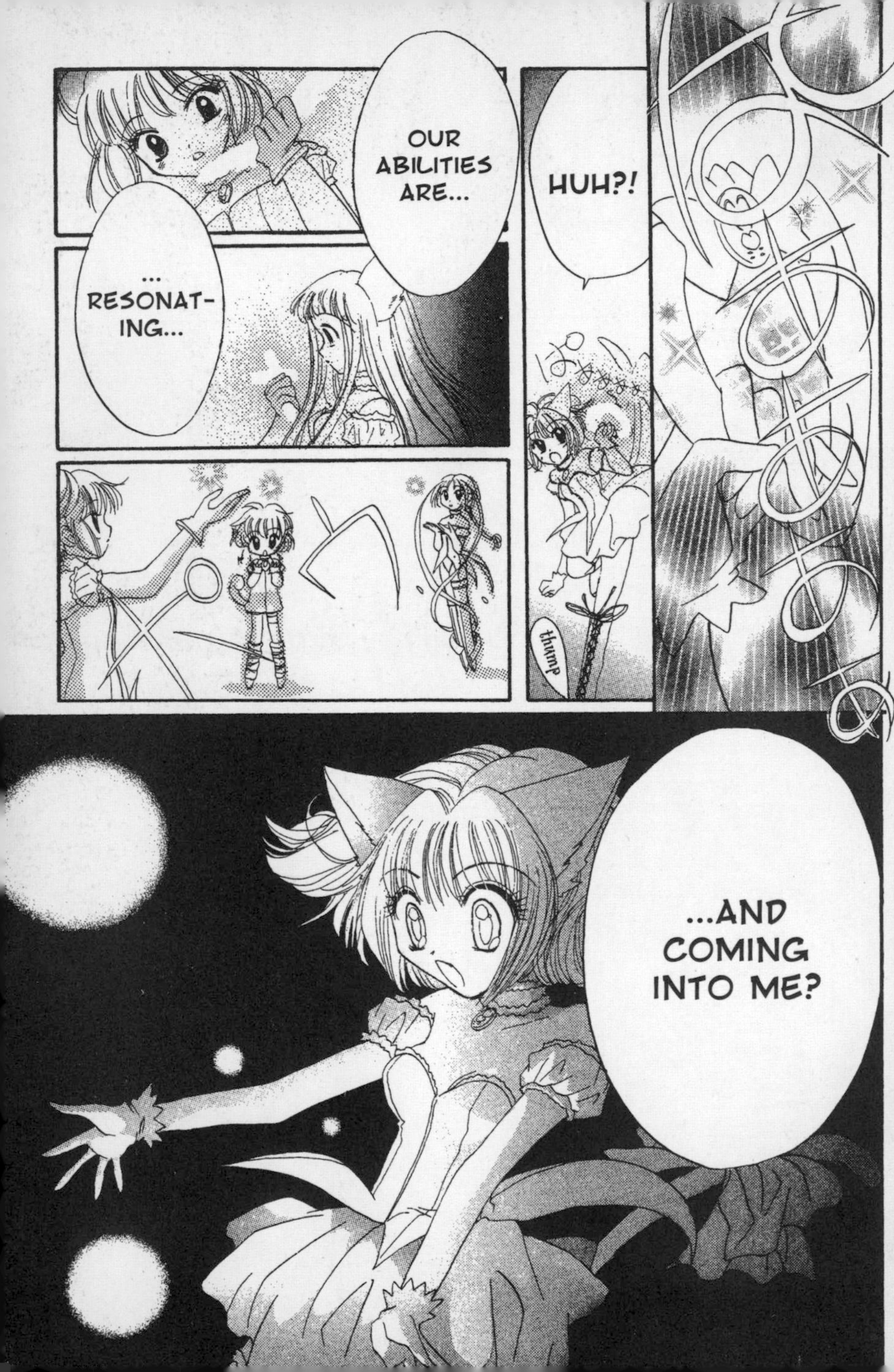
HUH?!
thump
OUR ABILITIES ARE...
...RESONATING...
...AND COMING INTO ME?

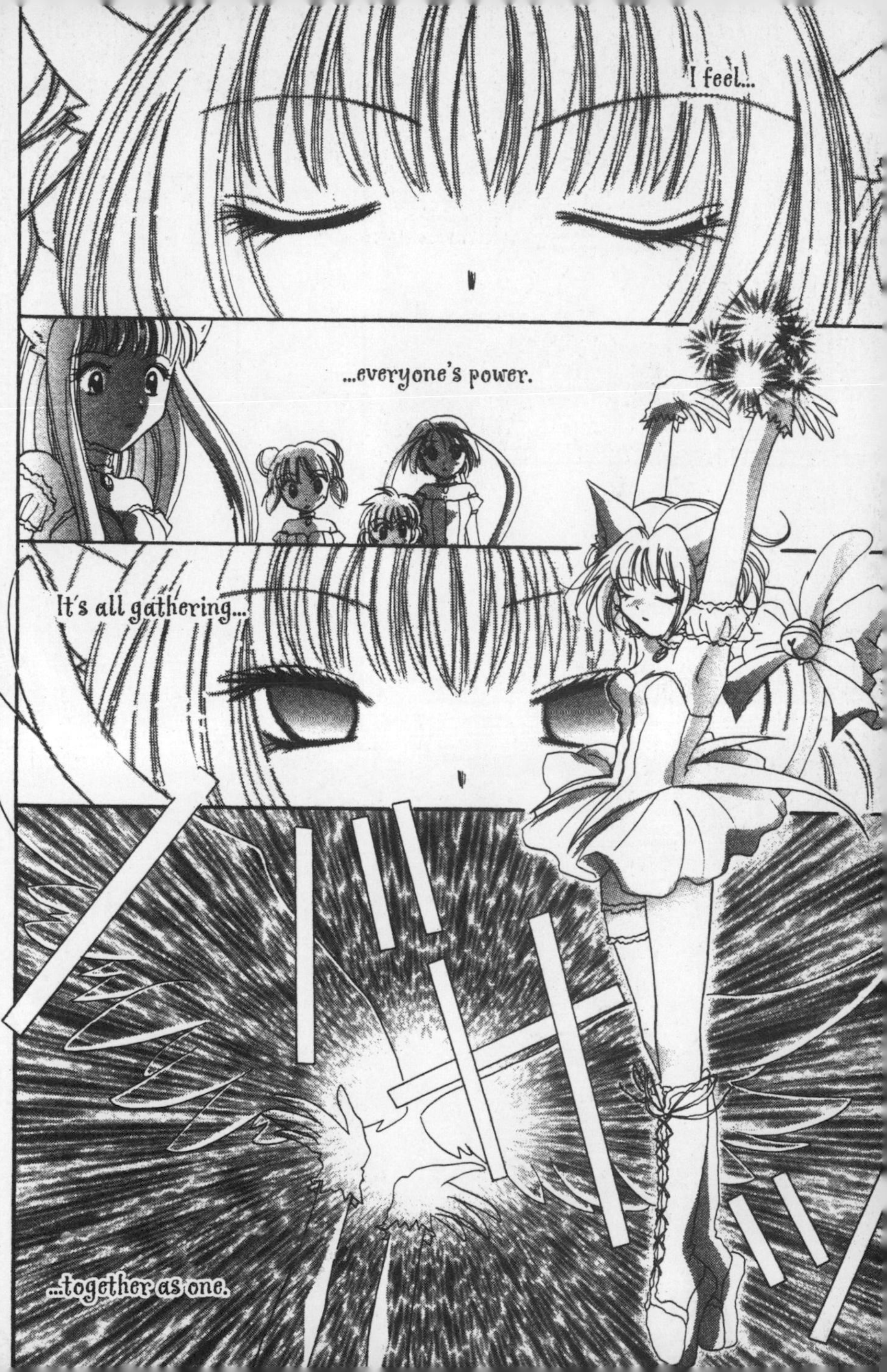
I feel...
...everyone's power.
It's all gathering...
...together as one.

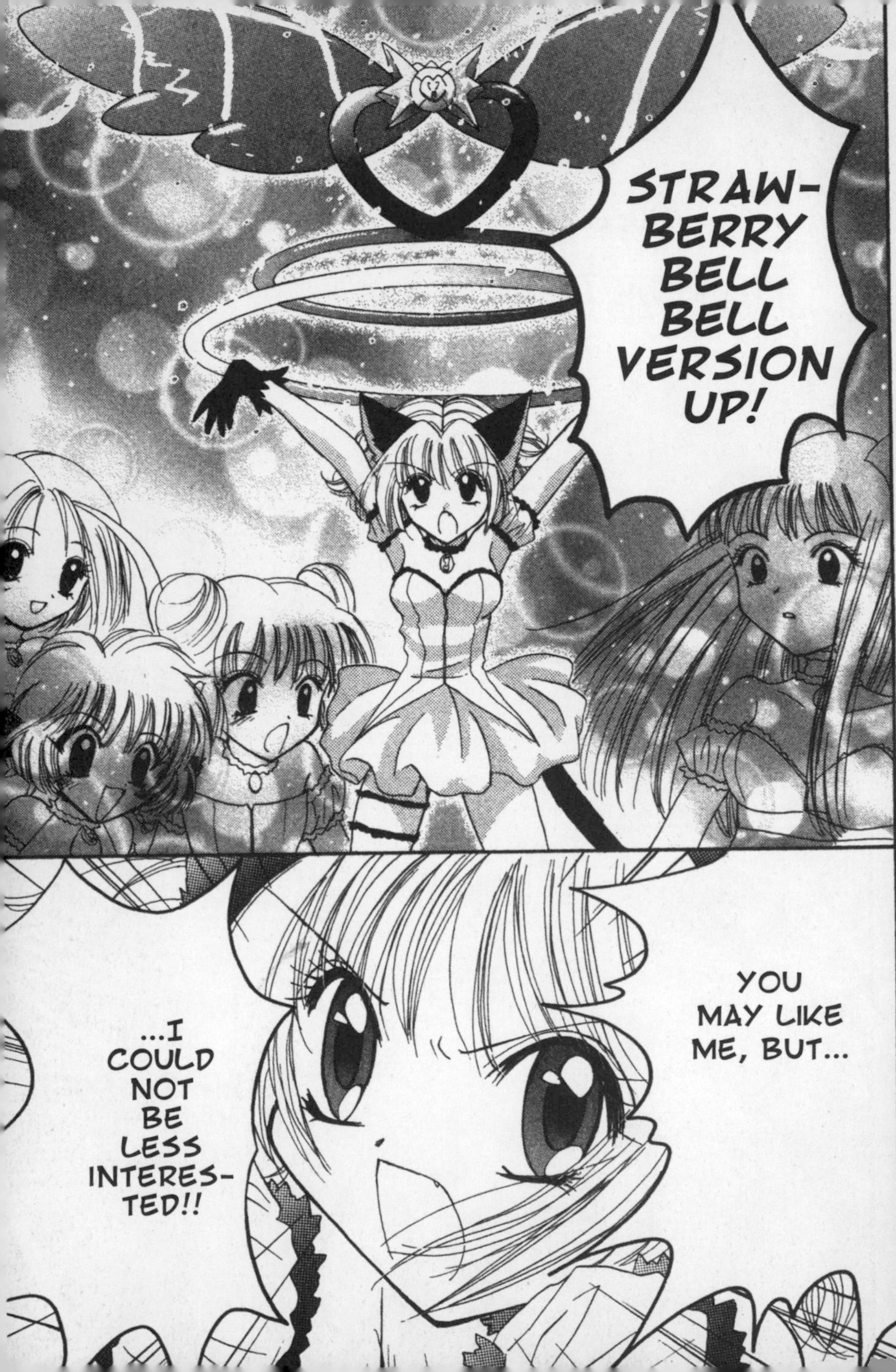
STRAW-
BERRY
BELL
BELL
VERSION
UP!
YOU
MAY LIKE
ME, BUT...
...I
COULD
NOT
BE
LESS
INTERES-
TED!!

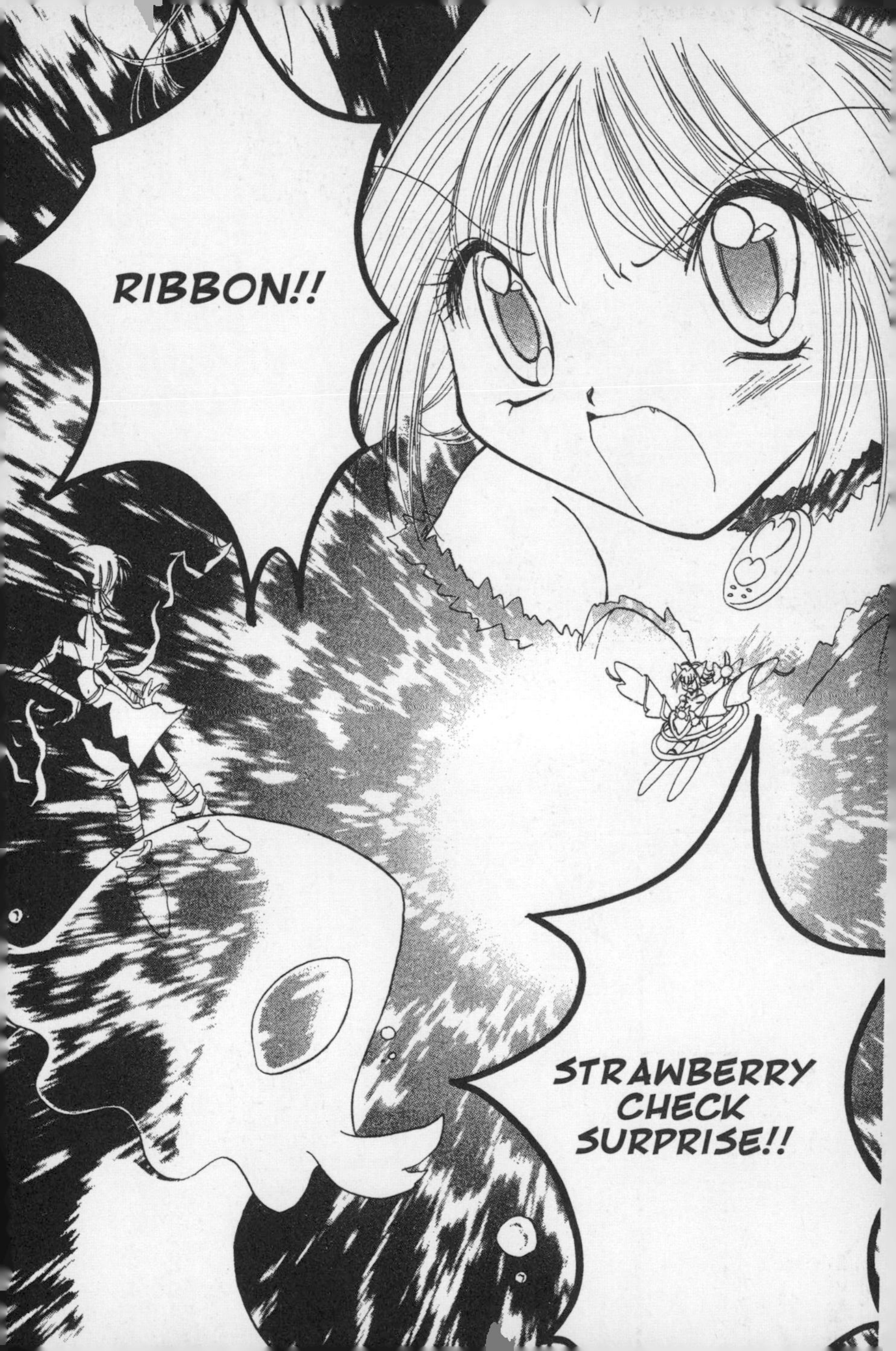
RIBBON!!
STRAWBERRY CHECK SURPRISE!!

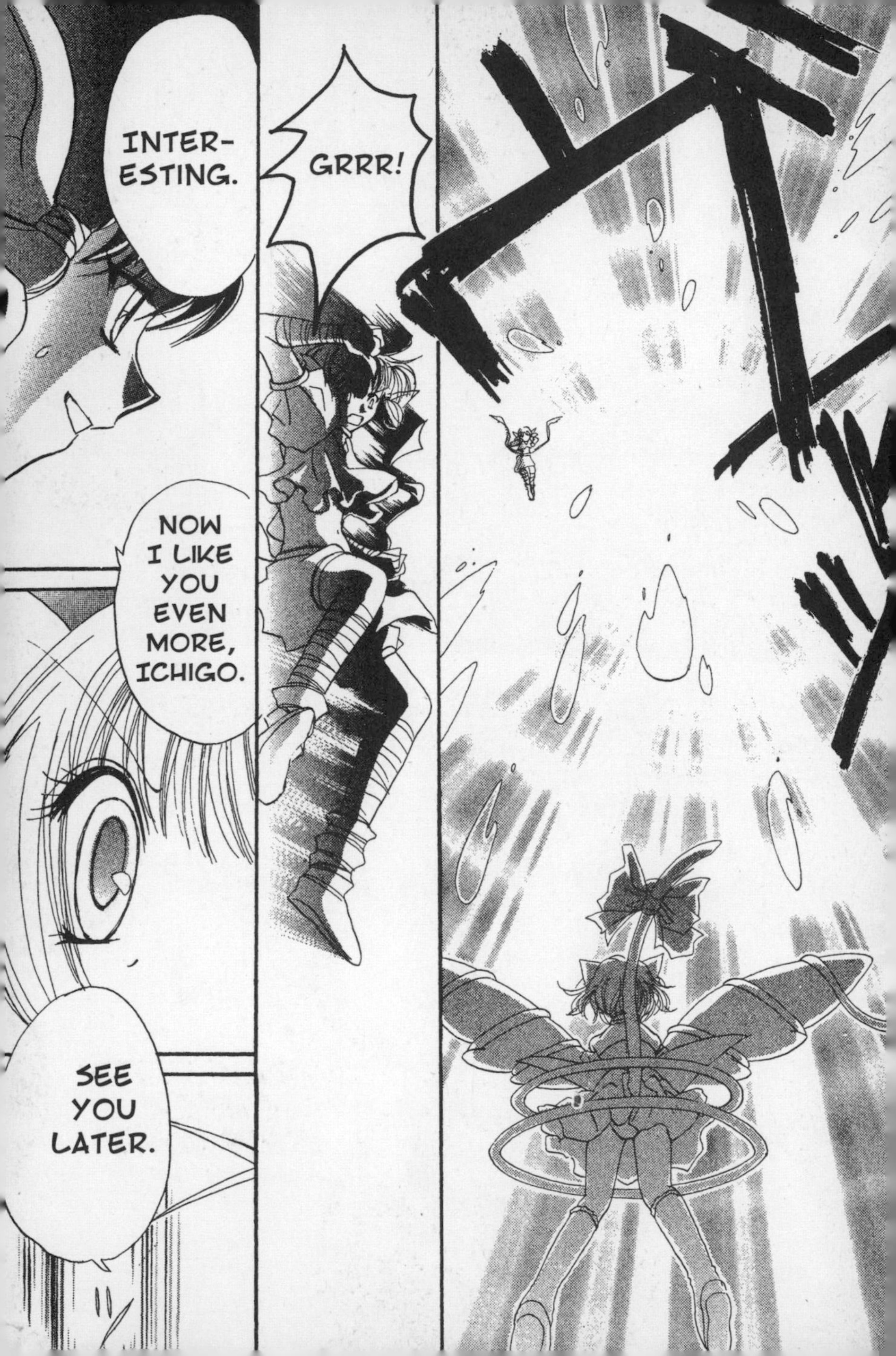
GRRR!
INTER-ESTING.
NOW I LIKE YOU EVEN MORE, ICHIGO.
SEE YOU LATER.

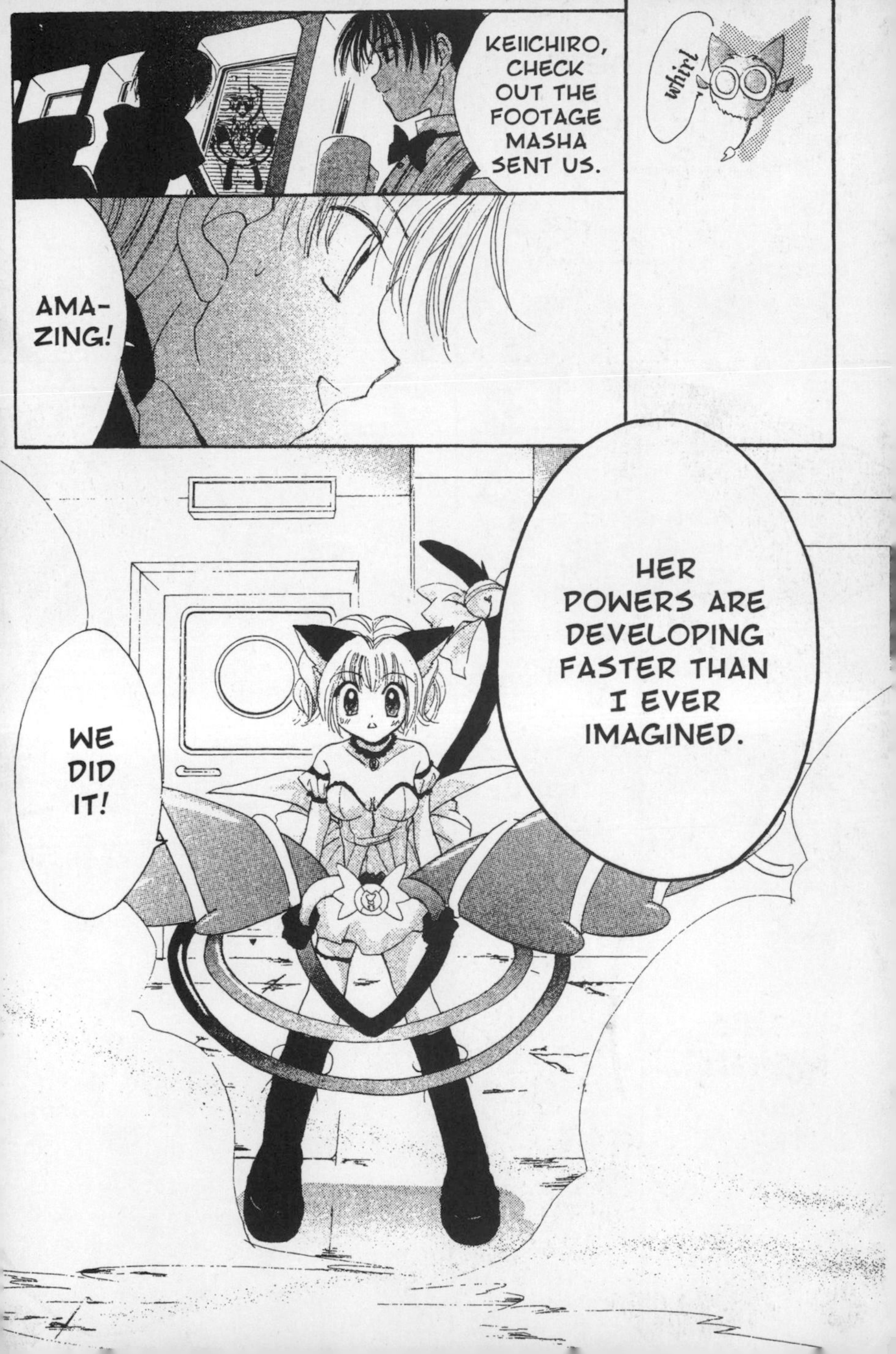
whirl
KEIICHIRO, CHECK OUT THE FOOTAGE MASHA SENT US.
AMA-ZING!
HER POWERS ARE DEVELOPING FASTER THAN I EVER IMAGINED.
WE DID IT!

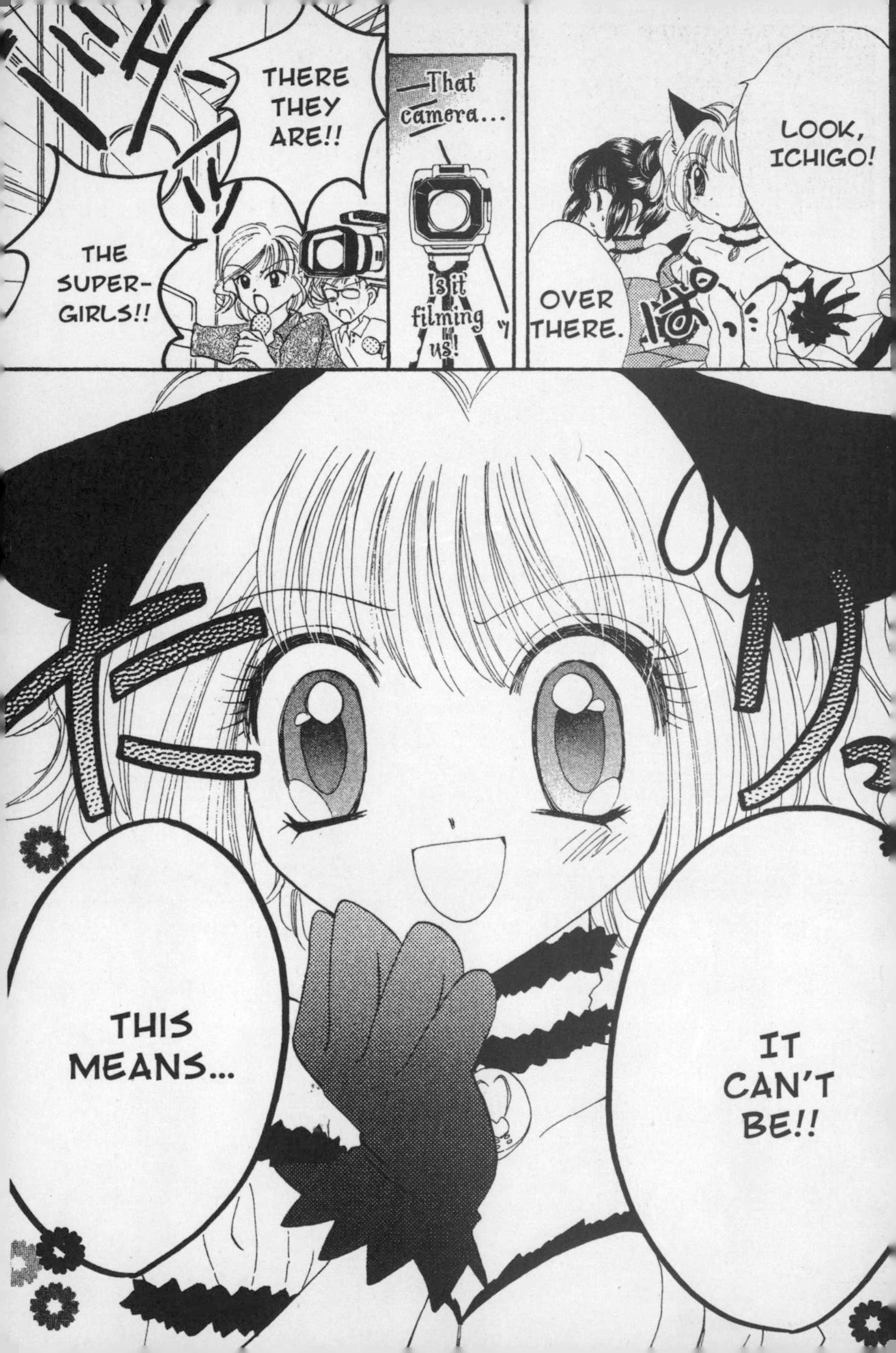
LOOK, ICHIGO!
OVER THERE.
That camera...
Is it filming us!
THERE THEY ARE!!
THE SUPER-GIRLS!!
IT CAN'T BE!!
THIS MEANS...

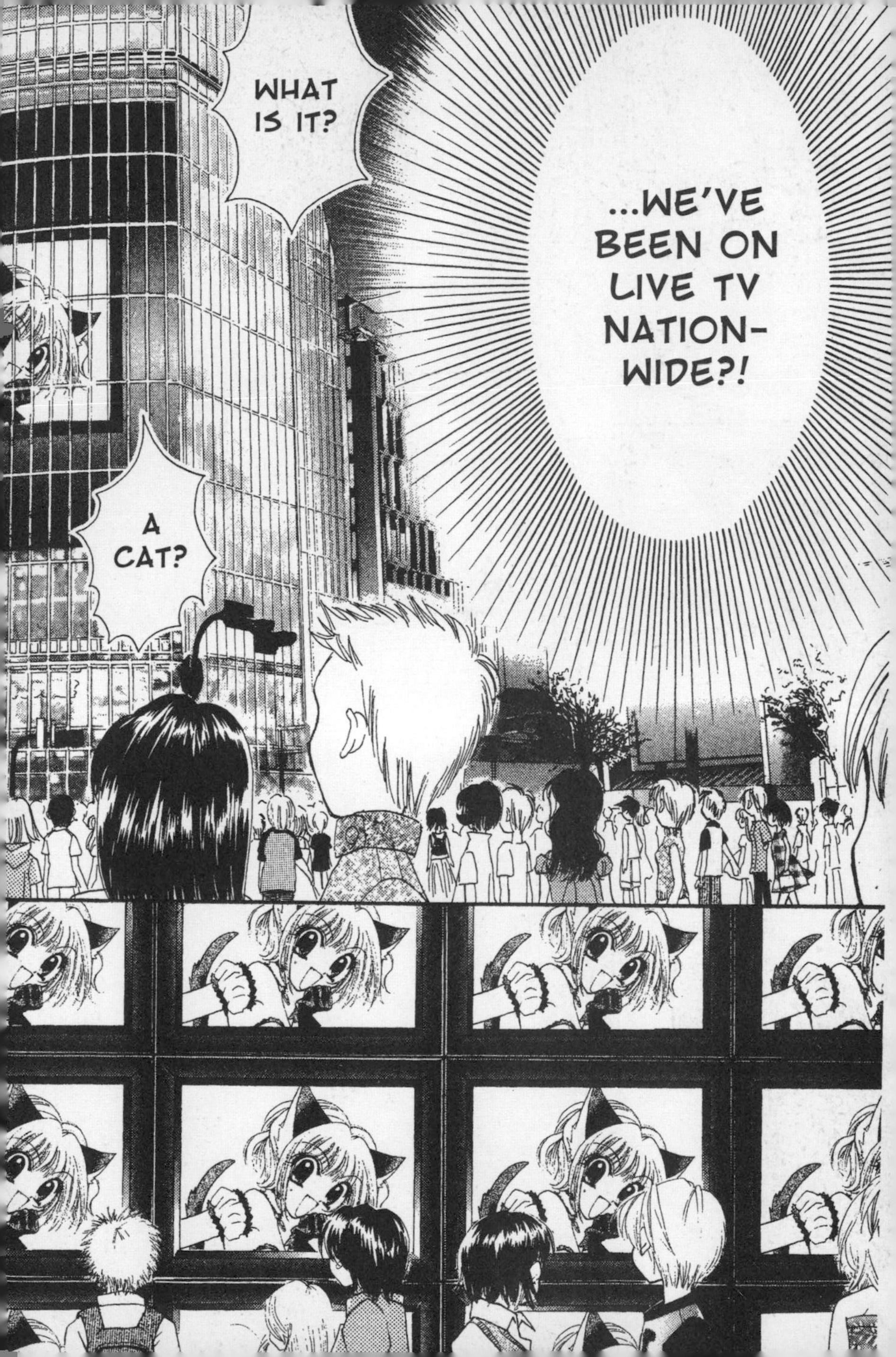
...WE'VE BEEN ON LIVE TV NATION-WIDE?!
WHAT IS IT?
A CAT?

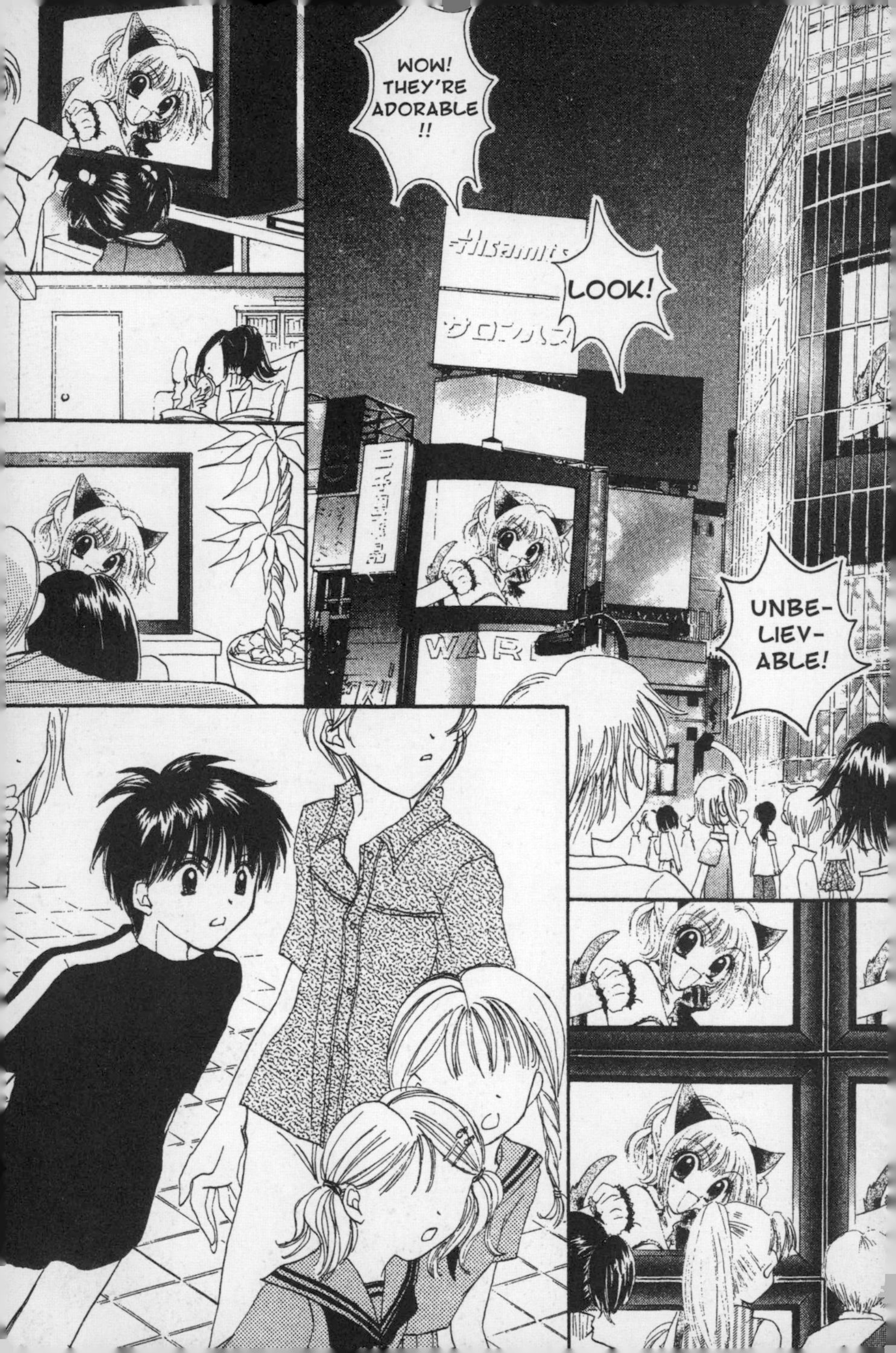
WOW! THEY'RE ADORABLE !!
LOOK!
UNBE-LIEV-ABLE!

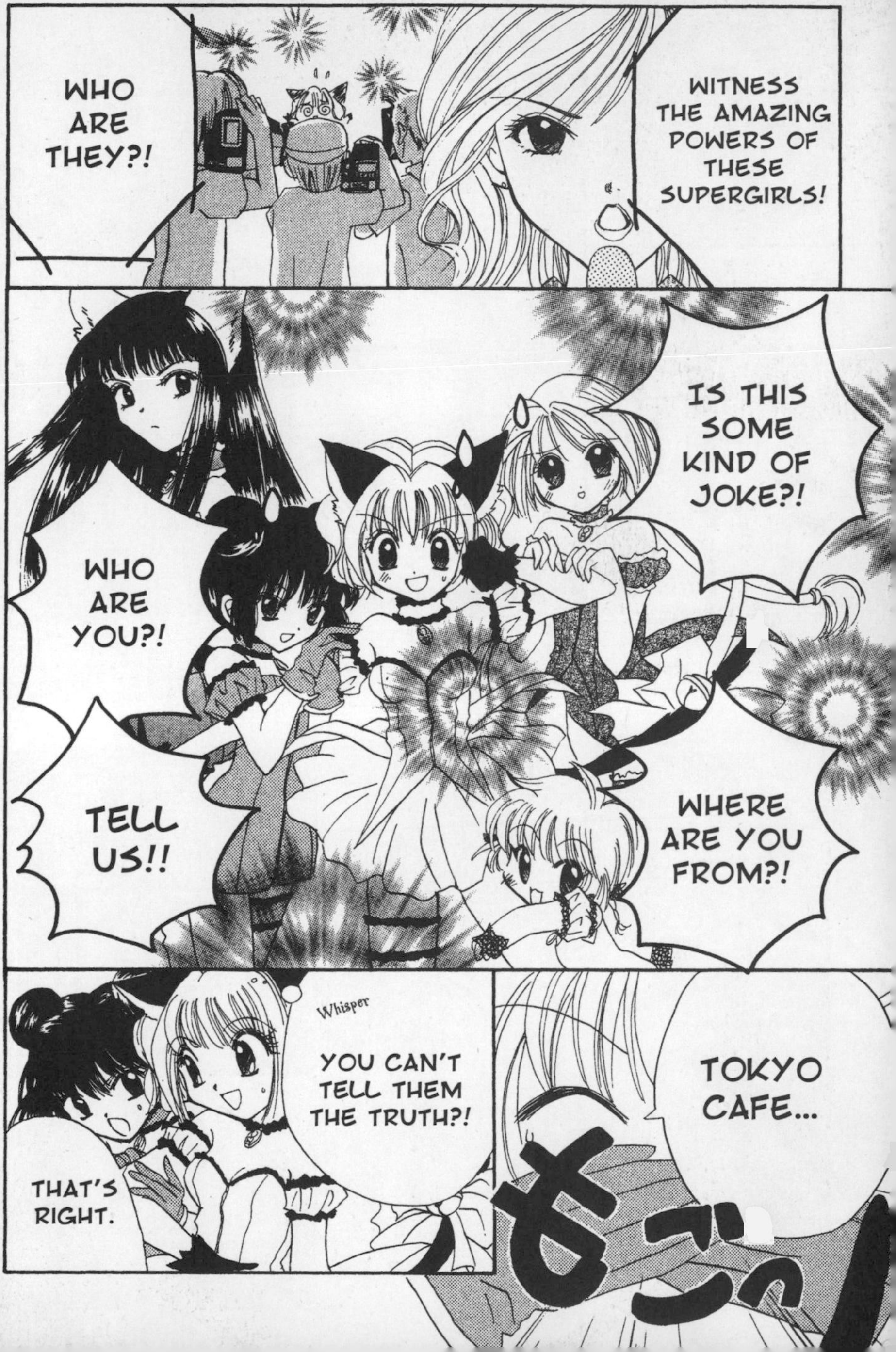
WITNESS THE AMAZING POWERS OF THESE SUPERGIRLS!
WHO ARE THEY?!
IS THIS SOME KIND OF JOKE?!
WHO ARE YOU?!
WHERE ARE YOU FROM?!
TELL US!!
TOKYO CAFE...
もごっ
Whisper
YOU CAN'T TELL THEM THE TRUTH?!
THAT'S RIGHT.

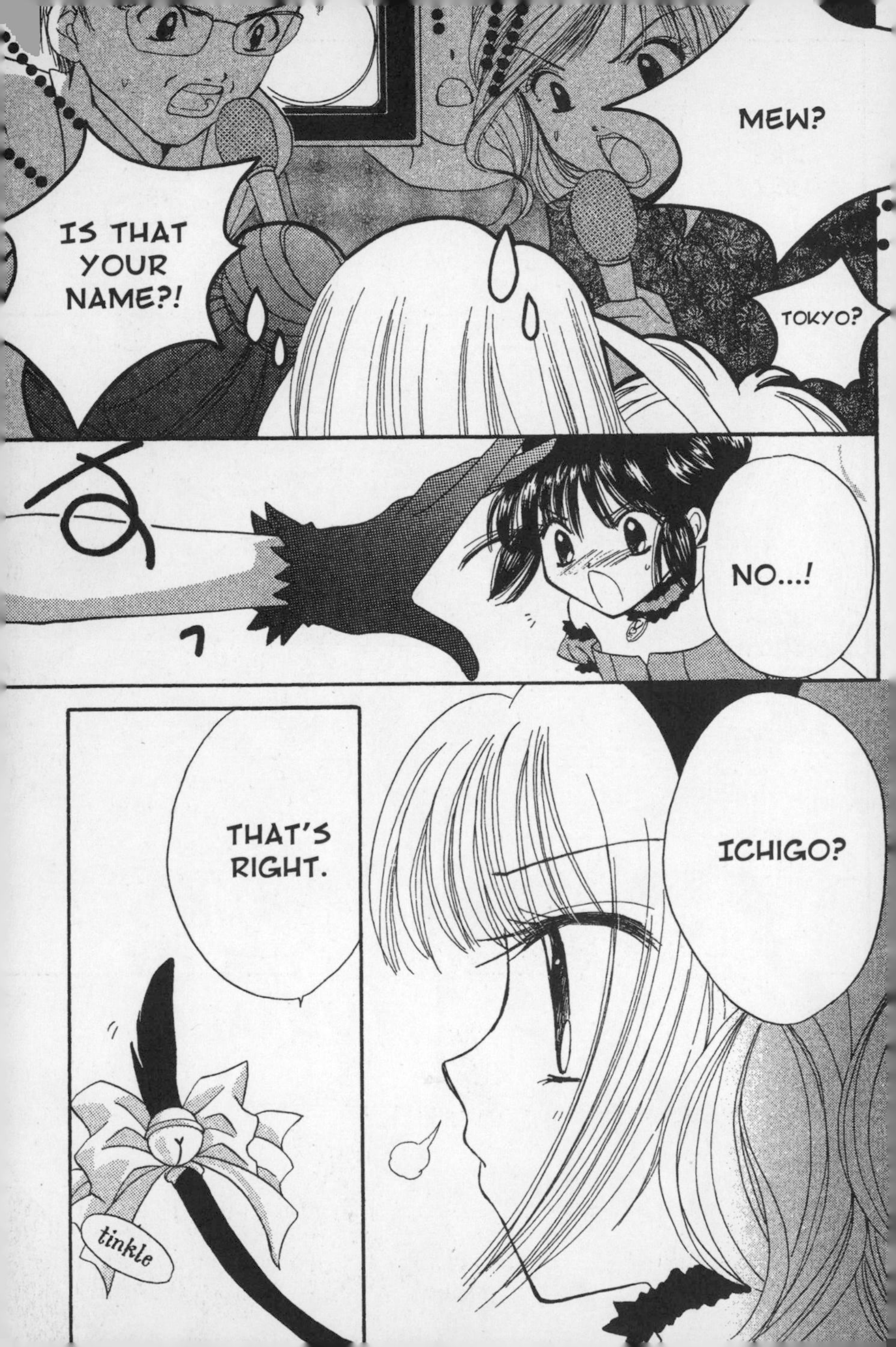
MEW?
TOKYO?
IS THAT YOUR NAME?!
NO...!
ICHIGO?
THAT'S RIGHT.
tinkle

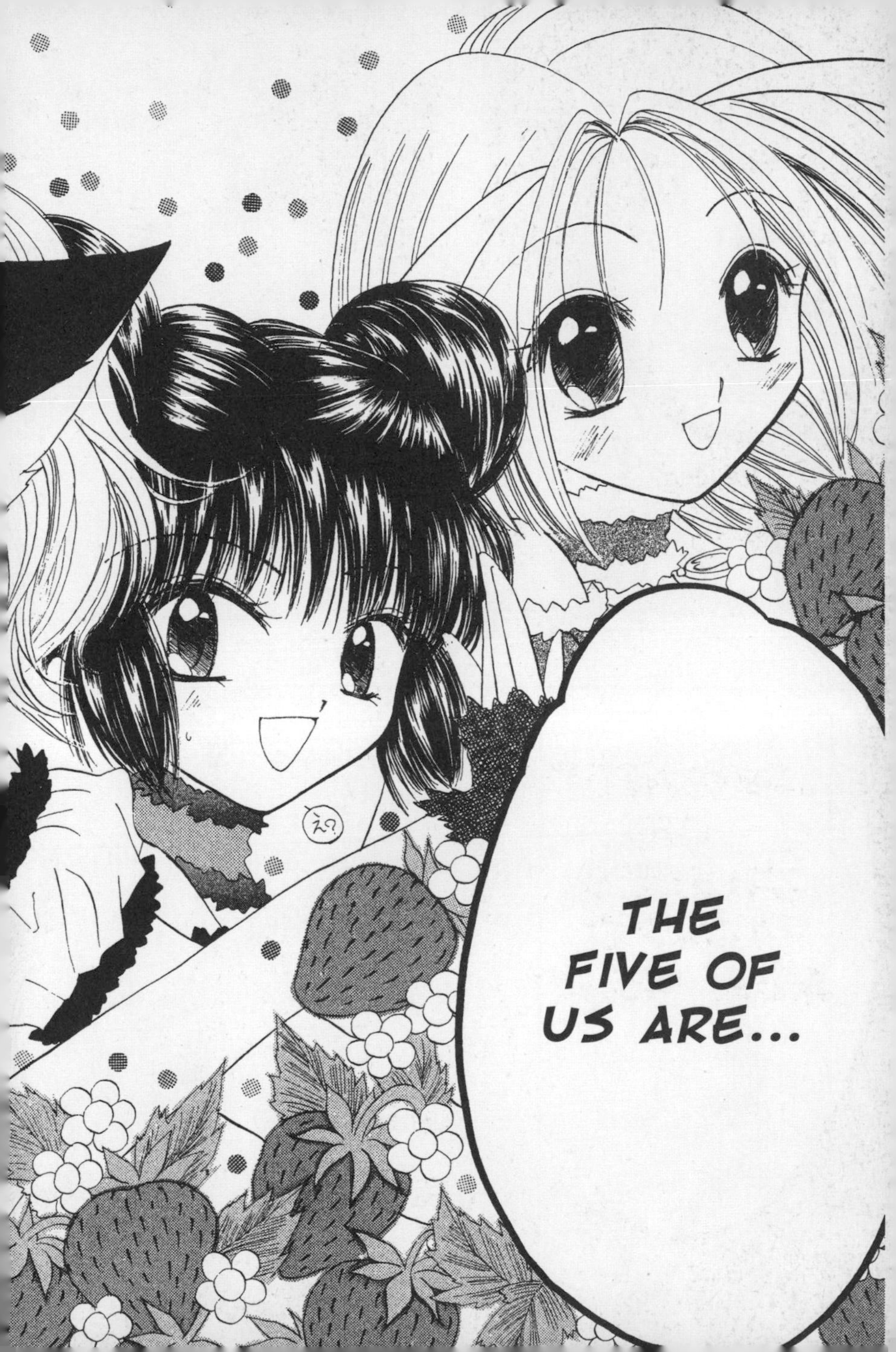

THE FIVE OF US ARE...
え?

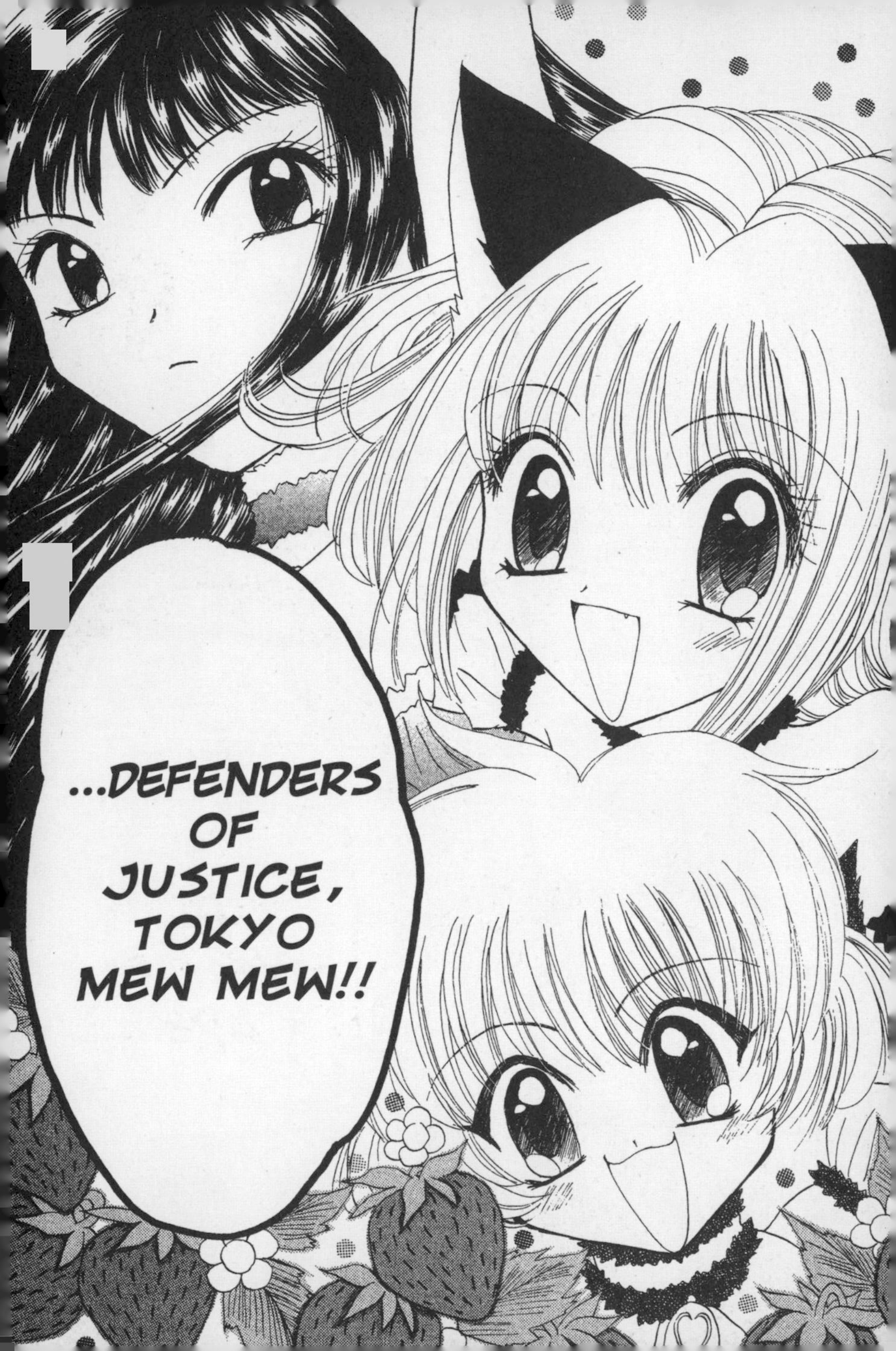
...DEFENDERS OF JUSTICE, TOKYO MEW MEW!!

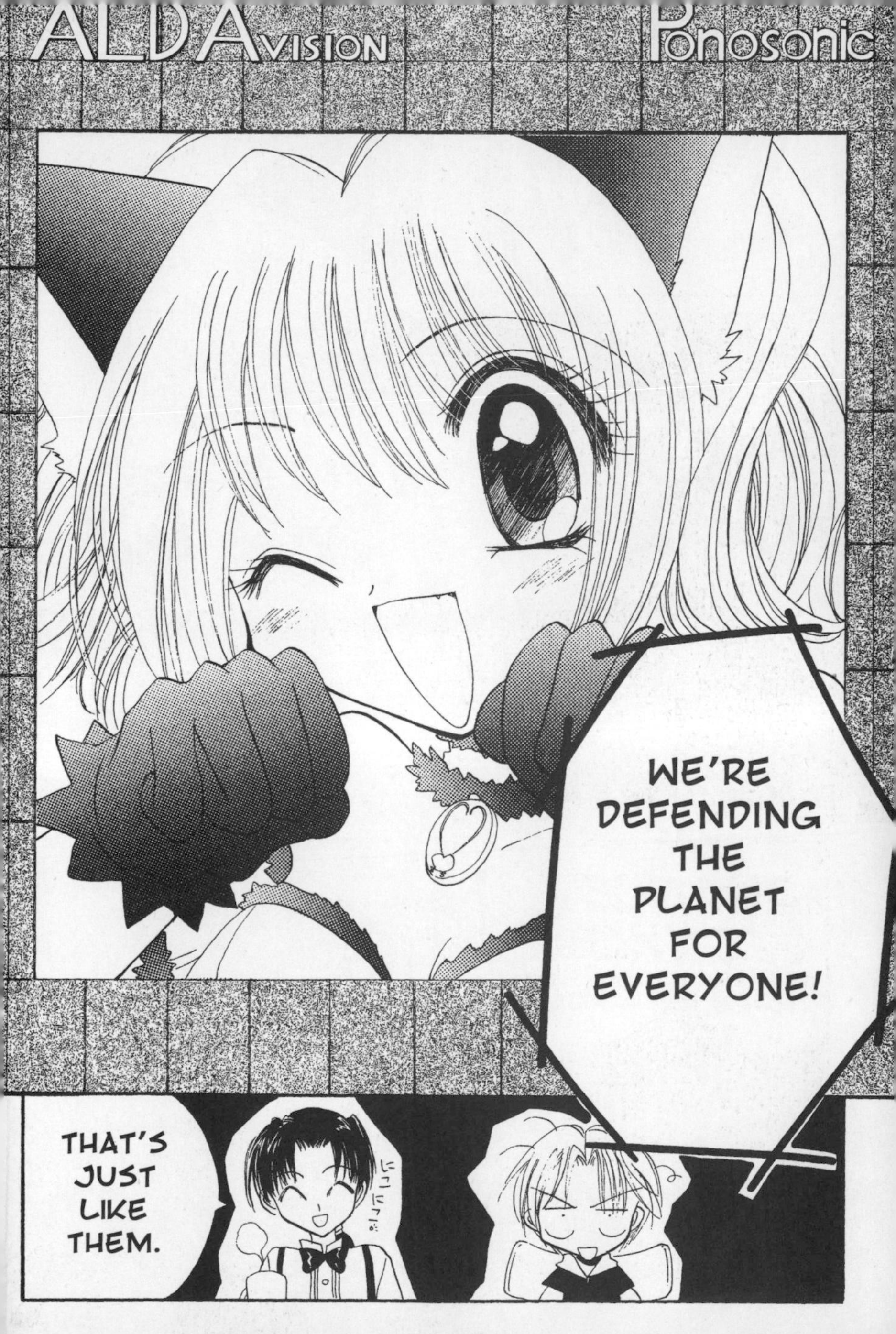
Ponosonic
ALDA VISION
WE'RE DEFENDING THE PLANET FOR EVERYONE!
THAT'S JUST LIKE THEM.

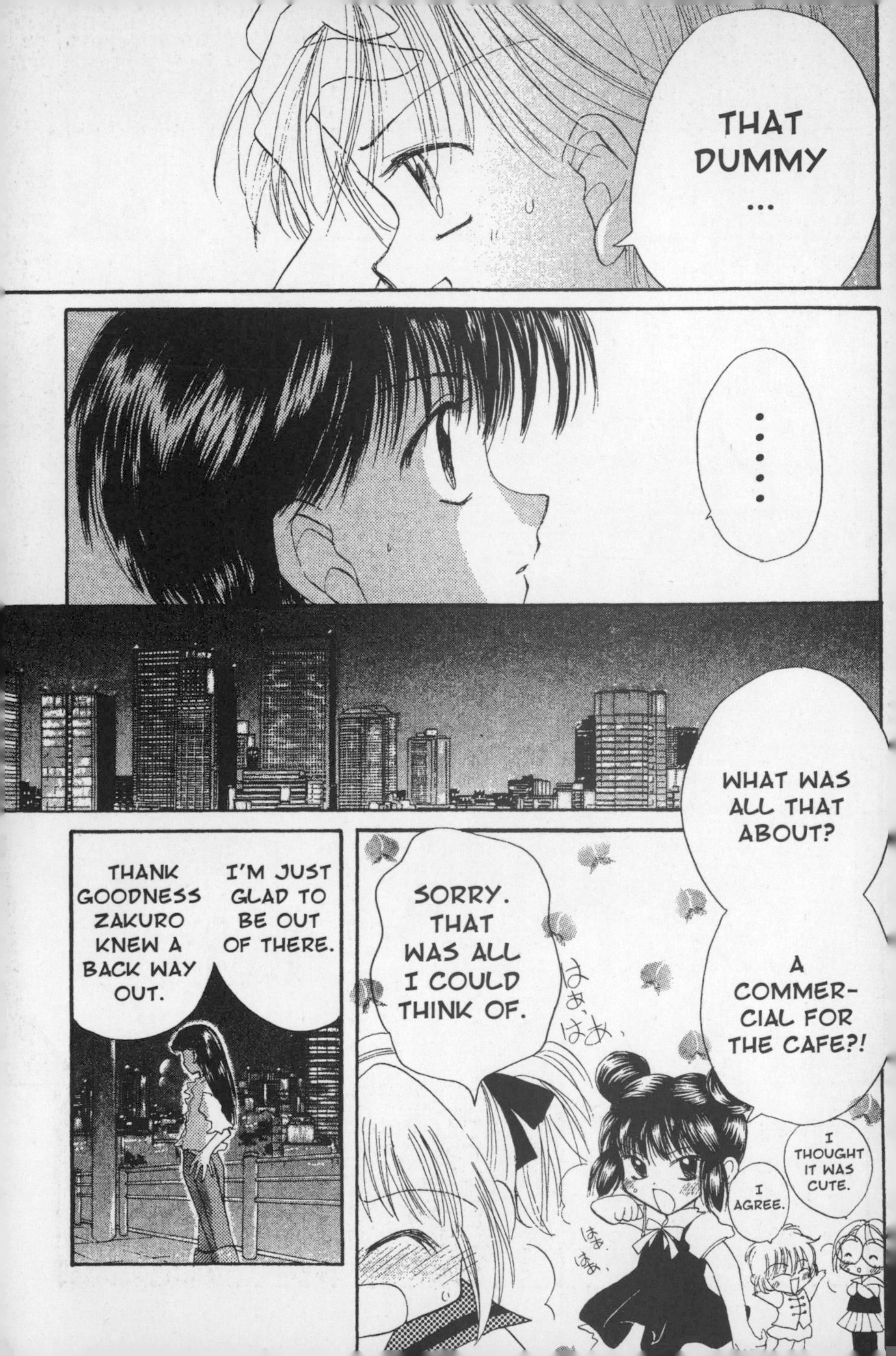
THAT DUMMY ...
• • • • •
WHAT WAS ALL THAT ABOUT?
A COMMERCIAL FOR THE CAFE?!
SORRY. THAT WAS ALL I COULD THINK OF.
はぁ、はぁ、
I THOUGHT IT WAS CUTE.
I AGREE.
I'M JUST GLAD TO BE OUT OF THERE.
THANK GOODNESS ZAKURO KNEW A BACK WAY OUT.

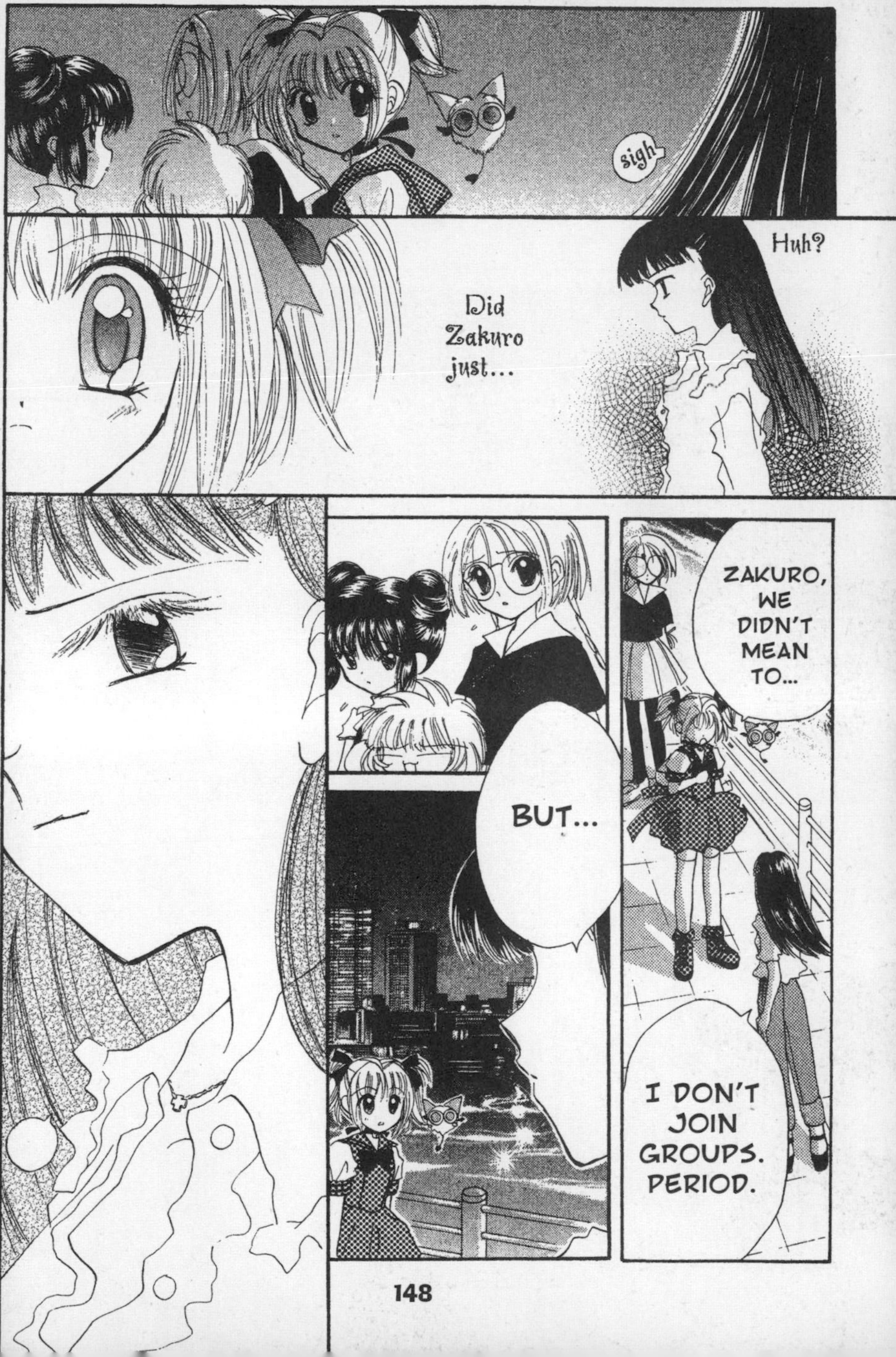
sigh
Huh?
Did Zakuro just...
ZAKURO, WE DIDN'T MEAN TO...
I DON'T JOIN GROUPS. PERIOD.
BUT...

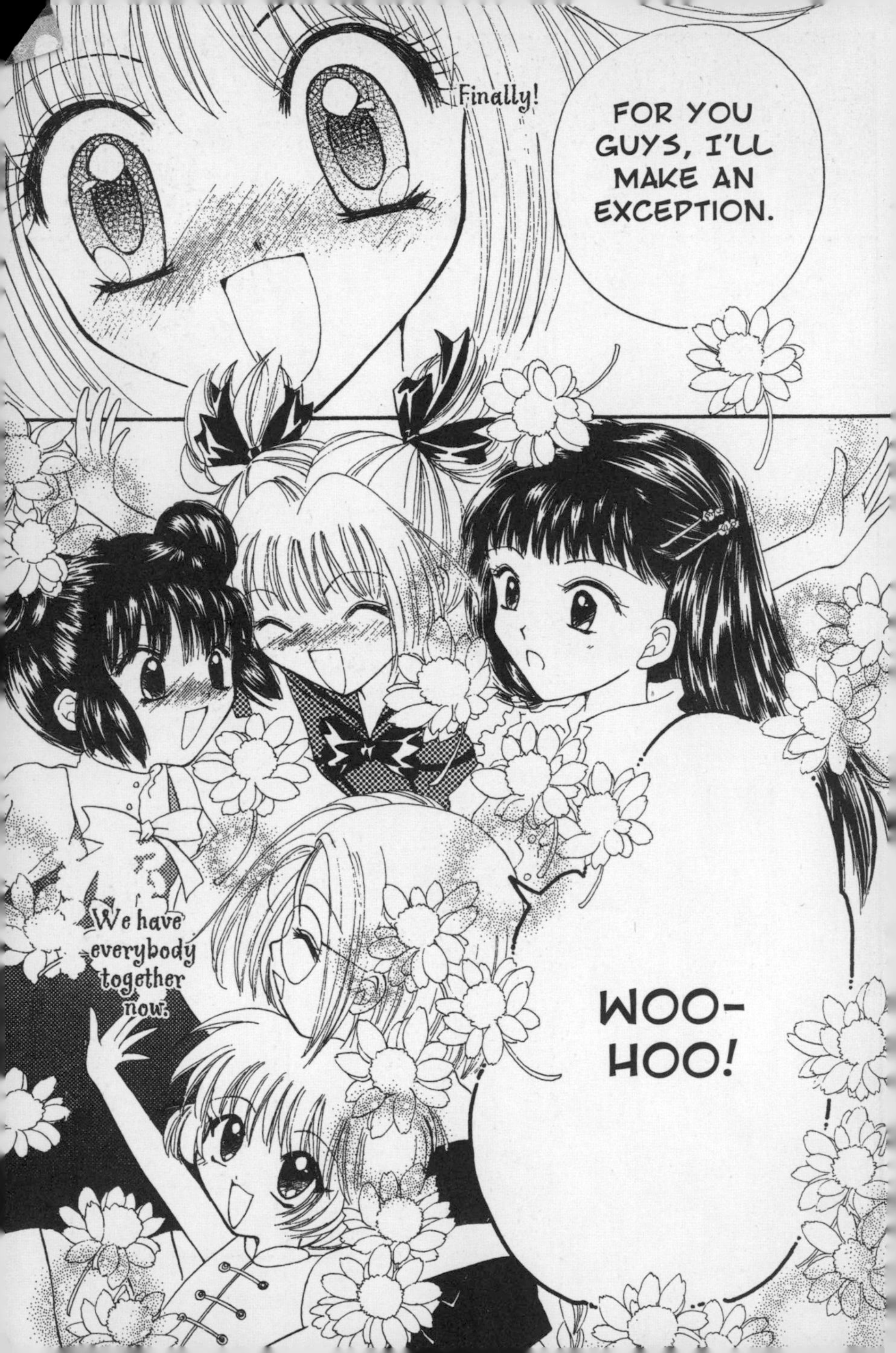
FOR YOU GUYS, I'LL MAKE AN EXCEPTION.
Finally!
WOO-HOO!
We have everybody together now.

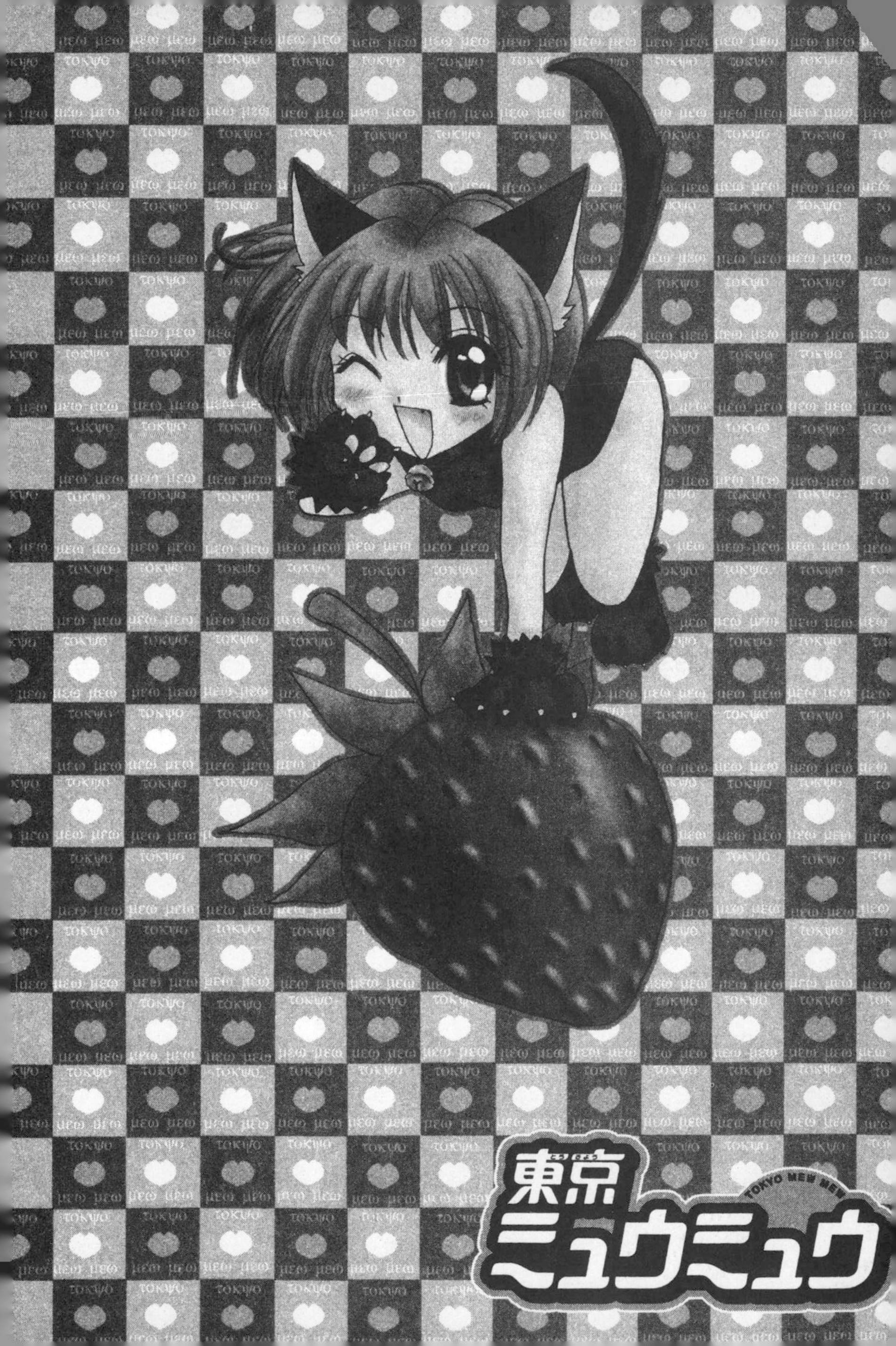
東京
ミュウミュウ
TOKYO MEW MEW

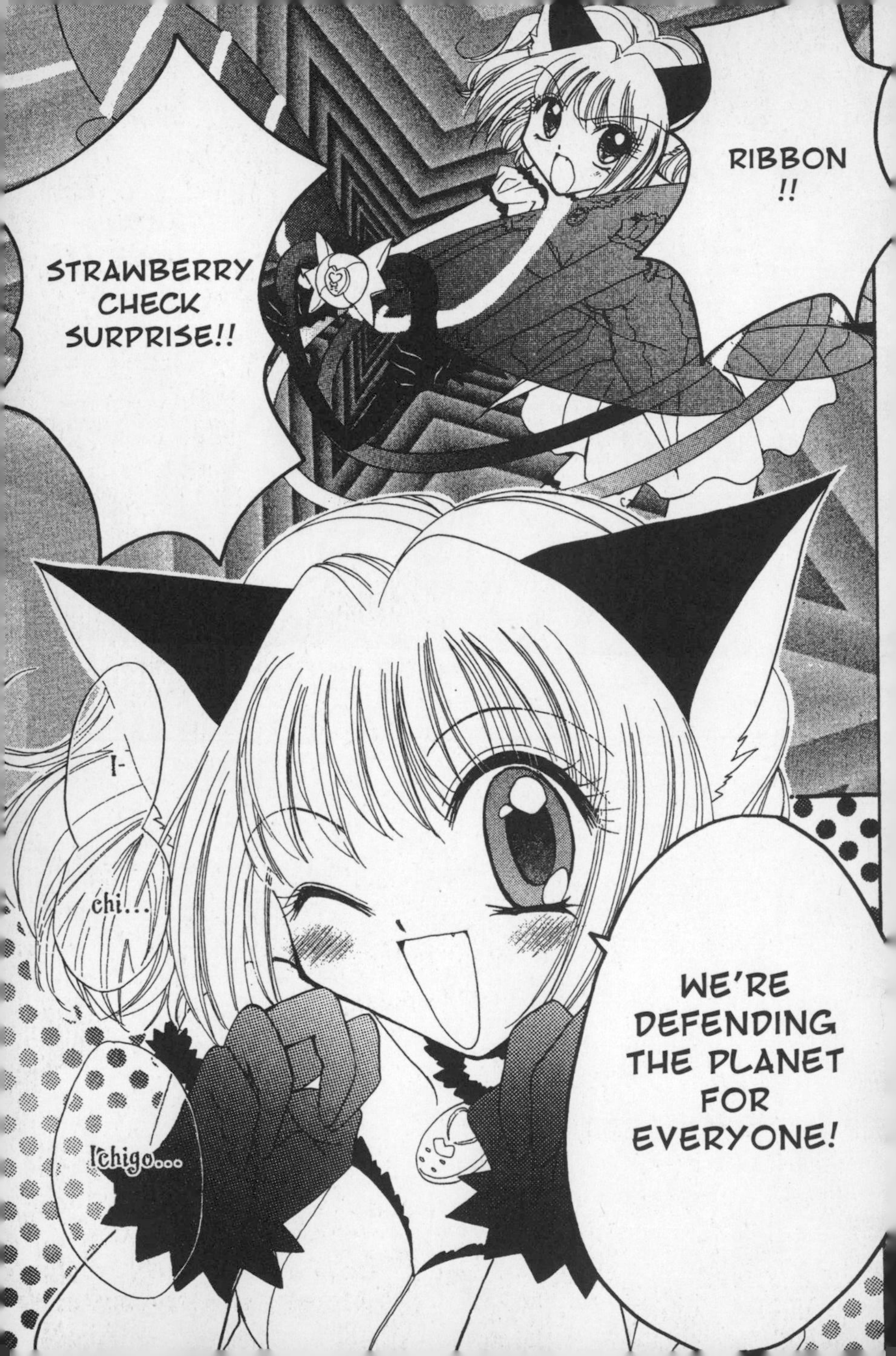
RIBBON !!
STRAWBERRY CHECK SURPRISE!!
WE'RE DEFENDING THE PLANET FOR EVERYONE!
I-
chi...
Ichigo...

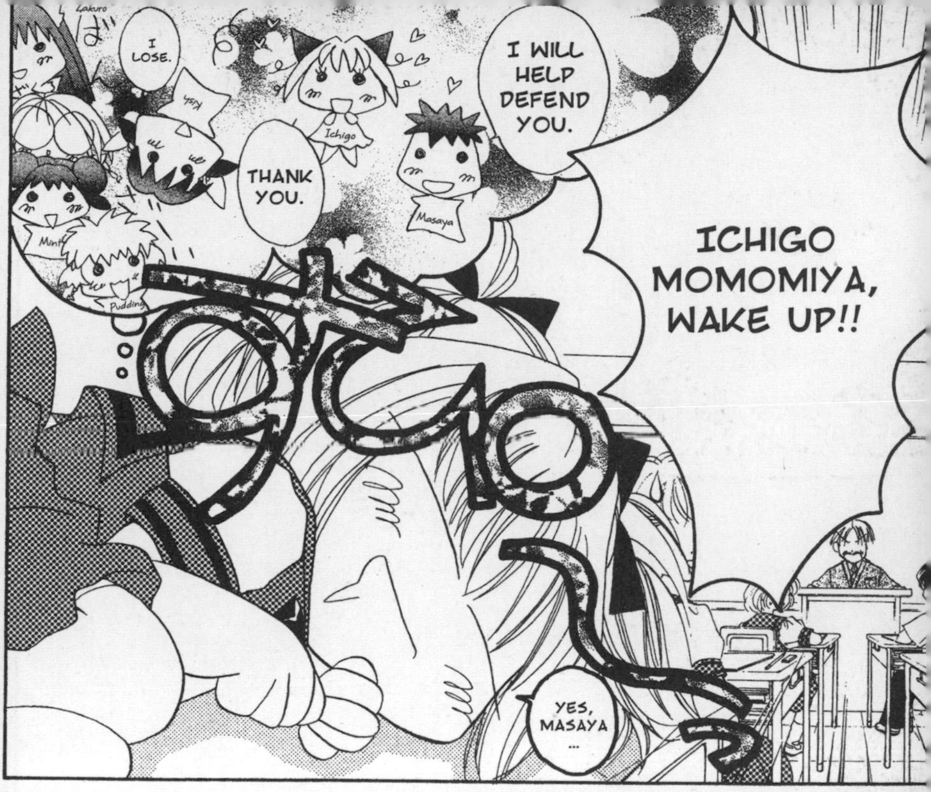
ICHIGO MOMOMIYA, WAKE UP!!
I WILL HELP DEFEND YOU.
Masaya
Ichigo
THANK YOU.
I LOSE.
Kish
Mint
Pudding
YES, MASAYA ...

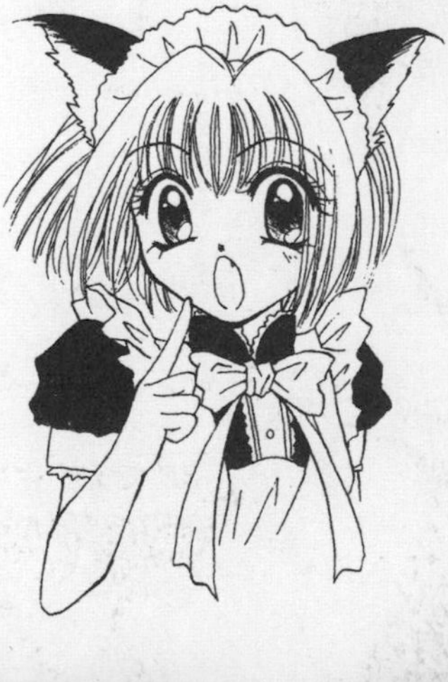

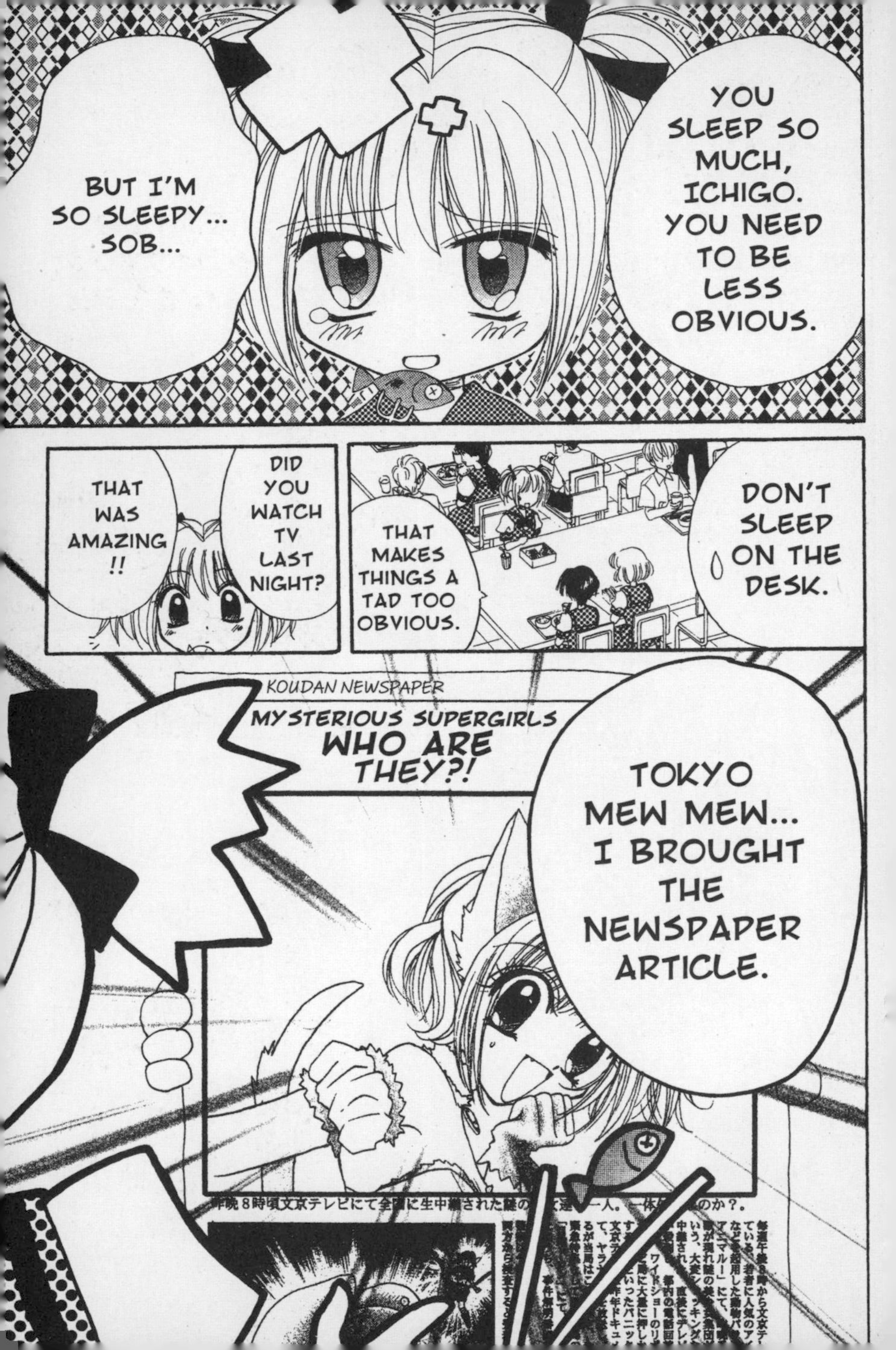
YOU SLEEP SO MUCH, ICHIGO. YOU NEED TO BE LESS OBVIOUS.
BUT I'M SO SLEEPY... SOB...
DON'T SLEEP ON THE DESK.
THAT MAKES THINGS A TAD TOO OBVIOUS.
DID YOU WATCH TV LAST NIGHT?
THAT WAS AMAZING!!
KOUDAN NEWSPAPER
MYSTERIOUS SUPERGIRLS
WHO ARE THEY?!
TOKYO MEW MEW... I BROUGHT THE NEWSPAPER ARTICLE.

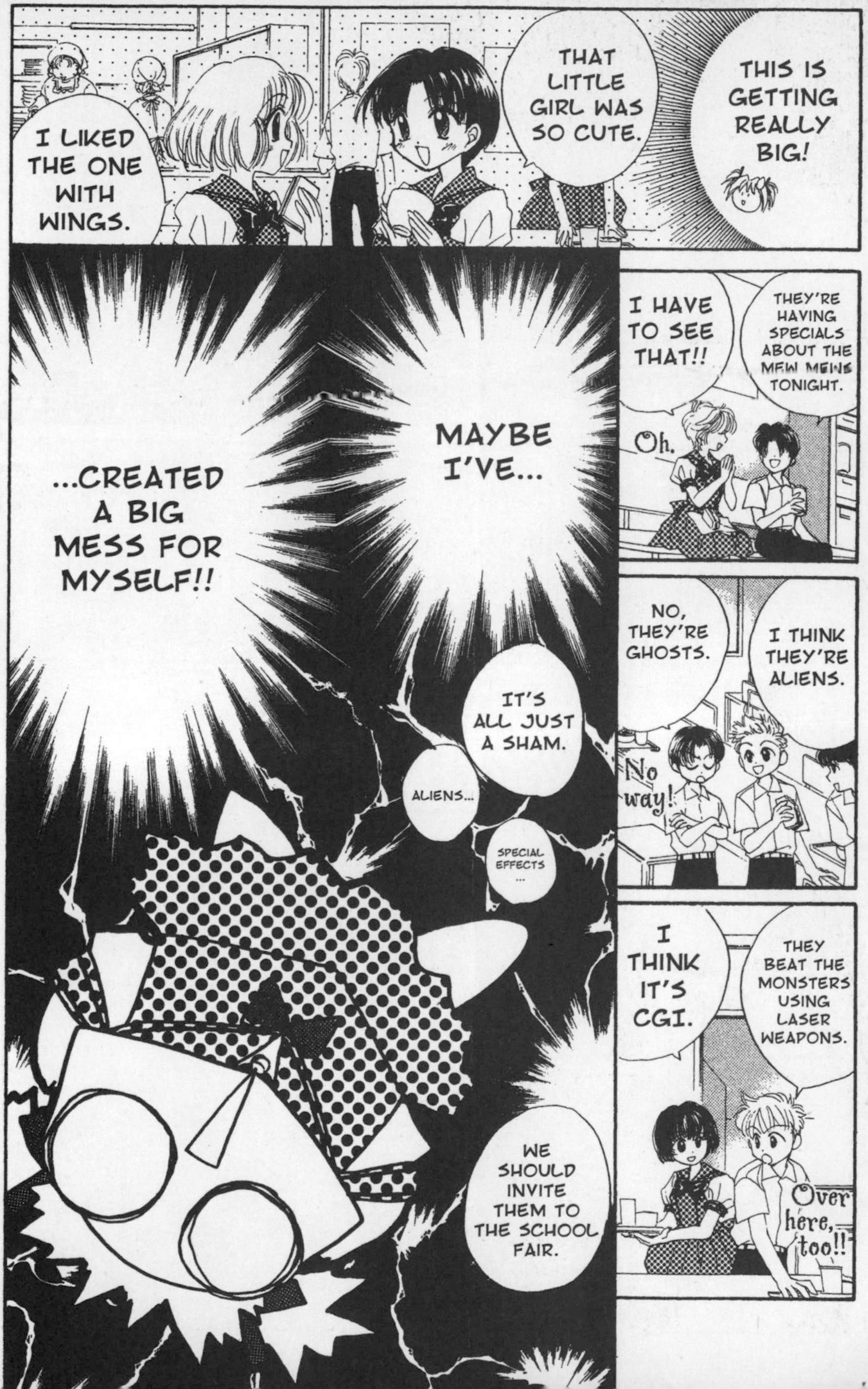
THIS IS GETTING REALLY BIG!
THAT LITTLE GIRL WAS SO CUTE.
I LIKED THE ONE WITH WINGS.
THEY'RE HAVING SPECIALS ABOUT THE MEW MEWS TONIGHT.
I HAVE TO SEE THAT!!
Oh.
I THINK THEY'RE ALIENS.
NO, THEY'RE GHOSTS.
No way!
THEY BEAT THE MONSTERS USING LASER WEAPONS.
I THINK IT'S CGI.
Over here, too!!
MAYBE I'VE...
...CREATED A BIG MESS FOR MYSELF!!
IT'S ALL JUST A SHAM.
ALIENS...
SPECIAL EFFECTS...
WE SHOULD INVITE THEM TO THE SCHOOL FAIR.

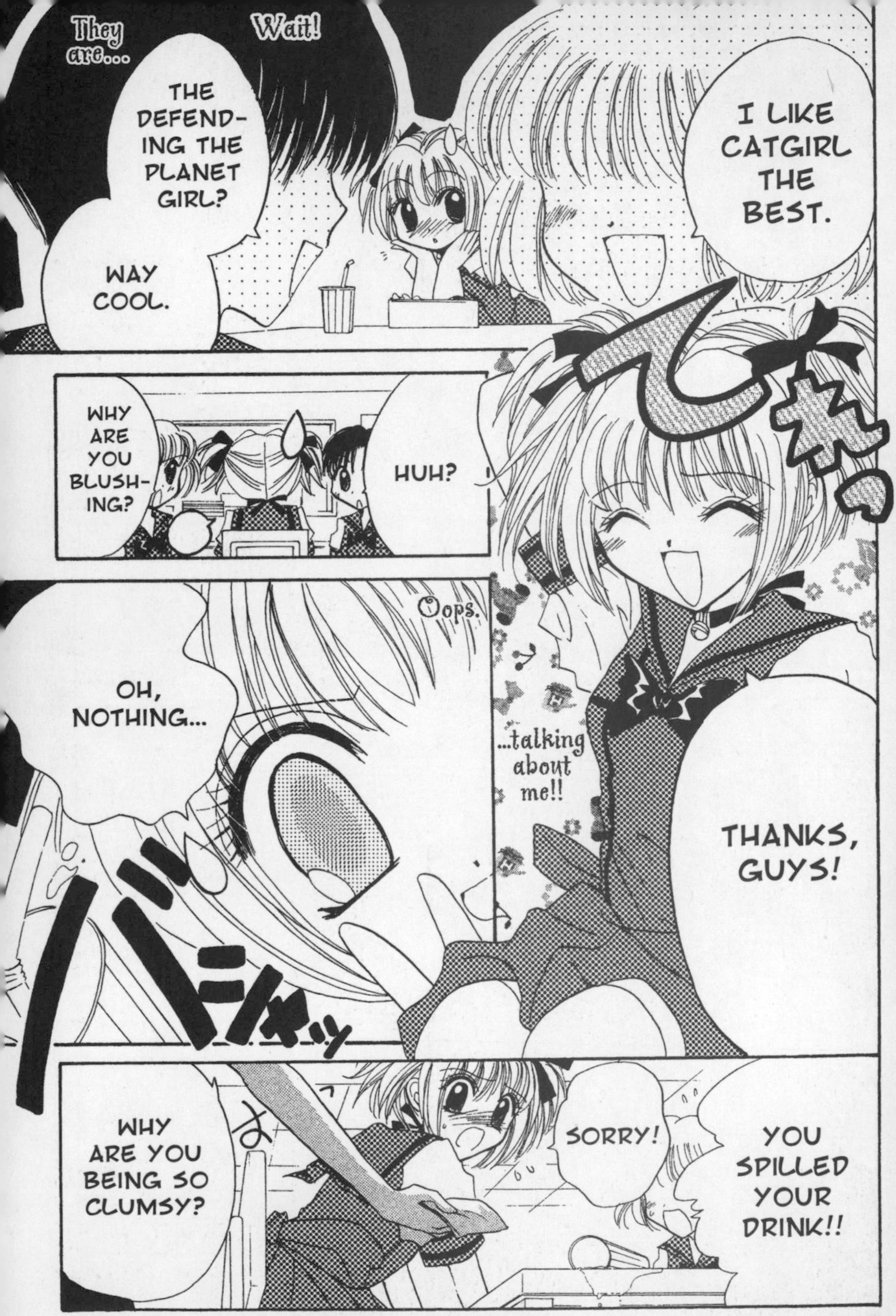

I LIKE CATGIRL THE BEST.
Wait!
They are...
THE DEFENDING THE PLANET GIRL?
WAY COOL.
...talking about me!!
THANKS, GUYS!
HUH?
WHY ARE YOU BLUSHING?
Oops.
OH, NOTHING...
YOU SPILLED YOUR DRINK!!
SORRY!
WHY ARE YOU BEING SO CLUMSY?

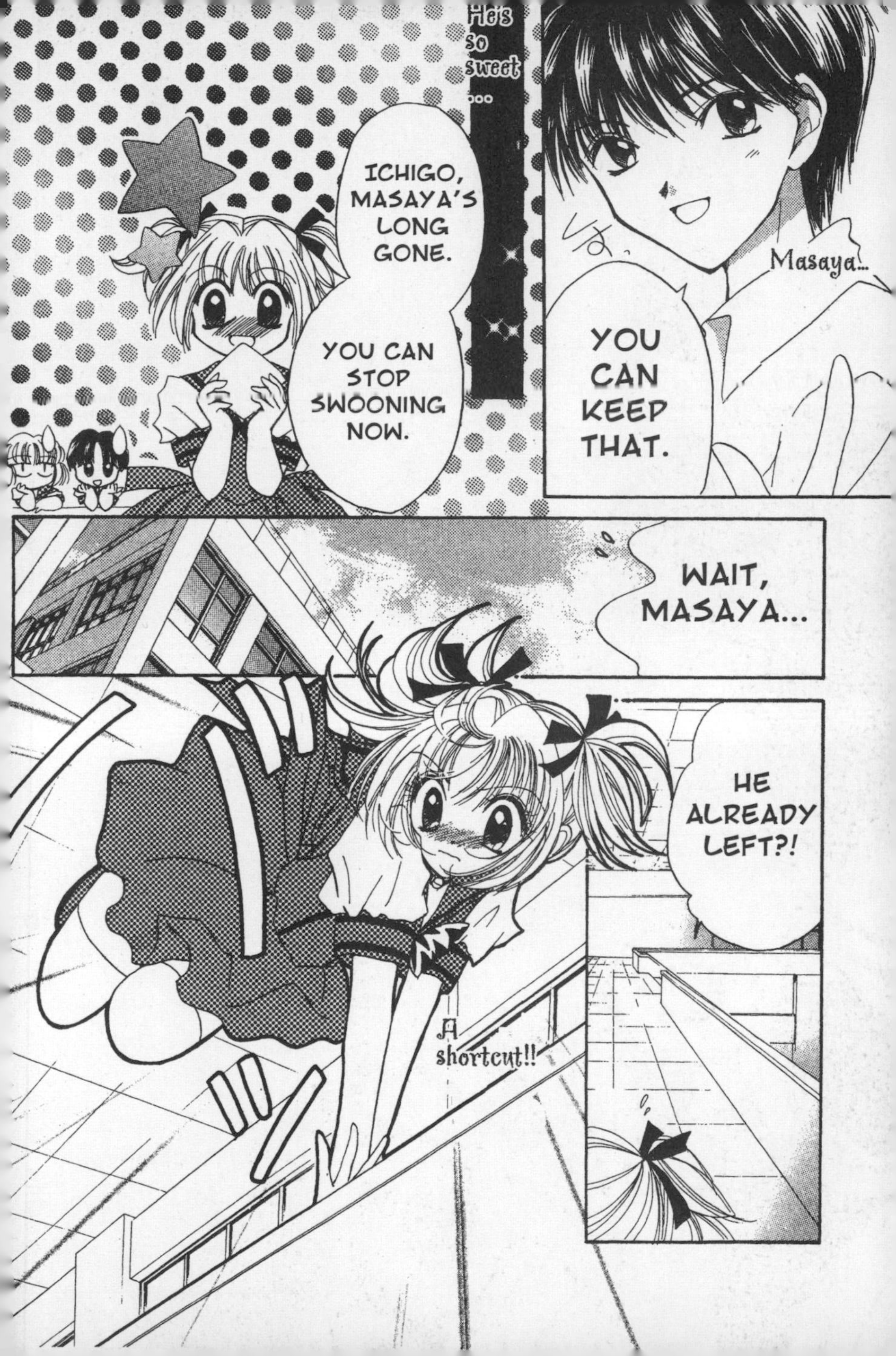
Masaya...
YOU CAN KEEP THAT.
He's so sweet...
ICHIGO, MASAYA'S LONG GONE.
YOU CAN STOP SWOONING NOW.
WAIT, MASAYA...
HE ALREADY LEFT?!
A shortcut!!

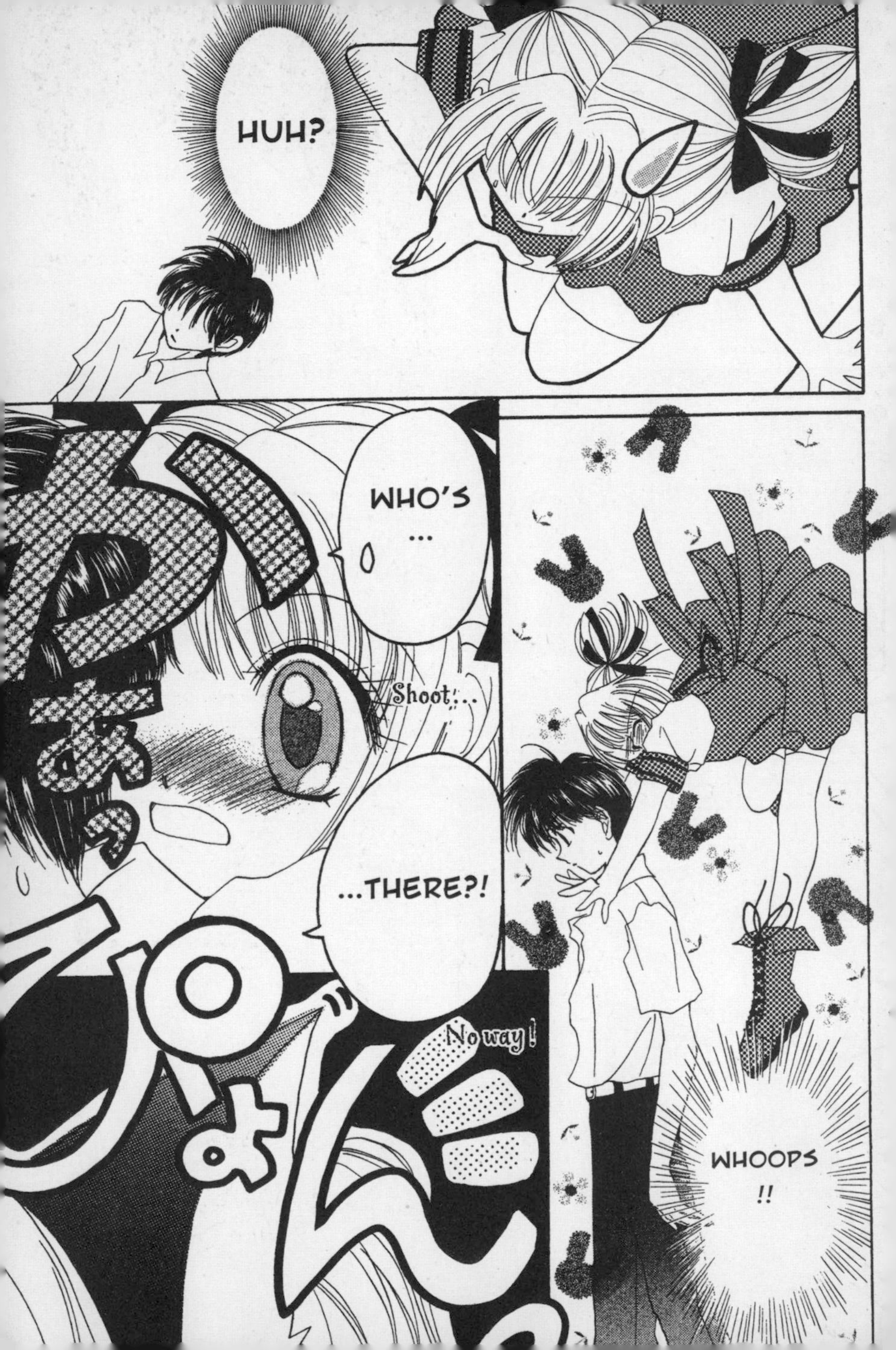
HUH?
WHOOPS !!
WHO'S ...
Shoot...
...THERE?!
No way!

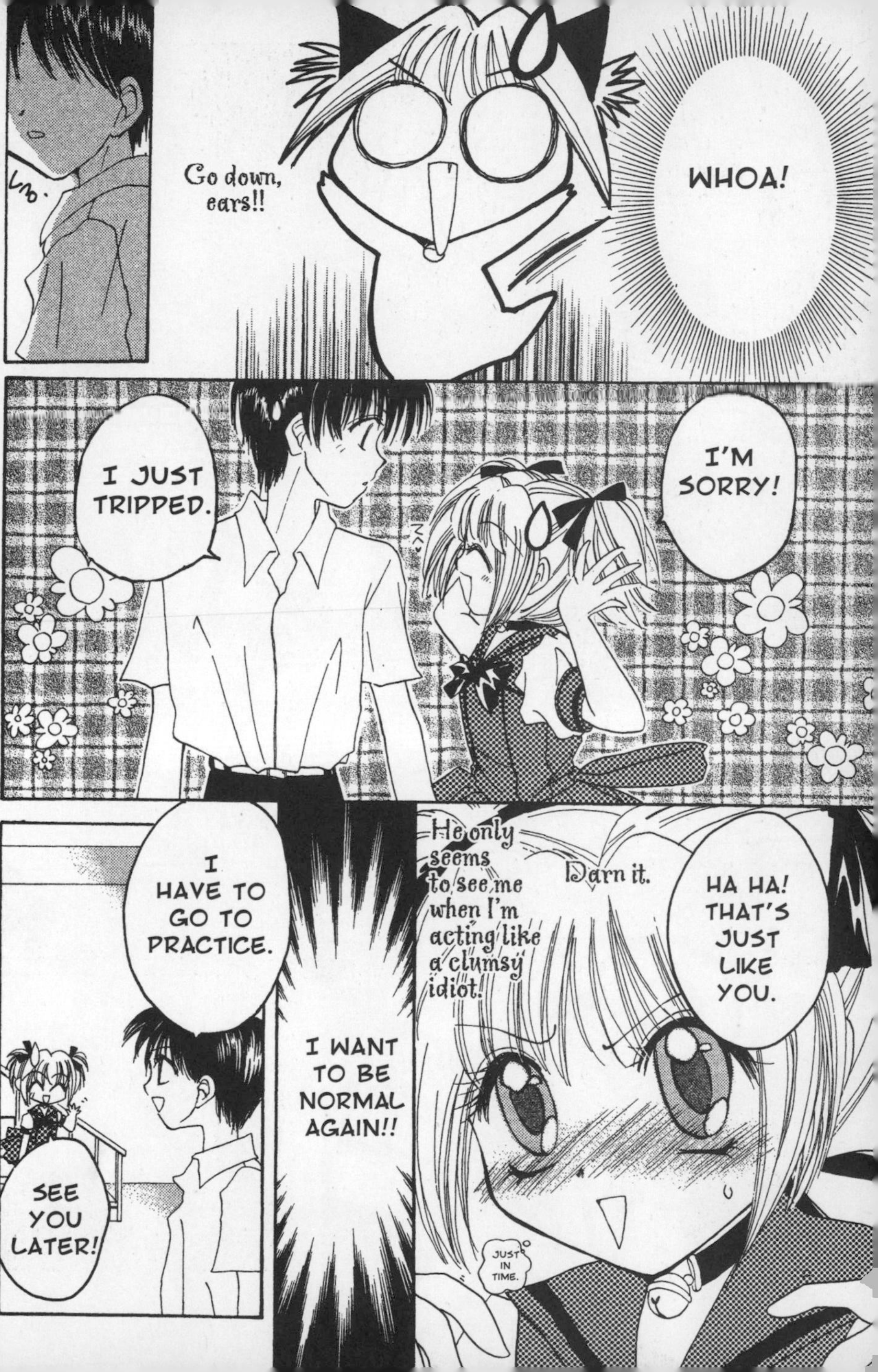
WHOA!
Go down, ears!!
I'M SORRY!
I JUST TRIPPED.
HA HA! THAT'S JUST LIKE YOU.
Darn it.
He only seems to see me when I'm acting like a clumsy idiot.
JUST IN TIME.
I WANT TO BE NORMAL AGAIN!!
I HAVE TO GO TO PRACTICE.
SEE YOU LATER!

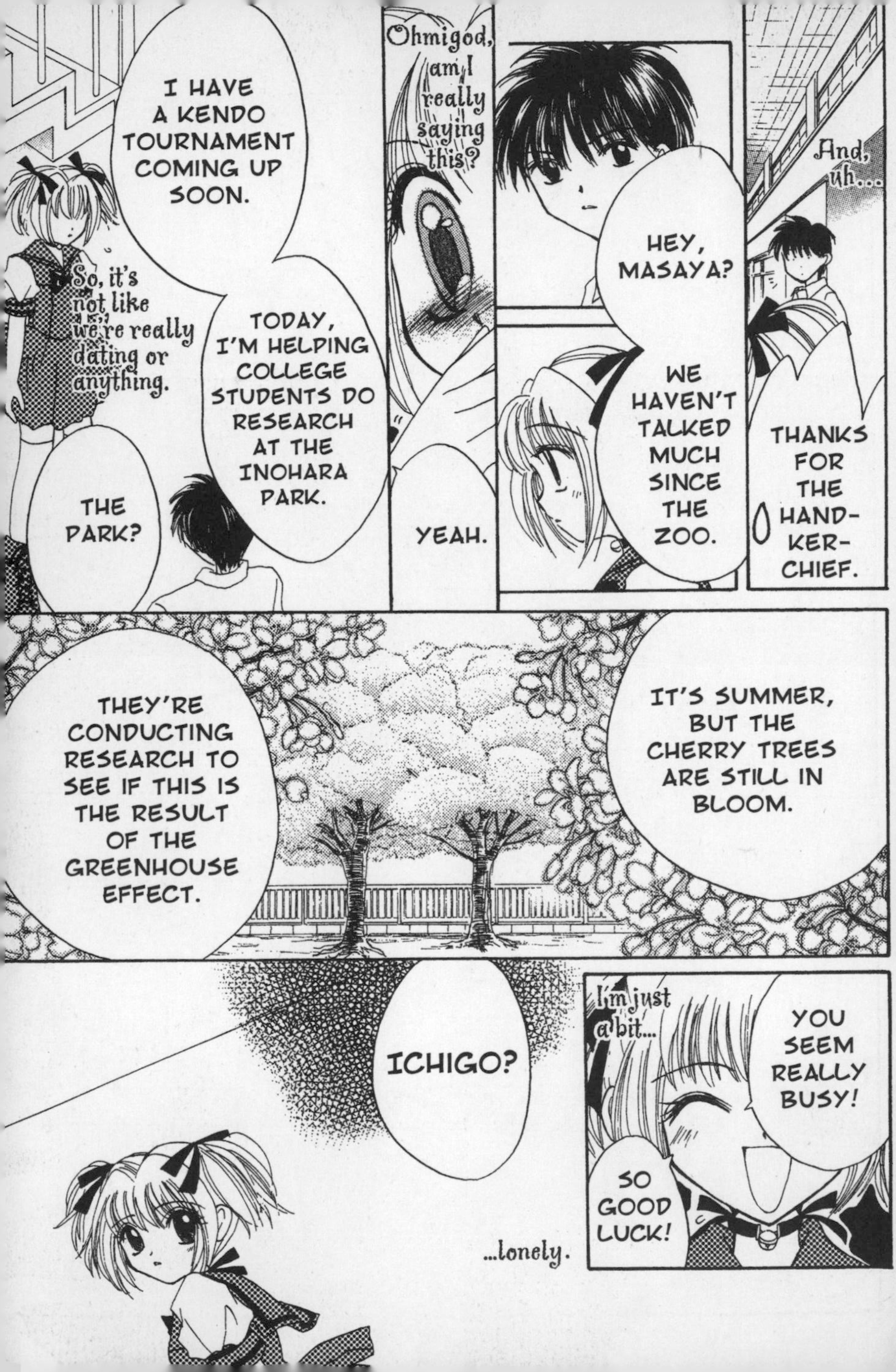
And, uh...
THANKS FOR THE HAND-KER-CHIEF.
HEY, MASAYA?
WE HAVEN'T TALKED MUCH SINCE THE ZOO.
Ohmigod, am I really saying this?
YEAH.
I HAVE A KENDO TOURNAMENT COMING UP SOON.
TODAY, I'M HELPING COLLEGE STUDENTS DO RESEARCH AT THE INOHARA PARK.
THE PARK?
So, it's not like we're really dating or anything.
IT'S SUMMER, BUT THE CHERRY TREES ARE STILL IN BLOOM.
THEY'RE CONDUCTING RESEARCH TO SEE IF THIS IS THE RESULT OF THE GREENHOUSE EFFECT.
YOU SEEM REALLY BUSY!
SO GOOD LUCK!
I'm just a bit...
ICHIGO?
...lonely.

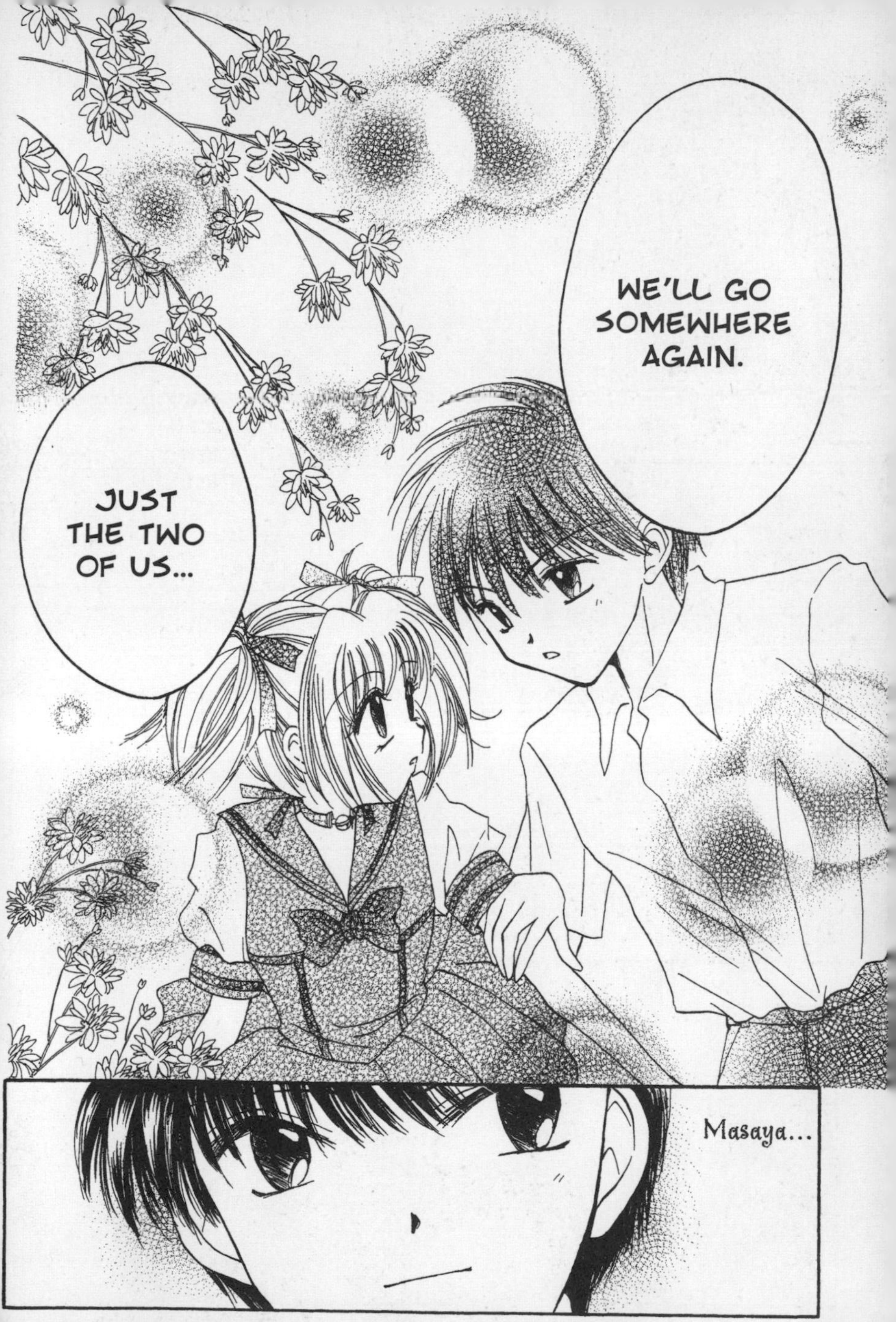
WE'LL GO SOMEWHERE AGAIN.
JUST THE TWO OF US...
Masaya...

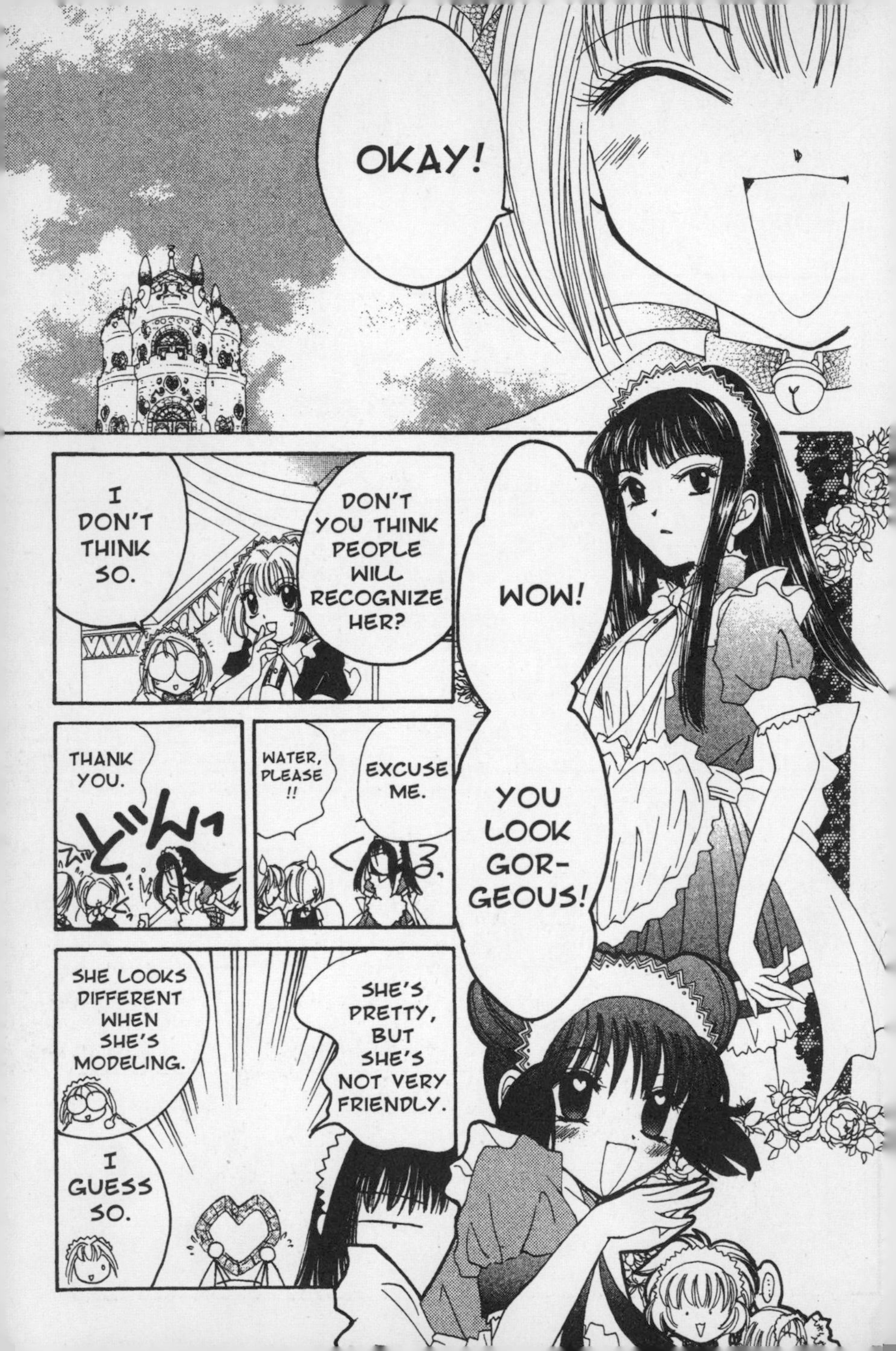
OKAY!
WOW!
YOU LOOK GORGEOUS!
DON'T YOU THINK PEOPLE WILL RECOGNIZE HER?
I DON'T THINK SO.
EXCUSE ME.
WATER, PLEASE!!
THANK YOU.
どん
SHE'S PRETTY, BUT SHE'S NOT VERY FRIENDLY.
SHE LOOKS DIFFERENT WHEN SHE'S MODELING.
I GUESS SO.

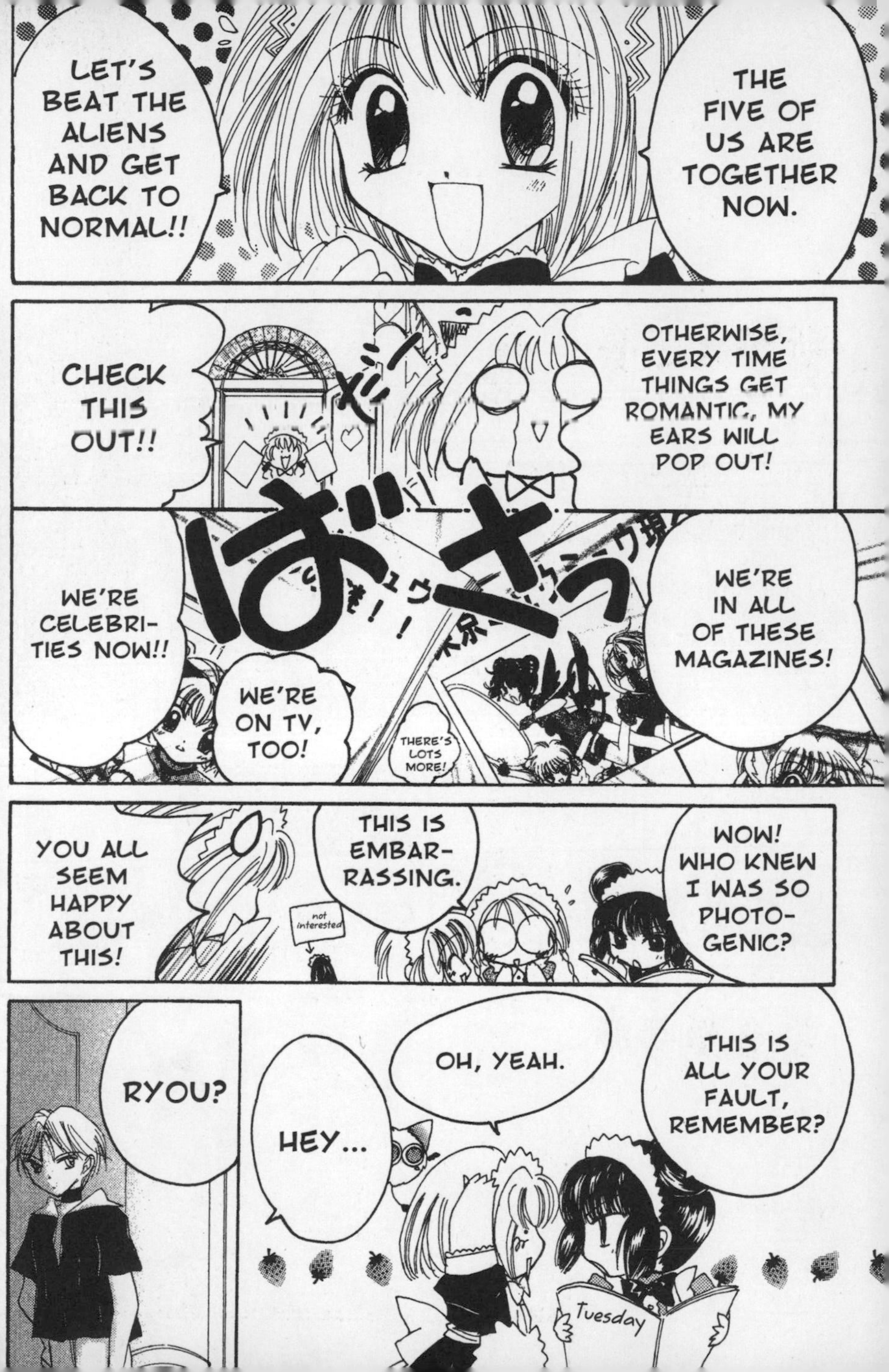
THE FIVE OF US ARE TOGETHER NOW.
LET'S BEAT THE ALIENS AND GET BACK TO NORMAL!!
OTHERWISE, EVERY TIME THINGS GET ROMANTIC, MY EARS WILL POP OUT!
CHECK THIS OUT!!
WE'RE IN ALL OF THESE MAGAZINES!
THERE'S LOTS MORE!
WE'RE ON TV, TOO!
WE'RE CELEBRITIES NOW!!
WOW! WHO KNEW I WAS SO PHOTOGENIC?
THIS IS EMBARRASSING.
not interested
YOU ALL SEEM HAPPY ABOUT THIS!
THIS IS ALL YOUR FAULT, REMEMBER?
OH, YEAH.
HEY...
RYOU?
Tuesday

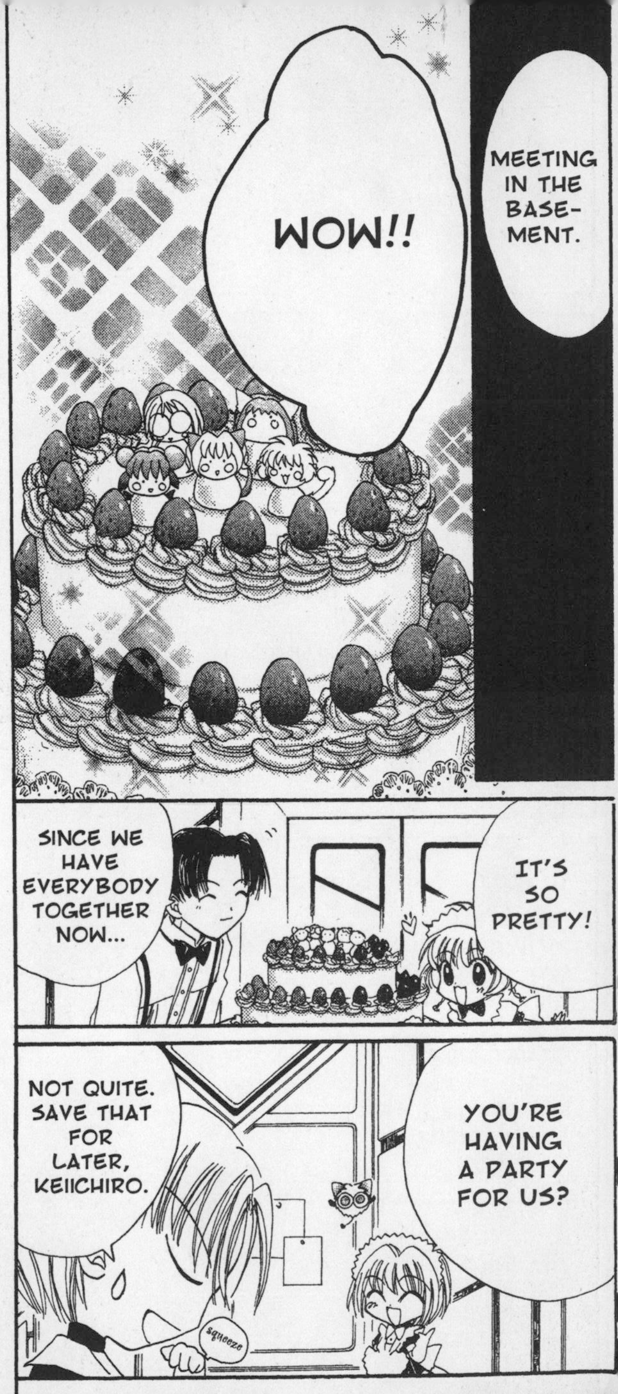
MEETING IN THE BASEMENT.
WOW!!
IT'S SO PRETTY!
SINCE WE HAVE EVERYBODY TOGETHER NOW...
YOU'RE HAVING A PARTY FOR US?
NOT QUITE. SAVE THAT FOR LATER, KEIICHIRO.
squeeze

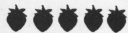

SPECIAL THANKS!!

REIKO YOSHIDA

RIMO MIDORIKAWA
MADOKA OMORI

HIDEAKI OIKAWA

HIJIRI MATSUMOTO
AYA SUZUKI

IZUMI UEDA

ASUMI HARA

M.SEKIYA
T.KAMAGATA

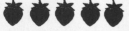

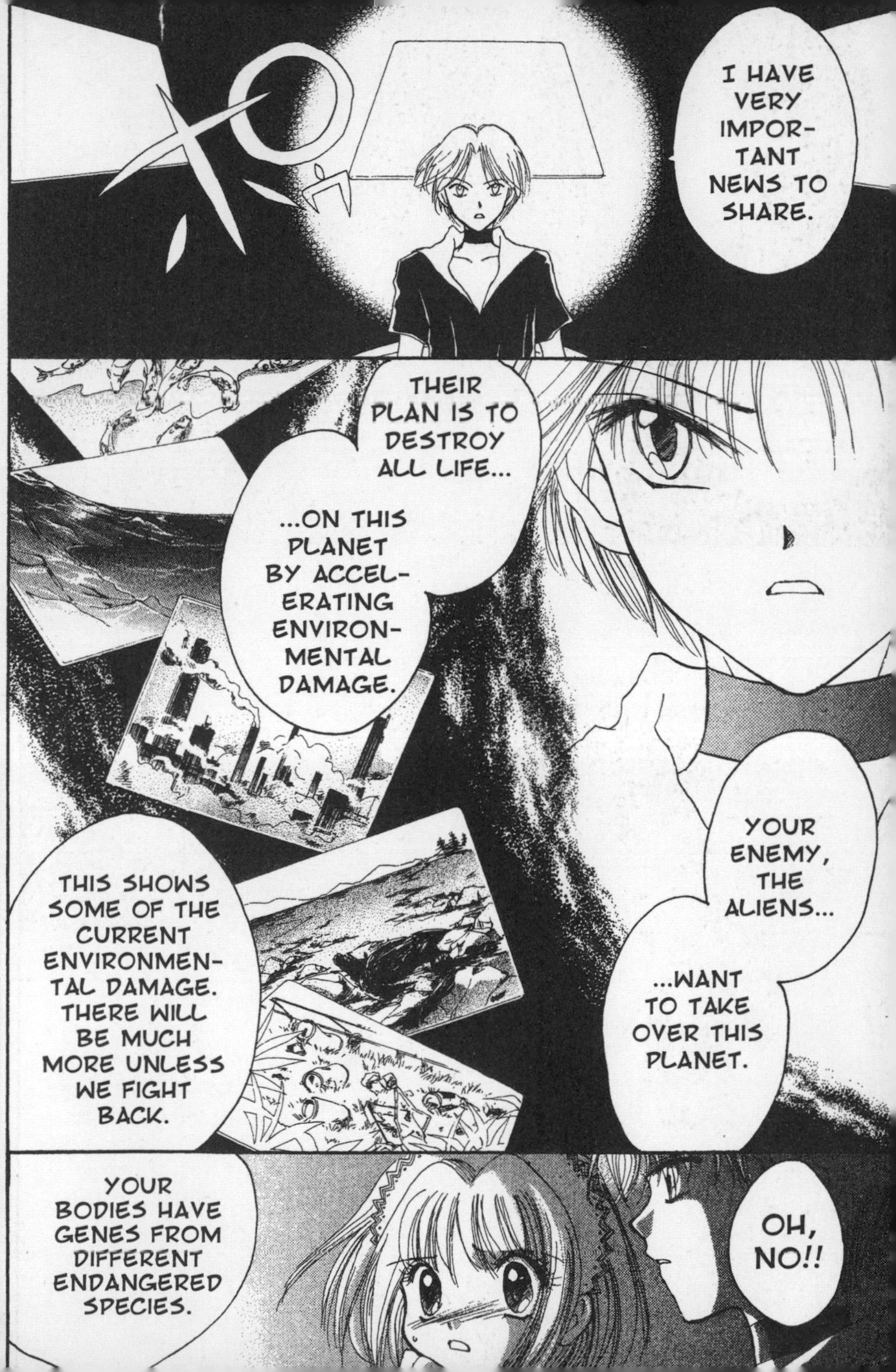
I HAVE VERY IMPOR-TANT NEWS TO SHARE.
YOUR ENEMY, THE ALIENS...
...WANT TO TAKE OVER THIS PLANET.
THEIR PLAN IS TO DESTROY ALL LIFE...
...ON THIS PLANET BY ACCEL-ERATING ENVIRON-MENTAL DAMAGE.
THIS SHOWS SOME OF THE CURRENT ENVIRONMEN-TAL DAMAGE. THERE WILL BE MUCH MORE UNLESS WE FIGHT BACK.
OH, NO!!
YOUR BODIES HAVE GENES FROM DIFFERENT ENDANGERED SPECIES.

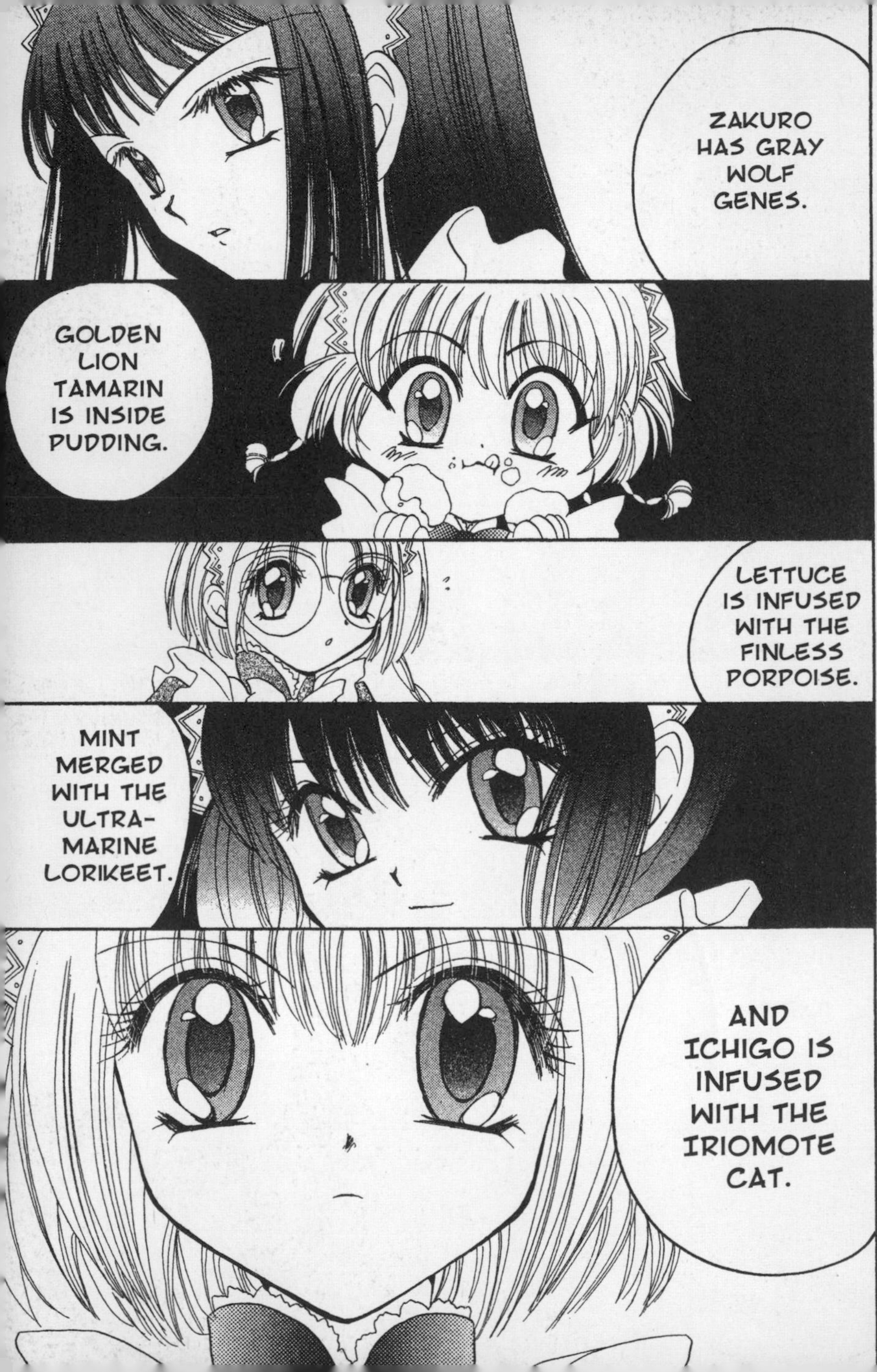
ZAKURO HAS GRAY WOLF GENES.
GOLDEN LION TAMARIN IS INSIDE PUDDING.
LETTUCE IS INFUSED WITH THE FINLESS PORPOISE.
MINT MERGED WITH THE ULTRA-MARINE LORIKEET.
AND ICHIGO IS INFUSED WITH THE IRIOMOTE CAT.

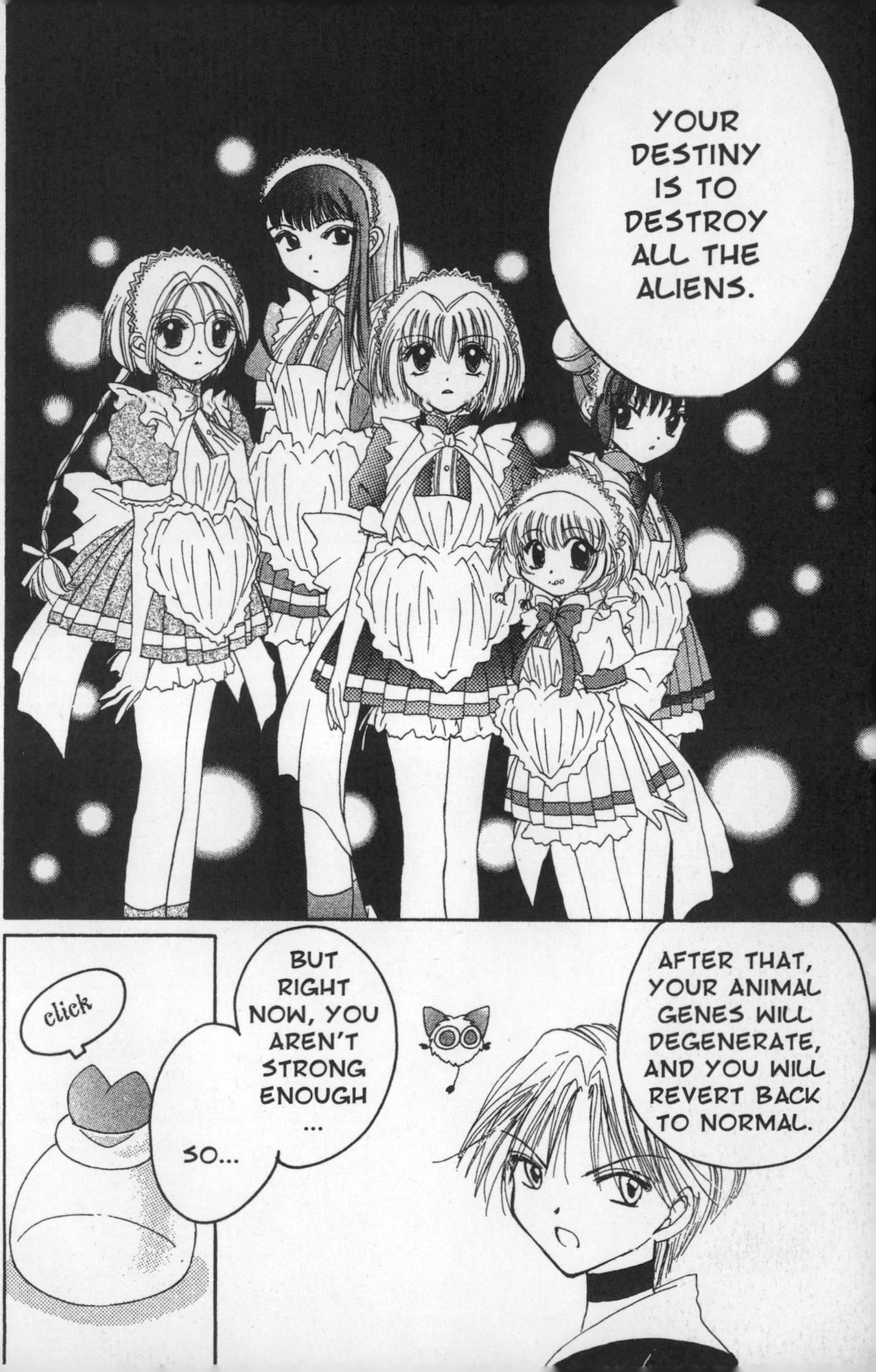
YOUR DESTINY IS TO DESTROY ALL THE ALIENS.
AFTER THAT, YOUR ANIMAL GENES WILL DEGENERATE, AND YOU WILL REVERT BACK TO NORMAL.
BUT RIGHT NOW, YOU AREN'T STRONG ENOUGH ...
SO...
click

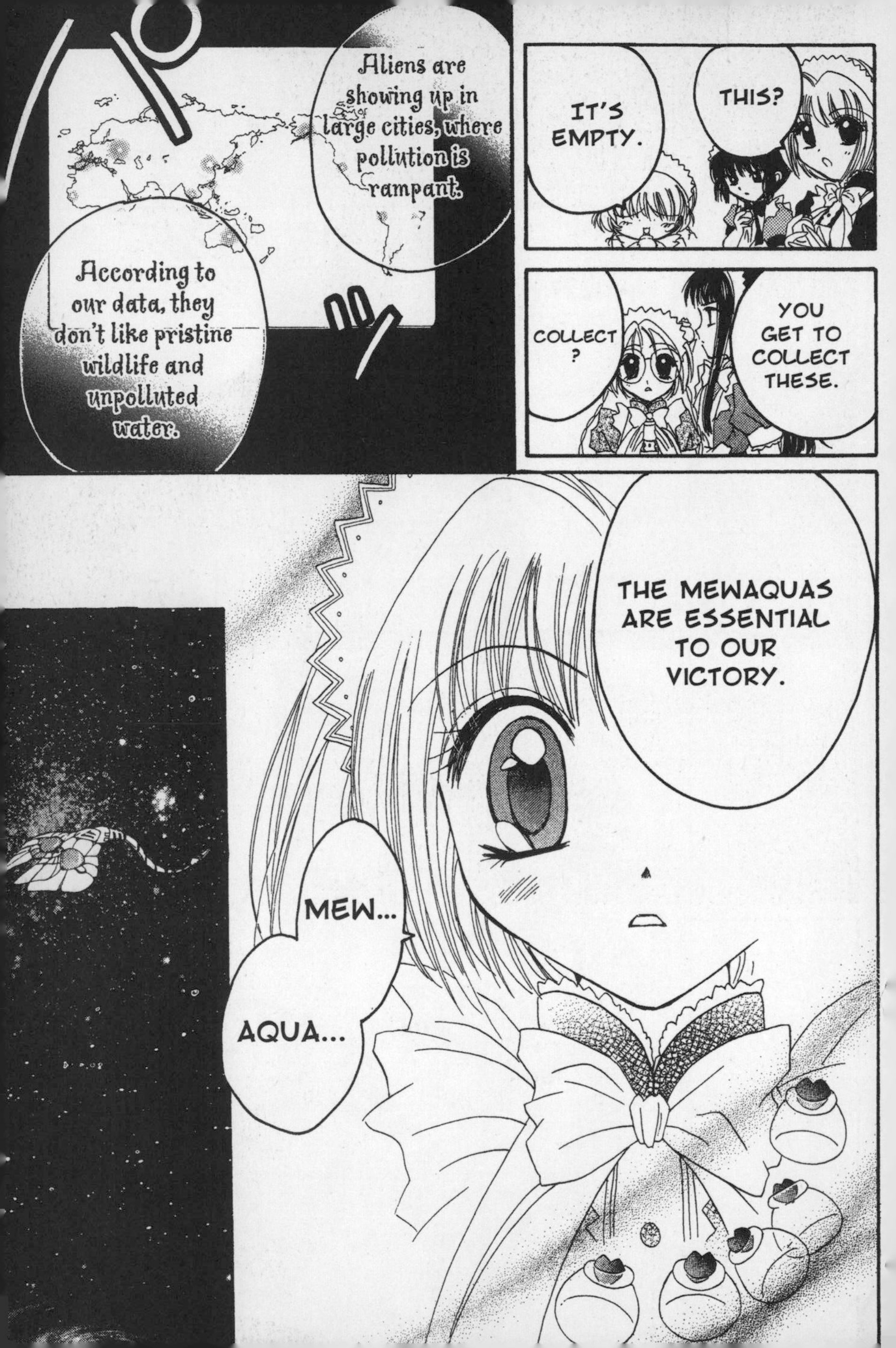
THIS?
IT'S EMPTY.
YOU GET TO COLLECT THESE.
COLLECT?
Aliens are showing up in large cities, where pollution is rampant.
According to our data, they don't like pristine wildlife and unpolluted water.
THE MEWAQUAS ARE ESSENTIAL TO OUR VICTORY.
MEW...
AQUA...

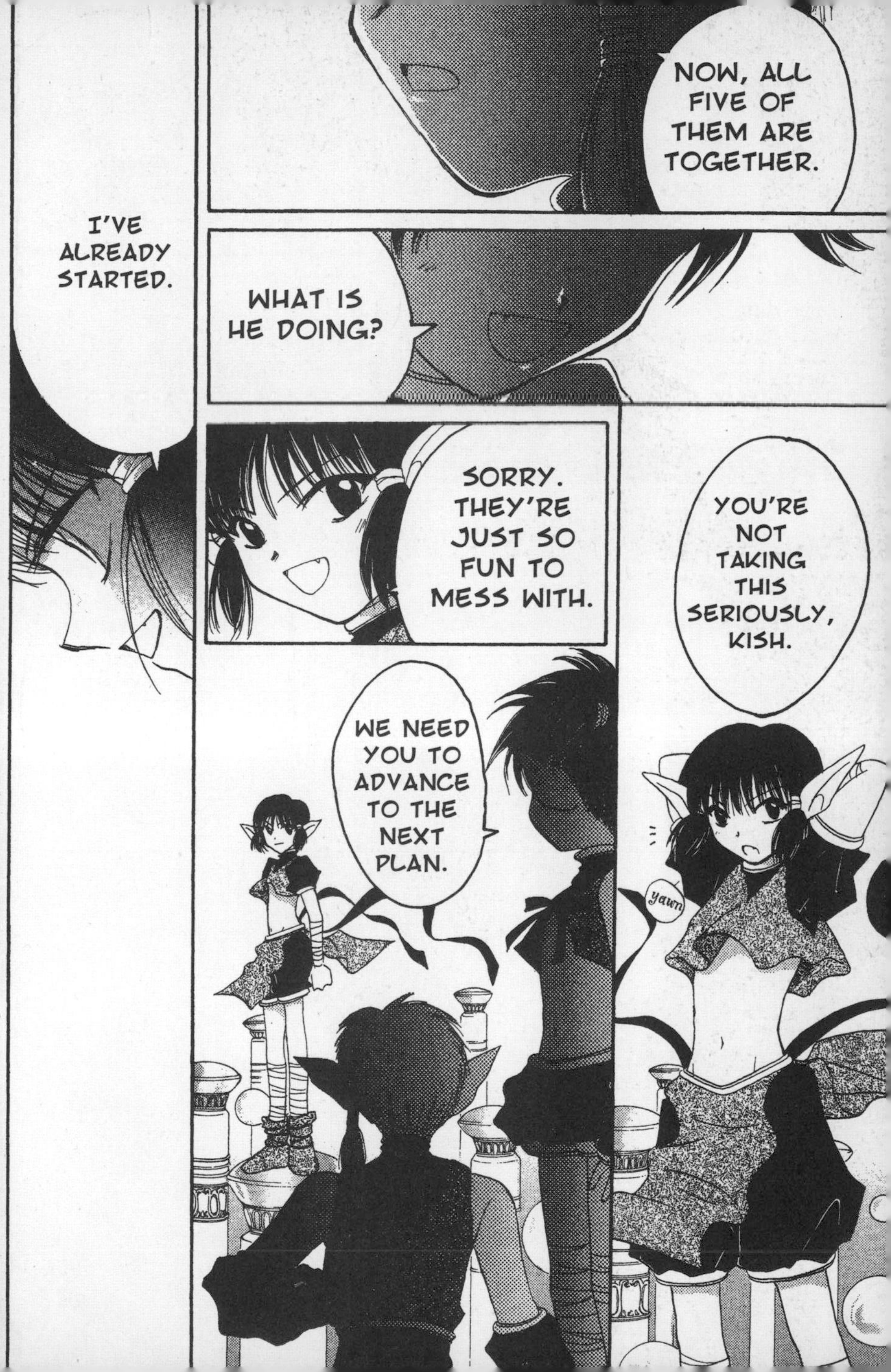
NOW, ALL FIVE OF THEM ARE TOGETHER.
WHAT IS HE DOING?
YOU'RE NOT TAKING THIS SERIOUSLY, KISH.
yawn
SORRY. THEY'RE JUST SO FUN TO MESS WITH.
WE NEED YOU TO ADVANCE TO THE NEXT PLAN.
I'VE ALREADY STARTED.

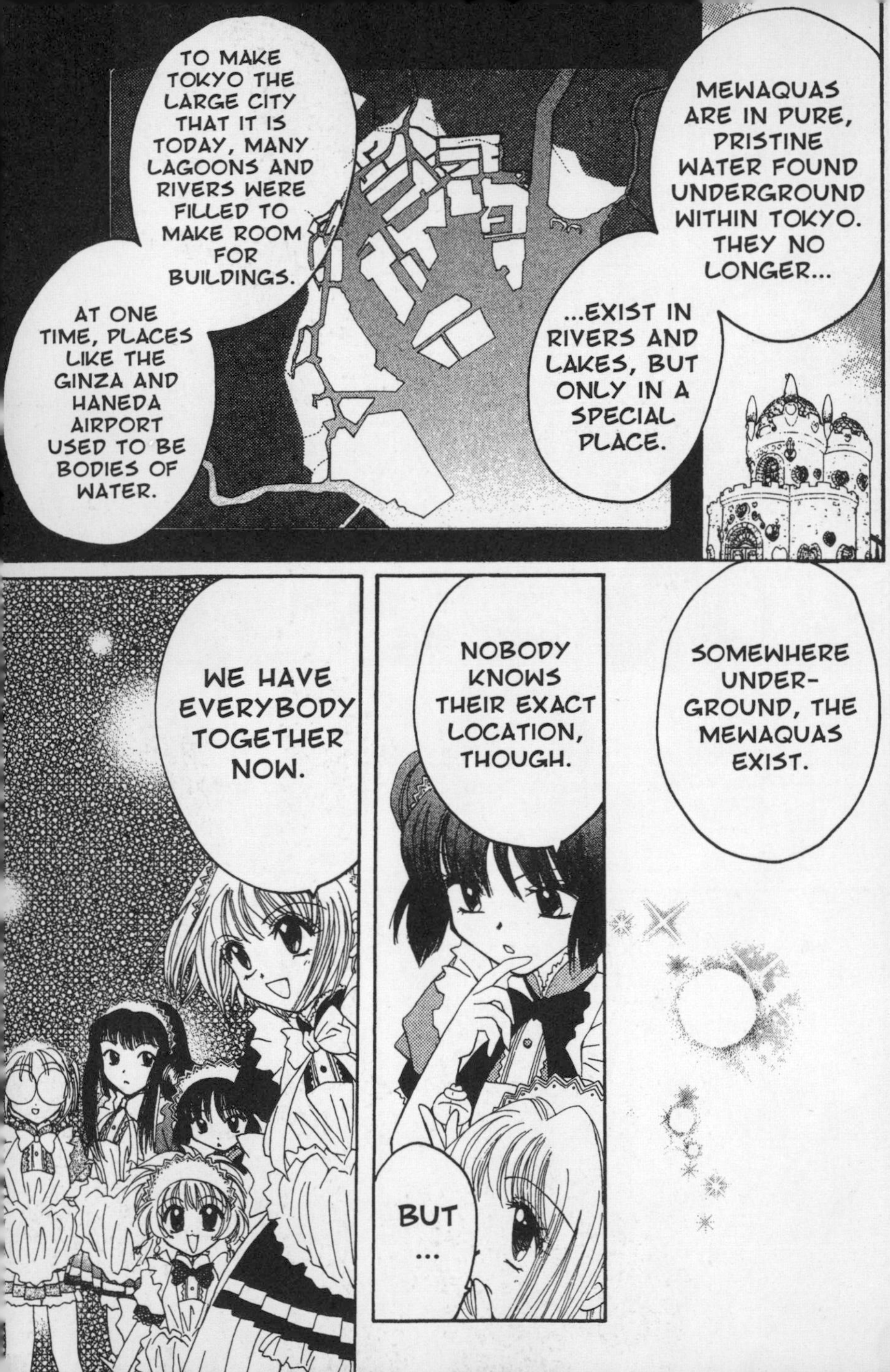
MEWAQUAS ARE IN PURE, PRISTINE WATER FOUND UNDERGROUND WITHIN TOKYO. THEY NO LONGER...
...EXIST IN RIVERS AND LAKES, BUT ONLY IN A SPECIAL PLACE.
TO MAKE TOKYO THE LARGE CITY THAT IT IS TODAY, MANY LAGOONS AND RIVERS WERE FILLED TO MAKE ROOM FOR BUILDINGS.
AT ONE TIME, PLACES LIKE THE GINZA AND HANEDA AIRPORT USED TO BE BODIES OF WATER.
SOMEWHERE UNDER-GROUND, THE MEWAQUAS EXIST.
NOBODY KNOWS THEIR EXACT LOCATION, THOUGH.
BUT ...
WE HAVE EVERYBODY TOGETHER NOW.

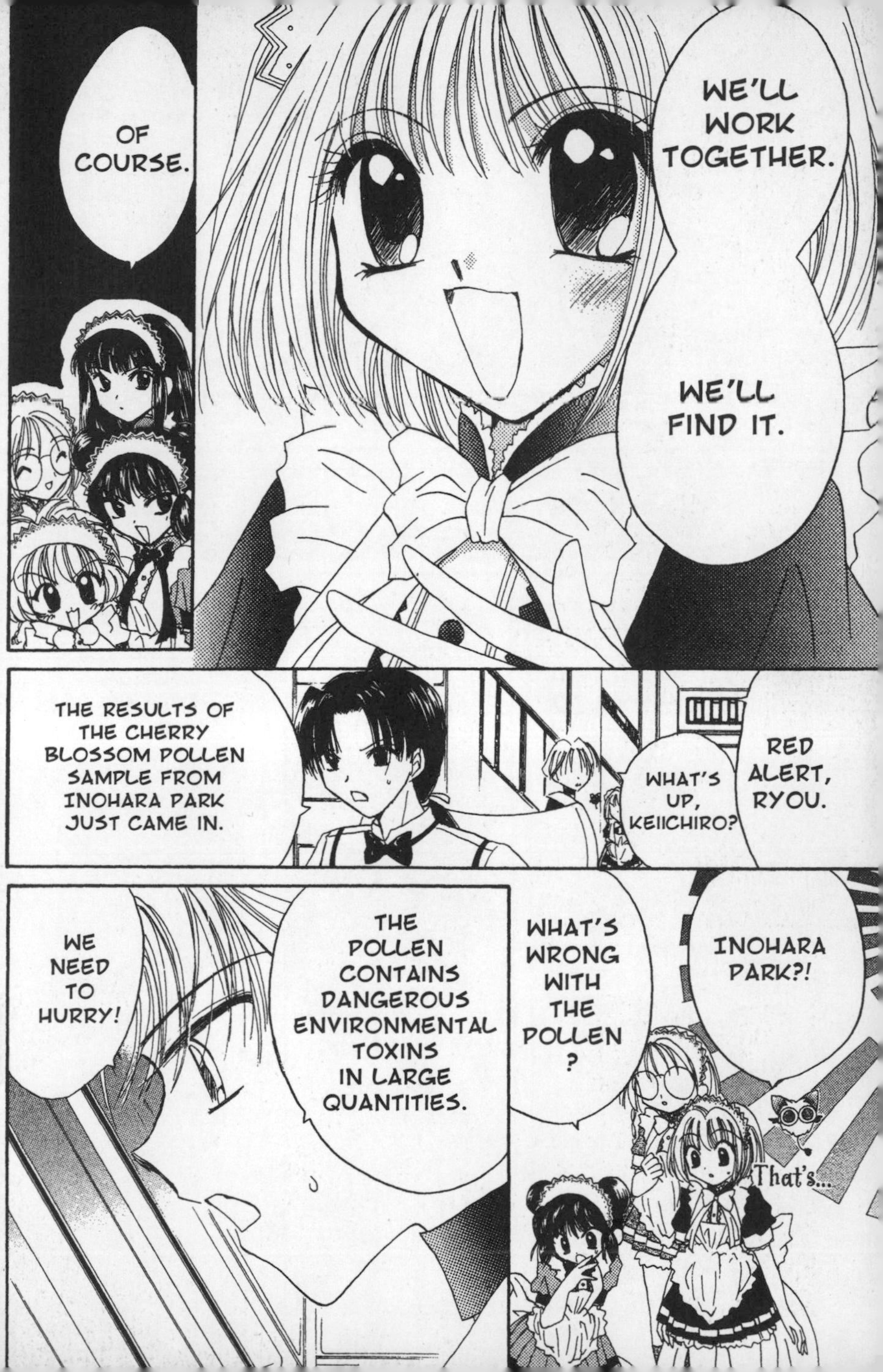
WE'LL WORK TOGETHER.
WE'LL FIND IT.
OF COURSE.
RED ALERT, RYOU.
WHAT'S UP, KEIICHIRO?
THE RESULTS OF THE CHERRY BLOSSOM POLLEN SAMPLE FROM INOHARA PARK JUST CAME IN.
INOHARA PARK?!
That's...
WHAT'S WRONG WITH THE POLLEN?
THE POLLEN CONTAINS DANGEROUS ENVIRONMENTAL TOXINS IN LARGE QUANTITIES.
WE NEED TO HURRY!

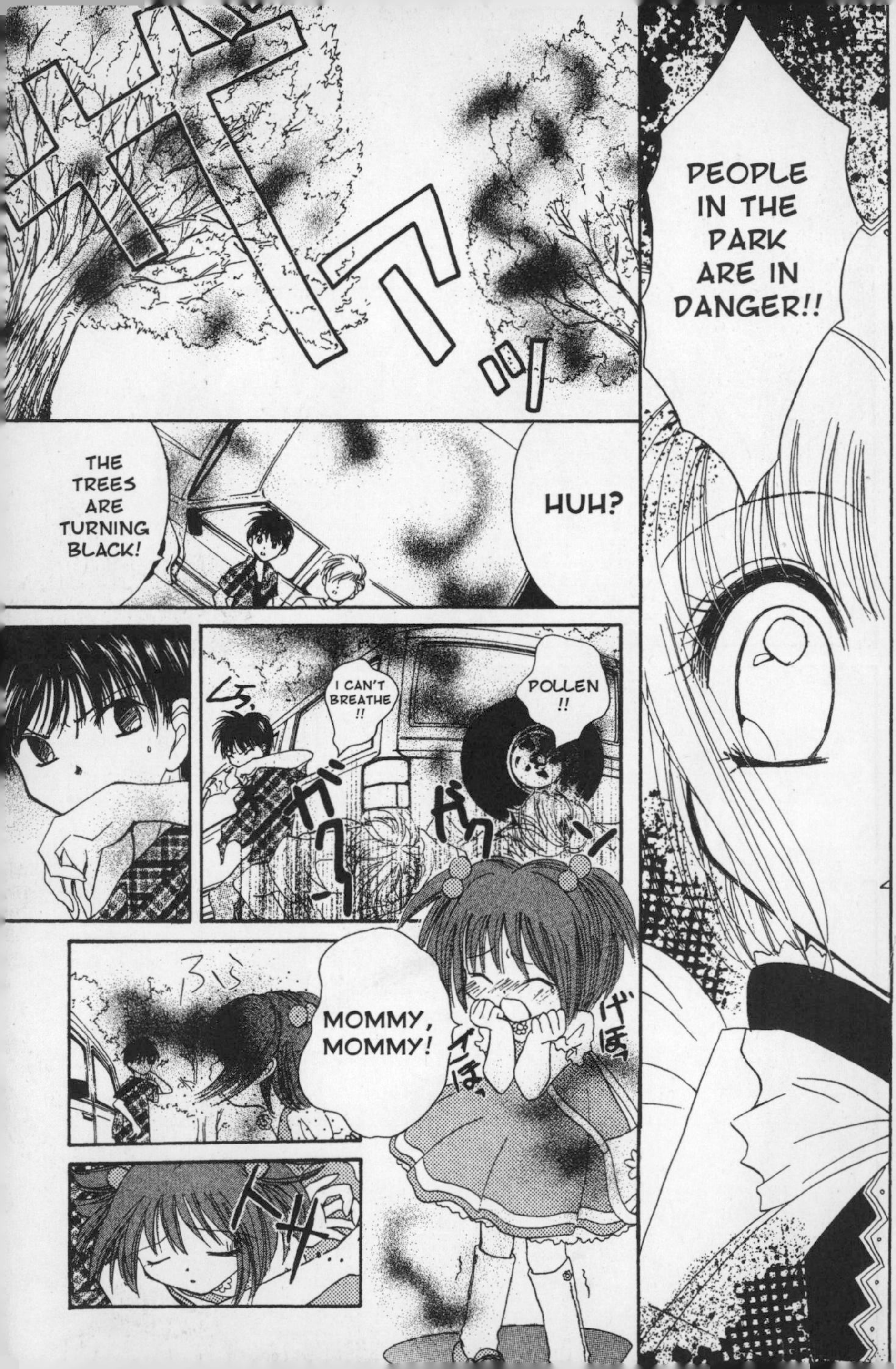
PEOPLE IN THE PARK ARE IN DANGER!!
HUH?
THE TREES ARE TURNING BLACK!
POLLEN!!
I CAN'T BREATHE!!
MOMMY, MOMMY!

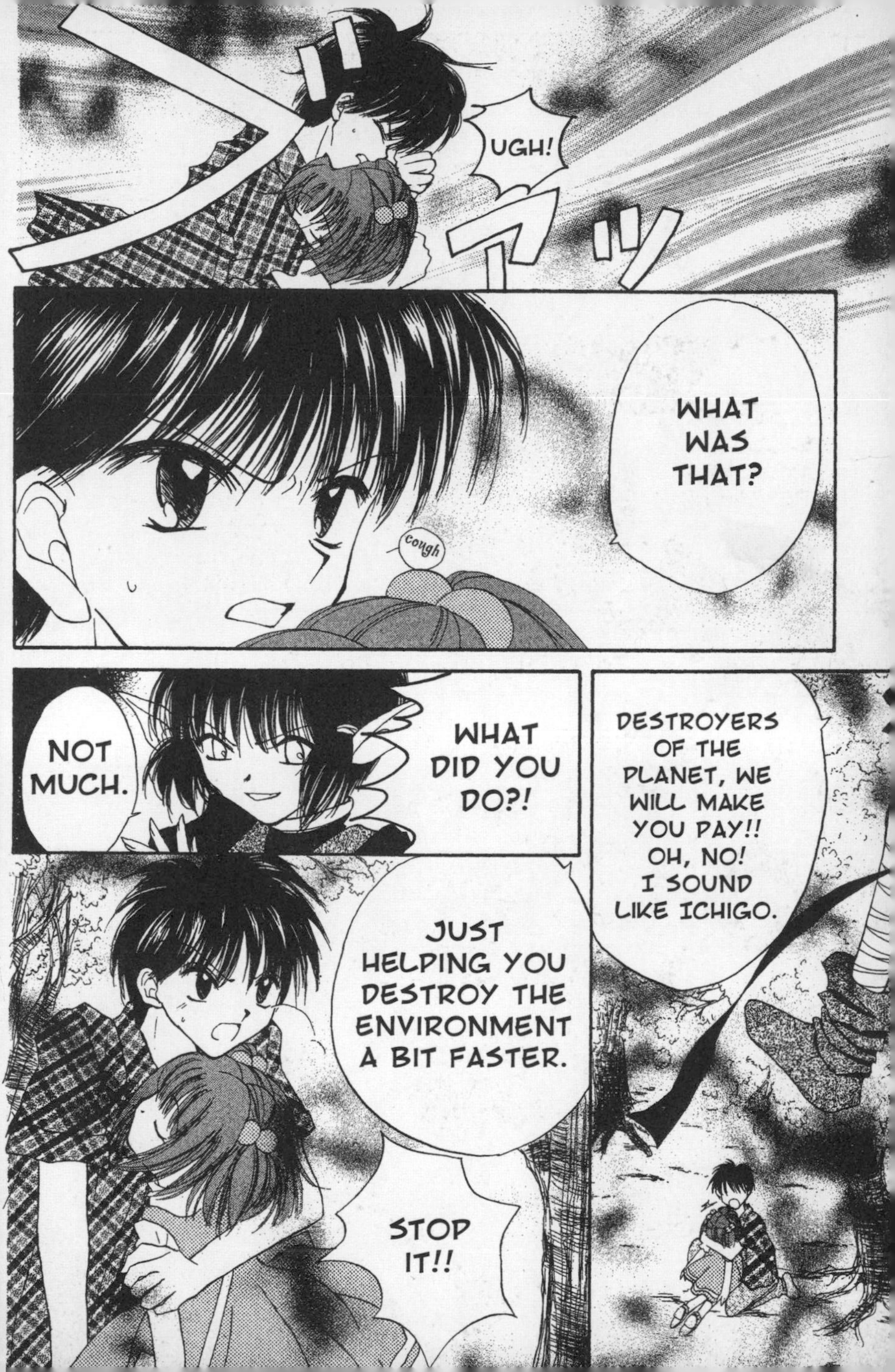
UGH!
WHAT WAS THAT?
cough
DESTROYERS OF THE PLANET, WE WILL MAKE YOU PAY!! OH, NO! I SOUND LIKE ICHIGO.
WHAT DID YOU DO?!
NOT MUCH.
JUST HELPING YOU DESTROY THE ENVIRONMENT A BIT FASTER.
STOP IT!!

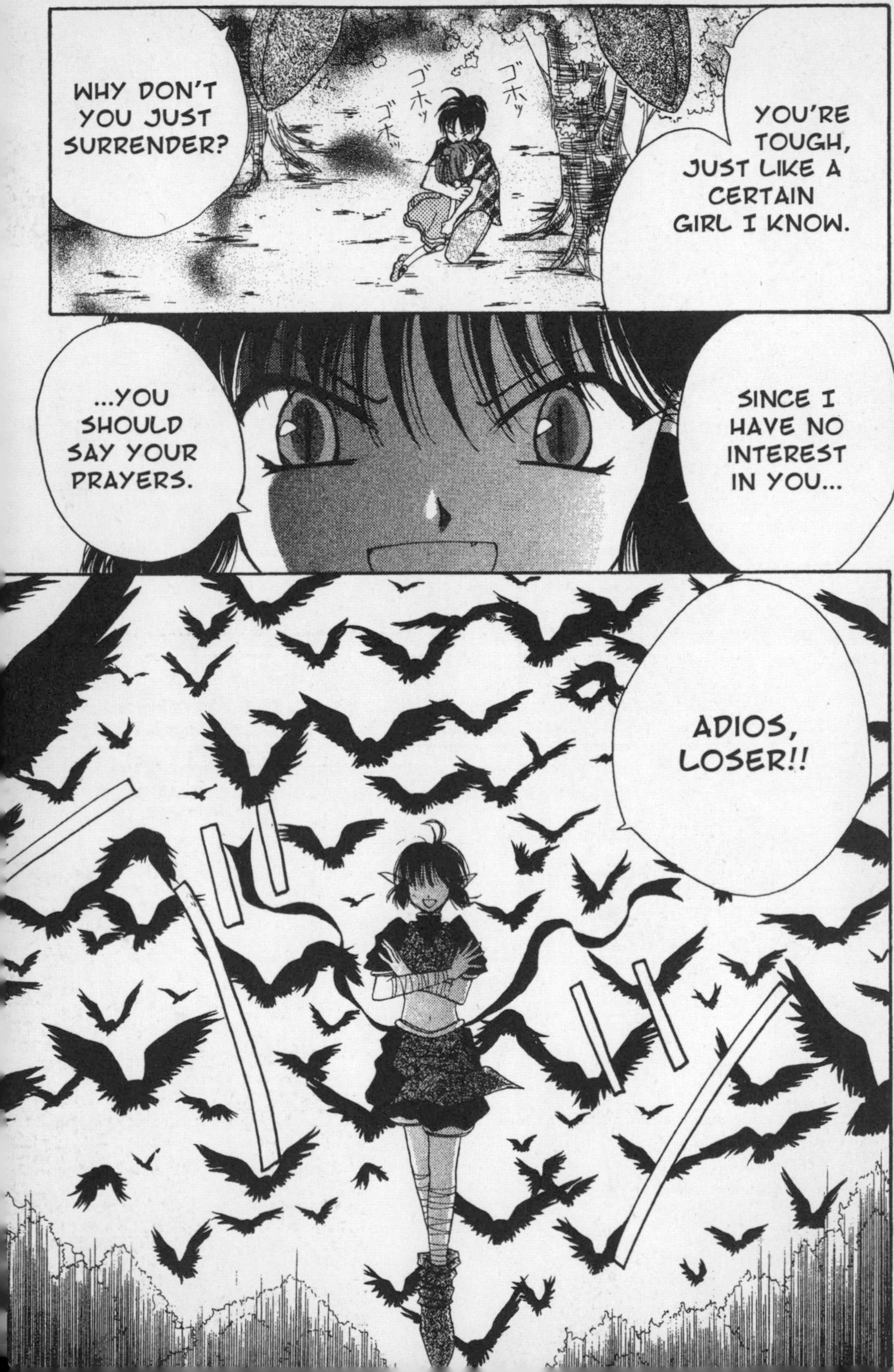
YOU'RE TOUGH, JUST LIKE A CERTAIN GIRL I KNOW.
ゴホッ
ゴホッ
ゴホッ
WHY DON'T YOU JUST SURRENDER?
SINCE I HAVE NO INTEREST IN YOU...
...YOU SHOULD SAY YOUR PRAYERS.
ADIOS, LOSER!!

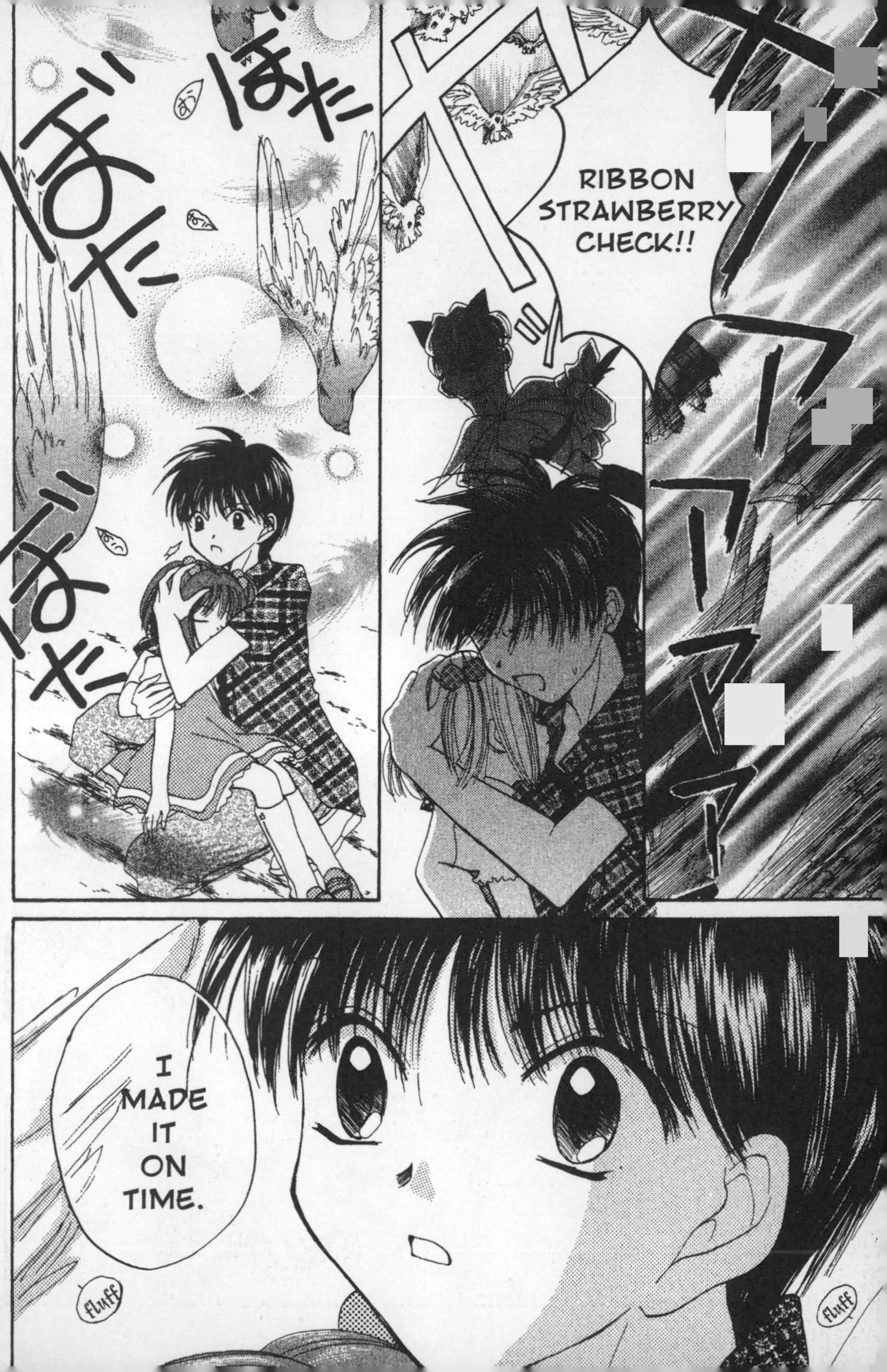
RIBBON STRAWBERRY CHECK!!
I MADE IT ON TIME.
fluff
fluff

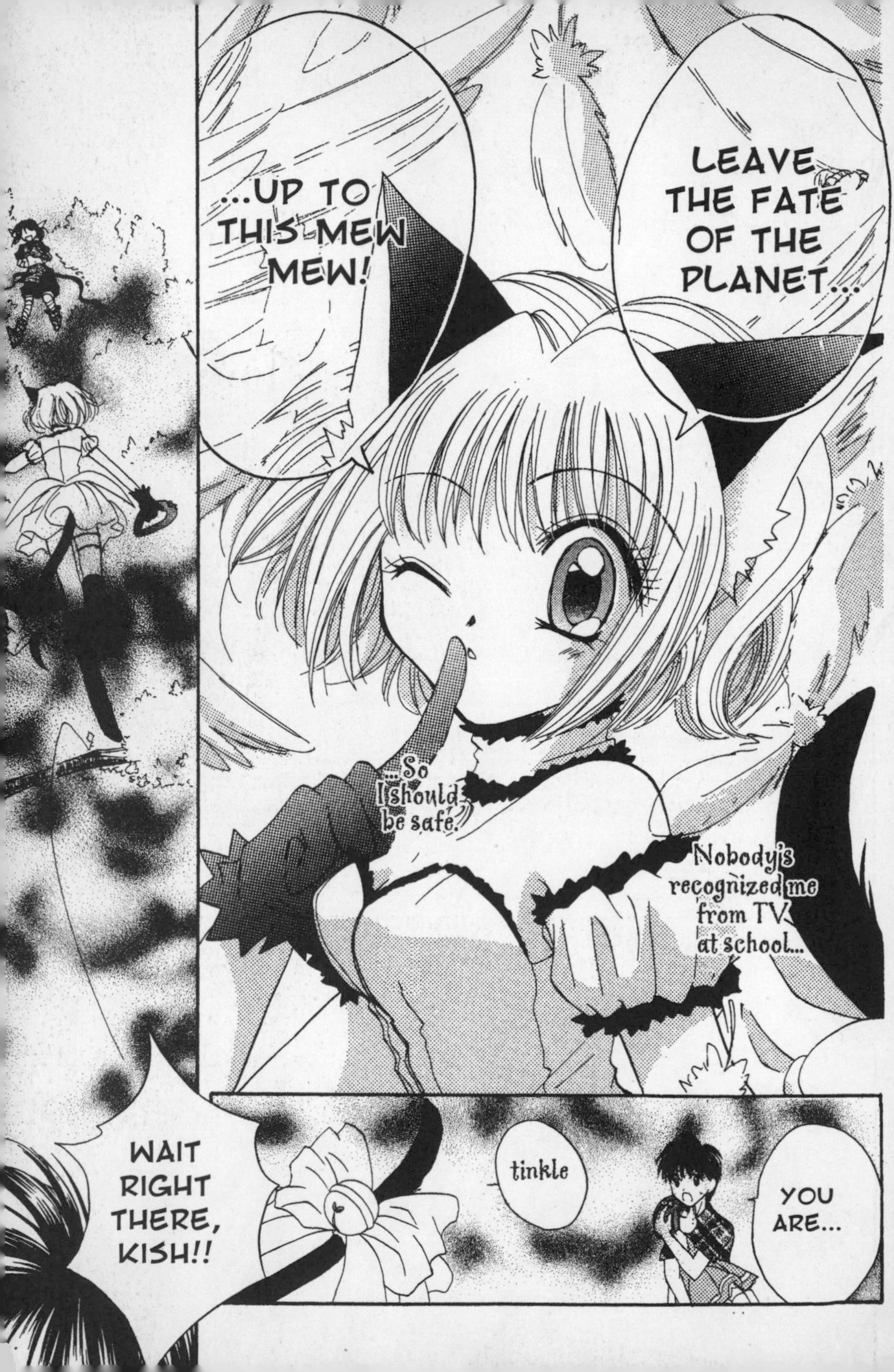
LEAVE THE FATE OF THE PLANET...
...UP TO THIS MEW MEW!
Nobody's recognized me from TV at school...
...So I should be safe.
YOU ARE...
tinkle
WAIT RIGHT THERE, KISH!!

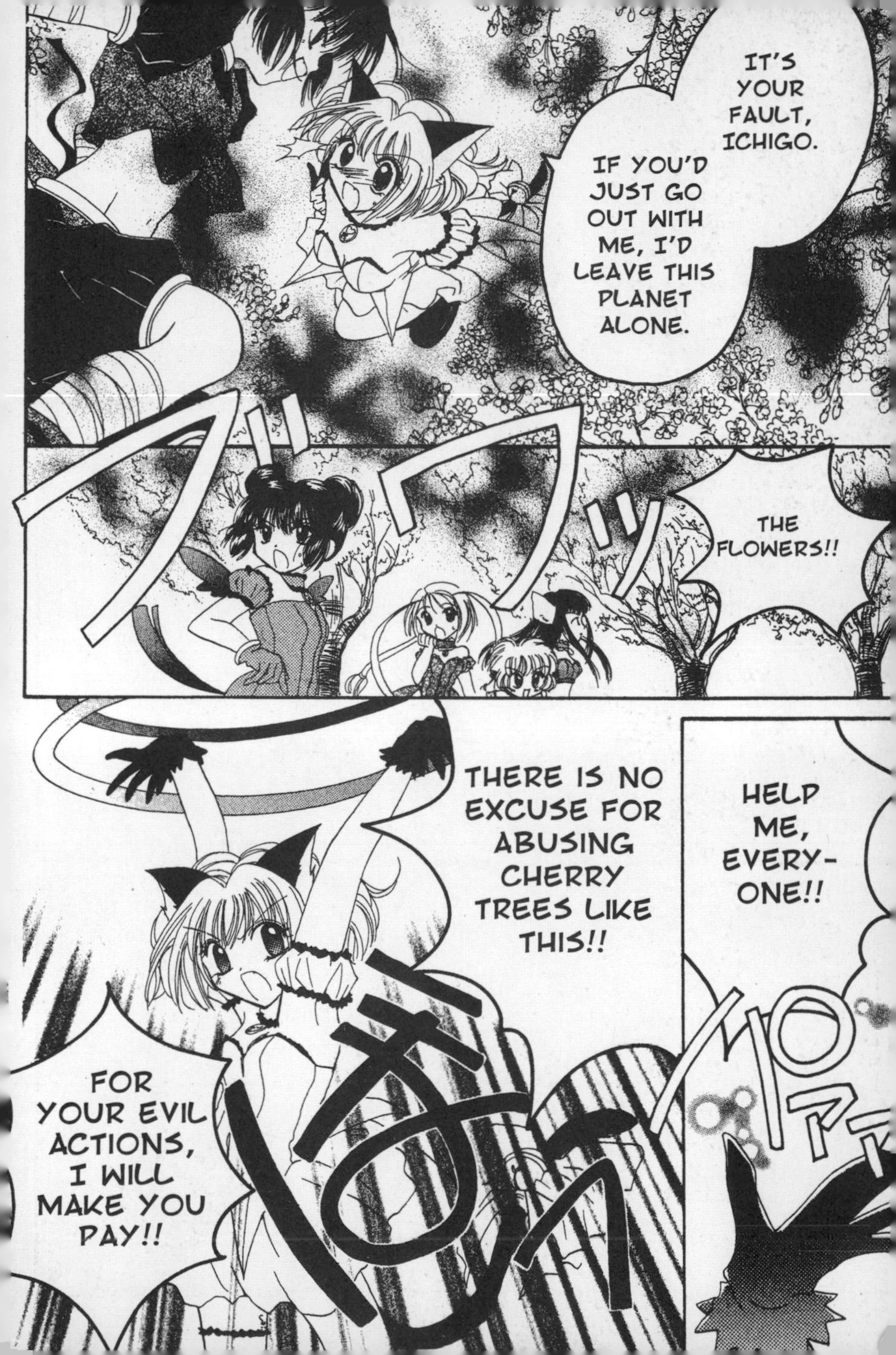
IT'S YOUR FAULT, ICHIGO.
IF YOU'D JUST GO OUT WITH ME, I'D LEAVE THIS PLANET ALONE.
THE FLOWERS!!
HELP ME, EVERY-ONE!!
THERE IS NO EXCUSE FOR ABUSING CHERRY TREES LIKE THIS!!
FOR YOUR EVIL ACTIONS, I WILL MAKE YOU PAY!!

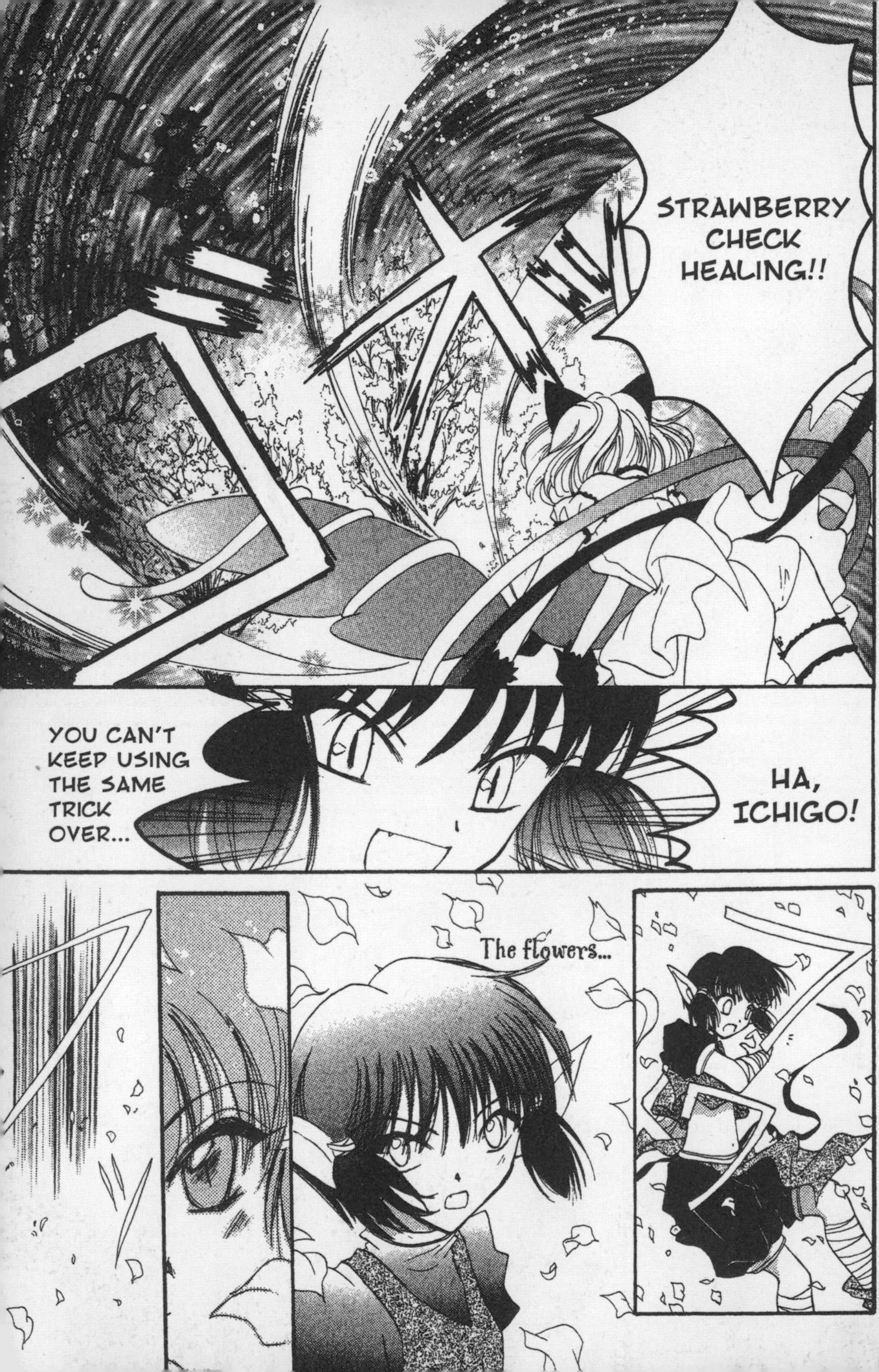
STRAWBERRY CHECK HEALING!!
HA, ICHIGO!
YOU CAN'T KEEP USING THE SAME TRICK OVER...
The flowers...

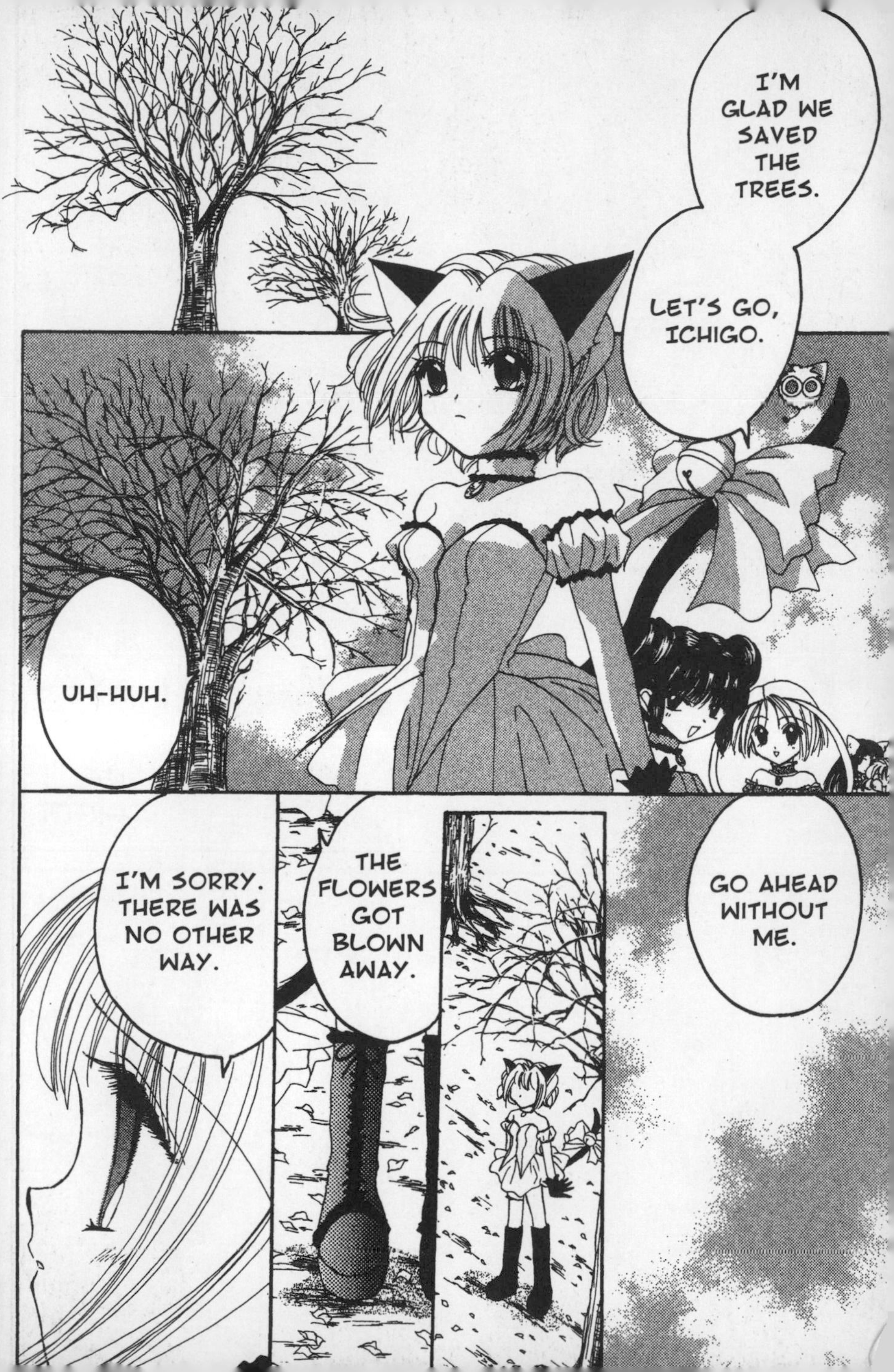
I'M GLAD WE SAVED THE TREES.
LET'S GO, ICHIGO.
UH-HUH.
GO AHEAD WITHOUT ME.
THE FLOWERS GOT BLOWN AWAY.
I'M SORRY. THERE WAS NO OTHER WAY.

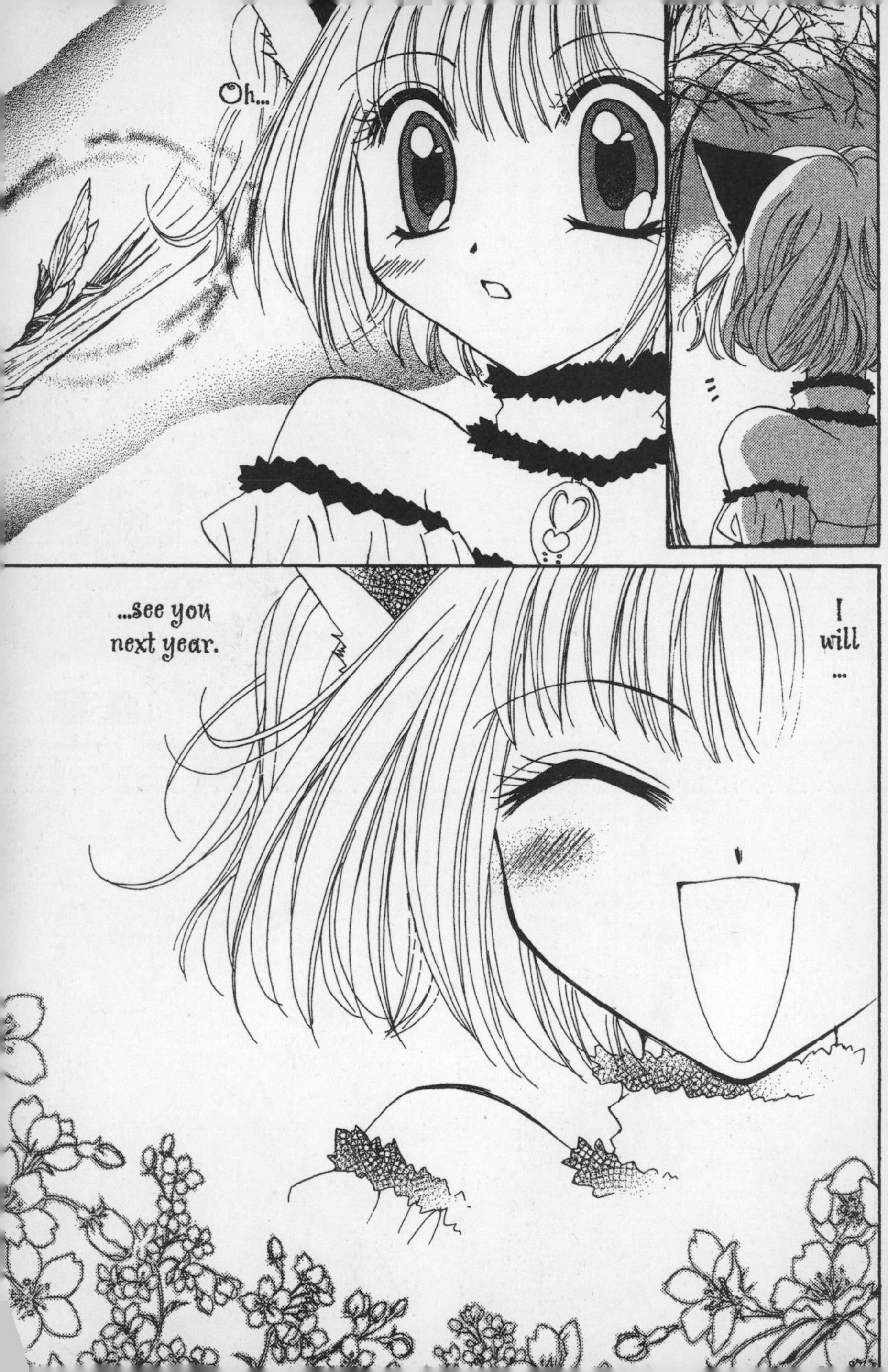
Oh...
I will ...
...see you next year.

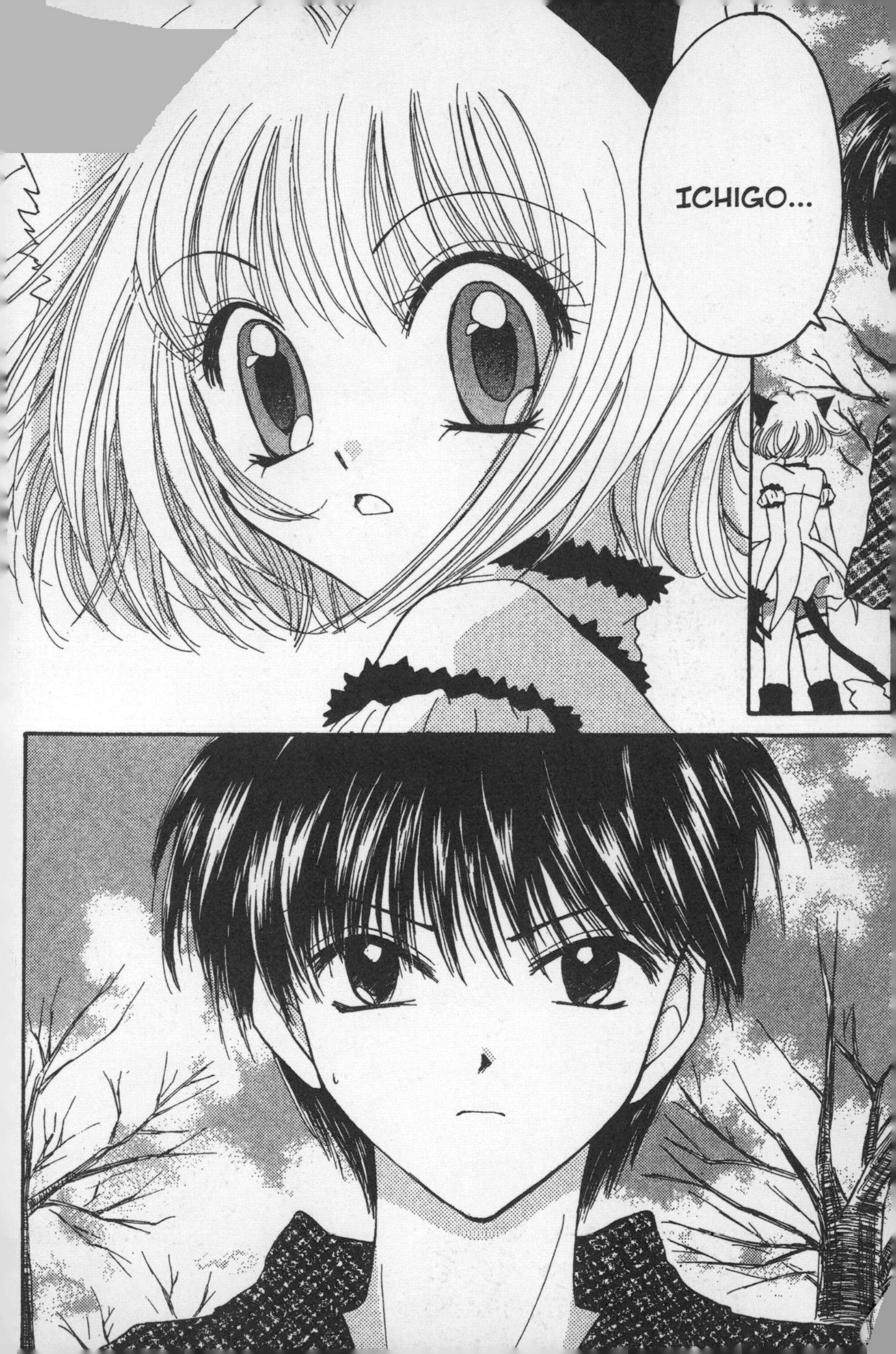
ICHIGO...

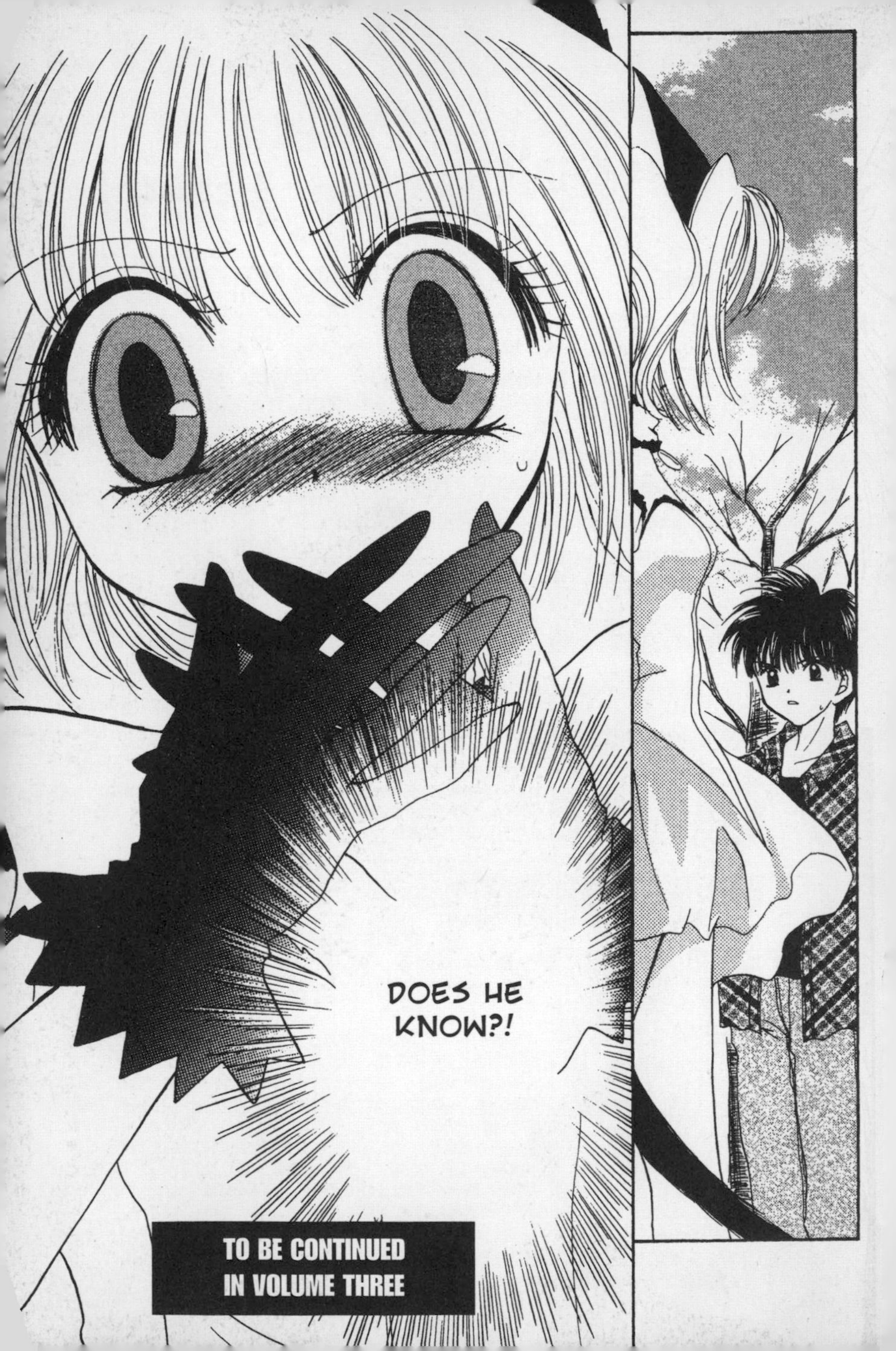
DOES HE KNOW?!
TO BE CONTINUED IN VOLUME THREE

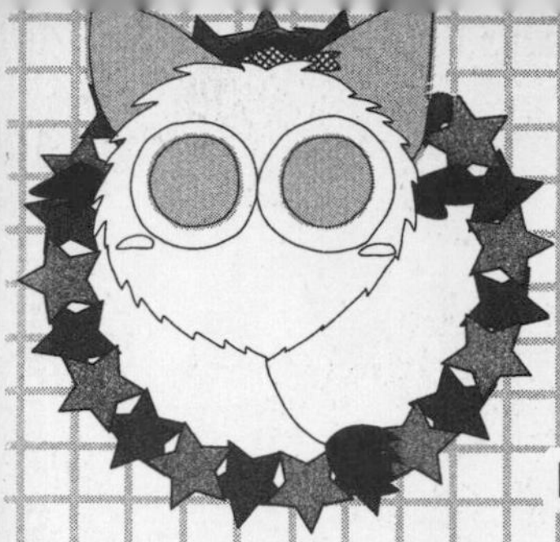

MASHA'S TOKYO MEW MEW

ENDANGERED SPECIES FILE

WHAT ARE ENDANGERED SPECIES?
ENDANGERED SPECIES ARE ANIMALS THAT ARE ON THE BRINK OF EXTINCTION. THERE ARE CURRENTLY 2,580 ENDANGERED SPECIES. THEIR NUMBERS ARE DECLINING FROM POACHING AND LOSS OF HABITAT. EVERYONE, LET'S ALL WORK TOGETHER TO SAVE ANIMALS FROM EXTINCTION!

ファイル FILE 4

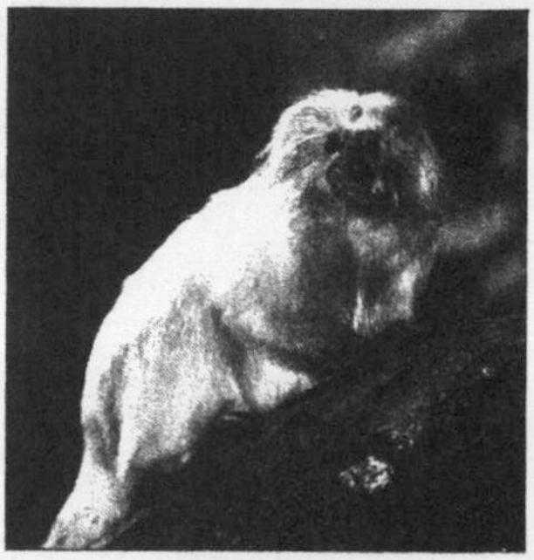

GOLDEN LION TAMARIN
(LEONTOPITHECUS ROSALIA ROSALIA)

AVERAGE BODY SIZE	20-30 CM.
AVERAGE TAIL LENGTH	20-30 CM.
AVERAGE WEIGHT	1.3-1.8 LBS.

HABITAT: THE GOLDEN LION TAMARIN ARE SMALL MONKEYS THAT BELONG TO THE MARMOSET FAMILY. THEY ARE NATIVE TO THE RAIN FORESTS OF BRAZIL, NEAR RIO DE JANEIRO. THEIR NAME COMES FROM THEIR GOLDEN, LION-LIKE FUR. THEY ARE CONSIDERED A SYMBOL OF RAIN FOREST CONSERVATION. THERE ARE CURRENTLY ABOUT 400 LEFT IN THE WILD. CONSERVATION EFFORTS FOR THIS SPECIES INCLUDE REFORESTATION, HABITAT PRESERVATION, AND RESCUE OF ORPHANED BABIES.

ファイル FILE 5

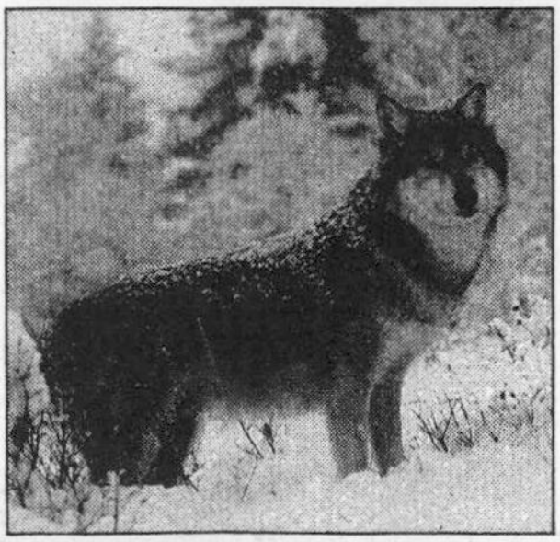

GRAY WOLF (CANIS LUPUS)

AVERAGE BODY SIZE	82-160 CM
AVERAGE WEIGHT	44-176 LBS. (MALE)
	40-121 LBS. (FEMALE)

HABITAT: THE GRAY WOLF'S HABITAT INCLUDES A LARGE SECTION OF NORTH AMERICA. A CARNIVORE, IT IS THE LARGEST WILD CANINE IN THE WORLD. IT IS AN EXCELLENT HUNTER, AND CAN BRING DOWN PREY MUCH LARGER THAN ITSELF. HUNTED HEAVILY FOR ITS FUR, HUMAN FEAR AND IGNORANCE FURTHER REDUCED ITS NUMBERS IN THE WILD. CURRENTLY, ABOUT 100,000 ARE LEFT IN THE WILD. THE LARGEST WOLVES COME FROM THE NORTHERNMOST REGION OF THEIR HABITAT.

THE FOLLOWING GIRLS WERE INFUSED WITH GENETIC MATERIAL FROM THESE ANIMALS. ▶ GOLDEN LION TAMARIN: PUDDING.
GRAY WOLF: ZAKURO.

東京ミュウミュウ

by Reiko Yoshida

Animal Fortune Telling Cards have recently become very popular. Which animal do you think represents you the best? An aloof but lovable cat? A classy and graceful Lorikeet? A mellow and relaxed porpoise? A fun and acrobatic monkey? A strong, smart wolf?

Many people would identify themselves with the cat, but the graceful Lorikeet should also be a popular choice. Porpoises make you want to protect them. Monkeys are such a blast, and the strong but silent wolf has many admirable qualities.

Personally, I feel closest to the porpoise. I like its relaxed, mellow demeanor. I tried snorkeling in the ocean once, with goofy looking goggles strapped to my face. Even in the seashore near Tokyo, the ocean was filled with fish. There is so much life in the ocean, even if it's not visible from the land. Sometimes I wish I could transform like Lettuce and swim in the ocean like a porpoise!

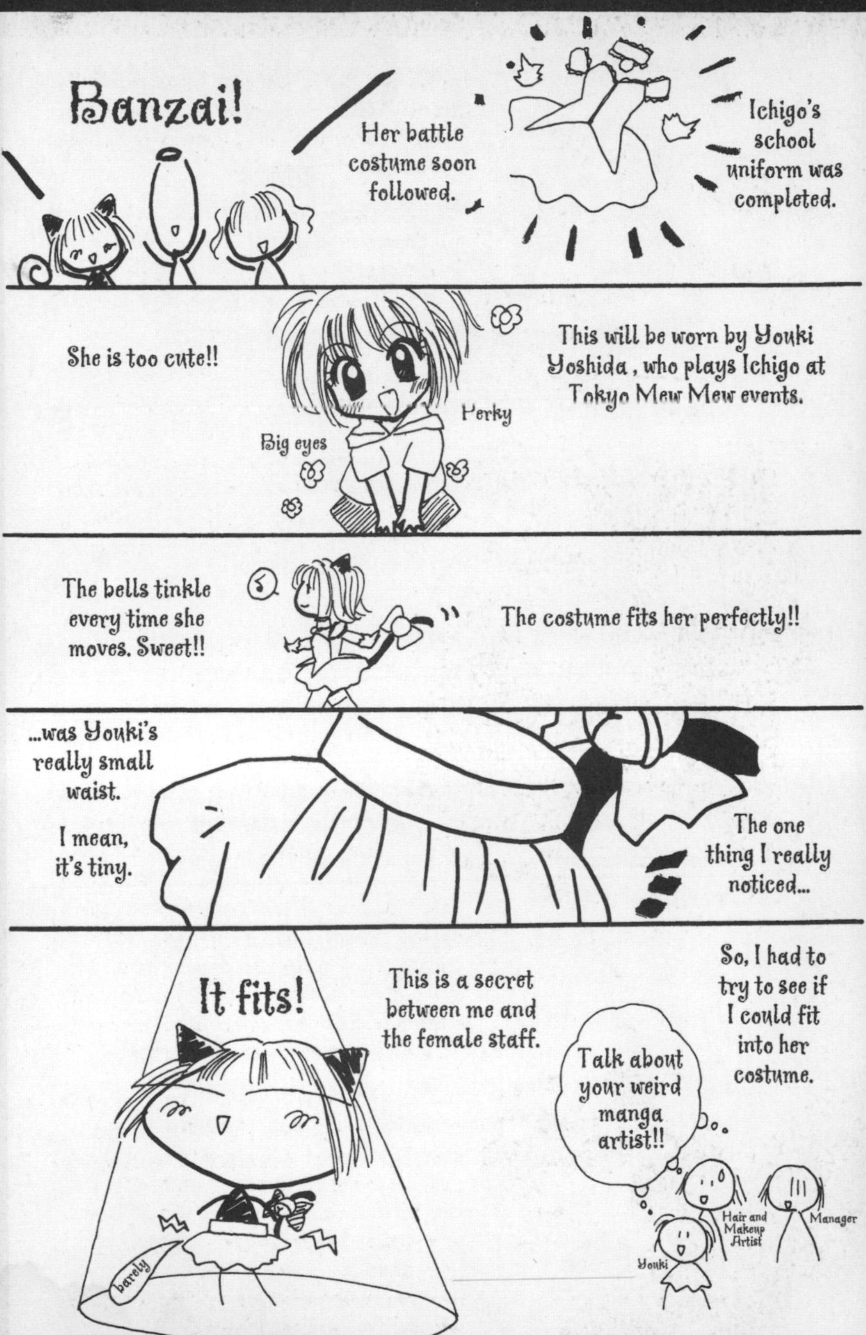

Ichigo's school uniform was completed.
Her battle costume soon followed.
Banzai!
This will be worn by Youki Yoshida, who plays Ichigo at Tokyo Mew Mew events.
Perky
Big eyes
She is too cute!!
The costume fits her perfectly!!
The bells tinkle every time she moves. Sweet!!
The one thing I really noticed...
...was Youki's really small waist.
I mean, it's tiny.
So, I had to try to see if I could fit into her costume.
Talk about your weird manga artist!!
Manager
Hair and Makeup Artist
Youki
This is a secret between me and the female staff.
It fits!
barely

Hello, it's me again, Ikumi!

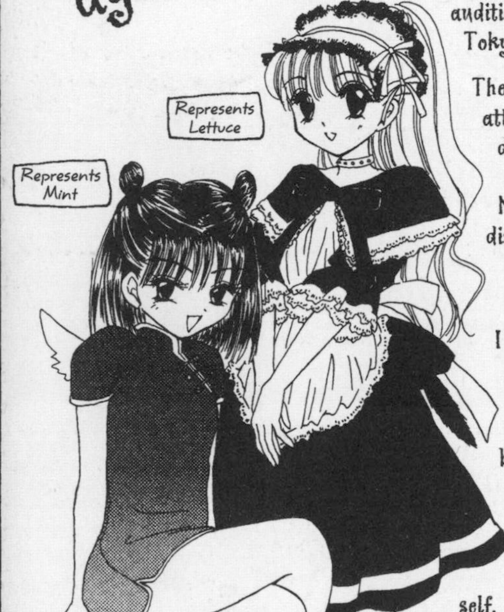
Represents Lettuce
Represents Mint
I like Chinese dresses.
I bought this at the discount store as a costume.

Hello, and glad to meet you! My name is Mia Ikumi. We're already on the second volume of Tokyo Mew Mew! I can't believe we're already on part two. How time flies.

It's been several months since the first volume was published. During that time, I've experienced a lot of new things. I was a judge at an audition, and I took a lunch cruise around Tokyo Bay. (Giggle!)

The most impressive experience was attending the Tokyo Mew Mew festival during Golden Week holiday. There was a gallery, and lots of new Tokyo Mew Mew collectibles and merchandise. I thoroughly enjoyed creating a poster for the festival, featuring all 12 characters!

I was amazed that the signing was two days long. The two illustrations to the left depict what I wore for the signings. I know, I'm weird. However, because of my bizarre look, a professional hair and makeup artist volunteered to do my makeup. I was really amazed. After she was done, I looked nothing like my usual self. I thought to myself, "Is this really me?" (a common sentiment found in girl's comics). I was glad I wore those costumes, because I got to experience that. On the second day, the makeup artist was waiting with makeup selected just for me. She is a wonderful person. I am really grateful to her.

Of course, a makeup artist can only do so much since they can't physically change the face structure. I don't know if anyone else who looked at me thought I was pretty, but I felt that she made me as beautiful as I could be. However, several of the male staff at the festival, among others, noticed her work and said they liked it. Not that you can trust their opinion on these things. (Smirk!)

The illustrations for these two pages were drawn using Youki Yoshida's picture, featured in Nakayoshi magazine. The girls in the illustration look younger, like they are 11 years old. The costumes are just like the photograph, though.

Once I met Youki in person, I realized these illustrations look nothing like her. Youki looks more like Ichigo in the comic book. Seriously. The first impression I had of her was "She has really big eyes!" I think she has the biggest eyes of anyone I know. My other impressions were that she was bubbly and cute, and how much she reminds me of Ichigo.

The more I see Youki, the more she reminds me of Ichigo. When I am doing my illustrations, I often feel like I am drawing Youki. I don't know if it's because she is a lot like Ichigo, or if it's because I'm impressed by how cute she is. I'm sure she will be attending many events in the future. You will miss out if you don't stop by and see her at an event. I will be seeing her next at the Tokyo Character Event Show. There will also be four other Mew Mew characters there, so come see us!!

I met the four girls who play the other characters at the audition. They are all pretty and slender, so I am already looking forward to seeing all five in their Mew Mew costumes. I will be attending the Tokyo Character Event Show. At least, it said so on the schedule my manager created. I won't be on the stage or anything, though. I'll just enjoy the five girls' performance from the VIP section. Hee hee.

The illustrations for the four other girls' costumes were completed several days ago. It's a lot of work to make costumes for four people. It's hard enough to just draw the costumes. I can only imagine how much work it is for the people who actually make them. Since they did such a wonderful job on Ichigo's costume, I'm sure the other costumes will be just as great. I'm excited.

So, I'll be cheering for Mew Mew at events all summer!!

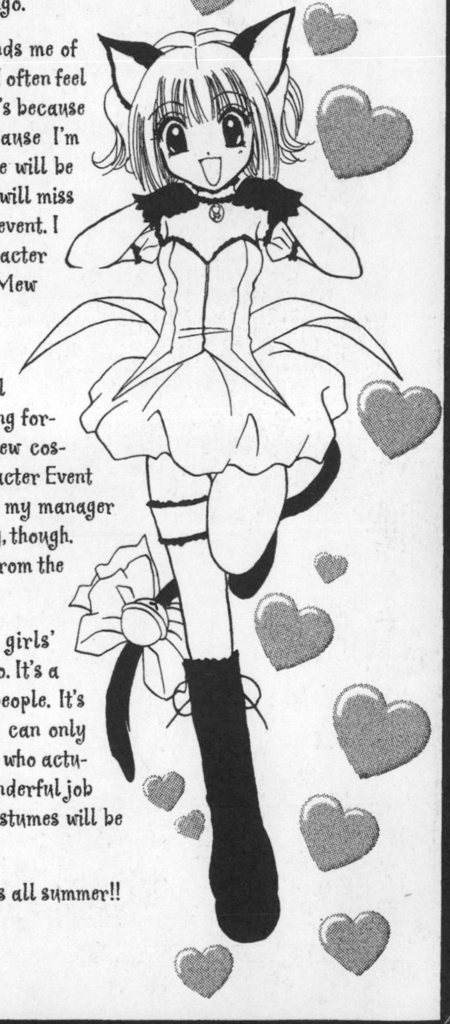

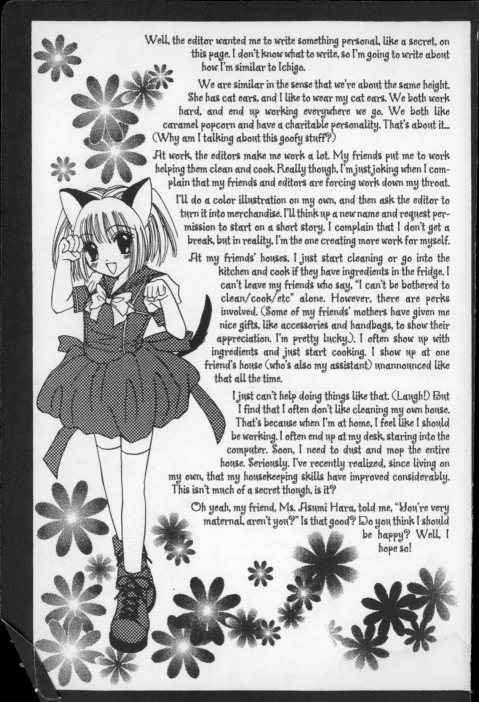

Well, the editor wanted me to write something personal, like a secret, on this page. I don't know what to write, so I'm going to write about how I'm similar to Ichigo.

We are similar in the sense that we're about the same height. She has cat ears, and I like to wear my cat ears. We both work hard, and end up working everywhere we go. We both like caramel popcorn and have a charitable personality. That's about it... (Why am I talking about this goofy stuff?)

At work, the editors make me work a lot. My friends put me to work helping them clean and cook. Really though, I'm just joking when I complain that my friends and editors are forcing work down my throat.

I'll do a color illustration on my own, and then ask the editor to turn it into merchandise. I'll think up a new name and request permission to start on a short story. I complain that I don't get a break, but in reality, I'm the one creating more work for myself.

At my friends' houses, I just start cleaning or go into the kitchen and cook if they have ingredients in the fridge. I can't leave my friends who say, "I can't be bothered to clean/cook/etc" alone. However, there are perks involved. (Some of my friends' mothers have given me nice gifts, like accessories and handbags, to show their appreciation. I'm pretty lucky.). I often show up with ingredients and just start cooking. I show up at one friend's house (who's also my assistant) unannounced like that all the time.

I just can't help doing things like that. (Laugh!) But I find that I often don't like cleaning my own house. That's because when I'm at home, I feel like I should be working. I often end up at my desk, staring into the computer. Soon, I need to dust and mop the entire house. Seriously. I've recently realized, since living on my own, that my housekeeping skills have improved considerably. This isn't much of a secret though, is it?

Oh yeah, my friend, Ms. Asumi Hara, told me, "You're very maternal, aren't you?" Is that good? Do you think I should be happy? Well, I hope so!

AFTERWARD

Yesterday, my friend told me that Disneyland was looking for cast members. The job was three days a week, including Saturdays. I'm telling you this because I really love Disneyland and wanted to work there. I could wear a character suit, or be an attendant at different attractions. For the longest time, I wanted to be like the girl at the Fantasyland store, selling ice cream with a radiant smile. She had such an amazing smile. It was as if she belonged there. Now, I'd rather sell caramel popcorn in front of Cinderella's castle. I'll eat caramel corn all day and watch the parades. Woohoo! That's my motivation...

While I did seriously think about this for a minute, I knew my editor would have a fit, so I decided against it. Yes, it was a very short dream. (Sob!)

Oh yes! Recently, Disneyland's nighttime parade, "Fantillusion" was canceled. I saw it many times until the very end, so I have no regrets. "The Electrical Dream Light" Parade is supposed to start soon!! After I finish my next manuscript, I will definitely check it out.

Changing subjects, I've recently started watching a pair of female, foreign comics called "Isabel and Benet." I've only caught a few minutes of their show on TV in the evening. I really like the fact that they speak Japanese so well, and have funny skits. I don't really have a favorite TV show. I just watch what strikes my mood at that time.

My assistant suggested lambs, so here are the characters as lambs.
What will they be next?

Final Thoughts

I am fortunate enough to work as a manga artist. Even in the manga field, I don't think many artists get to meet their characters in real life. I really feel lucky, and I'm blessed with a happy life. I don't want to rest on my laurels, though. Happiness is very difficult to come by. Happiness comes to you when you strive to find it from the bottom of your heart, and you work really, really hard for it.

Finally, to everyone who helped me with this project...

to everyone involved with this project in any way...

to everyone who has read this series...

Thank you very, very, very much!!

It's a blessing to bring joy to the people you love, and to find happiness within yourself.

Let's work hard together,

2001. 5. 23   -Mia Ikumi

COMING SOON...

TOKYO MEW MEW

VOLUME THREE

Finally, Ichigo has connected with all of the other girls who make up Tokyo Mew Mew. Together, they must battle the aliens before they take over the world! Between battles, Ichigo is worried that Masaya Ayoma knows her secret identity. Will they have a future as a couple if he knows the truth?! Find out the fate of the Mew Mews in the next book, Volume Three!

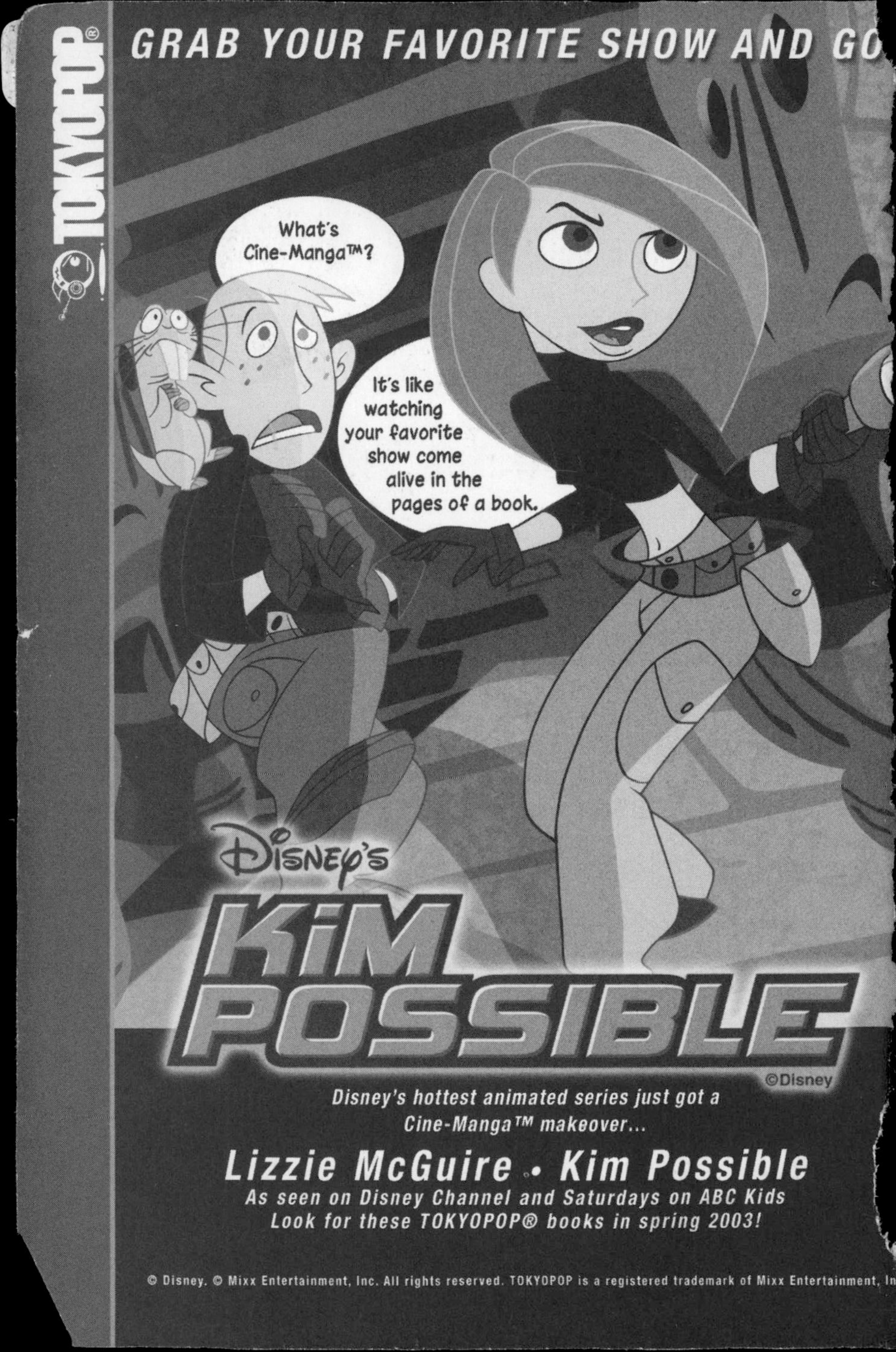
TOKYOPOP®
GRAB YOUR FAVORITE SHOW AND GO
What's Cine-Manga™?
It's like watching your favorite show come alive in the pages of a book.
Disney's
KIM POSSIBLE
©Disney
Disney's hottest animated series just got a Cine-Manga™ makeover...
Lizzie McGuire • Kim Possible
As seen on Disney Channel and Saturdays on ABC Kids
Look for these TOKYOPOP® books in spring 2003!
© Disney. © Mixx Entertainment, Inc. All rights reserved. TOKYOPOP is a registered trademark of Mixx Entertainment, In

STOP!

This is the back of the book.
You wouldn't want to spoil a great ending!

This book is printed "manga-style," in the authentic Japanese right-to-left format. Since none of the artwork has been flipped or altered, readers get to experience the story just as the creator intended. You've been asking for it, so TOKYOPOP® delivered: authentic, hot-off-the-press, and far more fun!

DIRECTIONS

1
2
3
4
5
6
7
8
9
10

If this is your first time reading manga-style, here's a quick guide to help you understand how it works.

It's easy... just start in the top right panel and follow the numbers. Have fun, and look for more 100% authentic manga from TOKYOPOP®!